THE RICHMOND CAMPAIGN OF 1862

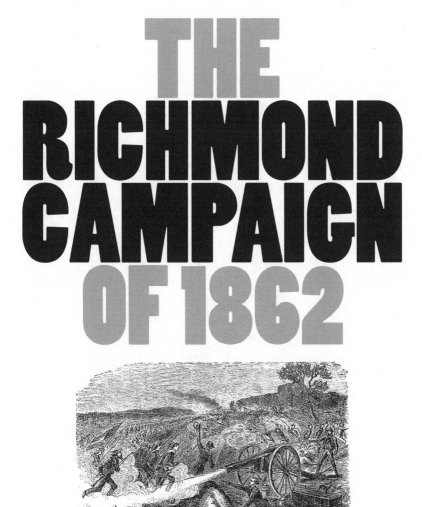

The Peninsula and the Seven Days

EDITED BY GARY W. GALLAGHER

The University of North Carolina Press

Chapel Hill and London

© 2000 The University of North Carolina Press

All rights reserved

Set in Bulmer and Poplar types

by G&S Typesetters

Manufactured in the United States of America

The paper in this book meets the guidelines for permanence and durability
of the Committee on Production Guidelines for Book Longevity of the
Council on Library Resources.

Library of Congress Cataloging-in-Publication Data

The Richmond campaign of 1862: the Peninsula and the Seven Days / edited
by Gary W. Gallagher

p. cm. — (Military campaigns of the Civil War)

Includes bibliographical references (p.   ) and index.

ISBN 978-0-8078-2552-5 (alk. paper)

ISBN 978-0-8078-5919-3 (pbk.: alk. paper)

1. Peninsula Campaign, 1862.   2. Seven Days' Battles, 1862.   3. Richmond
(Va.)—History—Civil War, 1861–1865.   I. Gallagher, Gary W.

E473.6.R54 2000   99-058608

973.7′32—dc21

| cloth | 04 | 03 | 02 | 01 | 00 | 5 | 4 | 3 | 2 | 1 |
| paper | 12 | 11 | 10 | 09 | 08 | 5 | 4 | 3 | 2 | 1 |

For the staff at the University of North Carolina Press

CONTENTS

THE RICHMOND CAMPAIGN OF 1862

MILITARY CAMPAIGNS *of the* CIVIL WAR

The 1862 Richmond campaign introduced warfare on a massive scale to the Eastern Theater. It ended eight quiescent months following the battle of First Manassas when the armies had watched each other warily along the northern Virginia frontier. The opposing commanders during that uneventful period were a well-matched pair who preferred planning to campaigning, contemplating lines of advance and retreat to fighting battles, and protecting their reputations to hazarding status and fame in the active pursuit of victory. Gen. George B. McClellan built the Union's Army of the Potomac into a formidable force that he declined to risk in active operations. A staunch Democrat, he also quarreled with his president and Republicans in Congress over what kind of war the North should wage. Gen. Joseph E. Johnston, the Confederacy's senior field officer in Virginia and McClellan's opposite number, expended endless energy bickering with President Jefferson Davis over rank and other matters tangential to the protection of the national weal.

McClellan finally bestirred himself to move in the spring of 1862, landing his army at Fort Monroe and undertaking a slow march up the Peninsula toward Richmond. By late April, Johnston had positioned his troops to block the Federal advance. The armies maneuvered and skirmished on the Peninsula throughout May, with the Confederates giving ground to the outskirts of the capital. Heavy fighting erupted in the battle of Seven Pines or Fair Oaks on May 31 and continued the next day. The grim list of more than 11,000 casualties from the two days of combat included General Johnston — whose disabling wounds obliged Jefferson Davis to reassign Robert E. Lee from his desk as a military adviser in Richmond to the field.

Lee spent the first three weeks of June preparing to take the initiative against McClellan. For his part, the Federal commander seemed content to grant his new opponent unlimited time to settle in as an army commander. The campaign climaxed in a furious week's fighting at the end of the month. Lee pressed the tactical offensive in what came to be known as the Seven Days battles, seeking to land heavy blows at Mechanicsville on the twenty-sixth, Gaines's Mill the twenty-seventh, Savage's Station the twenty-ninth,

Glendale the thirtieth, and Malvern Hill on July 1. Fending off Lee's somewhat clumsy blows, McClellan withdrew southward toward a secure base on the James River. The Federals eventually retreated to Harrison's Landing, where McClellan, who had shown no disposition to hit back at the rebels, hunkered down and issued a stream of requests for more men and supplies. Casualties for the entire campaign exceeded 50,000, more than 35,000 of whom had fallen during the Seven Days.

The Richmond campaign deserves attention for more than setting a new standard of slaughter in Virginia. It propelled Lee to the fore, where he immediately altered the strategic picture by dictating the action to a compliant McClellan. Lee's initial experience directing an army lacked tactical polish but nevertheless generated immense dividends. The Seven Days saved Richmond, inspirited a Confederate people numbed by dismal military news from other theaters, and helped set the stage for a strategic counteroffensive that would take the Army of Northern Virginia to Second Manassas and across the Potomac to Sharpsburg. On the Union side, the campaign dampened expectations of victory that had mounted steadily since the capture of Forts Henry and Donelson in February 1862. McClellan's failure also exacerbated northern political divisions relating to how the war should be waged, clearing the way for Republicans to implement harsher policies that would strike at slavery and other rebel property. The end of the rebellion had seemed to be in sight in April when McClellan prepared his forces to march up the Peninsula; by mid-July all but the most obtuse observers knew the war would continue in a more all-encompassing manner. Taken overall, the ramifications were such that the Richmond campaign must be reckoned one of the great turning points of the war.[1]

Few Civil War military operations offer more fruitful topics for scholarly investigation. The essays in this volume, the seventh of "Military Campaigns of the Civil War," follow the series' well-established pattern of addressing disparate elements of an operation. Once again a disclaimer is in order. The pages that follow do not present the chronological tactical story of the Richmond campaign. Every important commander does not receive his equal measure of analysis, and some battles receive only the most cursory attention. For a well researched and written narrative treatment, readers should consult Stephen W. Sears's *To the Gates of Richmond: The Peninsula Campaign* (New York, 1992). These essays collectively revisit famous scenes and personalities, search out some of the far-reaching outcomes of the campaign, and suggest the many ways in which events at the front and behind the lines interacted.

Readers and critics of earlier volumes in this series have asked that we do more to situate campaigns within the wider framework of the conflict. To that end, the opening essay shows how the Richmond campaign related to other military operations in the first half of 1862 and explores why its timing, location, and outcome had such important consequences. Much of the emphasis is on timing. McClellan's campaign unfolded against a backdrop of widespread Federal military success that promoted enormous optimism in the Union, as well as doubts among Confederates about the viability of their cause. The Seven Days sent shock waves through the North, where complacency evaporated amid political debates about how brutal an approach would be necessary to subdue the rebels. Because the Richmond campaign placed Robert E. Lee at the head of the Confederacy's biggest army, it soon became obvious that whatever strategy the North adopted in the Eastern Theater would confront enormous obstacles. Hindsight eventually would reveal that Lee's accession to command probably lengthened the conflict by more than two years.

Despite Lee's important role, George B. McClellan indisputably stood as the central figure of the Richmond campaign. It is thus appropriate that John T. Hubbell and William J. Miller make him the subject of the second and third essays — neither of which will offer any comfort to revisionists intent on burnishing "Little Mac's" reputation. McClellan invites analysis from any number of angles, as demonstrated by the vast body of work assessing such topics as his singular relationship with the Army of the Potomac's officers and soldiers, the possible psychological underpinnings of his military behavior, and why Abraham Lincoln retained him in command for so long.[2] Hubbell's assigned task in this volume was to provide a succinct overview of McClellan's conduct of the campaign. His essay touches on some of McClellan's strengths before rendering a bluntly negative evaluation of his performance. Either inept or insubordinate when it came to dealing with civilian superiors, McClellan treated President Abraham Lincoln abominably. He also refused to take responsibility for many of his own actions, manifested an aggravating passivity in the presence of the enemy, and directed untold complaints to Washington. Self-absorbed to the end, McClellan left the Peninsula insisting that he had overcome shoddy support from the Lincoln administration to render solid service during the campaign. As is so often the case with scholars of Civil War history, Hubbell found numerous insights in the writings of a participant — in this instance Peter S. Michie, a Union engineer who never served with McClellan but wrote a perceptive biography of the general in the late nineteenth century.

William J. Miller's essay on Union engineers underscores McClellan's tendency to manufacture excuses for his lack of decisive movement. In addition to lamenting the fact that his army was not larger, he claimed that bad roads, the weather, and the unpredictable Chickahominy River conspired to frustrate his plans. Sound military engineering could help overcome the last three factors, and Miller demonstrates that impressive efforts by Federal engineers proved insufficient for their army commander. Even when bridges and fortifications deemed essential to movement had been completed, McClellan chose to remain at rest. No one better understood this phase of the campaign than Brig. Gen. John G. Barnard, the army's chief engineer, who asserted that much of McClellan's carping was groundless. Instead of insisting that everything be perfect before he acted, McClellan should have pressed forward. Doing so probably would have saved Union lives and might have salvaged the general's reputation.

McClellan's most famous opponent during the Richmond campaign was "Stonewall" Jackson. Robert K. Krick canvassed obscure as well as more accessible sources to evaluate Jackson's notoriously flawed performance during the Seven Days. He allocates most of his attention to four episodes: Jackson's march from the Shenandoah Valley to Richmond; his late arrival at Mechanicsville on June 26; his dawdling march to Gaines's Mill on the twenty-seventh; and his costly lassitude at White Oak Swamp on June 30. Krick will have none of apologists who attempt to dress Jackson's failures in forgiving attire. He does give full weight to the general's exhaustion (noting as well that many other officers were equally exhausted during the Seven Days), concluding that by any reasonable yardstick the "Mighty Stonewall's" service, especially at White Oak Swamp, lacked its usual dash and aggressiveness and contributed little to southern victory.

Unlike Jackson's questionable actions during the Seven Days, which most Confederates overlooked or played down, Maj. Gen. John Bankhead Magruder's lapses proved to be immediately controversial. Savaged in the press and by many comrades, he defended himself against accusations that he had been drunk and that he had displayed personal cowardice. Peter S. Carmichael's essay reviews Magruder's role in the Richmond campaign. The general's many faults stand out clearly, among them his problem with drinking. But Carmichael also credits his strong points, arguing that for much of the campaign he did well. Like Jackson, he was exhausted, and that condition limited his effectiveness. His worst days came at Savage's Station and Malvern Hill, lapses for which Lee chose not to be as tolerant as he was with Jackson's. Carmichael assigns partial blame for Magruder's failures to poor staff work at army headquarters and to Lee's sometimes vague orders. Had the commanding general identified in Magruder the potential that he obviously saw in Jackson, Carmichael believes he would handled "Prince John" differently.

Although solid work in Texas lay ahead for Magruder after the Seven Days, notes Carmichael, he never escaped the damning shadow of his travails outside Richmond in 1862.

The sixth and seventh essays move away from generals and battles to the realms of society and politics. James Marten highlights the 1862 Richmond campaign in considering how proximity to the battlefront affected the lives of black and white noncombatants on the Peninsula and in Richmond. He describes how Confederate civilians reacted to the presence of large Union armies, adjusted to economic and social dislocation, and coped with sporadic irregular violence that plagued the rural countryside. Although most white residents remained loyal to the Confederacy in the near term, Marten suggests that the 1862 campaign abetted the development of fissures that later weakened the nascent slaveholding republic. Slaves underwent a more dramatic change in circumstances than their white neighbors. Union forces held out the promise of freedom to African Americans willing to accept the risk of trying to escape; those who stayed with their Confederate masters experienced a loosening of the bonds of slavery. In sum, notes Marten, the appearance of the Army of the Potomac in April 1862 began a process that transformed southeastern Virginia.

The Richmond campaign also figured prominently in the North's decision to wage a harsher war against the Confederacy. The most obvious component of the new policy involved freeing rebel slaves. William A. Blair looks at the road moderate northerners traveled toward the kind of war Radical Republicans and abolitionists had urged from the beginning. He finds that McClellan's defeat convinced most northerners that they could not count on hidden Unionist strength in the Confederacy. Stubborn rebels such as those who had turned the Army of the Potomac away from Richmond would maintain their resistance unless forced to give it up by United States military power. Radicals and abolitionists also played a major role, tempering their antislavery rhetoric to persuade fellow citizens that emancipation made sense as a war measure necessary to defeat the rebellion. After McClellan's retreat, Abraham Lincoln moved closer to the radicals, adapting their arguments to his goal of nudging the nation toward harder war. Keeping restoration of the Union in the foreground and pressing for emancipation as a means to help achieve the primary goal, Lincoln and the radicals succeeded in convincing the North to accept a major reorientation of the conflict.

Robert E. L. Krick and Keith S. Bohannon return to the battlefield to close the volume. In the penultimate essay, Krick looks at the climax of the battle of Gaines's Mill, by far the bloodiest of the Seven Days. His topic is Brig. Gen. W. H. C. Whiting's two-brigade division and its late-afternoon assault that breached Union lines near the Watt house. Krick draws on an impressive array of materials to make sense of the attacks, which, among other results, catapulted the soldiers of John Bell Hood's Texas Brigade to fame as the army's finest shock troops. Krick reminds readers that the offensive at Gaines's Mill was the largest ever mounted by any Confederate army, its 50,000 participants far exceeding the number involved in more famous attacks by George E. Pickett and James Johnston Pettigrew at Gettysburg and Stonewall Jackson at Chancellorsville. He also sees the attack on June 27 as a pivotal event that marked the first offensive tactical victory for Lee and the Army of Northern Virginia. The general and his soldiers built on that foundation to create one of the most famous and effective military partnerships in American history.

No episode in the Richmond campaign exceeded in dramatic power the futile Confederate attacks against massed Union artillery at Malvern Hill. In a war where Confederate guns often fought at a disadvantage in numbers and weight of metal, Malvern Hill stood out as especially hellish. The conventional understanding of artillery on July 1 juxtaposes Union guns slaughtering Confederate infantry against southern batteries being pounded into submission before they could have any impact on the battle. Keith S. Bohannon's essay revises this traditional picture in important ways. He agrees with earlier writers that Union batteries wreaked considerable havoc on southern infantry; indeed, he calls Malvern Hill the best day of the war for Brig. Henry J. Hunt's northern artillery. Superior training as well as superior equipment contributed to the Union artillery's excellent work. Yet Bohannon also asserts that Lee's assaults probably would have succeeded had it not been for Union infantry units that moved through their own batteries to engage Confederate attackers along the slopes of Malvern Hill. Moreover, Bohannon cites considerable evidence that the southern batteries, despite their inferior training and heavy casualties, inflicted significant losses on the defending Federals.

In terms of historical chronology, this volume stands first in "Military Campaigns of the Civil War." It joins *The Antietam Campaign* as one of a pair of titles that cover the opening and closing acts of the enormous operation that extended from June through October 1862. A future volume in the series will treat the campaign of Second Manassas, or Bull Run, thus completing a trilogy that will stand well on its own. Before that volume appears (probably in 2002), there will be one on the 1862 Shenandoah Valley campaign — itself an important adjunct to the Richmond campaign. Where the series goes after Second Manassas, whether forward to Petersburg or back to First Manassas, remains to be decided.

I wish to extend warm thanks to all the contributors. Bill Blair, Keith Bohannon, Peter Carmichael, Bob Krick, R. E. L. Krick, and Jim Marten are veterans of previous volumes in this series, as is cartographer George F. Skoch, and they all produced typically excellent work. John Hubbell and Bill Miller are new faces in this crowd whose contributions fit in seamlessly with those of their peers. The dedication expresses my gratitude to the staff at the University of North Carolina Press, many of whom I count as good friends as well as colleagues. I have worked on a number of projects at the Press over a period of fifteen years. During that time I have received unfailing kindness, cooperation, and encouragement from a group of people whose institutional hallmark is uncompromising professionalism laced with humanity. I hope there are many more projects in our future.

NOTES

1. Although Antietam in September 1862 and the tandem of Gettysburg and Vicksburg in early July 1863 most often are put forward as the military watersheds of the Civil War, a number of historians have emphasized the importance of the 1862 Richmond campaign. For example, Bruce Catton titled his chapters on the campaign in *Terrible Swift Sword* (Garden City, N.Y.: Doubleday, 1963), "Turning Point."

2. For a psychological discussion of McClellan, see the appendix in Joseph T. Glatthaar, *Partners in Command: The Relationship between Leaders in the Civil War* (New York: Free Press, 1994). For broader treatments filled with useful insights into the young general, see Bruce Catton's *Mr. Lincoln's Army* (Garden City, N.Y.: Doubleday, 1951) and Stephen W. Sears's *George B. McClellan: The Young Napoleon* (New York: Ticknor & Fields, 1988).

THE RICHMOND CAMPAIGN OF 1862

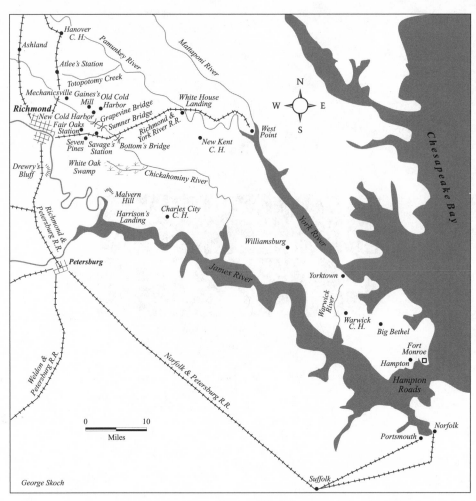

Area of operations, April–July 1862

G A R Y   W .   G A L L A G H E R

A Civil War Watershed

The 1862 Richmond Campaign in Perspective

T he 1862 Richmond campaign exerted immense influence on the
course of the Civil War. In the short term, its consequences rever-
berated through the armies that had maneuvered and fought up
Virginia's Peninsula to the Confederate capital, as well as affecting
the morale and expectations of untold thousands of civilians who
had followed the action from behind the lines. In the broader sweep of the
conflict, George B. McClellan's failure and Robert E. Lee's emergence as a
successful field commander marked a decisive moment in the Eastern Theater that in turn shaped the larger direction of the conflict. A seemingly ir-
resistible tide of Union military success between February and June 1862
receded rapidly after the Seven Days battles, opening the way for a stunning reorientation of the strategic picture in Virginia. Slightly more than two
months after the battle of Malvern Hill, the Army of Northern Virginia, having won a victory at Second Manassas that built on its success at the Seven
Days, stood poised to cross the Potomac River into United States territory.
This reversal of northern military fortunes canceled earlier projections of
victory within a framework that might have restored the Union much as it
had existed on the eve of war. Because their premier army had been humbled
by the rebels during the Richmond campaign, northerners had to confront
the prospect of pursuing a harsher kind of war to defeat the Confederacy.
That kind of war likely would bring the end of slavery and otherwise change
the nature of society in a restored United States. Confederates meanwhile
took heart at what they perceived as much improved chances of establishing
their slaveholding republic.

Anyone seeking to understand the 1862 Richmond campaign must take
into account a variety of factors, some of which often are missing from studies of Civil War campaigns and battles. It is not enough to look at the immediate strategic background, examine the tactical ebb and flow once the armies

engaged in combat, and count casualties and describe immediate post-battle movements to determine what had been won or lost. Civil War armies represented extensions of two democratic societies, and they operated within a complicated web of military, political, and social constraints. Although the Confederacy lacked the resources and manpower to defeat the North in an absolute sense, it could prevail if the northern people decided the war was too costly. Conversely, the North would win if the Confederate people proved unwilling to sacrifice any longer to achieve independence. The home fronts felt the impact of battles not only in terms of loved ones killed or maimed but also in the realm of political and social policy, and popular will in both societies fluctuated markedly in response to events at the military front. The most important operations, such as the 1862 Richmond campaign, cast shadows far beyond the time when armies marched away from battlefields.

Historians sometimes assess the impact of battles or the efficacy of generalship by examining casualties and gauging the immediate consequences for the respective armies. A pair of arguments from two influential books will illustrate this point. In *How the North Won: A Military History of the Civil War,* Herman Hattaway and Archer Jones argued that individual battles and campaigns counted for little during the Civil War because armies were unable to deliver knockout blows. Improved weaponry and the organizational character of the forces involved gave the defending party an advantage that guaranteed no commander would craft an American Cannae. "Understanding the indecisiveness and, therefore, the relative insignificance of battles," stated Hattaway and Jones, "is simply another way of perceiving the primacy of the defense when well-articulated and relatively maneuverable units of rifle-armed infantry dominated the battlefield." During the Civil War, "battles ceased to have their old importance and victors might well suffer proportionately or even absolutely higher casualties than the vanquished." The Seven Days fit this mold well, witnessing "attrition distinctly favorable to the Union" but being perceived as "a Confederate victory, because victory is customarily determined by who retreats from the battlefield." Hattaway and Jones observed that the 1862 Richmond campaign allowed Lee to avoid a siege for a time but only at hideous cost. The confrontation between McClellan and Lee had "resulted in frontal battles with heavy casualties on both sides and little real change in the strategic situation." [1]

Alan T. Nolan's *Lee Considered: General Robert E. Lee and Civil War History* focused even more than *How the North Won* on casualties as a crucial yardstick in evaluating military campaigns. Conceding that Lee's offensive during the Seven Days saved Richmond from McClellan's investing

GARY W. GALLAGHER

force, Nolan emphasized that Confederate dead and wounded totaled nearly 20 percent of the Army of Northern Virginia while in the Army of the Potomac the figure amounted to less than 11 percent. Such victories proved counterproductive because they bled precious manpower the Confederacy could ill afford to lose. Lee's devotion to the offensive during the 1862 Richmond campaign and elsewhere garnered favorable newspaper headlines but accomplished little else. "If one covets the haunting romance of the Lost Cause," asserted Nolan, "then the inflicting of casualties on the enemy, tactical victory in great battles, and audacity are enough." He went on to suggest that Lee's penchant for costly offensives, such as that waged against McClellan in June–July 1862, shortened the life of the Confederacy. Nolan quoted from Lt. Col. George A. Bruce, an early-twentieth-century critic of Lee, to buttress his argument that too many historians have heaped too much praise on Lee for his contributions to the southern war effort: " 'If the art of war consists in using the forces of a nation in a way to secure the end for which it is waged, and not in a succession of great battles that tends to defeat it,' a very different assessment of Lee's martial qualities is required." [2]

With casualties and the essential indestructibility of armies as analytical benchmarks, it is possible to interpret the 1862 Richmond campaign as a sprawling series of marches and battles that exacted a butcher's bill exceeding 50,000 casualties and left the contestants bloodied but intact. [3] The Federals withdrew only as far as Harrison's Landing on the James River, whence they continued to menace the Confederate capital. The South had lost irreplaceable manpower, but in many ways very little seemed to have changed and the war continued.

A full appreciation of the Richmond campaign requires far more attention to the larger picture. How did it figure in the entire tapestry of war during the first half of 1862? What were expectations behind the lines? How did Union and Confederate civilian morale change as a result of the campaign? How did the Army of the Potomac and the Army of Northern Virginia change? Was the conflict significantly different because of what happened on the Peninsula and at Richmond during that spring and early summer?

The military situation in the first half of 1862 followed a script decidedly favorable to the Union. Along the Mississippi River, United States forces made excellent progress toward the strategic goal, identified most famously by Winfield Scott in his so-called Anaconda Plan, of taking control of the great waterway and dividing the Confederacy into eastern and western parts. Well before the first shots at Mechanicsville opened the Seven Days fighting on the afternoon of June 26, Federal naval and land forces had seized Confederate strong points on the upper and lower Mississippi: Columbus,

Kentucky, on March 3; New Madrid, Missouri, on March 14; Island No. 10 on April 7; New Orleans on May 1; and Memphis on June 6. The stretch of river between Baton Rouge and Vicksburg remained in southern hands, but as a conduit for transporting goods and an outlet to the Gulf of Mexico for exports, the Mississippi had ceased to be part of the Confederacy.

Federal gains in the Western Theater rivaled those along the Mississippi. Henry W. Halleck, a much maligned and too often dismissed figure, presided over a spectacular run of victories in Middle Tennessee and northern Mississippi. With Ulysses S. Grant as Halleck's principal field commander, Union forces captured Fort Henry on February 6 and Fort Donelson ten days later, opening the Tennessee and Cumberland Rivers respectively, and stopped a Confederate counteroffensive in the horrific struggle at Shiloh on April 6–7. Don Carlos Buell's army occupied Nashville, with its crucial manufacturing, transportation, and distribution facilities, on February 25; just more than three months later, on May 30, Halleck himself led a mammoth northern force into the railroad center of Corinth, Mississippi. In less than four months, Federals had seized control of a vast swath of the Confederate heartland between Kentucky and Mississippi, a region rich in iron, industry, agricultural products, livestock, and other vital resources. Thomas L. Connelly has underscored the magnitude of this loss to the Confederacy, a judgment southern ordnance chief Josiah Gorgas rendered at the time. The failure to muster all available troops to defend Middle Tennessee before the fall of Henry and Donelson, wrote Gorgas on June 12, 1862, "was the great mistake of the War."[4]

Confederate failures at the margins joined those in major theaters. On the New Mexico frontier, Federals repulsed a small southern army of invasion in the battle of Glorieta on March 28. Three weeks earlier, Samuel R. Curtis had defeated Earl Van Dorn and Sterling Price at Pea Ridge in northwestern Arkansas. In North Carolina, Roanoke Island fell on February 8, New Bern on March 14, and Fort Macon near Beaufort on April 26. None of these actions by itself would have been terribly significant, but as small pieces of a large mosaic they merit attention.

No part of the puzzle loomed larger than Virginia, and Confederates could find little there to counter depressing news from west of the Appalachians and along the Carolina coast. Joseph E. Johnston's army, the largest rebel force in the Eastern Theater, abandoned its lines near Manassas Junction early in March and retreated from a second position along the Rappahannock River a month later. The action shifted to the Peninsula, where George B. McClellan and his Army of the Potomac landed at Fort Monroe and moved

GARY W. GALLAGHER

slowly toward Richmond. Confederates gave up Yorktown on the third of May, Williamsburg on the fifth, and Norfolk on the ninth. The ironclad CSS *Virginia* (popularly called the *Merrimac*), which had raised hopes in many a Confederate breast after its historic victories over several wooden warships on March 8, was scuttled on May 11. "No one event of the war," remarked Josiah Gorgas from his post in Richmond, "not even the disaster of Ft. Donelson created such a profound sensation as the destruction of this noble ship."[5] By the last week of May, 100,000 Federals under McClellan had reached the outskirts of Richmond, more than 30,000 under Irvin McDowell stood at Fredericksburg, and thousands of others lay in the Shenandoah Valley and western Virginia. The battle of Seven Pines or Fair Oaks closed the month with yet another southern failure, as Johnston's ill-executed assaults produced several thousand casualties but left intact the strategic status quo.

Thomas J. "Stonewall" Jackson's Shenandoah Valley campaign supplied the only significant bright spot in this dismal Confederate picture. Between May 8 and June 9, against a group of minimally talented opponents, the dour Virginian won several small victories that cheered Confederates hungry for good news from the battlefield. Jackson's reputation soared among a populace that typically exaggerated the military, as opposed to the psychological, importance of what he had accomplished. The Valley campaign was consequential but in no way offset the larger reality that McClellan's army was closing in on Richmond.

One last point about the military situation in early 1862 bears mention. Operations in the Eastern Theater almost certainly carried more weight than those elsewhere. This is not to say everyone looked to the East as the theater of decision — that surely was not the case. But a majority of civilians North and South, members of the United States Congress, and political leaders in London and Paris formed their primary impressions about how the war was going by reading accounts of eastern operations. Several factors explain this phenomenon. The centers of population clustered in the East, as did newspapers with the highest circulations. The largest and most prominent armies commanded by the most celebrated generals fought in the East, and they campaigned in the shadow of the respective national capitals. Some observers at the time, including Abraham Lincoln, lamented what they considered an undue focus on the East, as have a number of modern historians. Yet the fact remains that what happened during the 1862 Richmond campaign would exert all the more influence because of where it occurred.[6]

Fighting near Richmond would administer a major jolt to the northern political front. As the first year of the conflict closed and the second began, the northern political scene featured cautious optimism about prospects for victory amid debate and flux concerning war aims. The Republican Party made progress on its legislative agenda, passing the Homestead Act on May 20 and preparing to enact Senator Justin Morrill's land grant college legislation, a transcontinental railroad bill, and an internal revenue bill (the last three would become law on July 2–3, 1862). The Republican vision of moving the United States toward the late nineteenth century as an industrial and agricultural giant driven by free labor seemed to be on track.

But the northern public and Congress divided bitterly over emancipation and the question of what kind of Union they sought to restore. Most Democrats vociferously insisted they would risk lives and treasure to save the Union but not to free enslaved black people. The notion of striking at the South's social system by destroying slavery alienated Democrats, virtually all of whom would have seconded George B. McClellan's adamant opposition to adding freedom to Union as a northern war aim. As one student of Democratic politics during the Civil War has observed, the party "forcefully challenged the government's policies, particularly the administration's determination to use whatever means necessary to destroy the South and inflict blows against a social system in the name of winning the war."[7] The Republican majority overcame Democratic opposition, prohibiting the use of military power to return fugitive slaves to rebel owners on March 13, abolishing slavery in the District of Columbia on April 16, and prohibiting slavery in all Federal territories on June 19. Black and white abolitionists, Radical Republicans, and some moderate Republicans supported more sweeping legislation, and Abraham Lincoln, who wanted to control the issue himself, considered calling for emancipation as a measure necessary to defeat the Confederacy. McClellan's Richmond campaign served as a major wild card in this debate over emancipation. A Federal victory and the capture of Richmond, coming on the heels of so many northern successes elsewhere, might convince white southerners to abandon their cause. That in turn could end the war before the North decided to insist on emancipation as a precondition to restoration of the Union.

The northern public expected success from the Army of the Potomac as summer approached in 1862. This expectation derived from the many triumphs on battlefields from New Mexico to the Atlantic coast, the cumulative effect of which prompted newspapers to indulge in lavishly optimistic projections about McClellan's prospects for a decisive victory. Editors across the North claimed that Confederate morale had plummeted, as when a *New York Times* headline described "A PANIC THROUGHOUT THE SOUTH" in late April.

GARY W. GALLAGHER

Maj. Gen. George B. McClellan in an engraving that afforded northern readers
one of their first visual impressions of the young commander
Frank Leslie's Illustrated Newspaper, *June 15, 1861*

Eric T. Dean's examination of northern press opinion during the Richmond campaign revealed startlingly naive articles and editorials: "Toward the beginning of the [Peninsula] campaign, the *New York Tribune* predicted the end of the war in sixty days, the *New York Herald* in seventy-five days, and the *Indianapolis Daily Sentinel* within a few months." No paper exceeded the recklessly upbeat writings of the *New York Times,* which as early as March 12 assured readers that the "final blow may now be struck which shall annihilate the rebel army as an organized force, and crush the Government of the rebel Confederacy at its Capital."[8]

Northerners who read such accounts and followed the advances of United States armies understandably developed positive views about how the war would end.[9] Typical were Maria Lydig Daly, the wife of a Democratic judge in New York City, and Benjamin Brown French, a bureaucrat in Washington. On May 11, Daly reacted in her diary to a spate of good reports: "What splendid news! Norfolk taken, Portsmouth captured, the Navy Yard saved, the *Merrimac* ours, President Lincoln with the army before Norfolk! . . . Now there may be truth in what Mrs. McClellan told us yesterday, that the war would be over by the Fourth of July." A few weeks earlier, French had noted that the "Nation has been wonderfully excited, & Washington has, of course, been in a tumult. The news of victory after victory over the rebels has come and over them we have all rejoiced, and appearances indicate that the game of secession is nearly played out." French characterized the Confederate press as "despondent," adding that "every prestige of success is now with the Union-loving portion of the people." Senator Charles Sumner of Massachusetts, a Radical Republican who did not wish the war to end without emancipation, expressed mixed feelings in a letter to the Duchess of Argyll dated June 9. "It seems pretty certain that the *military power* of the rebellion will be soon broken," he noted. "What then? That is the great question. Seward assured me yesterday that it would 'all be over in 90 days.' I do not see it so."[10]

Sentiment in the Confederacy contrasted sharply with that in the North. Every Union military success had bred a southern failure, promoting war-weariness and an almost frantic need for victories to raise civilian morale. Shortages of food, territory lost to northern invaders, and stringent governmental actions added to a gloomy situation. By far the most important, and divisive, national legislation was the Conscription Act passed on April 16, 1862. The first comprehensive draft in American history, it sought to keep Confederate ranks filled at a time when enlistments had dwindled and thousands of twelve-month volunteers neared the end of their terms of service. Many adherents of state rights and individual freedom decried what they saw as a grotesque perversion of the ideals that had animated secessionists in 1860–61; others labeled the measure necessary to Confederate success. The debate raged as George B. McClellan inched inexorably toward Richmond. "There was a variety of opinion concerning conscription," one historian of the Confederate draft rather drolly observed. "Fundamentally, however, it did not harmonize with the individualistic instincts of Southerners and with their conception of genuine manhood."[11]

The fact that Confederate armies had been losing ground in every quarter overshadowed conscription as a cancer eating at southern morale and will. The southern populace yearned for victories — especially offensive ones delivered by generals who took the initiative rather than merely countering Union movements. Testimony from six witnesses touches on themes present in a mass of letters and diaries. John Beauchamp Jones, a clerk in the War Department whose famous diary recounted myriad aspects of life in wartime Richmond, often described civilians impatient with a defensive strategy. Throughout the month of May, he carefully noted each of the milestones along the road that carried McClellan's army to Richmond without a major battle. For example, on the eighth he wrote that "Norfolk and Portsmouth are evacuated! Our Army falling back! The Merrimac is to be, or has been, blown up!" Six days later he used fewer exclamation points in an equally dreary entry. "Our army has fallen back to within four miles of Richmond," he wrote. "Much anxiety is felt for the fate of the city. Is there no turning point in this long line of downward progress?" Comments by a refugee in Richmond echoed Jones's language. "A gentleman, high in position, panic-struck," observed Judith W. McGuire in her diary, "was heard to exclaim, yesterday: 'Norfolk has fallen, Richmond will fall, Virginia is to be given up, and tomorrow I shall leave this city, an exile and a beggar.' Others are equally despondent, and, as is too frequently the case in times of trouble, attribute all our disasters to the incompetency and faithlessness of those entrusted with the administration of public affairs."[12]

Two South Carolinians voiced similar concerns about the trajectory of Confederate military affairs. "Oh! Hattie, how many, many, sad reverses we've had since I received your letter," wrote Anna E. Kirtland to Harriet R. Palmer from Memphis on May 14. "It is useless to enumerate them. Of course you've read all about them. New Orleans was the saddest blow to us." Although Kirtland had heard that the fortifications at Vicksburg were invulnerable and would stop Yankee gunboats ascending the Mississippi, the long list of lost Confederate strongholds left her uncertain: "I've heard of so many impregnable forts that I have almost lost all faith in them." Henry William Ravenel placed his impressions on paper with no thought of sharing them with anyone. "When I think of our late disasters, I feel cast down, & almost at times disheartened," he admitted in his journal on May 17. Thanking God for what he termed "a sanguine & hopeful temperament," Ravenel added that he soon recovered "my buoyancy of spirits, & my strong unquenchable *Faith* in our ultimate success." Still, he foresaw a difficult road ahead that would demand an extreme effort. "We must fight on," he concluded, "for at the worst it can only end in ruin, & that is already announced to us as our portion by our insolent and boasting foe." [13]

From Caroline County, Virginia, Helen Stuart Bernard spoke for many of the thousands of Confederates who had seen Union forces overrun their locales by late spring 1862. "The record of the past fortnight would contain only the outpourings of a vexed spirit," she wrote bitterly. "The enemy are in full possession of the country all around us. . . . I am weary & sick with grief, indignation & excitement." Cut off from Richmond, Bernard and her neighbors had to "read Yankee papers," which were "jubilant over the fall of N[ew] O[rleans] & Norfolk, the destruction of the Merrimac & the retreat of our Army on the Peninsula." A banker in Lynchburg betrayed anger toward the Confederate government as well as disappointment when bad tidings arrived from the Peninsula. "News that Norfolk had been evacuated and the navy yard destroyed," recorded William M. Blackford in his diary on May 12: "The Merrimac was blown up. This is almost incredible, and yet so fatuous has been the course of our policy that it may be true." [14]

The absence of an army commander around whom the Confederate people could rally deepened the crisis. The first year of the war had seen four officers rise above their peers: P. G. T. Beauregard, the "Hero of Sumter" and co-victor at First Manassas; Joseph E. Johnston, who shared the laurels of Manassas and led the primary army in Virginia thereafter; Albert Sidney Johnston, the president's favorite, who directed affairs in the massive Western Theater; and Robert E. Lee, who brought to his Confederate service an impressive Revolutionary heritage and a reputation as Winfield Scott's favorite soldier. By the time of the Seven Days, Sidney Johnston lay dead of wounds at Shiloh after a decidedly mixed career in the field, and Beauregard had fallen out of favor with Jefferson Davis and gone into temporary exile after the fall of Corinth. In Virginia, Joe Johnston had retreated so often that many had come to question his abilities before he suffered a disabling wound at the battle of Seven Pines. Robert E. Lee stepped into Johnston's position with his public image much diminished because of controversial service in western Virginia and along the South Atlantic coast in 1861 and early 1862.

Lacking an untainted general commanding a major army, Confederates made Stonewall Jackson their paramount military idol. Jackson seized headlines by leading his demi-army in the Shenandoah Valley to victory in five small battles. A pair of newspaper accounts suggest the fervor of southern reaction. On June 1, the *Memphis Daily Appeal* remarked that "the hopeless may look upon Jackson's banner and feel their energies renewed, their hearts cheered, and their souls reinvigorated." Eleven days later the *Richmond Whig* reacted to news of Jackson's victories at Cross Keys and Port Republic: "[Jackson's] little army is the pride of the South and the terror of the North. . . . Oh, for a dozen Jacksons!" Typical of those entranced by Jackson's exploits, South Carolinian Emma Holmes breathlessly described the battle of First Winchester: "Stonewall Jackson has achieved another glorious victory near Winchester, or rather succession of them after three days fighting — each day defeating a portion of Bank's army & finally completely routing it 'in worse than Bull Run style' — large numbers of prisoners and immense quantities of camp equipage and stores of every kind have fallen into our hands." [15]

But Robert E. Lee rather than Stonewall Jackson would coordinate the defense of Richmond in June. He undertook his new duties without enjoying the nearly universal confidence among his fellow citizens that would be his hallmark a few months hence. Many civilians and soldiers who hungered for aggressive action doubted that Lee was up to the task. They thought he had performed timidly in western Virginia during the autumn of 1861 and deplored his penchant for entrenching while in Charleston during the winter of 1861–62. With vitriol typical of his writings, Edward A. Pollard described Lee in western Virginia as "a general who had never fought a battle . . . and whose extreme tenderness of blood induced him to depend exclusively upon the resources of strategy, to essay the achievement of victories without the cost of life." A North Carolinian who later would become an almost slavish admirer of Lee sounded a skeptical note upon learning that he had replaced Joseph Johnston. "I do not much like him," she wrote dismissively on June 2, "he 'falls back' too much." According to this woman, he had acquired a pejorative sobriquet even before his assignments in the fall and winter of 1861–62: "His knick name last summer was '*old-stick-in-the-mud*'. . . . There is mud enough now in and about our lines, but pray God he may not fulfil the whole of his name." [16]

These brief summaries of events and opinion during the first half of 1862 indicate how much was at stake as the armies on the Peninsula moved toward their climactic battles outside Richmond. Flushed with military success, the North confidently expected McClellan to deliver a crowning triumph that would crush the rebellion. How such a victory would influence the debate over emancipation remained to be seen. Confederates struggled to maintain hope in the midst of economic hardship, turmoil over the draft, a relentless drumbeat of failure on the battlefield, and the absence of an army commander in whom they could invest their hopes.

The Seven Days dramatically altered the military and nonmilitary ele-

Robert E. Lee and Stonewall Jackson in the field during the Seven Days battles, a postwar sketch by Alfred A. Waud. Although Lee is the central figure in this sketch, Jackson was the more famous commander in the spring and summer of 1862.
John Esten Cooke, Life of Gen. Robert E. Lee *(New York: D. Appleton, 1871), opposite p. 84*

ments of this picture. Although space prohibits a detailed review, a few observations will highlight the campaign's impact on the armies and the home fronts. Evidence of this impact, in turn, will serve as a reminder of the powerful connections between the military and civilian spheres during the Civil War.

The Army of the Potomac is a good place to begin to assess the Richmond campaign's ramifications. George B. McClellan's reputation suffered among those officers and men in the army who believed he had retreated unnecessarily, given up favorable ground after repelling Lee's attacks at Malvern Hill, and fumbled a brilliant opportunity to capture the enemy's capital. Months of hard work spent pressing the rebels toward Richmond's defenses had come to nothing when the powerful Union host withdrew to Harrison's Landing, there to set up camp along the humid banks of the James River. No

GARY W. GALLAGHER

one expressed greater outrage at this result than Brig. Gen. Philip Kearny, the combative commander of the Third Division of Brig. Gen. Samuel P. Heintzelman's Third Corps. McClellan's cautious approach to warfare frustrated Kearny, who poured out his unhappiness in letters to his wife. Writing from Harrison's Landing on July 1, Kearny charged that "McClellan's treasons or mismanagement has thrown on us a great many partial Battles, of much severity, which he should have spared us. But all of which he invited by his bad arrangements." Nine days later, Kearny claimed that "McClellan's want of Generalship, or treason, has gotten us into a place, where we are completely boxed up. . . . And out of which nothing short of most bold and dashing moves can extricate us to be of any service." A sergeant in the 19th Massachusetts used less inflammatory language to make a similar point: "We are at a loss to imagine whether this is strategy or defeat." Mixing sarcasm with disgust, a junior officer in the engineers noted how some of McClellan's admirers "deify a General whose greatest feat has been a *masterly* retreat." [17]

Far more numerous were soldiers whose disappointment at not taking Richmond failed to undermine their morale and confidence in McClellan. Three pieces of testimony will illustrate this point. A private in the 15th Massachusetts credited rebel generals with movements that compelled McClellan to retreat from the Chickahominy to the James, adding that the withdrawal "was one of the most brilliant achievements of the War." This soldier retained "the utmost confidence in George B. McClellan. No Gen. can expect to be successfull in each and every undertaking." A staff officer from Michigan alluded to diminishing hopes for success between May and late June. "At Yorktown I felt the most unbounded confidence," wrote Charles B. Haydon. " . . . After Fair Oaks & Stewart's raid the thought of beating them was less prominent in my mind than that it was impossible for them to beat us. The general feeling seemed to be let *them come.*" As for the Seven Days and the Union retreat, Haydon conceded, "Few expected what has followed." Yet he insisted that "perfect confidence & good feeling" prevailed, describing how "we all cheered most heartily for country, cause & leader" on July 4 when McClellan "came around to see us." Hannah Ropes, a matron at Union Hospital in Georgetown, D.C., spoke with some of the wounded from Fitz John Porter's Fifth Corps. "None of our men feel defeated at all by the battles near Richmond," she stated, "and those who are not disabled for life wish to go back as soon as they are well enough." [18]

Many Federal soldiers believed their government had failed to provide the men and material necessary for victory. Frederick Law Olmsted, general director of the U.S. Sanitary Commission, conversed with officers and enlisted men at Harrison's Landing immediately after the Seven Days. He concluded that the army believed it had fought well against a superior foe and only needed reinforcements to go after the rebels again. Some in the army were "utterly despondent and fault-finding," but "there is less of this than ever before, and fewer stragglers and obvious cowards. . . . Of what we saw after Bull Run there is not the slightest symptom." In a letter dated July 6, Olmsted urged Lincoln to send 50,000 fresh men to the Army of the Potomac. "Without these," he observed pessimistically, "the best army the world ever saw must lie idle, and, in discouragement and dejection, be wasted by disease." [19]

The Richmond campaign exacerbated the already poisonous distrust between Democratic generals in the Army of the Potomac and Republicans in Washington. Radical Republican senator Zachariah Chandler of Michigan, a member of the Joint Committee on the Conduct of the War, attacked McClellan unsparingly in the committee and on the floor of the Senate. Privately, Chandler called McClellan "an imbecile if not a traitor" who had "virtually lost the Army of the Potomac." Democratic newspapers defended the general, as when the *New York Herald* called for congressional committees to refrain from meddling in military affairs and opined that "only traitors and fools" would support Chandler.[20] In Lincoln's cabinet, Secretary of the Treasury Salmon P. Chase and Secretary of War Edwin M. Stanton lambasted McClellan's timid handling of the Richmond campaign and chronic pleas for more men and supplies. Three weeks after the battle of Malvern Hill, Chase "urged upon the President the importance of an immediate change in the command of the Army of the Potomac. . . . I said that I did not regard Genl. McClellan as loyal to the Administration, although I did not question his general loyalty to the country." [21]

Lincoln himself journeyed to Harrison's Landing on July 8–9 for a visit to army headquarters. The Richmond campaign marked the first of several in which the president could not get his eastern commanders to use their full strength against the Army of Northern Virginia, and what he saw on the James did not encourage him. McClellan had prepared a confidential letter for Lincoln, dated July 7 and later known as the "Harrison's Landing Letter," which called for continuance of a restrained form of warfare against the Confederacy. "Neither confiscation of property . . . ," insisted McClellan, "or forcible abolition of slavery should be contemplated for a moment." The United States should abide by the "highest principles known to Christian civilization." David Donald has aptly described the president's reaction to "Little Mac's" suggestion: "That policy had been pursued for over a year and Lincoln was convinced that it had failed. He was ready to move on." Two days after returning to Washington, Lincoln appointed Henry W. Hal-

GARY W. GALLAGHER

President Lincoln reviewing Union troops at Harrison's Landing on July 8, 1862.
Frank Leslie's Illustrated Newspaper, *August 2, 1862*

leck general-in-chief, a move, wrote Donald, that "signaled a repudiation of McClellan, and of McClellan's view of the war."[22]

Lincoln thus moved much closer to the abolitionists and Radical Republicans who had demanded seizure of slaves and other property belonging to rebels. Later in July, deeply affected by the outcome of the Seven Days, Lincoln would inform his cabinet that he intended to issue a proclamation of emancipation. Congress, meanwhile, put the finishing touches on the Second Confiscation Act, a measure designed to free all slaves held by rebels. Senator Sumner explicitly tied passage of this act on July 17 to Union military failure in the Richmond campaign. "The Bill of Confiscation & Liberation, which was at last passed, under pressure from our reverses at Richmond," wrote Sumner in early August 1862, "is a practical act of Emancipation."[23] Had McClellan been the victor in July 1862, he certainly could have pressed his case for a softer policy more effectively. The consequences for millions of enslaved African Americans might have been momentous.

Most northern civilians understood that the campaign had failed, though few of them believed it presaged Confederate independence. Some newspapers that had been wildly optimistic in April and May adopted a more prudent tone regarding what it would take to win the war.[24] Overall the North began to confront the unpleasant fact that enormous sacrifice and loss likely would be necessary.

McClellan's retreat hit especially hard because hopes had been so high. Two well-known diarists captured the sobering impact of the bad news.

Evaluating the campaign on July 4, Benjamin Brown French revealed the degree to which northerners had first been encouraged and then cast down by reports from the Richmond front. "I have been looking over my journal and am considerably amused to find how long we have all been expecting that Richmond would be taken!" he wrote. "And now the doings of the past week have driven back our immense army from within 4 miles of Richmond to 20! The loss of life has been immense. Our generals call it a strategic movement of McClellan to obtain a better base of operations! Two or three such strategic movements would annihilate our army." French did not doubt that Federal soldiers had fought well and believed they probably had been outnumbered. Although on July 4 he "almost despair[ed] of our ever taking Richmond," three days later he took heart from wounded officers in Washington who expressed complete confidence in McClellan. Those veterans harbored anger that the army had not been reinforced. As soon as McClellan received fresh troops, one officer told French, "he will take Richmond." New Yorker George Templeton Strong, a staunch Republican, concluded on the night of July 3 that McClellan had been "beat back by a superior force but not destroyed. The enemy was superior because we have been outgeneraled. The blame rests, probably, on the War Department. The remedy is speedy reinforcement." Eight days' reflection deepened Strong's melancholy: "We have been and are in a depressed, dismal, asthenic state of anxiety and irritabiliy," he wrote. "The cause of the country does not seem to be thriving just now." [25]

Politics colored reaction to the Richmond campaign among many northern civilians. Democrats tended to blame the Lincoln administration and Congress rather than McClellan, stressing that the army should have been reinforced before the final battles around Richmond. Thus did Maria Lydig Daly, who had been so enthusiastic about McClellan's prospects in May, lash out at Republicans in her diary on July 3. McClellan had shown himself "an able general" during the retreat to the James and now occupied a strong position. The defeat was not his fault but "that of his enemies, who, to ruin him, would sacrifice a whole army. . . . It is time that Democrats should have something to say. Three quarters of the army are composed of them, yet every Democratic general is persecuted, and the Republicans do their best to get them out of the way." Elizabeth Blair Lee, the sister of Montgomery and Frank Blair and wife of naval officer Samuel Phillips Lee, described the army on July 3 as "disgusted with the conduct of the Govt." She understood that 20,000 men had embarked to reinforce McClellan, adding editorially, "Oh if they had been sent a month ago!! we might have been spared much sorrow on both sides of the lines — " [26]

GARY W. GALLAGHER

In the realm of foreign affairs, the Richmond campaign carried far more clout with French and British observers than any of the Union successes west of the Appalachians. A recent study of French newspapers during the Civil War found that as McClellan advanced on Richmond "many Frenchmen confidently expected an early end to the war." But opinion changed abruptly "when General Robert E. Lee drove McClellan away from the gates of Richmond" and followed up with other strategically offensive movements. In Britain, McClellan's repulse helped fuel support for recognizing the Confederacy during heated debates in Parliament. American diplomat Charles Francis Adams believed that the Richmond campaign had canceled the capture of New Orleans as a factor favoring the Union and persuaded many in Britain that the Confederate capital would never be taken. In a letter written July 18, 1862, French diplomat Agénor-Etienne de Gasparin informed Lincoln that the "check sustained by the federal army before Richmond was certainly a situation of difficulty for the United States." The Frenchman went on to wonder why the North did not apply its greater military resources more effectively. Lincoln answered on August 4, claiming that the "moral effect was the worst of the affair before Richmond; and that has run its course downward." The president then betrayed frustration at the importance given events in Virginia compared to those farther west: "It seems unreasonable that a series of successes, extending through half-a-year, and clearing more than a hundred thousand square miles of country, should help us so little, while a single half-defeat should hurt us so much."[27]

The "half-success" at Richmond had a seismic effect on the Confederacy's war for nationhood. Lee's debut as a field commander marked the most important watershed in the development of the Army of Northern Virginia — and one of the crucial turning points of the entire war. His victory during the Seven Days, however marred by tactical lapses, thrust him into the limelight as the Confederacy's only post-Manassas army commander with a major victory to his credit. That status helped solidify his hold on the field command he had long wished to exercise. Lee's leadership in June and July 1862 began an eleven-month process by which he would mold the army into a finely tuned instrument that won notable victories, rapidly became the most important national institution in the Confederacy, and helped sustain morale in the face of mounting odds and hardships on the home front. Although eclipsed in the popular imagination by Stonewall Jackson during the Richmond campaign and for a time thereafter, Lee soon rose to become the unchallenged military idol of the Confederacy. Fellow citizens began to compare him to George Washington, Lee's own model of a man and leader. The comparison was apt because Lee and his army would come to function much as Washington and the Continental army had during the American Revolution. Beginning with the Seven Days, Lee would shoulder an increasing share of the burden of sustaining morale among his nation's citizenry.[28]

Although counterfactual speculation about what might have happened under different circumstances is usually pointless, Lee's rise to command offers a clear exception. It is easy to imagine the war taking a very different path if Joseph Johnston had escaped his wound at Seven Pines. He almost certainly would have retreated into Richmond (retreating is what Johnston preferred in almost all situations), there to be besieged and eventually conquered by McClellan. The avalanche of bad news from other theaters already had threatened to smother southern hopes for victory; the loss of its capital might well have destroyed the Confederacy. Lee's successful defense of the city reversed a downward trend and virtually guaranteed a much longer and more revolutionary struggle. James M. McPherson has ruminated about the "profound irony" inherent in Lee's victory: "If McClellan's campaign had succeeded, the war might have ended. The Union probably would have been restored with minimal destruction in the South. Slavery would have survived in only slightly modified form, at least for a time. By defeating McClellan, Lee assured a prolongation of the war until it destroyed slavery, the Old South, and nearly everything the Confederacy was fighting for."[29]

Lee had pursued the kind of strategic and tactical offensive best suited to satisfy the expectations of the Confederate people. Two days before the battle of Mechanicsville, war clerk Jones noted public concern that McClellan might lay siege to the city before its defenders struck a blow. "Our people are beginning to *fear* there will be no more fighting around Richmond until McClellan *digs* his way to it," he wrote. Military inaction brought "fits of gloom and despondency" among the people, but when they "snuff battle in the breeze, they are animated with confidence." Lee's conduct during the Richmond campaign spawned such confidence and won plaudits from many who previously had groused about his timid style of generalship. The Richmond *Dispatch* had been among those doubtful of Lee's abilities but reversed course quickly after the Seven Days. "The rise which this officer has suddenly taken in the public confidence is without precedent," reported the *Dispatch* on July 9. Less than a week later, the Richmond *Whig* asserted that "by the brilliancy of his genius" Lee had silenced critics, "established his reputation forever, and . . . entitled himself to the lasting gratitude of his country." In far-off Columbia, South Carolina, Grace Brown Elmore thanked God for Lee's "glorious fight" at the Seven Days. "Thou hast answered our prayers," she wrote in her diary on July 25, "and given us one who is well able to guide us through this fearful time, and lead us on to freedom."[30]

GARY W. GALLAGHER

In the afterglow of victory, some Confederates lamented Lee's failure to achieve more. Varina Davis stood among them, complaining to her husband that McClellan's army should have been destroyed rather than merely driven back. Jefferson Davis reflected the attitude of most Confederates in replying that "our success has been so remarkable that we should be grateful and believe that even our disappointments were ordered for our gain." After all, McClellan's larger army had been forced from its entrenchments by a less well equipped Confederate force, had abandoned millions of dollars worth of supplies, and had given up on a campaign that consumed months to plan. "Our troubles you perceive have not ended," stated Davis gently, "but our chances have improved so I repeat be of good cheer." Other witnesses remarked about people who shared Varina Davis's view. A soldier who left the battle line to visit Richmond shortly after Malvern Hill found no "signs of any jubilation over our series of victories." Everyone professed to have had faith that the Army of Northern Virginia would prevail, and "all regretted the escape of McClellan." J. B. Jones mentioned "some sage critics" dissatisfied that "Lee does not follow up his blows on the whipped enemy." They were wrong, he thought; the "serpent has been killed, though its tail still exhibits some spasmodic motions." If anything, Jones worried that most Confederates were "too jubilant . . . over our recent success near the city." Overconfidence could prevent the degree of commitment necessary for ultimate victory.[31]

A junior officer following events in Virginia from his station in Savannah offered an evaluation likely shared by many other Confederates. It revealed pride in the victory and a grasp of its larger implications, leavened with a wistful mention of possible opportunities lost. Lt. Charles C. Jones rejoiced in "the valor of our men and the success of our arms" that drove back "the hostile legions of the aggressor . . . in consternation and dread confusion." Sorry that Lee had not compelled the "unconditional surrender of McClellan and his boasted army of invasion," Jones understood that disadvantages of numbers and matériel had worked against the Army of Northern Virginia. He knew the campaign had improved the Confederacy's chances for independence — "the tide has indeed turned," as he put it — and spoke of the depressing effect this defeat would have in the North. It would undermine civilian morale, boost the peace party, and frustrate Union diplomatic efforts. "It must teach them the utter impracticability of any theory which looks towards a subjugation," Jones predicted, and "will completely upset all the boastful schemes, and give the direct lie to all the vain promises, of their corrupt administration."[32]

The Seven Days rapidly took on the aura of an unequivocal Confederate triumph. The observations of an English visitor to the battlefields in the autumn of 1862 doubtless reflected the opinions of the Confederates who accompanied him. "I had an opportunity, while at Richmond, of going over the celebrated battlefields which were the scene of the utter overthrow of the Federal army under General McClellan . . . when he was attempting to take the city," wrote W. C. Corsan. The Seven Days presented "a series of defeats inflicted on an enemy, probably succeeding each other more rapidly, and of a more crushing character, than can be found elsewhere in history." The beaten northern army fled to "a swamp — a defeated, terrified, demoralized mob." Only Federal gunboats at Malvern Hill and "consummate skill, and the greatest haste" during the retreat saved the Federals from "annihilation by their triumphant foes!"[33]

The Richmond campaign also began the phenomenon of Confederates focusing progressively more on the Eastern Theater to determine the health of their cause. Lee had given them their first major victory in nearly a year, helping to erase some of the sting from losses in the Mississippi Valley, Middle Tennessee, and along the Atlantic coast. Over the next year, Second Manassas, Fredericksburg, and Chancellorsville would spread the impression that all good news emanated from the theater where Lee and his army operated. Under these circumstances, and with the additional importance of Richmond as a psychological, industrial, and governmental colossus, it should come as little surprise that Confederates fixed their hopes as well as their gaze on Virginia.

As the armies watched each other below Richmond in July 1862, much of the recent campaign's impact already was apparent. Civilians and soldiers in the United States and the Confederacy could see the imprint of the campaign on political connections to military affairs, debate over war aims and policy, the command structures of the armies, civilian morale and attitudes, and the diplomatic front. They could only guess at some of the longer-term effects that stand out in retrospect. Modern students of the war should use that retrospective advantage to appreciate the full context within which the campaign was waged and the astonishing range of its immediate and long-range influence.

NOTES

1. Herman Hattaway and Archer Jones, *How the North Won: A Military History of the Civil War* (Urbana: University of Illinois Press, 1983), 692, 200–201. Hattaway and Jones included the western battles between Federals under Henry W. Halleck and Ulysses S. Grant and Confederates under Albert Sidney Johnston and P. G. T. Beau-

GARY W. GALLAGHER

regard in their analysis of clashes that piled up casualties but left the strategic picture relatively undisturbed.

2. Alan T. Nolan, *Lee Considered: General Robert E. Lee and Civil War History* (Chapel Hill: University of North Carolina Press, 1991), 82, 84, 106. For another work that stresses the degree to which Lee's bloody battles hurt the Confederacy, see Grady McWhiney and Perry D. Jamieson, *Attack and Die: Civil War Military Tactics and the Southern Heritage* (University: University of Alabama Press, 1982). This book opens with a description of the costly frontal assaults at Malvern Hill. Four historians who essentially restate Nolan's arguments without adding anything new in the way of evidence or analysis are Edward H. Bonekemper III, *How Robert E. Lee Lost the Civil War* (Fredericksburg, Va.: Sergeant Kirkland's Press, 1997); John D. McKenzie, *Uncertain Glory: Lee's Generalship Re-Examined* (New York: Hippocrene Books, 1997); Bevin Alexander, *Robert E. Lee's Civil War* (Holbrook, Mass.: Adams Media, 1998); and Michael A. Palmer, *Lee Moves North: Robert E. Lee on the Offensive* (New York: Wiley, 1998). For the counterargument that Lee's campaigns lengthened the life of the Confederacy, see Joseph L. Harsh, *Confederate Tide Rising: Robert E. Lee and the Making of Southern Strategy, 1861-1862* (Kent, Ohio: Kent State University Press, 1998), and chapter 3 of Gary W. Gallagher, *The Confederate War* (Cambridge, Mass.: Harvard University Press, 1997). In *Davis and Lee at War* (Lawrence: University Press of Kansas, 1995), xii, Steven E. Woodworth offers a thoughtful critique of Lee, concluding that his offensive-minded approach "was in fact one of two possible ways in which the South could conceivably have obtained its independence." (Woodworth believes the other way was a "thoroughly defensive, survival-oriented grand strategy so much praised by many modern scholars."). For a pair of very well-written earlier works that placed the Richmond campaign in a broad context, see Bruce Catton, *Terrible Swift Sword* (Garden City, N.Y.: Doubleday, 1963), and Clifford Dowdey, *The Seven Days: The Emergence of Lee* (Boston: Little, Brown, 1964).

3. Casualties at the three largest actions of the Richmond campaign were as follows: battle of Williamsburg (May 5) — 2,239 U.S. and 1,703 C.S.; battle of Seven Pines or Fair Oaks (May 31–June 1) — 5,031 U.S. and 6,134 C.S.; Seven Days battles (June 25–July 1) — 15,849 U.S. and 20,141 C.S. The total of 51,097 killed, wounded, and missing does not include casualties from smaller actions and skirmishing. Figures for Civil War casualties are notoriously unreliable. These were taken from E. B. Long, *The Civil War Day by Day: An Almanac, 1861-1865* (Garden City, N.Y.: Doubleday, 1971), 207, 220, 235.

4. On the value of the Tennessee heartland, see Thomas L. Connelly, *Army of the Heartland: The Army of Tennessee, 1861-1862* (Baton Rouge: Louisiana State University Press, 1967), especially pp. 3–15. For Gorgas's quotation, see Josiah Gorgas, *The Journals of Josiah Gorgas, 1857-1878,* ed. Sarah Woolfolk Wiggins (Tuscaloosa: University of Alabama Press, 1995), 42–43.

5. Gorgas, *Journals,* 45. Many contemporary accounts attest to the importance of the *Virginia.* See, for example, Fanny Hume, *The Fanny Hume Diary of 1862,* ed. J. Randolph Grymes Jr. (Orange, Va.: Orange County Historical Society, 1994), 94, and Edmund Ruffin, *The Diary of Edmund Ruffin,* ed. William Kauffman Scarborough, 3 vols. (Baton Rouge: Louisiana State University Press, 1972–89), 2:301.

6. For a useful discussion of the predominance of the East by a historian who often champions the West, see Richard M. McMurry, *Two Great Rebel Armies: An Essay in Confederate Military History* (Chapel Hill: University of North Carolina Press, 1989), 1–9.

7. Joel H. Silbey, *A Respectable Minority: The Democratic Party in the Civil War Era, 1860–1868* (New York: Norton, 1977), ix. McClellan consistently opposed adding emancipation as a goal for the Union. In November 1861, for example, he wrote: "*I* am fighting to preserve the integrity of the Union & the power of the Govt — on no other issue. To gain that end we cannot afford to raise up the negro question — it must be incidental & subsidiary" (George B. McClellan, *The Civil War Papers of George B. McClellan: Selected Correspondence, 1860–1865,* ed. Stephen W. Sears [New York: Ticknor & Fields, 1989], 128).

8. Eric T. Dean Jr., "'We Live under a Government of Men and Morning Newspapers': Image, Expectation, and the Peninsula Campaign of 1862," *Virginia Magazine of History and Biography* 103 (January 1995): 15–17.

9. Dean, "'Government of Men and Morning Papers,'" 22–23, prudently points out that it is difficult to demonstrate that "media-generated images and expectations actually influenced public opinion" in 1862. Such a connection could be proven only "if one had access somehow to public opinion surveys of the 1860s" — and even then, as the modern experience with polls has shown, the results might be debatable. While taking this into account, I believe it is safe to assume that newspaper coverage during the first five and one-half months of 1862 helped foster optimism among northerners.

10. Maria Lydig Daly, *Diary of a Union Lady, 1861–1865,* ed. Harold Earl Hammond (New York: Funk & Wagnall's, 1962), 126–27; Benjamin Brown French, *Witness to the Young Republic: A Yankee's Journal, 1828–1870,* ed. Donald B. Cole and John J. McDonough (Hanover, N.H.: University Press of New England, 1989), 388; Charles Sumner, *The Selected Letters of Charles Sumner,* ed. Beverly Wilson Palmer, 2 vols. (Boston: Northeastern University Press, 1990), 2:119.

11. Albert B. Moore, *Conscription and Conflict in the Confederacy* (New York: Macmillan, 1924), 17. Chapter 1 of Moore's pioneering work offers a range of testimony for and against conscription.

12. John Beauchamp Jones, *A Rebel War Clerk's Diary at the Confederate States Capital,* 2 vols. (1866; reprint, Alexandria, Va.: Time-Life, 1982), 1:123–24; [Judith W. McGuire], *Diary of a Southern Refugee during the War* (1867; reprint, Lincoln: University of Nebraska Press, 1995), 113.

13. Louis P. Towles, ed., *A World Turned Upside Down: The Palmers of South Santee, 1818–1881* (Columbia: University of South Carolina Press, 1996), 323–24; Henry William Ravenel, *The Private Journal of Henry William Ravenel, 1859–1887*, ed. Arney Robinson Childs (Columbia: University of South Carolina Press, 1947), 140–41.

14. Rebecca Campbell Light, ed., *War at Our Doors: The Civil War Diaries and Letters of the Bernard Sisters of Virginia* (Fredericksburg, Va.: American History Company, 1998), 32–33; Susan Leigh Blackford, ed., *Memoirs of Life in and out of the Army in Virginia during the War between the States*, 2 vols. (1894; reprint, Lynchburg, Va.: Warwick House, 1996), 1:145.

15. J. Tracy Power, "'There Stands Jackson Like a Stone Wall': The Image of General Thomas J. 'Stonewall' Jackson in the Confederate Mind, July 1861–November 1862" (M.A. thesis, University of South Carolina, 1984), 66, 83; Emma Holmes, *The Diary of Miss Emma Holmes, 1861–1866*, ed. John F. Marszalek (Baton Rouge: Louisiana State University Press, 1979), 168–69. Power argues that Confederate newspaper editors deliberately sought to transform Jackson into a national hero: "The major Confederate newspapers, particularly the influential quartet of the *Richmond Dispatch*, the *Richmond Enquirer*, the *Richmond Examiner*, and the *Richmond Whig*, established and embellished Jackson's reputation, and by their portrayal of him insured that the public perception of Stonewall would be as the preeminent hero of the Southern cause" (p. 81). Other scholars would counter that Jackson's accomplishments needed no boost from newspaper puffery to create a groundswell of public acclaim.

16. Edward A. Pollard, *Southern History of the War: The First Year of the War* (1862; reprint, New York: Charles B. Richardson, 1864), 168; Catherine Ann Devereux Edmondston, *"Journal of a Secesh Lady": The Diary of Catherine Ann Devereux Edmondston, 1860–1866*, ed. Beth Gilbert Crabtree and James W. Patton (Raleigh: North Carolina Division of Archives and History, 1979), 189.

17. Philip Kearny, *Letters from the Peninsula: The Civil War Letters of General Philip Kearny*, ed. William B. Styple (Kearny, N.J.: Belle Grove Publishing, 1988), 116, 125; Stephen W. Sears, *To the Gates of Richmond: The Peninsula Campaign* (New York: Ticknor & Fields, 1992), 347.

18. Roland E. Bowen, *From Ball's Bluff to Gettysburg . . . and Beyond: The Civil War Letters of Private Roland E. Bowen, 15th Massachusetts Infantry, 1861–1864*, ed. Gregory A. Coco (Gettysburg, Pa.: Thomas Publications, 1994), 109; Charles B. Haydon, *For Country, Cause and Leader: The Civil War Journal of Charles B. Haydon*, ed. Stephen W. Sears (New York: Ticknor & Fields, 1993), 263; Hannah Ropes, *Civil War Nurse: The Diary and Letters of Hannah Ropes*, ed. John R. Brumgardt (Knoxville: University of Tennessee Press, 1980), 56.

19. Frederick Law Olmsted, *The Papers of Frederick Law Olmsted*, vol. 4, *Defending the Union: The Civil War and the U.S. Sanitary Commission*, ed. Jane Turner Censor (Baltimore: Johns Hopkins University Press, 1986), 389, 392–93.

20. Bruce Tap, *Over Lincoln's Shoulder: The Committee on the Conduct of the War* (Lawrence: University Press of Kansas, 1998), 122–26.

21. On Chase and Stanton, see Salmon P. Chase, *The Salmon P. Chase Papers,* ed. John Niven, 5 vols. to date (Kent, Ohio: Kent State University Press, 1993–), 1:350; Gideon Welles, *Diary of Gideon Welles: Secretary of the Navy under Lincoln and Johnson,* ed. Howard K. Beale, 3 vols. (New York: Norton, 1960), 1:95–97. Welles recounted a meeting in August 1862 at which Stanton heavily criticized McClellan's handling of the entire Richmond campaign.

22. McClellan, *Civil War Papers,* 344; David Herbert Donald, *Lincoln* (New York: Simon & Schuster, 1995), 360–61. On Lincoln's change of policy, see also Mark E. Neely Jr., "Lincoln and the Theory of Self-Emancipation," in *The Continuing Civil War: Essays in Honor of the Civil War Round Table of Chicago,* ed. John Y. Simon and Barbara Hughett (Dayton, Ohio: Morningside, 1992), 46–50, 56–58. Neely concluded that by mid-July, Lincoln had decided that the "formidable power and dimensions of the insurrection" obliged the United States to take "extraordinary measures" against the Confederacy.

23. Sumner, *Selected Letters,* 2:122. On the relationship between the Seven Days and Lincoln's decision to push for emancipation, see Welles, *Diary,* 1:70–71. For a perceptive discussion of how the Richmond campaign fit into the movement toward a harsher northern war effort, see chapter 4 of Mark Grimsley, *The Hard Hand of War: Union Military Policy toward Southern Civilians, 1861–1865* (New York: Cambridge University Press, 1995).

24. Dean, "Government of Men and Morning Newspapers," 18.

25. French, *Witness to the Young Republic,* 400–401; George Templeton Strong, *The Diary of George Templeton Strong,* ed. Allan Nevins and Milton Halsey Thomas, 4 vols. (New York: Macmillan, 1962), 3:236–37, 239. In *Our Masters the Rebels: A Speculation on Union Military Failure in the East, 1861–1865* (Cambridge, Mass.: Harvard University Press, 1978), 99, Michael C. C. Adams argued that McClellan's failure to defeat a smaller rebel army promoted a widespread belief in the North that Confederate soldiers and generals might be superior to their Union opponents. "McClellan's contribution to Southern prestige in the North is easily stated," wrote Adams. "He was given a huge and splendidly equipped army, which he handled so clumsily as to make the military machine look impotent. . . . More serious was the failure of the Peninsula campaign. McClellan had acted so haltingly that he made his enemies look brilliant, even when they often were not."

26. Daly, *Diary,* 157; Elizabeth Blair Lee, *Wartime Washington: The Civil War Letters of Elizabeth Blair Lee,* ed. Virginia Jeans Laas (Urbana: University of Illinois Press, 1991), 160.

27. George M. Blackburn, *French Newspaper Opinion on the American Civil War* (Westport, Conn.: Greenwood, 1997), 57–58; Howard Jones, *Union in Peril: The Cri-*

sis over British Intervention in the Civil War (Chapel Hill: University of North Carolina Press, 1992), 133–36; Abraham Lincoln, *The Collected Works of Abraham Lincoln,* ed. Roy P. Basler, 9 vols. (New Brunswick, N.J.: Rutgers University Press, 1953–55), 5:355–56.

28. For a fuller development of the themes in this paragraph, see Gallagher, *Confederate War,* especially chap. 3; and Gary W. Gallagher, "The Idol of His Soldiers and the Hope of His Country," in Gallagher, *Lee and His Generals in War and Memory* (Baton Rouge: Louisiana State University Press, 1998).

29. James M. McPherson, *Battle Cry of Freedom: The Era of the Civil War* (New York: Oxford University Press, 1988), 490–91.

30. Jones, *Diary,* 1:135; Richmond *Dispatch,* July 9, 1862; Richmond *Whig,* July 15, 1862; Grace Brown Elmore, *Heritage of Woe: The Civil War Diary of Grace Brown Elmore, 1861–1868,* ed. Marli F. Weiner (Athens: University of Georgia Press, 1997), 35.

31. Jefferson Davis, *The Papers of Jefferson Davis,* ed. Haskell M. Monroe, James T. McIntosh, and Lynda Lasswell Crist, 10 vols. to date (Baton Rouge: Louisiana State University Press, 1971–), 8:280–81; [Thomas E. Caffey], *Battle-Fields of the South, from Bull Run to Fredericksburgh; with Sketches of Confederate Commanders, and Gossip of the Camps* (1864; reprint, Alexandria, Va.: Time-Life, 1984), 380; Jones, *Diary,* 1:141, 144.

32. Robert Manson Myers, ed., *The Children of Pride: A True Story of Georgia and the Civil War* (New Haven: Yale University Press, 1972), 923–24.

33. W. C. Corsan, *Two Months in the Confederate States: An Englishman's Travels through the South,* ed. Benjamin H. Trask (Baton Rouge: Louisiana State University Press, 1996), 87–88.

JOHN T. HUBBELL

The Seven Days of
George Brinton McClellan

istory and historians have not been kind to George Brinton Mc-
Clellan. His many critics have charged him with a multitude of
faults — passivity, indecisiveness, "demons and delusions," and
fears that bordered on actual cowardice. Stephen Sears ranks him
as "inarguably the worst" commander of the Army of the Potomac.
Yet his contemporaries expected great things from him. Early impressions,
in 1861, were of a poised, energetic, and engaging young officer. Indeed, a
"look of competence" was one of McClellan's "most noticed characteristics."
He looked good in uniform and on horseback, and he "made it a point to be
seen often" by his soldiers. Nor is command presence a small matter, especially among new soldiers. They would in time sort out the real leaders, but
on the eve of the great campaigns of 1862 a general who looked the part had
an advantage.

McClellan was at an advantage as well in terms of education and experience, and he had earned a small reputation as a military intellectual. Yet his
public experience, in the army and in the world of commerce, did not pre-
clude a habit of excuse-making, uninformed caution, and the blaming of superiors, military and political, for problems great and small. A noticeable
and unattractive social snobbery led him to give undue credit to his "aristo-
cratic" opponents and to sell short his own soldiers, no matter how he publicly flattered them. He was given to petulance and alternating bouts of ar-
rogance and self-pity, tendencies often revealed in the same letter, if not in
the same paragraph. His strategy could be grandiose without being grand,
in the sense of being realistically comprehensive. He showed scant regard for
military practicalities and small appreciation of terrain or logistics.[1] Napoleon was his hero, but as an army commander he was not Napoleonic, a trait
defined by Peter Michie as the "ready adaption of means to the end in view,
followed by celerity of movement to gain strategical advantage."[2]

McClellan was not the only public man to think in terms of a decisive battle in 1861, but he was the least likely or willing to do with what he had. On the Peninsula in 1862, what he had was considerable. That campaign and the army were his, for better or ill. He neither sought nor accepted advice, counsel, or even encouragement. For all his executive ability and experience, McClellan would not delegate authority, although when circumstances demanded leadership he was quite willing to delegate responsibility. He was secretive in that he only grudgingly shared information with his primary commanders or his civilian superiors. He never understood that it was his place to reassure and inform the president, not the opposite, as he demanded. His open contempt for his commander-in-chief poisoned the atmosphere at the beginning of the 1862 campaign.

Lord Charnwood's commentary is instructive on this point. "It counts for little" that McClellan privately expressed small regard for the government, "but it counts for more that he was personally insolent to the President." Lincoln's early and misplaced deference to the general "would not obscure to any soldier the full gravity" of McClellan's breach of manners. "It was not merely foolish to treat a kind superior rudely; a general who thus drew down a curtain between his own mind and that of the Government evidently went a very long way to ensure failure in war." Jacob D. Cox, one of the Union's more perceptive and effective volunteer officers, wrote: "The general who indoctrinates his army with the belief that it is required by its government to do the impossible, may preserve his popularity with the troops and be received with cheers as he rides down the line, but he has put any great military success far beyond his reach."[3] McClellan may not have indoctrinated his army, but he convinced himself that the government wanted him to fail.

The movement of the Army of the Potomac to the Peninsula was a major achievement for which McClellan deserves credit. It was the "stride of a giant," no matter that strategic boldness immediately gave way to tactical timidity. McClellan's excuse for his lack of celerity was that the navy was preoccupied by the CSS *Virginia* and because Lincoln, concerned with the safety of Washington, halted the deployment of Irvin McDowell's corps to the Peninsula.

McClellan's litany of complaints centered on his unwavering belief that he was vastly outnumbered and needed constant and immediate reinforcements. Lincoln had doubted the efficacy of the movement in the first place, and if McClellan's reports were accurate, the campaign had already failed. Further, Thomas J. Jackson's diversions and incursions in the Shenandoah Valley convinced the president that the capital was vulnerable to a quick strike. He also believed that McClellan had misled him as to the number of

*Union soldiers cheer on April 5, 1862, as George B. McClellan arrives
on the Peninsula to take command of the advance toward Yorktown.*
Frank Leslie's Illustrated Newspaper, *May 3, 1862*

troops actually protecting Washington. Thus his letter of April 9, 1862, a communication that combined explanations, impatience, and reassurances. Lincoln began with a sentence that would have been a clear warning to a general with even a modicum of sensitivity: "Your despatches complaining that you are not properly sustained, while they do not offend me, do pain me very much." The president's "explicit order" that Washington "be left entirely secure, had been neglected. It was precisely this that drove me to detain McDowell." The safety of the capital was a "question which the country will not allow me to evade."

Nor was Lincoln's concern misplaced. The idea that a national capital is a center of gravity in time of war does not demand Clausewitzian insight. The photographs of a Viet Cong machine gun squad on the grounds of the American Embassy in Saigon in 1968 guaranteed, even without Walter Cronkite's valedictory, that the Tet Offensive was a strategic success. But Abraham Lincoln's concern for Washington must be understood in conjunction with his understanding that the Union armies, East and West, must carry the war to the enemy. Thus he counseled McClellan: "And, once more let me tell you, it is indispensable to *you* that you strike a blow. *I* am powerless to help this." The deployment on the Peninsula, "instead of fighting at or near Ma-

JOHN T. HUBBELL

nassas, was only shifting, and not surmounting, a difficulty. . . . The country will not fail to note — is now noting — that the present hesitation to move upon an intrenched enemy" replicates earlier hesitations. Lincoln assured McClellan that "I have never written you, or spoken to you, in greater kindness of feeling, nor with a fuller purpose to sustain you, so far as in my most anxious judgment, I consistently can. *But you must act.*"

Lincoln might have added, act in the manner of Ulysses S. Grant at Shiloh. While Grant was properly criticized for allowing himself to be surprised on April 6, the blow came as he was moving toward the enemy. And at the end of that unhappy April day, when asked if he wished to order a retreat, Grant said no, that he would attack and beat his opponents on the next day, which he did.

Lincoln's reference to action reinforced his message of April 6, in which he pointedly advised: "I think you better break the enemies line from Yorktown to Warwick River, at once. They will probably use *time,* as advantageously as you can."[4]

McClellan's siege of Yorktown was less than a siege because the Confederates could leave at any time. Their retreat on May 3–4 surprised McClellan, who was not prepared to exploit the situation. He busied himself with staff work rather than going forward to seize his opening. On May 5 came a sharp engagement at Williamsburg. McClellan arrived late but claimed credit for defeating a superior force in what he called a "brilliant victory." He blamed his corps commanders for mishandling the battle and told Stanton that only his timely arrival prevented a defeat.[5] Yet for the next several days, writes Michie, there was a "lack of enterprise and aggressiveness that should not have characterized a pursuing army on the heels of one disheartened by its supposed defeat at Williamsburg."[6]

The Union victories at Yorktown and Williamsburg did not inspire dash or decisiveness in McClellan. He continued to procrastinate even as he described his actions as careful preparation for a general movement against Richmond. He also found time to argue with Lincoln about the organization of the Army of the Potomac. On May 9, a telegram, written by Lincoln but sent by Secretary of War Edwin M. Stanton, said that rather than be "trammeled, and embarrassed while in contact with the enemy" and "on the eve of a great battle," the commanding general should organize his army as it best suited him. On the same date, and privately, Lincoln wrote McClellan that his fussing over appointments and organization left the impression, "in quarters which we cannot entirely disregard," that he was more interested in elevating "one or two pets" and denigrating their rivals than he was in fighting.[7]

In late May, Stonewall Jackson moved north in the Shenandoah Valley, which posed a threat to Washington but left him open to isolation and destruction should McDowell move with "celerity and vigor." It also meant that McDowell's movement to Richmond would be deferred "for the present." If, as Lincoln believed, a significant Confederate force was away from Richmond, McClellan should seize the opportunity: "I think the time is near when you must either attack Richmond or give up the job and come to the defense of Washington." On the same day he told his general: "Apprehension of something like this [Jackson's incursion], and no unwillingness to sustain you, has always been my reason for withholding McDowell's force from you. Please understand this, and do the best you can with the force you have."[8] But McClellan still believed that he was outnumbered, that he needed McDowell, and that the president and secretary of war should grasp this elementary fact.

As McClellan closed on Richmond, he spoke often of a large battle to come but was "forced to take every possible precaution against disaster and secure my flanks against the probably superior force in front of me." Yet he did not expect Johnston to attack him: "I think him too able for that." On May 27, McClellan ordered Fitz John Porter to secure his right, having learned that McDowell's corps was halted because of Jackson's adventures in the Valley. Porter's victory at Hanover Court House was "glorious," said McClellan, a "complete rout" of the rebel forces. But there was "no doubt that the enemy are concentrating everything on Richmond," and he desperately needed reinforcements.[9]

Notwithstanding Porter's glorious victory, McClellan "assumed an almost passive attitude" in circumstances that demanded action. According to William Swinton, a reporter for the *New York Times* who held political opinions at odds with McClellan's, the Union commander should have shifted his base to the James River or deployed the whole army north of the Chickahominy for an attack on Richmond. Inaction "was more hazardous than the boldest devisement, and was an eminent example of that kind of false prudence that is often the greatest rashness." But when faced with choices, a need for generalship, McClellan could not act. His was an "ever-about-to-do nonperformance."[10]

On May 31, Joseph Johnston attacked the corps of Samuel P. Heintzelman and Erasmus D. Keyes on McClellan's left. McClellan ordered reinforcements but only after two hours of fighting. It was late afternoon before Edwin V. Sumner's lead division reached the field. On June 1, the Confederates were beaten back and returned to their lines. Johnston was severely wounded. When McClellan rode to the front he received a "splendid ovation" from the soldiers, but he could never seem to translate his personal popularity with the army into a positive force.[11] He did tell Stanton that his left was now within four miles of Richmond and that as soon as he could concentrate his army he would force a general engagement. In a message to the soldiers he called for a "crowning effort" to "meet and crush" the enemy.[12]

For all his outward confidence, McClellan was demoralized, ill with the fevers, and appalled by the "sickening sight of the battlefield, with its mangled corpses and poor suffering wounded!" His worries about his flanks notwithstanding, McClellan's neglect had invited Johnston's attack. When the assaults came, there was little cooperation between the Union corps commanders, nor did McClellan take control. As Michie put it, "the influence of General McClellan's personal direction was most meagre" at Seven Pines. A powerful counterstroke did not materialize because of his predilection for inaction and because of his "state of utter exhaustion." But even after he regained his health, McClellan's every communication, private and public, suggests "that his generalship was not up to the situation demanded."[13]

That Jackson in the Valley was Jackson away from Richmond was an advantage in Lincoln's mind, but not in McClellan's. The general even believed that P. G. T. Beauregard was bringing an army from the West, a belief that defied logic and evidence. And he confided to his wife that the administration seemed to want him to fail. While McClellan fretted inwardly and complained outwardly he might have inferred that the Confederates had attacked on May 31 with whatever strength General Johnston could muster. As Kenneth P. Williams has observed, McClellan "did not have the ability to estimate the strength of an enemy force by its battlefield behavior — an essential in a successful commander."[14]

McClellan was not thinking, nor had he ever, in terms of the tactical offensive. Rather he lapsed into a fog of self-pity and fatalism, interspersed with moments of prideful inflexibility and the belief that the "final salvation of the country" depended on his army and "the fate of my army depends upon me."[15] He advanced behind siege lines in the belief that his superior artillery and field engineering would fix the Confederates in their Richmond defenses. He even may have believed that Robert E. Lee the fighter would stand passively on the defense. But Lee, knowing that his army could not long withstand a siege, dispatched J. E. B. Stuart's cavalry to scout the Union positions and found that McClellan's right, Porter's corps, was "in the air" and more or less isolated north of the Chickahominy. Michie compared Lee's "distinctness of purpose and knowledge of the situation" with McClellan's dreamlike state and concluded that "it is not difficult to determine which . . . was at that time the greater master of the art of war."[16]

McClellan planned for a general advance on June 25 but, after hearing reports of massive Confederate reinforcements, began making his excuses to the secretary of war. He would do his best with the "splendid Army" he had the honor to command; "if it is destroyed by overwhelming numbers," he would "at least die with it and share its fate." If a "disaster" occurred, the fault would not be his. Michie writes: "It is difficult to understand the mental attitude that caused McClellan to write so despondent a message." Once again, "his strongly imaginative cast of mind unduly influenced" his reason.[17]

McClellan in fact held an advantage had he maintained the initiative, whether on the tactical offensive or defensive. He alerted his corps commanders to prepare for an attack, at which time he would counter decisively and in force. Or, if necessary, he would fight a defensive battle from prepared positions, making good use of his artillery. Lee had determined to concentrate on Porter, knowing that McClellan's left might carry Richmond's defenses in a counterstroke. Others shared his apprehension, but he really had no choice. According to Sears, Lee's intention to seize the initiative rested on his belief that McClellan would not strike on his left.[18] Lee acted from desperation and in the hope that he could cripple Porter's corps before McClellan could react. Of course Lee had other problems, namely that a key commander, the redoubtable Stonewall, recalled from the Valley, had only a slight grasp of what was expected of him. His very presence on the Peninsula was of consequence, in that it frightened McClellan, but on June 26, "There was little about him [Jackson] of the great captain."[19]

The battle began at 4:00 P.M., eight hours later than Lee wished. McClellan at 4:30 sent a telegraph message to his wife, full of reassurances that he would prevail and that the enemy was "falling into a trap." In a series of messages to Stanton, he described the "heavy engagement" on his right and at 9:00 P.M. told the secretary of war that he had carried the day and that his army was invincible.[20]

Porter held, thanks to his artillery, the quality of his field fortifications, and the steadiness of his infantry. As the Confederate attack stalled, McClellan evinced the high spirits of a winning general. He sensibly ordered Porter to a stronger position at Gaines's Mill on the Chickahominy. Alexander Webb remembered that Porter expected that his Fifth Corps would block Lee's offensive blows north of the Chickahominy while McClellan would advance the Union left against Richmond — an assumption that seemed to be shared by other staff officers. Porter later observed that discussions with McClellan early on the morning of June 27 left him with the impression that he was to oppose Lee's offensive "even to my destruction."[21]

At 10:00 A.M. on June 27, McClellan wired Stanton that the "troops on the other side [Porter] are now well in hand and the whole Army so concentrated that it can take advantage of the first mistake made by the enemy." Yet when Confederates renewed the attack at Gaines's Mill, McClellan neither reinforced Porter nor attacked on his left. In fact, McClellan was not in control of the situation nor did he want to be. He left Porter on his own while he concerned himself with extricating his army, which he now believed to be in peril. The feints and demonstrations against his left now became in McClellan's mind an overwhelming assault, where the "odds have become immense." "We hold our own very nearly," he informed the secretary of war at 8:00 P.M.: "I may be forced to give up my position. . . . Had I twenty thousand fresh and good troops would be sure of a splendid victory tomorrow." At the same time he wired his wife that the Federals had waged "a terrible fight against vastly superior numbers." He was "well but tired out. No sleep for two nights and none tonight."[22]

The commanding general of this magnificent army was paralyzed by fear, delusion, and exhaustion. Never did he go to the fighting.[23] With reference to McClellan's misapprehension of Confederate strength, especially on his left, Michie writes: "Language is scarcely strong enough to condemn in appropriate terms the inefficient administration of the source of information whereby so gross a miscalculation should have been evolved." The error is compounded when one considers that the armies were in close contact for over a month.[24]

Darkness may have saved Porter on June 27 as the Confederates had penetrated his defenses and no significant reinforcements were forthcoming. McClellan believed that all was lost and he must retreat to save his army. The army was not beaten, but the general was, most completely. At 10:30 P.M. he reported, "We have met a severe repulse today having been attacked by vastly superior numbers, and I am obliged to fall back between the Chickahominy and the James River." Shortly after midnight he sent the infamous telegram to Stanton, reporting that the army "was overwhelmed by vastly superior numbers even after I brought my last reserves into action." With "20,000 or even 10,000 fresh troops to use tomorrow I could take Richmond." The defeat came through no fault of the commanding general but because the administration had not properly supported him, and now "the Govt must not and cannot hold me responsible for defeat." He concluded with these incredible words: "If I save this army now I tell you plainly that I owe no thanks to you or any other persons in Washington — you have done your

Following McClellan's decision to retreat to the James River, the Federal flotilla on the Pamunkey River at White House (which burns in the center background of this wartime sketch by William Waud) prepares to depart for the new base of operations.
Frank Leslie's Illustrated Newspaper, *July 26, 1862*

best to sacrifice this Army." Because a supervisor in the telegraph office in Washington deleted McClellan's inflammatory final comments before passing the communication on to higher authority, neither Stanton nor Lincoln knew of this offensive language until many months later. That they necessarily did not respond immediately may have suggested to McClellan's fevered brain that they somehow agreed with him.[25]

Lincoln wired McClellan on June 28: "Save our Army at all costs. Will send reinforcements as fast as we can." He also reminded him that "I feel any misfortune to you and your Army quite as keenly as you feel it yourself. If you have had a drawn battle, or a repulse, it is the price we pay for the enemy not being in Washington." Then, more practically, Lincoln asked: "Please tell at once the present condition and aspect of things."[26]

McClellan's chorus of laying blame and self-pity and melodramatic and self-serving talk of sharing dangers with his brave soldiers cannot obscure the fact that he had distanced himself physically and psychologically (even spiritually) from his army, removed himself from active field command, and left it to his corps commanders to manage the retreat. They maintained unit integrity within their commands and at key moments coordinated action between and among corps. McClellan later boasted of his masterful "change of base," but he had little influence on the tactical situation. As Michie so aptly observes, army headquarters "during the whole of the retreat were unduly distant from the several fields of battle."[27]

Saturday, June 28, was a time of respite between periods of intense and close fighting. It was also, writes Sears, "a day of intense calculation on the part of the two commanders." Lee had the initiative but awaited McClellan's next move. He might stand and fight, retrace his advance down the Peninsula, or retreat to the James. Lee seemed to believe that the feared attack on Richmond was not likely, given that McClellan had not seized the moment on June 26–27. He also seems to have grasped, as Swinton later did, that McClellan did not act because the "operation overleaped by its boldness the methodical genius of the Union commander." That is, he was constitutionally unable to seize an opportunity that he had created and recognized. Lee meant no less than to "intercept" McClellan, to defeat him away from his entrenchments and before he reached a secure base. McClellan thought less in terms of a fighting, contested withdrawal than an escape. He ordered the destruction of materials even though others urged him not to because it would suggest to the men "that they were a defeated army, running for their lives."[28]

The first movement, across White Oak Swamp to Savage's Station, was successful because McClellan's corps commanders were effective and Lee's subordinates were not. On June 30, at Glendale, Lee attacked again, believing that he could strike the Union columns in motion, divided, and at a tactical disadvantage. As battle was imminent, McClellan left for Haxall's Landing on the James, "without telegraphic communications too distant to command the army." At 4:00 P.M. he boarded the gunboat *Galena* and that evening enjoyed dinner, with table linens and "good wine."[29]

McClellan's reputation has never recovered from his inexplicable and inexcusable absence from the fighting at Glendale. In a telegram to Stanton, at 7:00 P.M., he reported: "Another day of desperate fighting. . . . If none of us escape we shall at least have done honor to the country."[30] In fact, Sumner and Heintzelman managed to withdraw their corps and save the army without direction or orders from McClellan, who learned of the results only from aides who were at the scene. John Barnard calls McClellan's comments an "extraordinary avowal" for a field commander and with devastating sarcasm adds: "This is the first time we ever had reason to believe that the highest and first duty of a general, on the day of battle, was, separating himself from his army, to reconnoitre a place of retreat."[31] Michie called the general's absence from the field "astounding." In Stephen Sears's words: "With each day of the Seven Days his demoralization had increased and each day his courage to command decreased accordingly. By Day Six [Glendale] the demoralization was complete; exercising command in battle was now quite beyond him, and to avoid it he deliberately fled the battlefield. He was drained in both mind and body." A. A. Humphreys wrote, "Never did I see a man more cut down. . . . He was unable to do anything or say anything."[32] The Union rear detachments escaped from Glendale because of the disjointed Confederate attack, especially by Jackson, who seemed more bemused and bewildered than usual. Lee never managed to concentrate for a major strike.

At 8:30 P.M., McClellan rejoined Porter's headquarters at Malvern Hill. He had been away from his army for twelve hours, "worn out" but "still hope[d] to save the army." On July 1, he wrote to his wife, Ellen, that the army was united, "worn out and war worn." Yet "I have still very great confidence in them and they in me — the dear fellows cheer me as of old as they march to certain death and I feel prouder of them than ever. I am completely exhausted — no sleep for days — my mind almost worn out — yet I *must* go through it. I still trust that God will give me success and I cheerfully entrust to his will."[33] The utter and appalling bankruptcy of the spirit contained in this letter renders further comment unnecessary.

At 9:30 A.M. on July 1, McClellan returned to the *Galena* and departed for Harrison's Landing. Once again he made no provision for command on the battlefield, and Fitz John Porter by default became the Union commander on the seventh day, the battle of Malvern Hill. The Union army was concentrated and in a secure defensive position, even if McClellan's major concern seemed to be in keeping open a line of retreat to Harrison's Landing.

Sears writes that McClellan's actions early on July 1 "cast doubt not only on his competence but on his courage as well." Michie found no justification for McClellan. The army "was in jeopardy," and the situation demanded the best of a general. McClellan's personal presence "was a duty of the first importance, in comparison with which everything else was relatively of no military value whatever." Almost a century after the events on the Peninsula, one of America's great captains, Matthew B. Ridgway, wrote, "In time of battle, when victory hangs in the balance, it is necessary to put down any signs of weakness, indecision, lack of aggressiveness, or panic, whether the man wears stars on his shoulders or chevrons on his sleeve." McClellan's sergeants did well enough; their general failed them. Again, as General Ridgway put it, "The job of a commander was to be up where the crisis of action was taking place."[34]

McClellan returned to Malvern Hill in midafternoon, briefly inspected the defensive lines, and then took a position on the extreme right, near the James River. Lee's attacks were ill considered and poorly coordinated, perhaps because he wanted to punish the Union army without regard to the terrible price his soldiers would pay for a massed assault against well-placed artillery and infantry. When the fighting broke off at about 8:30 P.M., Fitz John Porter, and the army, sensed victory. McClellan ordered a retreat from a victorious battlefield. A huge downpour on the day following ruined the morale of soldiers who did not understand the orders. McClellan saved his printing press and issued a windy address to the army on July 4.[35] He seemed to be proud of himself, but the words were those of a deluded man.

Lincoln responded to the debacle of the Seven Days by asking northern governors for an additional 300,000 men. He had earlier asked Henry W. Halleck, inert at Corinth, for "twenty five thousand Infantry — no artillery, or cavalry — but please do not send a man if it endangers any place you deem important to hold." He explained to McClellan that it was "impossible to reinforce you for your present emergency. . . . If you are not strong enough to face the enemy you must find a place of security, and wait, rest and repair."[36] Lincoln might have been addressing McClellan himself, surely a man in need of rest and repair.

On July 2, when it appeared that the army was safe, Lincoln requested that his general "allow me to reason with you for a moment." McClellan's call for 50,000 men was "simply absurd." Those numbers were not readily available in the Washington area and the general's own plans for the defense of the capital confirmed this assessment. Then, more gently, Lincoln added: "If . . . you have the impression that I blame you for not doing enough, please be relieved of such an impression. . . . If you think you are not strong enough to take Richmond just now, I do not ask you to try just now. . . . Save the Army, material and personal; and I will strengthen for the offensive again, as fast as I can."[37]

By July 4, McClellan seems to have recovered his self-confidence. In two messages he reassured the president that the army was intact, if weakened. He also asserted that one day "it will be acknowledged by all competent judges that the movement just completed by this Army is unparalleled in the annals of war . . . we have preserved out trains, our guns, our material — and above all our honor." Lincoln replied: "A thousand thanks for the relief your two despatches . . . give me. Be assured the heroism and skill of yourself, officers and men, are, and forever will be appreciated. If you can hold your present position, we shall 'hive' the enemy yet."[38]

Lincoln was both reassured and disturbed when he visited the army on July 9. The soldiers were fitter than he expected, and key generals wanted to stay and fight. McClellan was vague, even evasive, and apparently not clear about his circumstances. He did seize the opportunity to hand the president a letter, dated July 7, in which he commented at length not about the best means of defeating Lee but rather about the civil policy that must be pursued if the country was to be saved. Of special interest was his belief that "a declaration of radical views, especially upon slavery, will rapidly disintegrate our present armies." But Lincoln needed a "Commander in Chief of the Army; one who possesses your confidence, understands your views and who is competent to execute your orders. . . . I do not ask that place for myself. I am willing to serve you in such a position as you may assign me and I will do so as faithfully as ever subordinate served superior."[39]

Within days McClellan was writing in the harshest of terms about the president, perhaps because Lincoln had named Henry W. Halleck general-in-chief without telling McClellan beforehand. All during July he quarreled with the administration, promising action and then explaining why he could not act. Lincoln was decidedly less understanding than six months earlier. Indeed, he had come to doubt that McClellan would fight no matter the availability of men and resources. The general's letters, especially to his wife, reveal a man obsessed with his own place and problems, at once boastful and fatalistic. Perhaps a just God had placed Abraham Lincoln in authority only to test his good and faithful servant, George Brinton McClellan.[40] The Army of the Potomac was ordered back to Washington in early August, and its commanding general's last letter from Fort Monroe was replete with anger and self-pity. He would have been better advised to have adopted James Thurber's credo: "Don't look back in anger. Don't look forward with fear. Look around you in awareness."[41]

NOTES

1. Stephen W. Sears, *George B. McClellan: The Young Napoleon* (New York: Ticknor & Fields, 1988), xi–91, passim. Sears's studies of McClellan are the place to begin an analysis of the general. Spirited defenses of McClellan, not entirely persuasive, are Thomas J. Rowland, *George B. McClellan and Civil War History: In the Shadow of Grant and Sherman* (Kent, Ohio: Kent State University Press, 1998); Joseph L. Harsh, "Lincoln's Tarnished Brass: Conservative Strategies and the Attempt to Fight the Early Civil War as a Limited War," in *The Confederate High Command and Related Topics,* ed. Roman J. Heleniak and Lawrence L. Hewitt (Shippensburg, Pa.: White Mane, 1990), 124–41; and Harsh, "On the McClellan-Go-Round," *Civil War History* 19 (June 1973), 101–18.

2. Peter S. Michie, *General McClellan* (New York: Appleton, 1901), 461. The second ranked graduate in the West Point class of 1863, Michie served along the South Atlantic coast and with the Army of the James in 1863–65. U. S. Grant described him as "one of the most deserving young officers in the service" and deemed him worthy

of "substantial promotion." Michie finished the war as a brevet brigadier general. His postwar career included a thirty-year stint as professor of natural and experimental philosophy at West Point and authorship of several books. See *Dictionary of American Biography* for a brief sketch.

3. Godfrey R. B. Charnwood, *Abraham Lincoln: A Biography* (1916; reprint, Lanham, Md.: Madison Books, 1996), 210–11; Jacob D. Cox, *Reminiscences of the Civil War*, 2 vols. (New York: Scribner's, 1900), 1:370–71. Michie, *McClellan*, 466–67, writes that McClellan's "grave error was unquestionably his failure to confer freely and frankly" with Lincoln and Stanton about the campaign, especially the safety of Washington.

4. Lincoln's letters to McClellan dated April 6, 9, 1862, are in Abraham Lincoln, *The Collected Works of Abraham Lincoln*, ed. Roy P. Basler, 9 vols. (New Brunswick, N.J.: Rutgers University Press, 1953–55), 5:182, 184–85.

5. Stephen W. Sears, *To the Gates of Richmond: The Peninsula Campaign* (New York: Ticknor & Fields, 1992), 81. Sears quotes Francis W. Palfrey, who later wrote: "Curiously enough, there was always something for McClellan to do more important than to fight his own battles."

6. Michie, *McClellan*, 282.

7. Lincoln, *Collected Works*, 5:208.

8. Ibid., 232–33, 235–37.

9. McClellan to Lincoln, May 26, 1862, McClellan to Stanton, May 27, 28, 1862, in George B. McClellan, *The Civil War Papers of George B. McClellan: Selected Correspondence, 1860–1865*, ed. Stephen W. Sears (New York: Ticknor & Fields, 1989), 277–79.

10. William Swinton, *Campaigns of the Army of the Potomac* (New York: Charles B. Richardson, 1866), 129, 140–41.

11. See Sears, *McClellan*, 192–96, on the battle of Fair Oaks/Seven Pines.

12. McClellan, *Civil War Papers*, 286–87.

13. McClellan to Mrs. McClellan, June 2, 1862, ibid., 287–88; Michie, *McClellan*, 312; Sears, *McClellan*, 195–96. Sears often speculates about the effect of McClellan's periodic illnesses and lack of sleep. The obvious inference is that he did not take care to remain fit, nor was it in his character to do so.

14. Sears, *McClellan*, 199; McClellan to Mrs. McClellan, June 22, 1862, in McClellan, *Civil War Papers*, 305; Kenneth P. Williams, *Lincoln Finds a General: A Military Study of the Civil War*, 5 vols. (New York: Macmillan, 1949–59), 1:185–86, 226. Writing about Yorktown, Michie wondered why a man of McClellan's "logical and analytical mind" could not grasp that it was "utterly impossible" for the Confederates to field an army of the size he imagined when the Federal government with all its resources could hardly manage such a feat. "This unaccountable weakness in McClellan's mental equipment," wrote Michie, "is always so conspicuously in evidence that its influence

in the formation of his plans of campaigns or his dispositions for battle can never be ignored" (Michie, *McClellan*, 469–70).

15. McClellan, *Civil War Papers*, 305. This theme pervades McClellan's letters to his wife, Ellen, in the weeks before the Seven Days.

16. Michie, *McClellan*, 324–28.

17. McClellan to Stanton, June 25, 1862, in McClellan, *Civil War Papers*, 309–10; Michie, *McClellan*, 329. Sears, *McClellan*, 201, observes that it was a "dangerous state of mind for a general certain to be tested to the limit before long."

18. Sears, *McClellan*, 207–8. There appears to be little evidence that Lee "read" McClellan. Lee acted when and as he did on June 26 because he had no other choices and because it was in his nature to so act.

19. Sears, *To the Gates of Richmond*, 197.

20. McClellan, *Civil War Papers*, 315, 316–17.

21. Sears, *McClellan*, 209; Alexander S. Webb, *The Peninsula: McClellan's Campaign of 1862* (New York: Scribner's, 1881), 187; Sears, *To the Gates of Richmond*, 210.

22. McClellan, *Civil War Papers*, 318, 321.

23. Sears, *To the Gates of Richmond*, 233–34.

24. Michie, *McClellan*, 347.

25. McClellan to Flag Officer Louis M. Goldsborough, 10:30 P.M., June 27, 1862, McClellan to Stanton, 12:20 A.M., June 28, 1862, in McClellan, *Civil War Papers*, 322–23; Williams, *Lincoln Finds a General*, 1:230. Williams speculates that Stanton probably read McClellan's complete dispatch when the general published his report of the campaign in 1863. For an excellent analysis of how McClellan arrived at his inflated estimates of Confederate strength, see chapter 6 of Edwin C. Fishel, *The Secret War for the Union: The Untold Story of Military Intelligence in the Civil War* (Boston: Houghton Mifflin, 1996).

26. Lincoln, *Collected Works*, 5:289–90.

27. Michie, *McClellan*, 352.

28. Sears, *To the Gates of Richmond*, 255, 260; Swinton, *Campaigns of the Army of the Potomac*, 147.

29. Sears, *To the Gates of Richmond*, 280.

30. McClellan, *Civil War Papers*, 326.

31. John G. Barnard, *The Peninsula Campaign and Its Antecedents* (New York: Van Nostrand, 1864), 46. Barnard's little book was his report on engineering operations of the Army of the Potomac and a pointed critique of McClellan's report on the Peninsula campaign.

32. Michie, *McClellan*, 354; Sears, *To the Gates of Richmond*, 281. Alexander Webb, *The Peninsula*, 189, gives credit to McClellan for building the army organization and for inspiring the "personal affection entertained for [him] by the officers and men of his army." These circumstances saved the situation after Gaines's Mill.

33. McClellan, *Civil War Papers,* 326.

34. Sears, *McClellan,* 221; Michie, *McClellan,* 361–62; Matthew B. Ridgway, *Soldier: The Memoirs of Matthew B. Ridgway* (New York: Harper, 1956), 121, 207.

35. McClellan, *Civil War Papers,* 339.

36. Lincoln, *Collected Works,* 5:296–97, 295, 298.

37. Ibid., 301.

38. McClellan, *Civil War Papers,* 336–39.

39. Ibid., 344–45.

40. Ibid., chap. 6.

41. Quoted in Stephen E. Ambrose, *Americans at War* (New York: Berkeley Books, 1998), 243.

WILLIAM J. MILLER

I Only Wait for the River

McClellan and His Engineers on the Chickahominy

B y the time George B. McClellan stood on the banks of the Chickahominy River in late May 1862, he was a troubled man. His operation on the Peninsula had transformed itself into something
vastly different from the campaign he had planned in Washington.
The expected opportunities for rapid marches and brilliant successes had not materialized. The hoped-for campaign of maneuver had been
strangled by bad maps, muddy roads, and a ponderous supply train. Lost
were the weeks spent in laying siege to Yorktown, and lost, too, were the
2,239 Federal soldiers killed or wounded in the fight at Williamsburg, a battle
McClellan had not wanted. Yet the Federal commander had persevered
through the unexpected and pressed on with his army of more than 100,000
men. Assisted by the Fabian defense of Confederate commander Joseph E.
Johnston, he had closed to within a dozen miles of Richmond. The "Young
Napoleon" seemed to many in those late spring days to be on the verge of
triumph. Yet he stood on the muddy banks of the Chickahominy not only
opposed by a powerful enemy but crippled by a vast inexperience. Never
had any American general attempted to wield such an enormous army as a
weapon. McClellan was literally and figuratively in unknown territory, and
therein lay his trouble.

The world turned thirty-five times while George McClellan stood on the
banks of the Chickahominy. The rains came and went, the sun and the stars
smiled in turn from the Virginia sky, the swamp grass grew long, the honey-
suckle bloomed, boys became men, men fell ill and died, and spring turned
to summer. And on the thirty-sixth day, Robert E. Lee attacked. McClellan
withdrew his army from the Chickahominy, not the author of victory but the
victim of circumstances. In bitterness he wrote to Secretary of War Edwin M.
Stanton: "I am in no way responsible for this."[1]

Had McClellan captured Richmond, he without doubt would have deemed himself in many ways responsible, and he would have found many to concur. But he did not succeed, and in absolving himself of blame he attracted many critics — none so well informed as his own chief engineer, Brig. Gen. John Gross Barnard. In Barnard's view, the Federal defeat in the Seven Days battles was the direct, perhaps inevitable, result of the army commander's decisions on the Chickahominy. McClellan had failed to grasp opportunities, wrote Barnard, had failed to recognize the potential of the single most powerful obstacle to his success, and, above all, had wasted time.

McClellan readily explained his inability to move from the Chickahominy. His contemporary letters, subsequent testimony before Congress, official report, and postwar writings include full measures of self-justification. Among other factors, McClellan cited bad roads, the depth of the river, and the need for bridges and defensive fortifications. Because all these reasons pertain to military engineering, Barnard was the ideal man to comment on their validity, and having heard them, he persisted in assigning McClellan blame for defeat in the Seven Days and the death of northern hopes for an early end to the war.

Barnard seems an unlikely critic. He later wrote that during and after the Peninsula campaign he entertained for the army commander "the warmest personal regard. . . . With no man have I ever, with a more absolute freedom from any other feeling than one of personal kindness, been so long closely associated." [2]

Barnard was not ambitious for high command in the army, nor was he especially active in politics. He had graduated second in the West Point class of 1833 and subsequently made a name for himself in the American and European engineering communities, as much for his scholarship as for his nearly thirty years of practical labor on construction projects across America. He had served as superintendent at West Point in 1855 and 1856, after which he had turned to what one friend called "his attack on mathematics." Barnard "had a love for science for science's sake. He was in the habit of saying that he sometimes wished he had devoted his whole life to such studies." He published professional papers on such subjects as the oscillation of pendulums, the movements of gyroscopes and tops, "deviation in elongated projectiles," and the tides. He loved his profession and he excelled at it, so in 1861 he was the logical choice to lay out the elaborate fortifications around Washington. That year, he accepted McClellan's invitation to be his chief engineer. The two men had a bit more than a nodding acquaintance from the Old Army. Barnard had become a widower in 1853 and a few years later

Brig. Gen. John Gross Barnard
Francis Trevelyan Miller, ed., The Photographic History of the Civil War, *10 vols.*
(New York: Review of Reviews, 1911), 5:230

had pressed suit to Mary Ellen Marcy, the teenaged daughter of a fellow officer. Rebuffed, Barnard married another woman in 1860. Miss Marcy married George B. McClellan the same year.[3]

To be the chief engineer in the Army of the Potomac was to be indispensable, for engineering lay at the heart of McClellan's philosophy of making war. He wished to purchase victory as cheaply as possible. He would not

WILLIAM J. MILLER

permit history to say his road to Richmond had been paved with the corpses of his soldiers. The solution, he believed, was to rely heavily on artillery and engineering. In those two arms, rather than in infantry assaults, would McClellan place his faith, and in building his army he increased the number of batteries by more than 900 percent and founded a body of engineer troops trained for field service.[4]

The roughly 2,000 engineer troops who went to the Peninsula were organized into the Engineer Battalion and the Engineer Brigade. The battalion was composed of Regular Army troops under Regular Army engineer officers, headed by Capt. James C. Duane, who literally wrote the book on military field engineering — his *Manual for Engineer Troops* was published in 1861 and became the bible for all Federal engineers. His command consisted of but three companies, each led by a lieutenant. Duane had graduated third in the West Point class of 1848, two years behind George McClellan. The two remained fast friends, and when McClellan had taken command of the army in 1861 he immediately tapped Duane to create the new Engineer Battalion.

The Engineer Brigade, though much larger than the battalion, was also quite small — consisting of two regiments, the 15th and 50th New York Volunteer Engineers. Though a great majority of the officers and men in the brigade were new to the military, few were new to the construction trades. Carpenters, masons, and machinists abounded in the ranks, and many of the officers had training or experience as civil engineers. The two regiments became a boon to McClellan because no army — especially, perhaps, that one, given the proclivities of its commander — ever had too many engineer troops. In the status-conscious Army of the Potomac, they were called the "Volunteer Engineers" to distinguish them from the more esteemed "Regular Engineers" of Duane's Battalion.[5]

The leader of the Engineer Brigade was another old Regular, Brig. Gen. Daniel P. Woodbury, who had left West Point high in the class of 1836. A "mild unassuming Christian gentleman," Woodbury took command of the Volunteer Engineers because illness struck the original commander, Lt. Col. Barton Stone Alexander. Alexander's claim to fame was the completion in 1860 of the Minot's Ledge Lighthouse off the coast of Massachusetts, a feat praised as one of the great technological accomplishments in the young nation's history — and he did it $30,000 under budget.[6]

When in mid-May McClellan decided to assail Richmond from the east using the Pamunkey River and the Richmond & York River Railroad as his supply line, neither he nor any of his officers knew much about the twenty-three miles of terrain between Richmond and the Pamunkey. Barnard de-

Troops and wagons crossing the Chickahominy River at Bottom's Bridge.
Frank Leslie's Illustrated Newspaper, *June 21, 1862*

scribed the Peninsula as "a terra incognita." "We knew the York River and the James River," he explained, "and we had heard of the Chickahominy, and this was about the extent of our knowledge." When he finally got a look at the Chickahominy, Barnard was not encouraged. He thought it "one of the most formidable obstacles that could be opposed to the advance of the army — an obstacle to which an ordinary river . . . is comparatively slight." [7]

The Chickahominy consisted of three parts. First was the stream itself, which was only a few feet deep and flowed sometimes in a single course but more often was broken by islets into several narrow channels. Second was the swamp, a belt of heavy timber three to four hundred yards wide filled with dense undergrowth. Last came the bottomland bordering the swamp — about a mile of open, generally cultivated fields with soil so spongy it was unsuitable for cavalry and artillery. Bluffs rose steeply from the edges of the fields on both sides of the river. Though these heights made fine defensive positions, the trees in the swamp below screened from view the bottom on the opposite side, making it difficult to detect enemy movements. [8]

The Federals found that Confederates had burned the major bridges over the Chickahominy and built light fortifications above the most critical crossing site at New Bridge. Before he could push on to Richmond, McClellan would have to repair the most important bridges and put the railroad, his supply line, in running order. The engineers were broken into detachments so they might work on several projects at a time. Some rebuilt small bridges and widened, graded, and corduroyed the roads between White House landing and the Chickahominy. A detachment of the 50th New York Engineers of Woodbury's brigade reached Bottoms Bridge on the morning of May 22, and by the end of the next day they had built two new trestle bridges, each

WILLIAM J. MILLER

120 feet long. According to Woodbury, seventy-nine regiments, more than nine hundred wagons, and several batteries of artillery crossed the two bridges on May 24. At about the same time, another detachment of the 50th began rebuilding the railroad bridge over the Chickahominy. The New Yorkers found a sawmill, some timber, and a handcar about three miles east of the bridge, and they lost no time putting all to good use. In five days, with help from infantry regiments and civilian builders recently arrived from the North, the Volunteer Engineers raised a new span. At nightfall on May 27, the first Union locomotive crept across the bridge, and McClellan's supply line was open beyond the Chickahominy.[9]

As they came to know the river better, the engineers found their attention drawn to New Bridge, where a major road crossed the Chickahominy. There the thick woods of the swamps dwindled away to create a clearing that permitted a glimpse of the Confederate side, the only such opening on the river for miles in either direction. Though the Confederates had destroyed the bridge, the turnpike ran undisturbed through the swamps and bottomland on an embankment. Barnard saw that this elevated causeway would be less likely to flood in wet weather and was strong enough to support heavy traffic. Though he expressed concern about the state of the road on the far shore, which he could not examine because the Confederates controlled the heights on the south side, the advantages offered on the northern bank made New Bridge, from an engineering perspective, an ideal crossing point. It thus was perhaps inevitable that New Bridge would become strategically critical.[10]

McClellan had divided his army to occupy both the north and south banks of the Chickahominy. The Third and Fourth Corps had forded the river at Bottom's Bridge on May 20, and the latter, commanded by Brig. Gen. Erasmus D. Keyes, had moved forward under McClellan's orders to the crossroads known as Seven Pines. The Second, Fifth, and Sixth Corps remained on the north bank, where Brig. Gen. Fitz John Porter's Fifth Corps held the westernmost position in the army, northwest of New Bridge. McClellan was forced into this awkward deployment because the railroad ran on both sides of the Chickahominy and he needed a strong presence north and south of the river to protect his supply line. Concerned about the divided state of his army, "Little Mac" looked to protect one of his flanks.[11]

Barnard spent much of the last week of the month looking at the army's front, particularly the Confederate position above New Bridge. From friendly lines near Fair Oaks, he rode northward over the farms of the Goldings and the Garnetts. Confederate batteries stood on the southern heights overlooking, if not the bridge, certainly the roadways leading from it. From the earliest days of the Union presence on the river, Confederate pickets in the woods and bottomland had harassed Federals attempting to survey or bridge the stream. The guns on the heights ensured that any attempt to cross at New Bridge would be costly. Barnard thought it "impossible" to carry the Confederate position from below, but as he became more familiar with the ground, he saw that it was not strongly defended and was susceptible on its flank.[12]

On the twenty-eighth he found pickets of Brig. Gen. Henry Naglee's brigade very close to the enemy batteries. Two days later, he reached the Golding house, about a mile and a half from the bridge and overlooking the road from the bottomland. The engineer was convinced that a vigorous push across those heights from the Seven Pines–Fair Oaks area would drive away the Confederate defenders. With the southern heights secure, the engineers could throw pontoon bridges across in an hour or two and thereby open the bridge for Porter's corps and the rest of the army on the north bank to unite with Keyes. With that accomplished, McClellan would have excellent, generally parallel roads from New Bridge and Seven Pines that favored a rapid, unified advance on Richmond.[13]

McClellan's chief topographical engineer, Brig. Gen. A. A. Humphreys, also saw the opportunity. Writing to a friend that the attempt on the Confederate heights "ought to have been made at once," he thought the position "could have been best approached from its flank, which was, strange to say, even as late as the 27th May open."[14]

In preparation for such a movement, Woodbury's Volunteer Engineers had worked an abandoned sawmill near New Bridge, turning out planking and stringers and stacking the milled lumber at protected places in the bottomlands. They had selected sites for two supporting bridges, one above and one below New Bridge, and assembled portions of the spans so they could dash forward when called upon and throw them over more quickly.[15]

But McClellan was not looking at New Bridge. He was not even looking at the Chickahominy. His gaze in those critical last days of May turned to a Confederate force near Hanover Court House, beyond his right flank. On the twenty-seventh, he sent Fitz John Porter to defeat or drive off the force, and for the next few days his attention seems to have been focused on what he termed Porter's "glorious victory." Barnard considered this expedition "really useless," at least when measured against the possibility of uniting the army and moving past the Chickahominy. Although McClellan had to be concerned about his flank and any threat to his supply line, such concern is no explanation for letting 85 percent of his army lie idle while it might have been achieving victories or strategic gains.[16]

In his report, McClellan declared that he could not advance in late May because he was waiting for the bridges to be built. He stated that the army needed "eleven new bridges, all long and difficult, with extensive log-way approaches." This was an exaggeration. Barnard reported that only three bridges were considered necessary at the time — four, including the rail-road bridge, which already had been repaired. Of the three, New Bridge was most critical to offensive operations. It could have been thrown across the river within hours and did not require "extensive log-way approaches." New Bridge was "by far the best crossing of the Chickahominy," observed Barnard, "and one no inundation could seriously impair." So while McClellan suggested in his report and his many letters to Washington and to his wife in May and June that his advance waited only on the completion of the bridges, Barnard knew differently. "So far as engineering preparations were concerned," he wrote, "the army could have been thrown over as early as the 28th."[17]

Barnard came to see May 28–30 as critical for two reasons. Had McClellan seized the offensive opportunity offered at New Bridge, he not only would have united his army and taken a strong stride toward Richmond, but he also would have placed himself beyond the reach of what he knew to be a considerable obstacle. The Chickahominy had not yet demonstrated its sus-ceptibility to flooding, but any river of significant size may flood. For that reason alone no army commander could wisely keep his army divided by such a barrier for any longer than necessary. The Chickahominy was not to be trifled with, and the best way to deny the river its power was to advance beyond it as quickly as possible. The river loomed as a potentially fearsome problem for a static Army of the Potomac; however, that army in motion, even if dependent on a few bridges for its supply line, need waste little concern about a river in its rear. McClellan chose not to put the river and all its troubles behind him.

The first opportunity at New Bridge passed away suddenly as Barnard rode toward headquarters after examining the Confederate position on May 30. "I returned from that reconnaissance," he wrote, "in the torrents of rain which commenced to fall that afternoon and which continued during the night, completely changing the whole aspect of affairs." [18]

The downpour hampered the critical efforts of engineers and infantry a few miles away near Seven Pines. Under orders from McClellan, Barnard had on May 28 laid out a defensive line, including a redoubt and rifle pits, half a mile west of the crossroads. Miles D. McAlester did most of the design work for Barnard, but, possibly because he was just a lieutenant, he had trouble commandeering enough labor to swing the necessary picks and shovels. The work on the redoubt did not begin until the twenty-ninth or thirtieth, and the delay might have cost some lives. On the afternoon of May 31, when the redoubt was "quite incomplete," the Confederates attacked at precisely that point. [19] Although the assault made good progress, the Federals were able to blunt it, thanks to the vigor and foresight of Second Corps commander Brig. Gen. Edwin Vose Sumner.

On May 27, Sumner had put his troops to work building two bridges. He had neither asked for nor received help from any engineer but left the design and construction to his own troops. The infantrymen had found the swamp "a mass of rank vegetation, huge trees, saplings, bushes, grapevines and creeping plants." Col. Edward Cross of the 5th New Hampshire and his men built on a site where the 1st Minnesota had abandoned a bridging effort. They constructed a trio of low spans over three small channels by felling large trees and laying a corduroy road over them. A wooden causeway snaked through the swamp for thirteen hundred feet, and the bridges were not more than three feet above the stream, so the builders spent long hours standing deep in muck and fetid water. Sumner had fortified the men with barrels of whiskey, and the labor continued steadily until the bridge was finished at sundown on the twenty-ninth. Men of the 81st Pennsylvania built a similarly rough bridge about a mile downstream. The spans were known as Sumner's Upper and Sumner's Lower, though because Cross's men had used vines to bind the timbers together they called their span Grapevine Bridge. [20]

These two bridges were the closest to the battlefield of the five Federal spans over the river (two at Bottom's Bridge, the railroad bridge, and Sumner's two crossings), yet McClellan had ordered neither built. Then came the

WILLIAM J. MILLER

Members of the 5th New Hampshire pose on Grapevine Bridge over the
Chickahominy River.
Francis Trevelyan Miller; ed., The Photographic History of the Civil War, *10 vols.*
(New York: Review of Reviews, 1911), 1:279

deluge on the thirtieth. "The lightning was blinding and incessant," wrote one of the New Hampshiremen, "the thunder one continual roar, and the rain fell in torrents, turning the gentle incline on which we were encamped into one complete sheet of water, which ran like a river. The storm lasted far into the night, turning every brook, rivulet and river into a raging torrent . . . and the Chickahominy was one wide sea of swift-rushing, muddy waters." [21]

The booming river was too much for the lower bridge, which gave way on the afternoon of the thirty-first.[22] The upper bridge held long enough for much of Sumner's corps to cross and march three miles to aid their hard-pressed comrades at Seven Pines and Fair Oaks. Had Sumner not taken it upon himself to build them, the nearest link between the northern and southern shores would have been the railroad bridge, two miles downstream, leaving Sumner's troops a march of more than eight miles to the battlefield.

But the crisis had not yet passed. Though darkness ended the fighting that day, McClellan's corps commanders expected to resume on the morning of June 1. By then the flood had swept away both of Sumner's bridges. The two wings of the army, whose deployment resembled a large V, were linked only by the railroad bridge at the base of the V — six miles from Seven Pines and at least eight from Porter's wing above New Bridge, leaving Porter fourteen miles from the battlefield. Yet, according to the Prince de Joinville of McClellan's staff, not until 7:00 P.M. did the army commander order the engineers to place the spans that had been prepared at the crossings near New Bridge.[23]

These bridges would have given Porter a march to the field of about four miles. But the stream had by that time swept away the stacked lumber and bridge sections the volunteers had assembled. The engineers worked through the night, fighting raging waters that repeatedly bore away portions of bridges. Capt. Ira Spaulding, laboring at the crossing above New Bridge, was thrice forced to rebuild portions of his structure when more than half-way finished. By midmorning, pontoons spanned the swollen river at New Bridge, connecting the two ends of the causeway at the main crossing. Spaulding and his men later finished a crib-and-trestle-and-pontoon bridge, known as the Upper Trestle Bridge, about a mile above New Bridge, and by 2:00 A.M. on June 2, men of the 15th New York Engineers under Capt. William A. Ketchum completed the Lower Trestle Bridge about a mile below the main crossing. Of Ketchum's structure, Woodbury wrote, "the unlooked-for and remarkable rise of water . . . rendered it necessary for the men engaged in the construction of this bridge to work for nearly twelve hours in the cold water, frequently having to dive to place the legs of the trestles and swimming to reach the opposite bank; and this, too, mostly in the darkness of the night."[24]

McClellan had been impatient. At 9:20 on the night of the thirty-first, he told his chief of staff, "If the Engineers cannot build the bridges tonight. . . . The sooner we get rid of the Corps of Engineers the better — communicate this to Barnard. It is absolutely necessary that several bridges be practicable for Artillery in the morning." New Bridge was ready at 8:15 A.M. and the Upper Trestle Bridge at noon, but McClellan availed himself of neither to roll artillery toward the battlefield. He could not do so because the heights above the two crossings remained in the hands of the enemy, having not been cleared when the opportunity presented itself a few days earlier.[25]

That these bridges played no part in the fighting at Seven Pines and Fair Oaks is less important than how they might have figured after the battle. They were in place on June 1 and 2 and ready to bear Porter's corps to unite with the portion of the army around Seven Pines. Barnard pronounced the moment ideal "to take advantage of a victory at Fair Oaks, to sweep at once the enemy from his position opposite New Bridge, and simultaneously to bring over by the New Bridge causeway our troops of the right wing, which would then have met with little or no resistance." In 1863, McClellan dismissed Barnard's argument: "The idea of uniting the two wings of the army

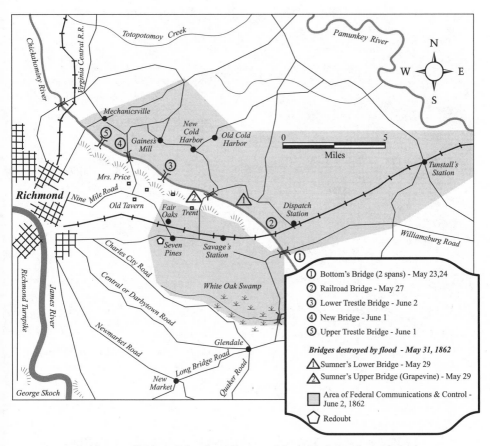

Bridges available to Federals on June 2, 1862 (with dates of completion)

The map legend reads:

① Bottom's Bridge (2 spans) - May 23,24
② Railroad Bridge - May 27
③ Lower Trestle Bridge - June 2
④ New Bridge - June 1
⑤ Upper Trestle Bridge - June 1

Bridges destroyed by flood - May 31, 1862

⚠ Sumner's Lower Bridge - May 29
⚠ Sumner's Upper Bridge (Grapevine) - May 29

◻ Area of Federal Communications & Control - June 2, 1862

⬠ Redoubt

in time to make a vigorous pursuit of the enemy, with the prospect of over-taking him before he reached Richmond, only 5 miles distant from the field of battle, is simply absurd, and was, I presume, never for a moment seriously entertained by any one connected with the Army of the Potomac."

But in 1862, McClellan himself entertained that very idea. In a dispatch at half-past noon on June 2, he told Stanton about the battle of the previous day. "The result," he wrote, "is that our left is now within four (4) miles of Richmond. I only wait for the river to fall to cross with the rest of the force & make a general attack." [26]

The general's disingenuousness or lapse of memory aside, he need not have waited for the river to subside on June 2, 1862. The water was high and did not look ready to drop soon, but even as McClellan scratched out his message to Stanton the span at New Bridge, with its elevated causeway through the flooded bottomlands, stood ready, as it had for twenty-six hours.

Alfred R. Waud's wartime sketch of a section of corduroy road near the
Chickahominy River constructed by Union engineers.
Library of Congress

The two trestle bridges might have been opened within hours if the engineers could work on the flooded approaches without fear of harassment from Confederates on the southern heights. In Barnard's view, the situation was plain: "General McClellan was not waiting for the bridges, but the bridges were waiting for General McClellan." [27]

June 1 is remembered as the date on which operations on the Peninsula took a critical turn. On that day, Robert E. Lee replaced Joseph Johnston as commander of the Confederate army defending Richmond and initiated a three-week program that resulted in victory in the Seven Days battles. Just as critical, however, was McClellan's failure to identify the Confederate position at Garnett's farm and Mrs. Price's on the heights above New Bridge as chief obstacles to his advance. He instead saw the river as his greatest problem and devoted his attention to overcoming it. The delay was fatal. Barnard wrote, "The opportunity of seizing this passage which the Battle of Fair Oaks offered having been lost, *then* the heavy labors of bridge building commenced." [28] The elaborate bridges built in the second and third weeks of June were not necessary to an advance *beyond* the Chickahominy; they were

WILLIAM J. MILLER

necessary to serving the enormous encampment *on* the Chickahominy. The longer McClellan remained on the river the more effort his troops would have to expend on building and maintaining an infrastructure to support itself. Delay thus compounded upon delay until General Lee needed no more time.[29]

In the aftermath of the battle of Fair Oaks, McClellan placed Alexander in charge of all the bridges with instructions to connect the two wings of the army. On June 3, Woodbury's New Yorkers completed a fine structure at Bottoms Bridge — a double-lane, 24-foot-wide span extending 120 feet across the river. During the rest of the first week in June, the engineers graded and corduroyed 3,000 feet of road, mostly near New Bridge, built five small bridges over creeks and gullies near New Cold Harbor, and laid two more bridges over the Chickahominy, raising their total to six spans in seven days.[30] The record is impressive, all the more so considering the weather with which they had to contend.

Rain fell on nine of the first ten days of June, the climax of an exceptionally rainy stretch during which precipitation, heavy or light, fell on nineteen of twenty-four days. Muddy roads made movement difficult, and the engineers, as well as fatigue parties from infantry regiments, labored incessantly to corduroy roads and maintain bridges and causeways. By June 10, McClellan told his wife, "the ground is so muddy we cannot use artillery — the guns sink up to their axle trees." That day, however, the rains ceased, giving way to the fine, hot weather — broken only infrequently by passing showers — that prevailed the rest of the month.[31]

Good weather in the middle of the month aided engineers at work on a final pair of major bridges over the river. On June 9, Woodbury's New Yorkers began a crossing three or four hundred yards above Sumner's Upper (Grapevine) Bridge. The site had been selected by Alexander in consultation with Woodbury, and the structure was designed to be invulnerable to the kind of flood the builders had witnessed at the end of May. The finished bridge wound through the bottomland for fourteen hundred yards, including its elevated corduroy approaches. Rising on forty cribs and six trestles, the span began bearing traffic on June 14. Distinguished by a sharp bend in its middle, it represented the supreme work of engineering on the Chickahominy, and its name — the Woodbury-Alexander Bridge — honored its designers.[32]

The second big project lay upstream. McClellan himself chose the site, and Duane's Regulars began work on June 10 or 11. Like the Woodbury-Alexander Bridge, Duane's bridge was intended to be substantial enough to withstand the punishment of the river at its wildest. Assisted by details from the Fifth and Sixth Corps, the engineers completed the twelve-hundred-foot-long, crib-and-trestle work on the seventeenth.[33]

While Alexander oversaw the bridge building, McClellan directed Barnard to lay out defensive works covering the entire front of the Army of the Potomac south of the Chickahominy. "I am forced to this by my inferiority in numbers," McClellan told the president, "so that I may bring the greatest possible numbers into action & secure the Army against the consequences of unforeseen disaster." Anchored in the center by "Casey's Redoubt" (Number 3), which had played such a conspicuous part in the battle on May 31, the line of fortifications included six redoubts or small forts and stretched for more than three miles from White Oak Swamp on the south (Redoubt Number 1) to the Chickahominy at Golding's farm (Redoubt Number 6). Strong, well-made infantry parapets connected the forts, which as a group had embrasures for forty field or siege guns. North of the Chickahominy, Barnard's men laid out four batteries. These gun emplacements, less elaborate than redoubts, were sited so they could work offensively against Confederate positions south of the river or defensively to protect the bridges. Two of the batteries stood above New Bridge, another nearby at Dr. Gaines's house, and a fourth at Hogan's house, near the Upper Trestle Bridge. Work on the batteries was essentially finished by June 20, allowing artillerists to move in, including two companies of the 1st Connecticut Heavy Artillery, who hauled ten pieces of siege artillery into two of the batteries near New Bridge.[34]

Given McClellan's long stay on the Chickahominy, these fortifications made good sense. A strong line of integrated works could hold an enemy attack at bay anywhere on the south bank long enough for reinforcements — even from the other side of the river — to reach the threatened point. Barnard's official report suggested that McClellan's intent with these fortifications was as much offensive as defensive; McClellan's explanation to Lincoln supports such an interpretation. With a smaller force (Barnard estimated 20,000 men could resist 100,000 attackers), McClellan could hold one section of the line and protect the army's supply line on the railroad while the main part of the army went on the offensive. Barnard believed, correctly, that McClellan had at last recognized the importance of the heights above New Bridge and that offensive operations would begin there.[35]

But as work on bridges and fortifications progressed, as the skies cleared and the ground hardened, and as Washington made good on promises of reinforcements, McClellan still declared himself unready to move. He informed Stanton on June 7, "I shall be in perfect readiness to move forward to take Richmond the moment that McCall reaches here & the ground will admit the passage of artillery." Three days later he wrote: "I wish it to be

WILLIAM J. MILLER

distinctly understood that whenever the weather permits I will attack with whatever force I may have." The last of George A. McCall's division of 9,000 Pennsylvanians joined McClellan's army on June 14. That same day, McClellan informed Secretary Stanton, "Weather now very favorable." [36] Still the army did not advance. On June 18, Lincoln wrote to McClellan to inquire about when the army might be ready to move on Richmond. "After tomorrow we shall fight the rebel army as soon as Providence will permit," answered McClellan the same day. "We shall await only a favorable condition of the earth and sky & the completion of some necessary preliminaries." [37]

The general did not explain precisely how Providence frustrated his advance, but the "necessary preliminaries" could only have been the completion of the line of fortifications. All else — including the earth and the sky — was favorable to an offensive at the time McClellan wrote. Those few days in the middle of the third week of June were critical in that all of McClellan's preparations, with the exception of the fortifications, had been completed. The bridges stood ready to carry men and vehicles, the roads had dried, the Union army was larger than it had ever been on the Peninsula, and the enemy had recently weakened himself at Richmond by sending reinforcements to the Shenandoah Valley. McClellan had even identified New Bridge as the critical point and expressed his intention to attack it. Yet he did not move. [38]

McClellan knew on June 18 that a few days' labor would complete his defensive works. He had decided not to move until the last shovelful of earth had been thrown — a decision Barnard thought foolish. Though the fortifications would not receive the finishing touches until the evening of June 21, they were, the chief engineer later pointed out, "ready enough *at any time* for an advance." [39]

On the morning of June 22, it might be argued that even by McClellan's lights the army was ready to advance. All his conditions had been fulfilled. Preparations on the river were complete. Heavy artillery was in place. The weather was perfect. Despite all these favorable elements, the Army of the Potomac lay idle through the twenty-second, the twenty-third, and the twenty-fourth. A week had passed since completion of the last bridge, and the only bridge *essential* for offensive operations had been standing unused for three weeks. Thus did McClellan let pass his fourth, best, and penultimate opportunity to move on Richmond. "I am compelled to state," commented E. D. Keyes some months later, "that I think Gen. McClellan does not excel in that quality of a general which enables him to know when to spring." [40]

Less than fifty miles to the west, Stonewall Jackson's army, the key column in Lee's plan to pry McClellan from his supply line, moved toward Rich-

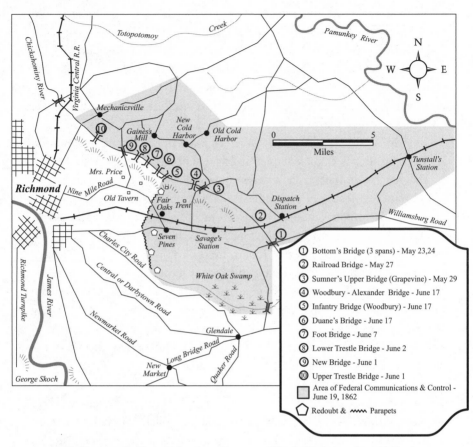

Bridges available to Federals on June 19, 1862 (with dates of completion)

mond from the Shenandoah Valley. The Valley Army was to turn Fitz John Porter's exposed northern flank on June 26, forcing the Federals to retreat from their forward positions. McClellan learned on the twenty-fourth of Jackson's approach, amid planning for what he termed "an advance of our picket line . . . preparatory to a general advance." This move, he hoped, would, "gain a couple of miles towards Richmond."[41] The equivalent of three Federal divisions advanced on the twenty-fifth and fought the battle of Oak Grove, withdrawing that evening having accomplished little.

June 26 was, according to McClellan's report submitted almost fourteen months later, "the day upon which I had decided as the time for our final advance." Yet in a dispatch to Stanton on the night of the twenty-fifth he mentioned no plans for an offensive. He wrote instead that he expected Jackson to attack his right the next day. He said the Confederates numbered 200,000 men and suggested that his army might be "destroyed by over-

WILLIAM J. MILLER

whelming numbers."[42] Despite these forebodings, the commanding general did not act. If he had planned a "final advance" for June 26, McClellan abandoned the idea as soon as he learned of Jackson's approach. He decided to continue on the defensive and receive the attack of what he believed were "overwhelming numbers." The Army of the Potomac remained idle through the morning and early afternoon of the twenty-sixth, until the Confederates finally mounted assaults near Mechanicsville after 3:00 P.M. The moment McClellan had spent weeks carefully preparing for had at last arrived.

Over the next six days, McClellan's army fought a series of defensive battles as it moved southward toward the James River. Some 34,000 men fell that week, 15,000 of them McClellan's. It may well have been for fear of losing so many men that McClellan had not moved from the Chickahominy in May or June. Though his letters in that period are full of references to a great battle, he was reluctant to bring on that engagement until he had taken every precaution to limit his casualties. He meant to secure the army against "the consequences of an unforeseen disaster" by improving communication between his two wings and building defensive works. This meant bridges, roads, and fortifications. On the Chickahominy, as at Yorktown, the engineers became McClellan's weapon of choice.

Although McClellan's myopic overreliance on engineering was prompted by a noble desire to save lives, it likely had the opposite effect. Military engineering consumes time, which in war, if spent lavishly, often costs lives (for example, illness claimed many Union soldiers while McClellan dawdled on the Peninsula). The young and inexperienced commanding general seemed not to lament the loss of precious hours and days. He waited; he deliberated; he prepared. In his own words, he was "cautious."

The Prince de Joinville, a staunch supporter of McClellan, mistook the reason for the army commander's free expenditure of days as yet another circumstance beyond the general's control. "To advance and meet the enemy upon his own ground," he wrote in 1862, "was an adventurous enterprise somewhat foreign to an American army. In that country men affect the slow, circumspect, methodical kind of war which leaves nothing to chance. This delay . . . is part of the national character." The prince did not suggest why Lee and Jackson had performed so out of national character that spring and summer, but he at least recognized the value of a day. In writing about one of McClellan's delays, the prince waxed poetic: "The opportunity, that moment which is ever more fugitive in war than in any other occupation of life, had taken wing."[43]

McClellan had let five such supreme moments fly: before the battle of Fair Oaks, after that engagement, after the bridges were complete, after the fortifications were complete, and immediately before the Confederate attack on June 26. "Such is the generalship," wrote Barnard, "which in delay, hesitation and uncertainty, incurs risks such as the rashest of daring and energetic generals seldom encounter."[44]

It seems unlikely that the Army of the Potomac would have suffered 15,000 casualties in any aggressive movement in May or June. Even if it had, losing so many men, or even more, might have been justified as the price of taking Richmond and perhaps ending the war. As it was, the 15,000 (and to that total must be added the as yet uncounted thousands of sick that left the army with "Chickahominy fever" in June) were paid out only to preserve the army, which would have to try again at greater cost. Like all misers, McClellan proved himself penny wise and pound foolish.

"I again repeat that I am not responsible for this," McClellan wrote on the day he left the river.[45] He later devoted months and thousands of words to proving his innocence and laying the blame for defeat where he believed it belonged. Historians continue to disagree about whether McClellan's plan was foiled by the meddling of political enemies or doomed by his alleged psychological instability. Whatever else might be said about the reasons for his failure on the Chickahominy, none can successfully argue that it was attributable to physical circumstances beyond his control. It was not the weather, nor was he forced to wait too long for bridges or for the Chickahominy to subside or for the roads to dry. Without doubt, all of these physical factors conspired to discourage movement, but never for more than a few days at a time and certainly not for five weeks. It was McClellan's continual rejection of opportunities to move from the river that rendered him susceptible to delays, each delay inviting more delays, and thus did the days and weeks pass away until Lee was prepared to attack. Barnard thought the weeks of waiting on the Chickahominy were the fault of McClellan, not of bad luck. To McClellan, wrote Barnard, "to *him,* and to the erroneous ideas disseminated concerning *his* capacity, merits and agency, the paralysis of doubt was due, as it was to him were justly ascribable the disasters which brought our military affairs to so low an ebb."[46]

Not until Ulysses S. Grant returned the Army of the Potomac to the vicinity of the Confederate capital in 1864 did the tide of northern optimism swell to a level near what it had been in 1862. Grant had more experience than McClellan had enjoyed two years earlier when he knocked on Richmond's door. Grant also had a better understanding of the equation most critical to success in war: he spent the lives of his men freely but did not waste time. As history knows, this formula brought Grant what McClellan could not obtain — Richmond, national victory, and the White House.

WILLIAM J. MILLER

Among those who helped Grant execute his campaign of relentless advance and continuous pressure was his chief engineer, John Gross Barnard.

NOTES

1. McClellan to Stanton, June 25, 1862, George B. McClellan, *The Civil War Papers of George B. McClellan, Selected Correspondence, 1860–1865*, ed. Stephen W. Sears (New York: Ticknor & Fields, 1989), 310.

2. John G. Barnard, *The Peninsula Campaign and Its Antecedents* (New York: Van Nostrand, 1864), 5.

3. Benjamin Alford, "John Gross Barnard," in *Thirteenth Annual Reunion, Graduates of the United States Military Academy* (June 12, 1882), 104–15; Allen Johnson and Dumas Malone, eds., *Dictionary of American Biography*, 20 vols. (New York: Scribner's, 1928–37), 1:626–27 (hereafter cited as *DAB*); Stephen W. Sears, *George B. McClellan: The Young Napoleon* (New York: Ticknor & Fields, 1988), 61, 63.

4. George B. McClellan, *McClellan's Own Story* (New York: Charles L. Webster, 1887), 115.

5. On the organization and command structure of the engineers in McClellan's army, see ibid., 119–25.

6. *DAB*, 10:485–86; Wesley Brainerd, *Bridge Building in Wartime: Colonel Wesley Brainerd's Memoir of the 50th New York Volunteer Engineers*, ed. Ed Malles (Knoxville: University of Tennessee Press, 1997), 134, 58; John G. Barnard, "Barton Stone Alexander," in *Tenth Annual Reunion, Graduates of the United States Military Academy* (June 12, 1879), 60–63.

7. U.S. War Department, *The War of the Rebellion: A Compilation of the Official Records of the Union and Confederate Armies*, 127 vols., index, and atlas (Washington, D.C.: GPO, 1880–1901), ser. 1, 11(1):126 (hereafter cited as *OR;* all references are to ser. 1); *OR* 11(1):110.

8. *OR* 11(1):111, 110.

9. *OR* 11(1):143–44.

10. *OR* 11(1):110–11.

11. McClellan to Lincoln, May 26, 1862, in McClellan, *Civil War Papers*, 277.

12. *OR* 11(1):113.

13. *OR* 11(1):111–12.

14. A. A. Humphreys to Archibald Campbell, July 28, 1862, Letterbook 7 (May, June, July 1862), A. A. Humphreys Papers, Historical Society of Pennsylvania, Philadelphia.

15. *OR* 11(1):143.

16. McClellan to Stanton, May 28, 1862, McClellan, *Civil War Papers*, 279; Barnard, *Peninsula Campaign*, 27. See also McClellan to wife, May 28, 1862, McClellan, *Civil War Papers*, 280.

17. Barnard, *Peninsula Campaign,* 31; *OR* 11(1):111.

18. *OR* 11(1):111–12.

19. U.S. Congress, *Report of the Joint Committee on the Conduct of the War,* 3 parts (1863; reprint, Millwood, N.Y.: Kraus, 1977), 1:606 (hereafter cited as *JCCW*); *OR* 11(1):113–14.

20. William Child, *A History of the Fifth Regiment New Hampshire Volunteers, in the American Civil War, 1861–1865* (1893; reprint, Gaithersburg, Md.: Ron R. Van Sickle Military Books, 1988), 64–65. Whatever validity the construction materials lent to the name of the structure, an old bridge near the same site had for many years been called Grapevine Bridge, so the name given the new structure by the Federals appears not to have been original.

21. Ibid., 69–70.

22. Ibid., 71.

23. Prince de Joinville, *The Army of the Potomac: Its Organization, Its Commander, Its Campaign,* trans. William H. Hurlbert (New York: Anson D. F. Randolph, 1862), 76.

24. *OR* 11(1):146–47.

25. McClellan, *Civil War Papers,* 284.

26. *OR* 11(1):113, 44; McClellan to Stanton, June 2, 1862, McClellan, *Papers,* 286.

27. Barnard, *Peninsula Campaign,* 26. McClellan mentioned the bridges in letters on June 2, 4, and 7.

28. Ibid., 31.

29. For a discussion of McClellan's difficulties in feeding his army and the attendant delays, see William J. Miller, "'Scarcely Any Parallel in History': Logistics, Friction and McClellan's Strategy in the Peninsula Campaign," in *The Peninsula Campaign of 1862: Yorktown to the Seven Days,* ed. William J. Miller, 3 vols. (Campbell, Calif.: Savas, 1997), 2:129–88.

30. *OR* 11(1):114, 145–48.

31. McClellan to wife, June 10, 1862, McClellan, *Civil War Papers,* 294; William J. Miller, "'Weather Still Execrable': Climatological Notes on the Peninsula Campaign," in *Peninsula Campaign,* ed. Miller, 3:184–87, 192.

32. *OR* 11(1):114–15, 148.

33. *OR* 11(1):115; Gilbert Thompson, "Work of U.S. Engineers: Military Bridges of the Army of the Potomac on the Chickahominy, 1862," *National Tribune,* July 11, 1901. Barnard and Alexander both thought Duane's bridge was completed on the nineteenth, but Thompson, who helped build it, states that the structure was finished on the seventeenth.

34. McClellan to Lincoln, June 20, 1862, McClellan, *Civil War Papers,* 304; Barnard, *Peninsula Campaign,* 42; *OR* 11(1):115–16, 148.

35. Barnard, *Peninsula Campaign,* 42; *OR* 11(1):116.

36. McClellan to Stanton, June 7, 10, 14, 1862, McClellan, *Civil War Papers,* 291, 296, 299.

37. McClellan to Lincoln, June 18, 1862, ibid., 303. See also Lincoln to McClellan, June 18, 1862, in Abraham Lincoln, *Collected Works of Abraham Lincoln,* ed. Roy P. Basler, 9 vols. (New Brunswick, N.J.: Rutgers University Press, 1953–55), 5:276.

38. McClellan to wife, June 15, 1862, McClellan, *Civil War Papers,* 301.

39. Barnard, *Peninsula Campaign,* 34.

40. *JCCW,* 1:614.

41. *OR* 11(1):49; McClellan to wife, June 23, 1862, McClellan, *Civil War Papers,* 307.

42. *OR* 11(1):51; McClellan to Stanton, June 25, 1862, McClellan, *Civil War Papers,* 310.

43. Joinville, *Army of the Potomac,* 71, 76.

44. Barnard, *Peninsula Campaign,* 32.

45. McClellan to Stanton, June 28, 1862, McClellan, *Civil War Papers,* 323.

46. Barnard, *Peninsula Campaign,* 4–5.

ROBERT K. KRICK

Sleepless in the Saddle

Stonewall Jackson in the Seven Days

O ne of the most acute of Confederate observers declared emphatically that Gen. R. E. Lee "undoubtedly" would have destroyed the
entire Federal army around Richmond in the early summer of 1862
but for "the incredible slackness, & delay & hanging back, which
characterized Gen. Jackson's performance of his part of the work."
The same commentator cited a wide spectrum of theories about the possible
causes of Jackson's failures but adroitly chose to conclude simply that Stonewall had been "for a while, not Jackson; being temporarily under the shadow
of a superstition." [1]

This essay will focus on four apparent lapses in June 1862 that stand at
odds with the remainder of Thomas J. "Stonewall" Jackson's remarkably energetic career: the march from the Shenandoah Valley to near Richmond; the
tardy arrival of Jackson's column near Mechanicsville on June 26; sluggishness in reaching the Gaines's Mill battlefield on June 27; and, most striking
of all, Jackson's egregious failure to act at White Oak Swamp on June 30.

The story has much to do with exhaustion. It begins, therefore, with Jackson's incredibly daring, risky, and aggressive campaign in Virginia's Shenandoah Valley. That epic chapter in American military history reached its
climax with two victories in two days, at Cross Keys and Port Republic. Just
before those two strenuous days, Jackson's unceasing exertions already had
left him "completely broken down," an aide wrote in a private letter. [2]

The surcease provided by six days in the Valley after Port Republic must
have restored the general somewhat, but his burdens remained sizable, if a
bit reduced. Then Jackson launched the army on rigorous new ventures that
required all he had to give. It is easy to imagine that his personal reservoir of
strength and energy was far from full as he headed for a whole new theater
of war.

While his army moved eastward beyond the Blue Ridge, Jackson undertook a round of exhausting personal activities that eventually so enervated him as to prevent normal functioning. On June 21 — a Saturday, as would become significant — Jackson started for Richmond, whence Lee had beckoned him for a discussion of the forthcoming campaign to raise the siege on the capital city. Jackson prefaced the trip with his customary elaborate attention to secrecy: he lied to the preacher and friend who was his host about the direction he was heading.[3]

When the general climbed aboard a freight train and started to roll in the direction of Richmond, he was perfectly situated to accomplish the trip in a prompt and efficient fashion. He ought to have reached Lee's headquarters in good time on Sunday morning, amply rested (he had gone to sleep on a postal clerk's bunk in the mail car), and then been able to return without undue stress. Instead, the general climbed off at Frederick's Hall in Louisa County before midnight, intent on observing his Sabbath. Jackson also gave his entire army, bent as it was upon a crucial strategic movement, all day off duty on Sunday, June 22. A railroad employee who saw Jackson aboard the train described him as a "little bow legged." More to the point, the general was a little weary and about to become infinitely more so.[4]

At about 1:00 A.M. on the twenty-third, his Sabbatical entanglements unloosed, Jackson mounted for a wearying horseback ride of about sixty miles in twelve hours to meet with Lee. Once again the general prefaced his departure with some artful evasions, this time about a breakfast he had no intention of eating.[5]

After the meeting with Lee and his subordinate commanders, Jackson spent a full night in the saddle for his return ride on June 23–24. He cannot have had more than a little sleep, and most likely none at all. Behind him, secrecy remained a top priority. Jackson's brother-in-law Gen. D. H. Hill wrote to his wife with an oblique reference to "one of the sons-in-law of Rev. Dr. Morrison [father of both generals' wives]." Hill noted that the meeting was being kept secret "even from the dignitaries of the government, most of whom are fools."[6]

While Jackson galloped tiredly across central Virginia, his troops were alternately slogging and riding toward Richmond. Employing what they referred to as the "rails and ties" system, they would ride in railroad cars for a spell, then dismount and walk on the ties while another unit had a chance to ride. A Confederate congressman who saw one of the troop trains marveled at how tightly the men jammed into the cars and clung to their roofs, "and, in fact, seemed to cover them all over like clusters of bees." Getting to Richmond from the Valley also posed a considerable logistical nightmare that was exacerbated by Jackson's secrecy. The army's redoubtable cursing quarter-

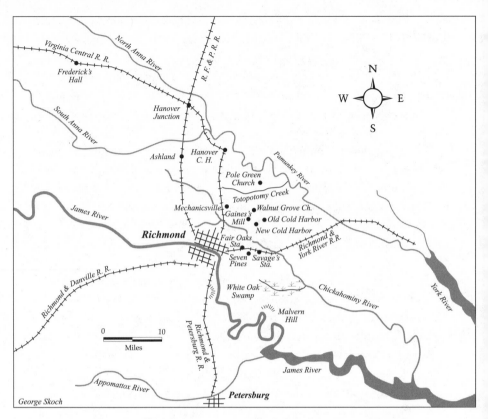

Area of Stonewall Jackson's movements during the Seven Days Campaign

master, Maj. John A. Harman, managed the feat in "spite of growls" that he was allowed to "know nothing" of the final destination of the whole business.[7]

The march was complicated by the fact that three infantry brigades newly arrived in the Valley had to spin around and retrace their steps. The commands of Evander M. Law, John Bell Hood, and Alexander R. Lawton had hurried west as a feint. These new, green formations (some men, remarkably, still carried pillows with them) hardly could be accounted an integral part of Jackson's army, but they moved under his directions. Valley survivors grumbled bitterly when the fresh newcomers rode the cars while weary veterans marched afoot.[8]

Confederates who had won fame as "foot cavalry" in the Valley found their route inhospitable. It was a "rough, hard road country — our feet suffered," one marcher complained. A Georgia captain put in charge of accumulating stragglers soon had more than 1,000 of them in hand. As part of the column streamed past Albemarle's elegant Edge Hill, Mrs. A. L. Rives sang opera arias for them. More pragmatically, ladies of the neighborhood passed out "the greatest quantity of provisions [to the] poor creatures."[9]

The hard roads of piedmont Virginia gave way to miry bogs as the army drew closer to Richmond. One of the rainiest springs for decades had raised the water in the South Anna so high that the march had to swerve onto a longer route with worse roads. Marchers bewailed having to negotiate "deep rivers and miry swamps . . . until completely exhausted . . . suffering of this night excelled anything that I have ever experienced . . . completely drenched." A member of the 38th Georgia expressed a prevailing notion when he wrote: "I donte like Jackson mutch, he runs us too mutch and too hard." One of the general's staff calculated that an average day's march covered nineteen miles.[10]

What is there to criticize in a march that moved that expeditiously despite so many encumbrances? The weak point in Jackson's execution of this critical mission was his insistence on stopping all day on June 22 to observe the Sabbath. The general was fond of insisting, "I can march my corps further in . . . 6 days and resting the 7th, and get through in better condition." His medical officer defended the halt (of the army, not necessarily of Jackson himself) because rest "was absolutely necessary for the good of the troops." The same man admitted, however, that on June 22, Jackson's "motive was a religious one." That focus was made apparent on Thursday, when the general had instructed an aide to see that "the cars continue to run constantly . . . until tomorrow midnight, as he does not wish them to run on Sunday."[11]

Jackson reveled in the chance to attend church twice that day. Once was in the camp of Hood's Texas Brigade, whose troops had not yet seen the legendary Stonewall. They jammed the meeting place to see him — and paid a heavy price when the Rev. Dr. Robert L. Dabney delivered a marathon sermon titled "The Believer Born of Almighty Grace." On page 35, Dabney declared, "Yes; but I suppose that the Spirit of all truth does not select tropes such that the figurative resemblance to the truths contained under them would be false." And at page 35 the preacher was by no means finished. One of the Texans nicely simplified the sermon's predestinarian dogma: "[Dabney] declared that a man born to be drowned could not be hanged or shot, and in effect, 'what is to be, will be (even if it never happens).'"[12]

During each moment of the twenty-four-hour halt around Frederick's Hall, Jackson was falling further behind schedule. As the maneuver element of a complex military combination designed to save his country's capital, Jackson clearly ought to have done whatever was necessary to meet his obligations. Even if some rest was indicated, a half-day's halt would have gone

Stonewall Jackson and his staff (clockwise from top right: Robert Lewis Dabney, William Allan, Alexander Swift Pendleton, Joseph G. Morrison, David B. Bridgford, Henry Kyd Douglas, James Power Smith, Hunter Holmes McGuire, Jedediah Hotchkiss, and Wells J. Hawks). Dabney's performance during the Seven Days left much to be desired.
Stonewall Jackson House Collection 51.38

ROBERT K. KRICK

far toward solving that problem without rupturing the timetable. The army was headed toward a series of battlefield crises in which hours and minutes became crucial; to have marched for one-half of that Sunday, or even for a few hours, might have had tremendous consequences later in the week. Defending the halt for non-Sabbitarian reasons founders on the simple fact that most of the army had been marching for only four days by this time. Furthermore, the "rails and ties" system had afforded most of the men some casual riding time to break up the marches. Incapacitating weariness cannot have throttled Jackson's famous foot cavalry as early as June 22.

Despite Thomas Jackson's unswervingly pious approach to life's challenges, there is no other major question about modulating his military demeanor on Sundays, either before or after June 22. In fact, contemporaries noted whimsically that the general seemed always to fight then rather than during the week, citing as an example three Sunday battles out of the six fought during the Valley campaign. That suggests that Jackson's bad judgment in this matter probably reflected the exhaustion that already was numbing his critical faculties, with further consequences destined to unfold in the following week. During the rest of the war, Sunday did not stand in the way of Jackson's temporal duty; on June 22, it did.

Whatever salutary impact the day off might have had for the line companies, Jackson himself gained nothing from the day of desuetude. Two long rides surrounding two sleepless nights leveled him. On the night of the twenty-fourth, one of the staff noticed Jackson demonstrating the most anomalous behavior: he spent an hour reading a novel. It "seemed to weary him." No one ever remarked on a similar interlude in the arms of fiction during the entire war — probably during Jackson's entire life. Soon thereafter a local boy serving with a Virginia cavalry regiment encountered Jackson on a lonely road, in the middle of the night, unaccompanied. When the chance for some badly needed rest offered, the duty-driven Jackson was too bewildered to accept.[13]

On the night of June 25, the single most important commodity that might have been applied to the Confederate cause in Virginia was a good night's sleep for Stonewall Jackson. The weariness of his body had already affected his judgment so adversely, however, that instead he stayed up all night long. "Under the stress of his great anxiety and heavy responsibilities," his wife wrote proudly if fatuously, "he gave not one moment to rest or sleep during the night, but devoted the whole of it to the most energetic preparations *and to prayer.*"[14]

Without deprecating the advantages of piety, it is easy to see that Jackson made a wretched choice of activities for those hours of darkness. The irresponsible depletion of his physical reserves begun with the two nights of post-Sabbath sleepless riding had utterly drained the general's reserves. Now he plunged into a red, hazy zone from which nothing good could be expected to result.

Focusing several columns from divergent tangents on a battlefield rarely works. Lee was hoping to achieve just such a coup on June 26. Jackson's maneuver element was to turn the right of Gen. George B. McClellan's army in the vicinity of Mechanicsville. All of Jackson's movements for ten days were aimed at that goal. By the time he arrived near where he would have been most useful, impetuous Confederates from Lee's force around Richmond had launched headlong assaults east of Mechanicsville that ended in tactical disaster. Jackson bore no direct responsibility for those spendthrift tactics, but his failure to fulfill his role set the stage for them.

One of the often-asked questions about the campaign is whether Jackson's lethargy — so obvious four days later — affected his advance on June 26. The record shows that in fact Jackson did everything, weary enervation notwithstanding, that reasonably could have been expected of him. Losing a day's march on June 22 affected affairs on the twenty-sixth, of course, but the approach by Jackson's column on that day can hardly be faulted. This is the only one of the four subjects examined in this essay in which Jackson seems to be immune to criticism.

A young soldier in the 33rd Virginia of the Stonewall Brigade noted in his diary that on the morning of June 26, he lay down in bivouac at 2:00 A.M. and marched again at 3:00 A.M. A Texan also recorded his regiment's departure at 3:00 A.M. An artillerist wrote that overnight on the twenty-fifth to twenty-sixth he and his mates were "so exhausted we dropped down and fell asleep," then scrambled to march again soon thereafter without any breakfast. Those experiences, and many more like them, belie the notion of slothful camp protocol.[15]

Once on their feet, the troops kept "moving steadily along," in the words of a soldier in the 31st Virginia. Their route was through "low marshy country verging at times to huge swamps," with "frog ponds and stagnant waters everywhere." The mugginess of those swamps on a "dreadfully hot" day (high near 90 degrees) proved stifling to marching men.[16] The sopping heat and muddy roads meandering through flat countryside posed a disconcerting change of pace to an army and a general famous for long, brisk marches on the familiar Valley Pike.

One problem along the march, as usual during his tenure with the army, came at the hands of the maladroit Rev. Dabney. He later boasted that an alarum about enemy cavalry to the left prompted him on his own authority

ROBERT K. KRICK

to halt the entire column and send a regiment in that direction. "This caused some delay," he calmly reported, and in any event was a false alarm. Fortunately for the Confederates, Dabney was quite far back in the column, so his adventure probably did relatively little harm. The head of the army never noticed, and the telescoping of a moving column imposed delays on the rear in any case.[17]

A relative handful of Federal soldiers offered resistance to the head of the column, but they were tenacious men, and they enjoyed the tremendous advantage that abets delaying tactics in heavily wooded country. No matter how many Confederates marched in the deep column, only a few men at its front could do anything about the harassing screen opposing them. Dr. Hunter Holmes McGuire, who rode next to Jackson most of the day, described steady, aggressive pressure against the Federal rear guard. McGuire wrote: "The whole of the march from Ashland nearly to Pole Green Church was a fight. We had skirmishes the whole of the way, and occasionally we had a sharp little combat." The calmly reliable doctor went so far as to style Jackson's efforts on the twenty-sixth "almost superhuman exertions."[18]

Eager hands promptly removed trees felled in the road as obstructions, but doing that work over and over again inevitably resulted in delays. Federals had of course destroyed the rude bridges that crossed streams and swamps, further retarding the march. Potable water — as distinct from the ubiquitous swamp water — was so scarce that Confederate cavalry watered their horses out of canteens.[19]

The best evidence of the firmness with which Jackson prosecuted this march comes from the Texans who led it. General John Bell Hood's men were destined to develop into perhaps the best brigade in the Army of Northern Virginia — unquestionably they must be recognized as at least one of the best. No one ever questioned the Texans' aggressiveness. Jackson attested to their commander's merit when he said of Hood, "Oh! he is a soldier!" On June 26, Hood's sturdy troops led the way, the 5th Texas in front of the rest by about one-half mile. A twenty-five-man picket scouted another half-mile in front of the regiment. The Lone Star soldiers had instructions to take "great care . . . to keep . . . out of sight of the enemy's scouts." The advantage that accrued to defenders on narrow roads in swampy country restricted even Hood's men to a slow, if steady, rate of advance. Their recollections attest to the difficulties they encountered.[20]

At last, near 4:00 P.M., the foremost Texans arrived at the considerable declivity of Totopotomoy Creek. They found the bridge over the "small creek with deep banks" in flames. The sound of axes cutting trees echoed from just around the bend on the far side. Scouts reported the enemy in wait in the same direction. Southern artillery fired in that direction while Confederate infantry and engineers repaired the bridge in good time using handy fence rails (within weeks Jackson would be arresting officers in clusters for appropriating fence rails in similar fashion elsewhere). A Texan noted that "the delay in moving was shorter than one would have supposed," but more precious daylight slipped away while they labored. The roar of fighting from the direction of Mechanicsville filled the air. Jackson was too late to affect that affair directly, but his presence above the far Federal right would oblige the enemy to retreat overnight.[21]

E. P. Alexander, the tartest of the general's prominent contemporary critics, declared that on June 26 Jackson "marched only 14 miles over good roads & had no opposition." The march was something more than fourteen miles in length; it was over execrable roads; and it faced steady opposition.[22]

One specific criticism sometimes leveled at Jackson was his failure to locate and employ good guides. In fact, he had annexed to his use most of a full company of cavalry from Hanover County. They experienced some confusion because long Federal occupation had leveled woodlots and cut wagon paths in every direction, altering the face of the countryside. These local lads were, however, the best asset anyone could have found — "excellent guides, trusted men." The insurmountable problem was that there were no useful alternative routes available.[23]

Given the deadly ennui that beset Jackson before and after the twenty-sixth, it is easy to imagine that had he possessed his accustomed energy, he would have found something clever to do. What that might have been on this day, though, is hard to imagine. A startling aspect of operations throughout the Seven Days was the virtually complete absence of staff work. A reliable means of turning an army commander's will into performance by tens of thousands of soldiers simply had not been formulated. Lee was noticeably, and understandably, concerned about Jackson's arrival. Yet not a single staff officer, or even a courier or orderly, went from Lee to Jackson all day long. The route would have been difficult, but knowing Jackson's status — perhaps even prompting his progress — would have been invaluable to Lee. In his diary, Lee's aide Charles Scott Venable wrote darkly of "waiting for Jackson." Another staff member heard Lee express worry about Jackson's whereabouts to Jefferson Davis. Venable commented obliquely that "communication with Jackson [was] delayed by bad roads and creeks up." The breakdown of staff work, or more precisely its virtual absence, affected most Civil War campaigns but none more so than the Seven Days.[24]

Stonewall Jackson spent the night of the twenty-sixth at the Hundley home, Laurel Meadow, affording him the invaluable opportunity to restore

ROBERT K. KRICK

Lee and Jackson during the Seven Days, an early postwar sketch by Adalbert J. Volk that (unlike Waud's treatment of the same subject reproduced on page 14) gives Jackson the dominant position.

Emily V. Mason, Popular Life of Gen. Robert Edward Lee
(Baltimore: John Murphy and Company, 1872), p. 106

his faculties with some rest. As was his custom throughout this fortnight, however, the general ignored his exhaustion. The host family noticed that he "did not sleep in the room assigned to him but spent the night in the dining room writing dispatches." [25]

On the morning of June 27, a tableau worthy of a photographer unfolded at Walnut Grove Church when Lee and Jackson met to discuss their options. Most men of both generals' armies had not seen the others' leader, and they crowded around in masses. "There had to be a guard posted around the generals," a North Carolinian wrote, "to keep the men back." Unfortunately, Jackson's characteristic secretiveness held such powerful sway that, Rev. Dabney grumbled, "he did not tell me one word of the instructions . . . from Lee." [26]

Worse, Jackson did not make himself clear to his guide when the march resumed, telling him simply to head for Cold Harbor. The guide reasonably enough led him toward the nearest of two places so named, New Cold Harbor. A sharp turn southward, at right angles away from his intended route (toward Old Cold Harbor), did not trigger any alarm in Jackson, who apparently was too deep in a fatigued haze to notice even so abrupt a deviation. Since none of the staff had any hint of the general's intentions, the mistake cost much needless marching and hours of delay. When the guide responded crisply to Jackson's befuddled complaint, Jackson expressed his reliance on God to bail him out. That did not work out, despite Jackson's later assertion that divine providence had in fact turned the mistake into a blessing. Subsequent canards against the underinformed pilot ("we were misled by guides," wrote the usually reliable William Allan) are belied by the early accounts. [27]

When, at long last, the head of the column got back into "the little country road, our really intended route," so much time had been lost that the troops ran into D. H. Hill's force converging from a different direction. Dabney and others described with intense relish how Jackson snubbed Gen. W. H. C. Whiting when Whiting worried about the approaching column. But Dabney admitted that Jackson then halted while *all* of Hill's command straggled past. [28]

Laboring as he was under a serious handicap, Jackson urgently needed a real chief of staff, functioning efficiently. Instead he had Dabney. The general would not have used a perfect chief of staff well, but even the most rudimentary staff assistance could have kept the column pointed properly on June 27. Jackson had gotten away with ignoring staff functions in the Valley. The difference here was that he was too impaired to manage everything in person. The Stonewall of Kernstown and Winchester — or any other period of the war — would have noticed a deflection by his entire force of ninety degrees away from its goal. In late June 1862, he was not himself.

Lee, meanwhile, spent another day "awaiting anxiously" the appearance of his subordinate at the designated point. Lee even rode across the rear of the Confederate line north of Boatswain's Swamp under heavy artillery fire in search of his leftward element. When Lee met his tardy lieutenant, he deflected some of Jackson's troops to the west. Eventually Stonewall sent J. Keith Boswell across the field to report to Lee "that we had come upon the enemy." After Jackson finally managed to reach the Old Cold Harbor

ROBERT K. KRICK

intersection, another confusing episode unfolded about getting the troops into position. For the rest of his life Dabney insisted that Maj. John A. Harman had horribly mangled Jackson's intentions by bungling his orders. A nugget of truth doubtless lurked in Dabney's allegations, but little genuine substance. Jackson watched over all of this while sucking on a lemon. The general's mood was "evidently disturbed," a Maryland soldier noticed. "His usual quiet and cool manner now evinced restlessness and anxiety. [He would] ride up and down the road, listening intently." Jackson's wife's memoir spoke of "unwonted excitement" and "riding restlessly." Other accounts talk of prayers and terse orders.[29]

When at last the day of bitter fighting at Gaines's Mill ended in the first great victory for Lee's Army of Northern Virginia, Stonewall was obviously prostrated by exhaustion. He acknowledged to an aide that his *horse* "was utterly broken down" but admitted nothing about his own condition. Dabney itched to announce his petty complaints about Harman to the general, but the chief of staff's brother prudently talked him out of it: "No, you see he is too much fatigued to wish to talk on *any* subject." Late that night Jackson lay down on the ground between his friend Gen. J. E. B. Stuart and one of the cavalryman's aides. When asked, "Where's your staff?" Jackson replied, "Off somewhere in comfortable quarters — I am playing orderly tonight."[30]

This "playing orderly" obviously constituted a stupendous waste of military talent and time under the best of circumstances. In Jackson's benumbed personal condition it probably seemed entirely natural. His nonchalant installation two months earlier of Dabney as chief of his staff, nine days after he had asked Dabney to join him as a chaplain, showed a dreadfully imperfect notion of what staff should be. To prepare the dour preacher for his crucial military post, Jackson "allowed . . . two days with Halleck's *Articles of War* — 'a thin octavo volume' — and put him in office." The bright young men who had been on the staff right along were stunned. One of them later jotted notes to himself about Dabney in the margins of his books: "What Dr. Dabney accomplished as a staff-officer none of the staff ever knew. He [only] looked wise & clerical in camp & was full of criticism of others. . . . I never heard of his doing anything on the *battle-field*. In camp & prayer meeting he was invaluable." Meanwhile, the brilliant young Alexander S. "Sandie" Pendleton, who eventually would become a strikingly successful chief of Jackson's staff, had a limited role. At Gaines's Mill, Jackson the predestinarian calmly used Sandie, over the objections of J. E. B. Stuart, to carry orders on a route where four predecessors had been killed.[31]

During these Seven Days, during which Jackson's ability to function deteriorated steadily, he desperately needed staff help. Dabney was Jackson's fault; excessive secrecy was Jackson's fault (or, perhaps, the defect of a virtue); but neither of those shortcomings was unique to this campaign. What made them loom so large was Jackson's inability, unique to this week, to run the army himself. Stonewall had repeatedly demonstrated the ability to be an eminently successful staffless warrior. In the campaign around Richmond, though, his diminished capacity highlighted those fundamental defects for the first — and only — time during his amazing career.

General Jackson's performance on June 28–29 continued to be below par. During those two days he faced the mission of pushing across the Chickahominy River and pursuing McClellan's retreating army. There is not enough space in this forum to examine all of Jackson's difficulties during the Seven Days. These two too-quiet days deserve study beyond the scope available here. Such work surely will reveal Jackson as not himself. In cursory review, it must be said that special pleading can cipher away many of the details, but on those two days Jackson cannot be portrayed as matching the legend he crafted in so many other places. Three witnesses depicted Jackson at this time as depleted and bereft. An artillerist described the general as "stark and stiff [and] worn down to the lowest point of flesh consistent with effective [?] service." One of Gen. John B. Magruder's staff who saw Jackson on horseback at 3:00 A.M. commented that "the strain . . . was excessive in a campaign like this. Want of sleep and . . . great physical fatigue was undergone in addition." A South Carolina journalist also discerned some of Jackson's problem. The general was "inclined to take 'cat naps,'" he wrote, "and before and during the . . . battles around Richmond he took little regular slumber." [32]

Two thoughtful participants in the campaign described the overarching problem on June 28–29 as the absence of staff work. "Had our army been as well organised at this time as it became afterward, & as seasoned," wrote Porter Alexander, "June 28th would doubtless have brought us active movement for new dispositions." William W. Chamberlaine, in a splendid but little-known memoir, mused: "It seems to me now that a numerous staff was needed to keep the Commanding General posted as to the movements of the different columns and to keep the Commanders of the different columns informed of the movements of each other, to ensure cooperation." In his own report Jackson offered no analysis, instead summarizing the results of the two days in four terse lines. [33]

A popular explanation of Stonewall's listlessness on June 29 is based on the calendar: the twenty-ninth was Sunday. That theorem leaps to mind on the basis of the overt, conscious delay Jackson made the week before at Frederick's Hall. Surviving evidence about Jackson's behavior on June 28–29, however, shows relatively more activity on the twenty-ninth than the twenty-eighth, if still less than the defense of the national capital warranted.[34]

Even Lee's sharp disappointment over Jackson's lack of production during the week cannot have prepared the army commander for June 30. That Monday was Jackson's worst day of the war, and by a factor of several multiples. While Gens. James Longstreet and A. P. Hill fought desperately on Frazier's Farm and around the Glendale intersection, Jackson halted within easy hearing of their fight opposite a relatively vulnerable Federal flank. There he slept away — sometimes literally, and steadily in a figurative sense — one of the brightest opportunities of the war.

Jackson's morning started briskly enough. His men reported marching at 2:30 A.M., or at least by 3:00 A.M. It was at least ten o'clock, though, when they fetched up on the north bank of White Oak Swamp on a crest above a destroyed bridge. Jackson, with care worthy of the Mexican War artillery subaltern he once had been, cut a covered way, arranged his ordnance behind some trees, and then opened a bombardment across the swamp. "The fire so opened . . . was kept up until dark," Jackson declared laconically in his official report. Since sunset did not arrive until 7:17, that sentence spanned many crucial hours. A book about the campaign that appeared soon after it ended called this "probably the heaviest fight of field artillery . . . during the war." That overstated the case, but in fact heavy fire raged for a time before the exchange became desultory.[35]

Jackson sat calmly, as always, under the enemy artillery fire. His chief of staff busied himself scooping up spilled molasses with crackers from a broken Yankee hardtack box. No one initiated anything more for some time as thousands of Confederates stood awaiting Jackson's orders in "this deep, tangled wilderness," as a 37th Virginia captain called it. Some stinging small-arms fire came across White Oak Swamp at the southerners, retreating Federals had torn up the bridge, and the vicinity was fearfully ugly, boggy countryside. Five known crossings threaded through White Oak Swamp in reasonable proximity, however, and other cowpaths warranted investigation. A dozen or more boys from adjacent Hanover County stood at Jackson's beck and call as guides. The Confederate legend who had been executor of the Snake Grade and the Gooney Manor Road at Front Royal would have located several workable options, picked the best of them, and gone to war.[36]

But the Stonewall Jackson of the Seven Days did absolutely nothing. The roar of a bitter fight of unexcelled valor by troops under A. P. Hill and James Longstreet filled the heavens, but Jackson did nothing. For a time, he literally lay on the ground and slept under a tree. One staff officer mused that "it looked to me as if on our side we were waiting for Jackson to wake up." [37]

Two prominent Confederates stood at center stage as the primary witnesses of the mysterious drama of White Oak Swamp. Neither Gen. Wade Hampton nor Col. Thomas T. Munford can be counted as Jackson sycophants. Both men were a bit disaffected, Hampton expressing displeasure with Lee and Munford grumbling about being the senior colonel in the army. Nor can Hampton or Munford properly be damned for Longstreet-like rancor or dishonesty or stories that transmogrified over time. Both must be considered solid witnesses.

Hampton described his bizarre dealings with Jackson in at least three versions. One of them is widely used and one but little. Munford wrote at least two accounts; the more important one is a manuscript not usually cited in this connection. [38]

By Hampton's account, Jackson rode through the swamp with some cavalry and came back alone. Hampton (who still commanded infantry, not cavalry, at this stage of the war) and an aide or two went exploring to the left of the main crossing. He remembered the ground as "not at all boggy . . . stream . . . shallow, with a clear sandy bottom . . . 10 or 15 feet wide." Beyond the swamp Hampton discovered an exposed Federal flank and crawled close to his unsuspecting enemies. When he returned, undetected, the Carolina brigadier went to Jackson, who asked whether Hampton could make a bridge. Yes, he replied, for infantry but not for artillery. Hampton did so with a fifty-man detachment, still without alerting the northerners. [39]

The successful bridge builder located Jackson sitting on a pine log and reported. "He drew his cap down over his eyes, which were closed, and after listening to me for some minutes, he rose without speaking" and "walked off in silence." In another account Hampton described Jackson's only reaction as "H-M-M?" and "UM-H-M-M." In one of his versions, Hampton recalled the denouement after an awkward pause in reverse — with he himself getting up and leaving in silence. The absence of reaction almost certainly betrayed an organism simply bereft of the capacity to react. Hampton was talking to a sickly shell of Stonewall Jackson. [40]

The noise of fighting by his friends made Jackson "eager to press forward," he declared in his official report; but in fact he probably could not have reacted to a swarm of hornets settling on his brow. A North Carolina soldier marveled when Jackson "never flinched" as a ball smacked into a tree just above his head and attributed the lack of reaction to courage of legendary proportions. Stonewall had plenty of that, demonstrated on many fields. On June 30 he also was devoid of the rudimentary functioning of a nervous system. [41]

ROBERT K. KRICK

Hampton told R. E. Lee his story in 1868, and Lee "said that he never had understood why the delay had occurred." No one else had understood either. Lee's contemporary official report summarized Jackson's June 30 in two disappointed sentences totaling twenty-two words. Maj. John Walter Fairfax of Longstreet's staff, who showed up in hopes of generating help for his hard-pressed friends fighting at Glendale, must have gone away as bewildered as Hampton.[42]

Even before his fruitless engineering exploits, Hampton had scouted to the right. On this same ground in 1864, Hampton (by then commanding all of the army's cavalry) would successfully cross the swamp to outflank Federals on the other side. That later venture also came to naught.

Tom Munford's story buttressed most of Hampton's account from a different perspective but carefully redefined one key circumstance. Munford splashed across White Oak Swamp through the torn-up poles and other debris at the site of the destroyed main bridge. His mission was to gather in some Federal artillery from which the crews had been driven by Jackson's barrage. Some "very annoying" rifle fire and pesky artillery deflected Munford's horsemen from that mission. They trotted downstream and easily found a cattle trail across the swamp that led them home.[43]

Munford mused after the war: "I thought, all the time, that he could have crossed his infantry where we re-crossed. I had seen his infantry cross far worse places, and I expected that he would attempt it." The colonel clarified an apparent mistake in Hampton's narrative, however, about the nature of the swamp. During the same 1864 campaign in which Hampton outflanked this crossing on its right, he came to be intimately familiar with the ground. The summer of 1864 bore little resemblance, however, to the earlier period. In Munford's words: "Genl Hampton often Picketed that vicinity in after times, and has confounded it with a dry season. The night before we arrived at White Oak swamp, we had I think as heavy a rain as I ever remember. . . . and the swamp was *belly deep* to the *horses* and *very rough.*"[44]

Hampton's glib account of the ease of crossing obviously must be discounted to some extent on that basis; but the nature of the swamp hardly matters. Any other week, Stonewall Jackson would have mastered it in the course of his duty. There can be little question, water level aside, about — in the words of a Confederate writer — "what might have happened had the Jackson of the Valley had the opportunity presented" on June 30.[45]

When added to a week of similar, if somewhat less egregious, low-intensity performances, White Oak Swamp shrieks for explanation. What was wrong with Mighty Stonewall? One theory, popular in modern writing, is that Jackson's temperament, riveted in place by sundry childhood experiences appealing to psychobabblers, left him receptive only to specific orders. Thus his delay at White Oak Swamp was a halt awaiting directions through channels — behavior dictated by his psyche. Such a notion is utterly untenable on the basis of the rest of the general's career. At First Manassas he had taken firm tactical initiatives without the least direction, answering the exigencies of the case; in the Valley he conspired to stretch, if not disobey, outdated orders to meet the needs that he recognized. Subsequently, at Chancellorsville (and elsewhere), Jackson would adapt promptly and with the utmost skill to existing circumstances to win great victories. In fact, his entire career is a paean to the necessity of seizing the moment. He may have been dully awaiting direction above White Oak Swamp — but if so, it was because he was not the Jackson of the other eighty-four weeks of his war, not because to do so was Stonewall Jackson's way.[46]

Examining what went wrong with Thomas Jackson that June week requires invoking the axiom that intelligence and judgment consist in large part of discerning differences between things that seem similar and similarities between things apparently different. What was different about Stonewall in that one week than in the rest of his two years of aggressive prowess? Observers wondered if he was sulking (a notion propounded mostly by proficient sulkers), confused in unusual country, jealous of the Richmond army, eager to spare his own troops, useless when facing good generals, or out of his depth with so large a force. Yet Jackson never before or after was unmanned by responsibility, prone to sulking, confused, jealous, or unduly (if at all) sparing of his men. Quite the reverse was true in each case.[47]

What Jackson *was* during the Seven Days, was exhausted beyond the ability to function adequately. In his classic *R. E. Lee,* Douglas Southall Freeman charted Stonewall's known loss of sleep during the period June 23–30 and demonstrated that he had precious little opportunity for rest. Subsequent evidence nibbles a bit more at the hours of potential repose. Such an analysis, of course, can tell us only when he was awake. Even presuming that all the uncharted hours were given over to sleep, which is very far from certain, Jackson faced a crushing burden of weariness. Every responsible officer in each army was similarly afflicted, obviously, but only Jackson undertook a hundred-mile roundtrip on horseback on two consecutive sleepless nights to begin the campaign. Even R. E. Lee, whose sturdy constitution demanded relatively little rest, was close to being prostrated by July 1 (the commanding general was sixteen years older than his famous lieutenant).[48]

Furthermore, Thomas Jackson was a man who absolutely required sleep — in his wife's words, he "sometimes was so overpowered by sleep that he could not resist it," and "his slumber might prove so profound as to render it difficult to arouse him." In several wartime letters, Stonewall complained of suffering because of losing needed sleep and made plans to get more. The general's tendency to spend church services in the arms of Morpheus prompted much amused comment, and he sometimes nodded off in the midst of an interview or at other unseemly moments. A staffer, when just getting to know him, remarked with surprise how sedentary Jackson's routine remained when military exigencies allowed: "The General spends most of the time in his room. . . . says but little and eats but little." Under normal circumstances, Jackson not only slept a lot but did so in a firm routine, "perfectly regular and systematic."[49] No fortnight during his life afforded less regular opportunities for sleep than late June 1862.

A recent thoughtful study of the impact of loss of rest on military officers declares that careful research has established an inalterable fact: "no act of will or ethical passion, no degree of training" can overcome the destruction of one's faculties after several days of sleep deprivation. A section of the study headed "Perverse Outcomes of Overvaluing Self-Denial" does not mention Stonewall Jackson, but it describes precisely the kind of anomalous behavior that he displayed during the Seven Days. "Pretending to be superhuman is very dangerous," the study concludes. Relying on a perceived divine mandate to be more than human proved to be the same thing for General Jackson.[50]

The worst of Jackson's days during this bad week clearly came on June 30, at the climax of the weary spell and under the cumulative effects of exhaustion piled upon exhaustion. To make matters worse, the eve of that bad thirtieth of June at White Oak Swamp was the hottest and wettest night of the week. Notions then prevalent about the bad effect of mysterious "miasmas" from the swamps reflected awareness of the debilitating effect of damp heat. The temperature still stood at 76 degrees at 10:00 P.M., and remained in the seventies at 7:00 A.M. the next morning after a torrential downpour overnight. Jackson reported wearily to his wife, "I had a wet bed last night, as the rain fell in torrents. I got up about midnight, and haven't seen much rest since." A Confederate colonel called the overnight downpour as heavy as he saw "at any time during the war." Another officer wrote of the "deadness of the atmosphere in this wilderness of low . . . marshy ground . . . the sun . . . superheating the humid atmosphere, causing prostrations of many and great discomfort to all."[51]

Not surprisingly, Stonewall Jackson's prostration led to genuine physical sickness as well, and that completed the formula for malaise and ineptitude. "During the past week," the general wrote home, "I have not been well, have suffered from fever and debility." For the decade and a half between the

Mexican War and the advent of Civil War, Thomas Jackson had grumbled steadily, indeed incessantly, about his health in conversation and in letters. His auditors must have grown monumentally weary of the relentless plaints. As though by a miracle, however, field service in the war instantly halted Jackson's chronic complaining. Whether because active operations left no time for comfortable hypochondria, or because the energetic regimen of active operations cured genuine nagging problems, Stonewall Jackson mentioned none of the woes that had so beset Major Jackson. It was just this once during the war, in the Richmond swamps, that Jackson got sick. The general told a minister friend that he felt worse during this onset than at any time since a serious illness in Mexico fifteen years earlier and blamed the "malarial region" for his problem. That suggests that the "fever and debility" he felt seemed malarial to him. The effect on the army's operations was debilitating indeed.[52]

Admission of "fever and debility" to Mrs. Jackson was not the general's only acknowledgment, through the haze that must have been upon him, that things simply were not right. At a rude dinner table on the evening of June 30, Jackson fell asleep with a biscuit between his teeth. Then, rousing briefly, he said, "Now, gentlemen, let us at once to bed, and rise with the dawn, and see if to-morrow we cannot *do something.*" The erratic behavior of course had been evident long before suppertime. One staffer thought that his chief was "more wearied and depressed than he had ever been seen to be before." Another declared, "He appeared to me to have less of his usual push and quick decision." A Maryland cavalryman detailed to headquarters made plans to get away from Jackson, who "had been in a bad humor for several days," evidently because he "had been completely worn out."[53]

The man whose very name stood for aggression, whose critics assail him today for too much fire and brimstone, was incapable of doing the right thing — in fact was incapable of doing anything whatsoever by June 30. A captain and aide-de-camp claimed that Jackson "once said the only objection he had to Genl Lee was that he did not hate the Yankees enough." Now, on perhaps the best single day of the war to do something assertive in that regard, Jackson simply was not at home. The congruence of this fabulous opportunity with the one brief window of Jacksonian ennui is stunning to contemplate in a statistical context. Maybe the God in whom Jackson reposed so much trust really was on Julia Ward Howe's side.[54]

Two of Jackson's aides who later wrote major histories summarized the dreadful failure of June 30. Nothing uncovered since they wrote can unhinge their conclusions. William Allan acknowledged the difficulties posed by Yankees and swamps but declared emphatically that "they were not such obstacles as usually held Jackson in check." Robert L. Dabney concluded that his hero, in whose defense he usually employed hagiography, had run out of fuel: "The labor of previous days, the sleeplessness, the wear of gigantic cares, with the drenching of the comfortless nights, had sunk the elasticity of his will and the quickness of his invention, for the once, below their wonted tension."[55]

Jackson apparently hit bottom on June 30. The next day, at Malvern Hill, he played no crucial role, but he seems to have stabilized somewhat — although it must surely have been in a considerable fog. The general rode toward the converging army at Malvern Hill after daylight in company with one of Longstreet's staff. An aide to Stuart found Jackson "in good spirits." A stranger who saw the general on July 1, however, described the evident, visible impact of "constant exposure" and "loss of sleep," which between them "left little to impress the imagination" about "this unattractive personality." During the battle, Jackson found opportunity to snarl again at Whiting with his accustomed asperity, perhaps exacerbated by exhaustion. A shower of Federal artillery rounds knocked limbs off trees over the general's head and threw dirt on a dispatch he was writing. His communiqués to J. E. B. Stuart during the morning spoke of being engaged and solicited divine aid.[56]

On the morning of July 2, Jackson's medical officer needed guidance from his chief and found him asleep. Dr. McGuire shook the general again and again, but without success. Jackson was "difficult to wake," McGuire recalled, "as he was exhausted and very sound asleep. I tried it myself, and after many efforts partially succeeded." Later that day at a conference of the army high command, "Jackson was very quiet," a far-from-novel state, "only answering in a brief, deferential tone." When Jefferson Davis showed up, Jackson was amply alert to recognize in the president a deadly enemy to his worldview and treated his civilian overlord with icy formality. The general was awake enough to be dismayed at the lack of an avid pursuit of McClellan and prudent enough to oppose a frontal assault on him soon thereafter.[57]

As the leaders of the Confederacy evaluated the campaign that saved Richmond, they could find much of which to be proud: the nascent nation's capital had survived a dire threat, ensuring the further life of their revolutionary endeavor. They also recognized the unmistakable fact that a golden opportunity for greater results had slipped through their fingers. Many men in positions of authority recognized Jackson's unhappy role in producing that disappointment.

Six months later, Gen. J. E. B. Stuart returned from a meeting with the army commander and told an aide, "Gen. Lee says he 'wishes he had a dozen Jacksons for his lieutenants.'" In July 1862, however, Lee was "deeply, bitterly disappointed" in Jackson. Charles Scott Venable of Lee's staff wrote that "the slowness of Jackson's movements" on the thirtieth "lost one of the [great] opportunities." Colonel (later major general) Jeremy F. Gilmer, well connected both personally and by marriage, wrote scornfully of the unwarranted attention given to Stonewall by the newspapers.[58]

Few of the public noticed. In the afterglow of driving away the invaders, a redeemed Richmond wallowed in euphoria that overwhelmed most introspection. Contemporary accounts described Jackson's operations against the Federal right flank as a surprise and a success: "Shall we ever forget the work of Jackson in the battles before Richmond?" trumpeted a popular journal. Quarrels and rumored duels, such as that between A. P. Hill and Longstreet, occupied the public mind. Some officers recognized the extent of their triumph and concluded that those who expected more were naive. Northerners, including veterans of the campaign, accepted the Jackson of legend and told fairy tales about Stonewall striding briskly among the prisoners threatening to cut off their ears with his sword.[59]

Lee, unfairly, was the subject of more animadversions than Jackson, such as the pronouncement of one staff major that the campaign "must forever stamp [Lee] a mediocrity." The Georgian who wrote a few weeks later, before any other campaigns had supplied new evidence, reflected much opinion: "Lee . . . will do very well; but the idol of the army, as well as of the people, is the gallant Stonewall." Such a judgment of the results of the Seven Days was neither rational nor just, but it certainly was prevalent.[60]

Even though by May 1863 Jackson, "as if to make up for [the Richmond campaign] had ever since been almost two Jacksons," a great opportunity had been lost forever. The first book on the campaign, written at the time and published within a few weeks, graphically counted the cost of the mistakes: "The dark forests . . . echo with the wails of the wounded and dying men. There is a bloody corpse in every copse, and mangled soldiers in every thicket of that ensanguined field."[61] Those thousands of southern casualties had bought three more years of life for their country — but they had not won the overwhelming, pivotal, early war triumph that might have turned the war's tide militarily, in men's minds North and South and in men's minds across the Atlantic.

An aide to a Georgia brigadier witnessed a piece of history in the swamps around Richmond that had nothing to do with musketry but everything to do with the grasping of opportunities. When Charles H. Smith arrived at General Lee's headquarters in quest of orders, he found the general operating out of two large tents with camp tables set up inside. Smith noticed a man lying comatose on the ground, his head and body under a table, "his

ROBERT K. KRICK

feet out upon the straw. His slouched hat was over his head and eyes, his sword was unbuckled, and his boots were on and spurred. His . . . clothes seemed faded and worn. . . . When the adjutant handed me the instructions, I ventured to point to the sleeping man and to ask, 'Who is he?' 'That is Stonewall,' he said; 'he has had no sleep for forty-eight hours and fell down there exhausted.'" [62]

NOTES

1. Edward Porter Alexander, *Fighting for the Confederacy: The Personal Recollections of General Edward Porter Alexander,* ed. Gary W. Gallagher (Chapel Hill: University of North Carolina Press, 1989), 96, 196.

2. Alexander S. Pendleton to mother, June 7, 1862, in William G. Bean, ed., "The Valley Campaign of 1862 as Revealed in Letters of Sandie Pendleton," *Virginia Magazine of History and Biography* 78 (July 1970): 364.

3. J. William Jones, "'Stonewall' Jackson," *Confederate Veteran* 12 (April 1904): 174.

4. Hunter H. McGuire, "The Seven Days Fighting about Richmond," undated typescript, Museum of the Confederacy, Richmond, Virginia (cited hereafter as McGuire, "Seven Days Fighting," MC); Edward Porter Alexander, *Military Memoirs of a Confederate: A Critical Narrative* (New York: Scribner's, 1907), 115; diary of James P. Hawkins, Southern Express Company, June 21, 1862, typescript by Joanna L. Smith, Lexington, Virginia, 1996.

5. Jones, "'Stonewall' Jackson," 174; R. L. Dabney to Jedediah Hotchkiss, March 31, April 14, 1896, Hotchkiss Papers, Library of Congress (repository cited hereafter as LC, and Hotchkiss cited hereafter without given name). The Dabney letter dated March 31 includes a detailed and amusing apologia for that officer's bungling of his responsibilities for the marches throughout the approach to Richmond.

6. D. H. Hill to "My Dear Wife," June 24, 1862, Schoff Collection, University of Michigan, Ann Arbor. Hill's remarks about the capacity of government dignitaries serves nicely to remind us that history is a continuum.

7. James H. Wood, *The War: "Stonewall" Jackson, His Campaigns and Battles . . . as I Saw Them* (Cumberland, Md.: Eddy Press, 1910), 68–69; A. R. Boteler, "Stonewall Jackson in the Campaign of 1862," Shepherdstown *Register,* February 18, 1882; [Alexander M. Garber], *"Stonewall Jackson's Way": A Sketch of the Life and Services of Maj. John A. Harman* (Staunton, Va.: "Spectator" Job Print, 1876), 23–24. The Boteler source, which has not been cited by historians heretofore, contains much minute and valuable detail about the approach to Richmond.

8. John Henry Cammack, *Personal Recollections* (Huntington, W.Va.: Paragon Ptg. & Pub. Co., 1920), 50–51; G. W. Nichols, *A Soldier's Story of His Regiment (61st Georgia), and Incidentally of the Lawton-Gordon-Evans Brigade* [Jesup, Ga.: n.p., 1898], 40–41.

9. William A. Fletcher, *Rebel Private Front and Rear* (Beaumont, Tex.: Press of the Greer Print, 1908), 23; James Cooper Nisbet, *Four Years on the Firing Line* (Chattanooga, Tenn.: Imperial Press, n.d.), 108–9; Sarah C. Rives to Alfred Landon Rives, June 23, 1862, Alderman Library, University of Virginia, Charlottesville (typescript supplied by my friend Barclay Rives of Keswick; repository hereafter cited as UVA).

10. Dabney to Hotchkiss, March 31, April 14, 1896, Hotchkiss Papers, LC; Thomas Nelson Page, *Robert E. Lee, the Southerner* (New York: Scribner's, 1909), 105; John Riley Phillips (31st Virginia), *A Soldier from Valley Furnace* (Wheeling, W.Va.[?]: n.p., 1997[?]), 38–39; M. A. Bentley (38th Georgia) to "Pap Mar Sisters and Brothers," July 12, 1862, copy in author's possession; McGuire, "Seven Days Fighting," MC.

11. The sternly pious Rev. Dr. Robert L. Dabney, who provided much evidence of Jackson's exhaustion in his contemporary writings, felt obliged in 1896 to denounce as "miserable skeptics" anyone thinking that Jackson "had exhausted his energies by his night ride . . . in order to avoid Sunday travel" (Dabney to Hotchkiss, March 24, 1896, Hotchkiss Papers, LC). Another strong allusion to Jackson's avoidance of Sunday marching is in [Ivy W. Duggan], "Army Correspondence," Sandersville *Central Georgian,* July 30, 1862. The quote about train schedules is from Boteler, "Stonewall Jackson in the Campaign of 1862."

12. Robert L. Dabney, *The Believer Born of Almighty Grace: A Sermon . . . Preached at Frederick's Hall, Va., in Hood's (4th) Texas Brigade, June 22d, 1862* (Richmond, Va.: Presbyterian Committee of Publication, ca. 1871); George T. Todd, *Sketch of History, the First Texas Regiment* (Jefferson, Tex.: Jefferson Jimplecute, 1909), unnumbered leaves. In introducing the printed version of his sermon, Dabney simply described the halt as being "for the Sabbath."

13. Dabney to Hotchkiss, March 31, 1896, Hotchkiss Papers, LC; T. W. Sydnor to Hotchkiss, undated [about January 1898], Hotchkiss Papers, LC.

14. Mary Anna Jackson, *Memoirs of Stonewall Jackson* (Louisville, Ky.: Prentice Press, 1895), 291–92. The emphasis is in the original. For a striking description of Jackson's appearance at this time, see William W. Blackford, *War Years with Jeb Stuart* (New York: Scribner's, 1945), 71.

15. George Daniel Buswell diary (33rd Virginia), June 24–26, 1862, copy in the author's possession; Nicholas A. Davis, *The Campaign from Texas to Maryland with the Battle of Fredericksburg* (Richmond, Va.: Office of the Presbyterian Committee of Publication of the Confederate States, 1863), 42; John G. Herndon (Charlottesville Artillery), "Reminiscences of the Sixties," copy in author's possession.

16. Phillips, *Soldier from Valley Furnace,* 39. The nearest solidly reliable temperature reading is from nearly one hundred miles farther north, where at 2:00 P.M. the mercury read 84 degrees. Given that the high temperature probably arrived a bit later in the afternoon, and crediting one hundred more miles of southerly latitude, the high must have approached 90. Temperature data are from the manuscript "Weather Jour-

nal Recording Observations at Lewinsville, Virginia, and Georgetown, D.C., June 1858–May 1866," microfilmed as CL-1064 at the National Weather Records Center, Asheville, N.C. (repository hereafter cited as NWRC).

17. Dabney to Hotchkiss, March 31, 1896, Hotchkiss Papers, LC.

18. McGuire, "Seven Days Fighting," MC; Hunter H. McGuire to Hotchkiss, March 30, April 14, 1896, Hotchkiss Papers, LC.

19. Page, *Robert E. Lee*, 105–6; Hotchkiss to G. F. R. Henderson, May 1, 1896, Hotchkiss Papers, LC; R. L. T. Beale, *History of the Ninth Virginia Cavalry* (Richmond, Va.: B. F. Johnson, 1899), 23; George W. Booth, *Personal Reminiscences of a Maryland Soldier* (Baltimore: Press of Fleet, McGinley, 1898), 44.

20. Fletcher, *Rebel Private*, 24–26; John W. Stevens, *Reminiscences of the Civil War* (Hillsboro, Tex.: Hillsboro Mirror Print, 1902), 24–25; McGuire to Hotchkiss, March 30, 1896, Hotchkiss Papers, LC. Four other articles, not quoted directly in the text, throw useful light on the Texans' brisk advance: J. T. Hunter, "At Yorktown in 1862 and What Followed," *Confederate Veteran* 26 (March 1918): 112; John Coxe, "Seven Days' Battles around Richmond," *Confederate Veteran* 30 (March 1922): 92; J. B. Polley, "Hood's Brigade and the 'Bucktails,'" *Confederate Veteran* 24 (February 1916): 73; and William B. Hamby, "Fourth Texas in Battle of Gaines's Mill," *Confederate Veteran* 14 (April 1906): 183.

21. Dabney to Hotchkiss, March 31, 1896, Hotchkiss Papers, LC; McGuire to Hotchkiss, April 14, 1896, Hotchkiss Papers, LC; Decimus et Ultimus Barziza, "Graphic Description of the Battle of Gaines' Mill," Richmond *Daily Whig*, August 4, 1862 (republished in the Houston *Tri-Weekly Telegraph*, April 3, 1865); George W. Beale, *A Lieutenant of Cavalry in Lee's Army* (Boston: Gorham Press, 1918), 33–34; Davis, *Campaign from Texas to Maryland*, 43–44; Fletcher, *Rebel Private*, 26; Ada C. Lightsey, *The Veteran's Story* (Meridian, Miss.: Meridian News, Printers and Binders, 1899), 17–18. In his letter, McGuire reported that Capt. Claiborne Mason's pioneer detachment, proficient and veteran bridge builders, was with Jackson most of the Seven Days, but McGuire was not positive that Mason and his men were present at Totopotomoy Creek.

22. Alexander, *Fighting for the Confederacy*, 100.

23. J. Churchill Cooke, "With Jackson around Richmond," *Confederate Veteran* 39 (1931): 248; McGuire to Hotchkiss, March 30, 1896, Hotchkiss Papers, LC. The Rev. Dabney's brother, the commonwealth's attorney for Hanover County, served as a guide. One of the 4th Virginia Cavalry men who did guide duty on his home ground was Robert Coalter Tomlin (Richmond *Daily Whig*, June 11, 1863). There is good primary evidence about local guides in Page, *Robert E. Lee*, 104–7, 304. In a letter dated July 4, 1862 (copy in the author's possession), J. H. Timberlake wrote, "The Hanover Cavalry [Company G, 4th Virginia Cavalry] with the exception of some three or four has been an escort for Genl Jackson."

24. Dabney to Hotchkiss, March 31, 1896, Hotchkiss Papers, LC; Charles Scott Venable diary (typed excerpts), June 26, 1862, University of South Carolina, Columbia (repository hereafter cited as USC); Henry L. P. King diary, June 26, 1862, Southern Historical Collection, University of North Carolina, Chapel Hill (repository cited hereafter as SHC). In a separate memoir, "Personal Reminiscences of the Confederate War" (UVA), Venable wrote more mildly of "Jackson not coming up in time."

25. Hanover County Historical Society, *Old Homes of Hanover County, Virginia* (Hanover, Va.: Hanover County Historical Society, 1983), 28.

26. Capt. Nicholas B. Gibbon memoir (28th North Carolina), *Mecklenburg Genealogical Society Quarterly* 3, no. 3 (n.d.): 132; Dabney to Hotchkiss, March 3, 1896, Hotchkiss Papers, LC.

27. Jackson's silly assertion about the heavenly conversion of the delay into an asset, as expressed by his wife undoubtedly on the strength of his own comments, is in Jackson, *Memoirs,* 293–94. See Page, *Robert E. Lee,* 304–5, for another version; but note that the Lincoln Sydnor cited there had enlisted a few days before and may be confusing what he heard from T. W. Sydnor about other scouting during this week (see T. W. Sydnor 1898 letter cited in note 13 above). By 1896, even Dabney was blaming "the mistake of our guides" (Dabney to Hotchkiss, March 3, 1896, Hotchkiss Papers, LC), although his own contemporary account told the story accurately. An interesting tale from one of the Hanover cavalrymen, about Jackson sending him in vain after civilian guides for this march, is in an untitled article by H. S. Anderson in the Ashland *Herald-Progress,* February 18, 1924.

28. Dabney to Hotchkiss, March 3, 1896, Hotchkiss Papers, LC. A lengthy narrative of this episode and the rest of the campaign through Dabney's eyes is his article "What I Saw of the Battle of the Chickahominy," *Southern Magazine* 10 (January 1872): 1–15. It does Dabney no credit to note that this decidedly self-serving piece was published anonymously.

29. Venable, "Personal Reminiscences," 43, UVA; J. K. Boswell to "Dr. Hotch" [Dear Hotchkiss], July 11, 1862, Hotchkiss Papers, LC; William Allan memoir, SHC; Jackson, *Memoirs,* 294; Booth, *Personal Reminiscences,* 45; J. William Jones, "The Old Virginia Town, Lexington," *Confederate Veteran* 1 (January 1893): 19; Jay B. Hubbell, ed., "The War Diary of John Esten Cooke," *Journal of Southern History* 7 (November 1941): 533. Jedediah Hotchkiss defended Jackson's quiescence on the left at Gaines's Mill in a letter to R. L. Dabney, March 4, 1896, Hotchkiss Papers, LC. Dabney's certainty that he knew the inside story prompted him to declare, in typically immodest (and typically foolish) fashion, "Since the death of Gen. R. E. Lee I am the only man living who knows how the battle of Gaines Mill was fought and won" (Dabney to Hotchkiss, March 3, 1896, Hotchkiss Papers, LC). For some unaccountable reason, it has become popular to debunk Jackson's fondness for lemons. In this instance, multiple witnesses recorded the general's indulgence.

30. William Allan memoir, SHC; Hubbell, ed., "John Esten Cooke," 532; Dabney to Hotchkiss, March 3, 1896, Hotchkiss Papers, LC.

31. Thomas C. Johnson, *The Life and Letters of Robert Lewis Dabney* (Richmond, Va.: Presbyterian Committee of Publication, 1903), 261–64; Jedediah Hotchkiss, *Make Me a Map of the Valley: The Civil War Journal of Stonewall Jackson's Topographer,* ed. Archie P. McDonald (Dallas, Tex.: Southern Methodist University Press, 1973), 124; manuscript marginalia in H. Kyd Douglas's copy of Mrs. Jackson's 1892 memoir of her husband, 254, 305, at Antietam National Battlefield, Sharpsburg, Md.; W. G. McDowell, "Lt. Col. A. S. Pendleton," *Rockbridge County News,* January 21, 1909.

32. Robert A. Stiles, *Four Years under Marse Robert* (New York: Neale, 1903), 98; Joseph L. Brent, *Memoirs of the War between the States* (New Orleans: Fontana Printing Company, 1940), 189–90; unidentified 1862 South Carolina newspaper clipping, copy in possession of the author.

33. Alexander, *Fighting for the Confederacy,* 104–5; William W. Chamberlaine, *Memoirs of the Civil War* (Washington, D.C.: Press of Byron S. Adams, 1912), 23–24; U.S. War Department, *The War of the Rebellion: A Compilation of the Official Records of the Union and Confederate Armies,* 127 vols., index, and atlas (Washington, D.C.: GPO, 1880–1902), ser. 1, 11(2):556 (hereafter cited as *OR* with page numbers, all citations to this series, volume, and part).

34. Alexander, *Fighting for the Confederacy,* 105, 113; Alexander, *Military Memoirs,* 144–45. Jackson's communiqué to J. E. B. Stuart dated 2:50 P.M. on the twenty-ninth (box 2, J. E. B. Stuart Papers, Henry E. Huntington Library, San Marino, Calif. [repository hereafter cited as HEHL]) briskly outlines operations on that Sunday evening, although it admittedly does not crackle. Fifteen minutes after he indited that document, Jackson endorsed upon an order (original in the same Stuart Papers) to Stuart from Lee's chief of staff, concerning watching the Yankees downstream, that he would "remain . . . near my present position."

35. Alexander, *Military Memoirs,* 146; James W. Beeler diary (Carpenter's Battery — 3:00 A.M.), Winchester–Frederick County Historical Society Collection, Handley Library, Winchester, Va.; *OR,* 556–57; [Edward A. Pollard], *The Seven Days' Battles in Front of Richmond* (Charleston, S.C.: Steam-Power Presses of Evans & Cogswell, 1862), 16–17. The Richmond sunset is from *Richardson's Almanac* (Richmond, Va.: J. W. Randolph, [1861]), unpaginated leaves. Sundown remained unchanged for the rest of the campaign at that point so close to the solstice. That probably casts less new light on the situation than at first it seems to do. For Jackson's arrival with Magruder's troops south of the Chickahominy on the evening of the twenty-ninth, see Ivy W. Duggan letter of July 8, 1862, Sandersville *Central Georgian,* and Thomas Lewis Ware letter of June 29, 1862, SHC. Both Duggan and Ware belonged to the 15th Georgia of Toombs's brigade. Ware, like many another Confederate, was disappointed to find Jackson "quite an ordinary looking man." The John Hinsdale journal (Hinsdale Family

Papers, William R. Perkins Library, Duke University, Durham, N.C.) uses almost identical words in describing the general on this same day.

36. Elbert M. Williamson, *Confederate Reminiscences* (Danville, Va.: Privately printed, 1935), 2–3; Willis Jefferson Dance, *Elbert Madison Williamson* (Danville, Va.: Privately printed, 1969), 10–11; Wood, *The War,* 76–77; Cooke, "With Jackson around Richmond," 248. Now that Jackson had moved into Henrico County, his Hanoverians were no longer in their immediate home neighborhoods, and there is no available evidence about Henrico boys joining as guides; even so, the cavalry detachment was still on relatively familiar ground.

37. McHenry Howard, *Recollections of a Maryland Confederate Soldier and Staff Officer* (Baltimore: Williams & Wilkins, 1914), 148.

38. The three Hampton accounts are in Alexander, *Military Memoirs,* 149–51; Alexander, *Fighting for the Confederacy,* 108–9; and Charles Marshall, *An Aide-de-Camp of Lee,* ed. Frederick Maurice (Boston: Little, Brown, 1927), 108–12. The Munford accounts are cited in notes 43, 44 below. Evidence from the Hampton accounts is used throughout the following paragraphs without further reference to the sources, except that notes identify the origins of direct quotations. Staff officer Rawlins Lowndes validated Hampton's narrative in a terse (thirty-one words) note to E. P. Alexander dated April 1, 1901 (Alexander Papers, SHC) that is made far more important by an accompanying good sketch of the ground.

39. Hampton in Alexander, *Military Memoirs,* 150. A letter from M. A. Miller to Hotchkiss, May 26, 1896, asserts that Claiborne Mason and his detachment of black pioneers were at hand for bridge building earlier than June 30. The William Allan memoir, SHC, agrees with Miller. If that was the case, Jackson's failure to use that skillful crew on the thirtieth made his lassitude even more arrant. In his letter of April 14, 1896 (Hotchkiss Papers, LC), McGuire told Hotchkiss that he ate supper with Mason "somewhere between Gaines' Mill and White Oak Swamp," but that he could not recall "how long [Mason] was with us."

40. Hampton in Alexander, *Fighting for the Confederacy,* 108.

41. *OR,* 557; T. Frank Forrest, *An Old Soldier's Career* (Stewart, Miss.: n.p., 1906?), third and fourth unnumbered leaves. A fanciful tale about Jackson behaving forcefully at this time with some Yankee prisoners, and fearing earthworks, is in Alfred L. Castleman, *The Army of the Potomac, behind the Scenes, a Diary of Unwritten History* (Milwaukee, Wisc.: Strickland, 1863), 192–93.

42. Charles Scott Venable diary, June 30, 1862, USC; Hampton in Alexander, *Military Memoirs,* 151; *OR,* 495.

43. Thomas T. Munford to Wade Hampton, March 23, 1901, in Alexander, *Military Memoirs,* 148–49; Thomas T. Munford to E. P. Alexander, August 8, 1907, Alexander Papers, SHC; Cooke, "With Jackson around Richmond," 248.

44. Munford to Hampton in Alexander, *Military Memoirs,* 149; Munford to Alexander, August 8, 1907, SHC.

45. Alexander, *Military Memoirs,* 151.

46. Jackson's sole autobiographical apologia serves as a text for the notion that he was behaving woodenly rather than woozily. On overhearing some wondering staffer, the general curtly snapped, "If General Lee had wanted me he could have sent for me." No similar Jacksonian justification, or even explanation, of anything that happened during the war is of record. Hunter H. McGuire in G. F. R. Henderson, *Stonewall Jackson and the American Civil War,* 2 vols. (London: Longmans, Green, 1898), 2:57. A modern exposition of the theory of Jackson as rigidly dutiful is in James I. Robertson Jr., *Stonewall Jackson: The Man, the Soldier, the Legend* (New York: Macmillan, 1997), 495–98.

47. An excellent summary of the theorems forwarded to explain Jackson's difficulties during the campaign is in Douglas Southall Freeman, *R. E. Lee: A Biography,* 4 vols. (New York: Scribner's, 1934–35), 2:572–82.

48. Ibid., 579–80, 200. For an emphatic rejection of the exhaustion thesis, see Alexander, *Fighting for the Confederacy,* 98. James Power Smith, in "Stonewall Jackson: His Character" (*Confederate Veteran* 19 [October 1911]: 497), offered a typically pietistic benediction.

49. Jackson, *Memoirs,* 345, 151–52, 168, 109; Susan Leigh Blackford, ed., *Memoirs of Life in and out of the Army in Virginia,* 2 vols. (Lynchburg, Va.: J. P. Bell, 1894), 1:165–66, 184; Hotchkiss, *Make Me a Map of the Valley,* 17.

50. Dr. Jonathan Shay, "Ethical Standing for Commander Self-Care: The Need for Sleep," *Parameters* 28 (Summer 1998): 93–105. I have my friend H. W. "Heinie" Henzel to thank for bringing this apposite and current research to my attention.

51. Manuscript "Weather Journal Recording Observations at Lewinsville, Virginia, and Georgetown, D.C., June 1858–May 1866," NWRC; Jackson, *Memoirs,* 297; Munford to Alexander, August 8, 1907, Alexander Papers, SHC; Wood, *The War,* 76. William Allan (memoir, SHC) called the night "very hot" and wrote of "the effluvia" being "almost unbearable." The usually reliable Dr. H. H. McGuire insisted in his letter to Hotchkiss dated April 14, 1896 (Hotchkiss Papers, LC), that Jackson had crawled into an ambulance with McGuire and not gotten wet. The general's own contemporary account to his wife of course takes easy precedence. For a fine investigation of 1860s attitudes toward swamp "miasmas," see Richard M. McMurry, "Marse Robert and the Fevers: . . . Medical Ideas as a Factor in Civil War Decision Making," *Civil War History* 35 (September 1989): 197–207.

52. Jackson, *Memoirs,* 302. The comparison to Mexican illness and talk of the "malarial region" is from a letter to Rev. James Ewing cited in Clifford Dowdey, *The Seven Days: The Emergence of Lee* (Boston: Little, Brown, 1964), 198. Dowdey provided

neither notes nor sources, but he was well connected with many first-generation descendants of veterans and saw much good material in that fashion. I have been unable to locate the letter to Ewing. Dowdey also offers a concise summary of the stress-fatigue thesis (pp. 196–200, 368).

53. Robert L. Dabney, *Life and Campaigns of Lieut.-Gen. Thomas J. Jackson* (New York: Blelock, 1866), 467; Jackson, *Memoirs,* 298; R. L. Dabney to Hotchkiss, April 22, 1896, cited in Freeman, *Lee,* 2:581; John Gill, *Reminiscences of Four Years as a Private Soldier in the Confederate Army* (Baltimore: Sun Printing Office, 1904), 67.

54. William McWillie notebooks, Mississippi Department of Archives and History, Jackson.

55. William Allan, *The Army of Northern Virginia in 1862* (Boston: Houghton Mifflin, 1892), 121; Dabney, *Life and Campaigns,* 466–67. For an enlisted man's view that echoes this thesis, see Booth, *Personal Reminiscences,* 49–50.

56. James Longstreet to E. P. Alexander, August 26, 1902, Alexander Papers, SHC; Blackford, *War Years with Jeb Stuart,* 79; Brent, *Memoirs,* 199; separate recollections of Capt. William L. Balthis and Carter Berkeley, both of the Staunton (Va.) Artillery, Hotchkiss Papers, LC; John G. Herndon, "Infantry and Cavalry Service," *Confederate Veteran* 30 (May 1922): 172; Leroy Wesley Cox memoir, copy in the author's possession; dispatches from Jackson to Stuart at 9:40 and 11:20 A.M., July 1, 1862, box 2, J. E. B. Stuart Papers, HEHL.

57. Walter Clark, comp., *Histories of the Several Regiments and Battalions from North Carolina in the Great War, 1861–'65,* 5 vols. (Goldsboro: Nash Brothers, Printers, 1901), 2:560; R. L. Dabney quoted in Mrs. Mary A. Jackson, "Stonewall Jackson the Campaigner," *Hearst's Magazine* 24 (November 1913): 770; Hunter H. McGuire to Hotchkiss, May 28, 1896, Hotchkiss Papers, LC; R. E. Lee to Mrs. T. J. Jackson, January 25, 1866, Hotchkiss Papers, LC. The invaluable G. Campbell Brown memoir (Brown-Ewell Papers, Tennessee State Library and Archives, Nashville) describes riding most of the night with Gens. R. S. Ewell and D. H. Hill, then finding Jackson "about 6 a.m. . . . two miles back at his wagons, eating breakfast." Evidently McGuire's difficulty playing at alarm clock was in the very early hours. Brown also is an early and solid authority for the story that Jackson "quietly . . . assured [Ewell] there was no danger" of any offensive movement by McClellan. Another description of Jackson just after the campaign said that "he makes one think of an old fox hunter" (James Branscomb letter to "My Dear Sister," July 15, 1862, Alabama Department of Archives and History, Montgomery). Captain Blackford also reported (*War Years with Jeb Stuart,* 80–82) an interesting story about Jackson's rationale for treatment of the dead the next morning.

58. John Esten Cooke diary in Hubbell, ed., "War Diary," 537; Alexander, *Fighting for the Confederacy,* 96; Venable, "Personal Reminiscences," 45, UVA; Jeremy F. Gilmer to "My dear Loulie," August 17, 1862, Gilmer Papers, SHC.

59. [Pollard], *Seven Days' Battles,* 6–7; *Southern Literary Messenger,* July–August 1862, 504; "A Prussian Officer," *The Defence of Richmond against the Federal Army* (New York: George F. Nesbitt, 1863), 10–11; William H. Powell, *The Fifth Army Corps* (New York: G. P. Putnam's, 1896), 105.

60. Samuel W. Melton to his wife, July 6, 1862, USC; "From Jackson's Army," Columbus (Ga.) *Weekly Sun,* September 2, 1862.

61. Alexander, *Fighting for the Confederacy,* 196; [Pollard], *Seven Days' Battles,* 45.

62. Charles H. Smith, *Bill Arp from the Uncivil War to Date* (Atlanta: Hudgins, 1903), 42–43.

PETER S. CARMICHAEL

The Great Paragon of Virtue and Sobriety

John Bankhead Magruder and the Seven Days

nder a cold, steady rain on July 2, 1862, Confederate burial parties feverishly worked at Malvern Hill, disposing of the human wreckage left from Robert E. Lee's final attack against George B. McClellan's Army of the Potomac. A day earlier the Federals had repulsed repeated Confederate charges before retreating to Harrison's Landing, an unassailable position along the James River. With McClellan's withdrawal, the Seven Days campaign ended and so did Maj. Gen. John Bankhead Magruder's brief career with Lee's Army of Northern Virginia. Inside the battlefield's most recognizable landmark, the Crew house, Magruder sat behind a table engrossed in paperwork. He looked terrible, dangerously pale, the veins in his face swollen and purple.[1]

The demands of campaigning had wrecked the general's nerves, exhausted his stamina, and brought him dangerously close to a physical and emotional breakdown. As staff officers and couriers scurried in and out of the house, Magruder wrote a short note to Secretary of War George W. Randolph. He bluntly asked for an immediate transfer to the Trans-Mississippi Department, a command he had received the previous May. Richmond authorities had postponed his orders, upon his request, so that he could defend his native state. While McClellan regrouped, Magruder wanted permission to leave for the Western Theater, though Richmond was still in danger. The Army of the Potomac, coiled up along the James River, could strike the Confederacy's capital at any moment. Some of Magruder's subordinates warned that the army was not prepared to resist a Union advance.[2] No one could predict that the fighting would subside for an extended period. Yet Magruder lost no time in asking for his release. Without an objection, Lee accepted the request and instantly relieved him of all duties with the Army of Northern Virginia.[3]

Relations between Magruder and Lee ended in controversy. Countless officers alleged that Magruder had been intoxicated and behaved like a coward at Malvern Hill. These charges, often scurrilous in intent, tarnished what had been a solid performance during the Peninsula campaign. The ugly rumors followed Magruder to the Trans-Mississippi and nearly resulted in the loss of his new command. Although the general ranked among the most formidable drinkers in the antebellum Old Army, charges of his drunkenness and cowardice at Malvern Hill lacked hard evidence. They were largely based on Magruder's reputation as an incorrigible tippler, not on eyewitness accounts of his drinking in the field.[4] Lee probably realized that his subordinate was a victim of army gossip and a target of the press. He consequently never brought Magruder up on charges or demanded a court of inquiry.

The commanding general's aversion to making public the army's internal disputes largely explains why he wanted a clean break with Magruder. To expedite matters, Lee refused to defend Magruder publicly or prolong his stay in the Army of Northern Virginia. Recent scholarship suggests that Lee may have allowed Magruder to leave in part because the excesses in his personal life reminded the commanding general of his dissipated father, "Light Horse Harry."[5] If the pious Lee had held all subordinates to his own moral yardstick, it would have resulted in a purge in the Army of Northern Virginia of staggering proportions. What officers did in their private lives mattered little to Lee, who evaluated lieutenants by what they did on the battlefield, not off it.

In Magruder's case, Lee counted two critical failures during the Seven Days campaign. The more serious transgression occurred at Savage's Station on June 29, when Magruder disobeyed Lee's personal instructions to advance rapidly. Lee's orders were not discretionary, and Magruder understood this. His disobedience bitterly disappointed the commanding general, who considered June 29 his best opportunity to crush McClellan's rear guard. Although Lee's plans at Savage's Station unraveled for complex reasons that did not involve Magruder, the latter should not, as in some recent scholarship, be cleared of his own critical mistakes or viewed as Lee's scapegoat.[6] Magruder's stock fell even further with his reckless management of the Confederate right wing at Malvern Hill. His inability to organize a proper assault and loss of composure in front of the troops, and Lee's perception that he did not obey orders, convinced the commanding general that Magruder was unreliable. Apart from what Lee might have believed about Magruder's drinking and other personal weaknesses, "Prince John" showed at Savage's Station and Malvern Hill that he could not be entrusted with the weighty responsibilities of high command.

The twisted fault lines of Magruder's personality did not suddenly appear

Maj. Gen. John Bankhead Magruder

Robert Underwood Johnson and Clarence Clough Buel, eds., Battles and Leaders of the Civil War, *4 vols. (New York: Century, 1887–88), 2:209*

in war but emerged early in life. Born in 1807 in Port Royal, Virginia, he early on incurred the disdain of young females in the area. A Fredericksburg woman wrote that as a boy Magruder "was the butt of all the girls, he was stupid and conceited."[7] Young Magruder valiantly tried to remain a perpetual adolescent. After entering the first class at the University of Virginia, he eagerly joined the raucous activities of his classmates. University officials expelled many for their riotous behavior, but Magruder remained for a year until he secured an appointment to West Point in 1828. He seemed immune to the academy's rigorous environment, violating rules with impunity and routinely sneaking away from his barracks to visit Benny Havens's tavern, where he cultivated his taste for liquor. He spent so much time at the tavern that he almost reached the two hundred demerits stipulated for expulsion.

PETER S. CARMICHAEL

His participation in the famous "Eggnog Riots" of 1826 nearly resulted in his ejection. While many cadets chased officers from their quarters with clubs and other weapons, Magruder and Jefferson Davis peacefully sipped grog in the privacy of their rooms. Magruder also wasted time playing the flute with cadet William Nelson Pendleton, the future artillery chief of the Army of Northern Virginia. Despite his unruly behavior, Magruder ended his career at West Point a captain of the Battalion of Cadets with a respectable standing of fifteenth in the class of 1830. After an initial assignment to the infantry, he transferred to the 1st Artillery, a branch of service to which he devoted himself throughout his antebellum career. In the war with Mexico, he served competently, receiving two brevets for bravery.[8]

A regal bearing, flamboyant mannerisms, and a penchant for extravagant parties made Magruder a highly visible if not a popular officer in the Old Army, earning him the nickname "Prince John." He cut a striking figure, standing some six feet tall, with dark hair and mustache. He dressed impeccably, though a slight lisp and a tendency to use profanity detracted from his refined appearance. He walked with an unmistakable stride, which some considered ridiculously pompous. His eccentricities, however, endeared him to most fellow officers, especially those who enjoyed his elaborate military reviews. While stationed in Texas with Zachary Taylor's army in 1845–46, he set up a theater and mounted many plays, including a rendition of *Othello*. Magruder also impressed guests with exquisite dinner parties. At a reception honoring some British officers, Magruder rented the finest available china, glassware, and furniture. Impressed by the lavish display, one guest remarked that "American officers must be paid enormously. What is your monthly pay?" "Damned if I know," answered Prince John with an air of indifference. He then turned to his servant and asked, "Jim, what is my monthly pay?" The servant remained discreetly silent.[9]

Magruder's expensive tastes far exceeded his meager army pay. Always tottering on the brink of financial ruin, he told his lawyer in 1840 that he was "very hard pressed" and sorry "to be obliged to give you so much trouble. I must therefore rest in seeing myself largely your debtor for the present."[10] Marriage saved him from financial ruin. He found a source of financial assistance in Esther Henrietta Von Kapff, the daughter of a wealthy Baltimore merchant. They were married in 1831 and eventually had two daughters and a son. The couple's relationship deteriorated rapidly after the nuptials, and they rarely spent time together. Magruder almost never spoke of his wife and children to army colleagues, many of whom believed him to be single. Mrs. Magruder kept residence in Baltimore while he traveled to his various military posts. When her daughter became ill in 1850, she moved to Europe, returning only twice to see her husband before his death in 1871. Although the relationship proved emotionally barren, the Von Kapff family fortune gave Magruder the fiscal support he needed. He frequently asked his wife to pay his debts and organize social gatherings when he returned to Baltimore on furlough. His personal excesses, alcoholic bouts, and carefree lifestyle probably drove her to Europe. One observer noted that Magruder "managed to alienate her devoted attachment, to make her separate from him & leave him to the irregular life which was anything but happy or respectable." [11]

His troubled marriage intensified Magruder's longings for a bachelorlike existence. He continued to drink and behave with the youthful ardor of his West Point days. After a binge in Baltimore, he found himself locked out of his hotel. He stumbled next door to a stage office, where he passed out on a pile of mail sacks. The next morning the stagecoach arrived to pick up the mail and one passenger. The driver thought Magruder was the passenger and, unable to wake him, hauled him aboard and headed to Washington. Arriving the next morning still in an alcoholic stupor, Magruder left the driver no choice but to drop him off on a bench. When he awakened, Prince John was completely disoriented. To get his bearing, he visited a nearby tavern for an early morning toddy. He then walked outside, progressing down Pennsylvania Avenue until he spotted the Capitol. His mind swirled in confusion. How could he be in Washington? He fortunately encountered a West Point classmate, Thomas Lee, and called out: "My God, Tom, how glad I am to see you! Will you, for God's sake, tell me where I am?" Magruder's drinking escapades understandably became legendary among his fellow officers in the Regular Army.[12]

Three days after Virginia left the Union on April 17, 1861, Magruder resigned from the United States Army. Confederate authorities briefly detained him in Richmond before sending him to the Peninsula on May 21 to assume command of 3,500 soldiers between the James and York Rivers. On June 10, 1861, some of his troops defeated the Yankees at Big Bethel, a minor victory but one Magruder ranked as equal to Winfield Scott's exploits in Mexico. His secondary role in the skirmish did not stop Magruder from portraying himself as the great captain on the field. The press reinforced his image as one of the Confederacy's most promising generals. In such a climate, promotion quickly followed. On August 7, he received a major general's commission.[13] The following April he justified the additional rank when he masterfully defended the lower Peninsula against McClellan. Magruder's impressive earthworks and dammed streams blocked the Union advance at Yorktown. Although badly outnumbered, Prince John put on his finest show by shifting his troops and placing "Quaker guns" along the line. His theatrics created the illusion that the Confederates planned to attack. "Genl. Magruder was well fitted for the task confided to him," observed his staff officer Joseph L. Brent. "He had the faculty of an engineer in discovering strong and weak localities intended to be defended, and allowed no detail to escape him in the way of preparation." Brent was especially impressed by Magruder's ability to devise "many methods of exhibiting an aggressive strength" that deceived McClellan.[14]

Magruder's creative tactics stalled the Army of the Potomac for an entire month, giving Joseph E. Johnston time to shift his army from northern Virginia to the Peninsula. When Johnston assumed overall command in mid-April, Magruder clashed with his new superior. Johnston described the work of Magruder's engineers as amateurish and insisted that the Yorktown line be abandoned. Jefferson Davis trusted Johnston's judgment and assumed that Magruder's efforts were inadequate. To make matters worse, Johnston dismissed Magruder's arguments to hold McClellan at Yorktown, electing to begin the withdrawal to Richmond in early May.[15]

Magruder controlled the right wing of Johnston's retreating army, some 17,500 men, but his nominal superior was Gustavus W. Smith. Magruder deeply resented being subordinate to Smith, whose commission as major general bore an earlier date. Intense exchanges between the two men followed, and petty bickering continued until Magruder refused on May 23 to obey Smith's orders. On that same day, Confederate authorities directed him to report to Richmond to receive his new assignment as commander of the Trans-Mississippi Department. Such an important post must have thrilled the ambitious Magruder, but he convinced Randolph to hold the transfer until the end of the campaign. Despite personal problems with his superiors, he wanted to help defend his native soil. Johnston wanted nothing more to do with Magruder and had reassigned his troops to Lafayette McLaws. Randolph prevented the transfer, however, insisting that Magruder return to his command.[16] Acrimony between the two officers might explain why Johnston relegated Magruder to a secondary role at the battle of Seven Pines on May 31.

Although Magruder squabbled with his superiors, he succeeded in gaining the devotion of his troops. It should come as no surprise that the hard-drinking Louisiana Tigers became one of Magruder's pet units. During Mardi Gras season in early 1862, some Tigers held a burlesque parade in the town of Williamsburg that ended at Magruder's headquarters. One Louisianan, a baby-faced private named Billy Campbell, decided to dress up as a woman. A comrade who introduced Campbell as a sister of another soldier escorted him into Magruder's office. Magruder, who had an eye for the ladies, quickly became enamored of his "female" guest. Taking her by the hand, he engaged her with drink, food, and entertaining conversation. Meanwhile, some Tigers sneaked into the room above Magruder, ripped a mattress apart, and pushed feathers through the cracks in the floor. Amid the laughter and cascading feathers, the Tigers shouted that it was a "Louisiana snowstorm." Campbell slipped away in the confusion, leaving the bewildered general to contemplate the female guest lost in the Louisiana snow.[17]

The added responsibilities of being a major general did not end Magruder's womanizing and drinking. In early 1862, he had an affair with the wife of his chief medical officer. Magruder and the woman flirted and danced in public, sometimes staying together until the early morning hours. Such scandalous behavior horrified observers. "During the night the great Paragon of virtue and Sobriety Gen[.] Magruder," wrote staff officer Richard Leach, "was so drunk that he fell from the arm of the whore he was dancing with and would have been burnt to death had he not been pulled from the fire by one his Orderlies." Leach pitied the woman's husband, who "came up to my room drunk a few night ago and took me by the arm and said several times that he had rather be dead and dammed and in Hell than married." Leach could not understand why a clergyman in the army named Osborne would endorse Magruder and take "him into the pulpit." "Strange world is it not," he asked.[18]

Magruder must have been relieved when Lee took command of the Army of Northern Virginia shortly after Johnston's wounding at Seven Pines. Nothing suggested that relations between Johnston and Magruder would improve. Moreover, when Prince John had advocated that the Confederates retain the Yorktown line, Lee had backed his proposal over Johnston's arguments for retreat. If Lee entertained reservations about Magruder and his questionable personal life, he kept them to himself. More critical issues occupied his time, and they revolved around a Union army poised to take Richmond. By the last week of June, Lee proposed a complicated scheme to save the city. With McClellan's army divided by the Chickahominy, he gave Magruder some 25,000 men, including troops from Benjamin Huger, to defend against the 65,000 Federals south of the river. The remaining one-third of the Union force, some 30,000 soldiers north of the Chickahominy, would be the object of Lee's planned offensive. Lee assembled 65,000 soldiers from the divisions of D. H. Hill, A. P. Hill, James Longstreet, and "Stonewall" Jackson's Army of the Valley, intending to envelop the isolated Union right flank commanded by Fitz John Porter while Magruder and Huger kept the bulk of the Army of the Potomac out of Richmond. Magruder's assignment, wrote staff officer Brent, was considered "the post of honor as well as of danger."[19]

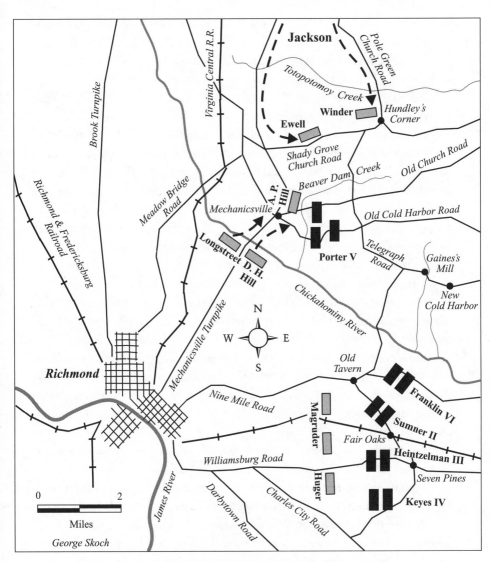

Battle of Mechanicsville, June 26, 1862

Minor skirmishing along Magruder's front faded in and out on June 25, the first of the Seven Days. The next day, Jackson's dawn attack against Porter never materialized. The silence troubled Magruder, who expected to hear gunfire north of the Chickahominy. He worried that his lightly manned defenses could not withstand a major attack and feared that Confederate inactivity might encourage the enemy to advance. To keep McClellan off balance, Magruder returned to the role that had earned him wide acclaim at Yorktown. He shifted troops back and forth, opened an intermittent artillery fire, and made an occasional attack with his skirmishers while making certain that McClellan's soldiers witnessed the dramatics. Prince John's charade succeeded beautifully. The Federals patiently waited for Lee to take the initiative. Not until 3:30 P.M. did he strike, and Porter defeated the piecemeal Confederate attacks at Beaver Dam Creek before retreating to a position near Gaines's Mill the following morning.[20]

Although Magruder's ruse had worked exceedingly well, he doubted that his theatrics would fool McClellan again. He told his subordinates that the fighting at Beaver Dam had revealed that the Army of Northern Virginia was concentrated above the Chickahominy. Such information must reveal to McClellan that Richmond lacked enough defenders, making Magruder's lines open to attack on June 27. After conferring with his staff, he concluded that "our position was so inherently weak" that McClellan could break "our line." Further study of the available maps revealed other potential problems. Most of the Union forces opposing him were closer to Richmond than the Confederate troops above the Chickahominy. No longer could D. H. Hill, Longstreet, and A. P. Hill provide immediate support in an emergency. Lee's offensive had dangerously isolated Magruder's and Huger's soldiers. The commanding general could reinforce Magruder only by sending troops back to Mechanicsville, a march of some ten miles that would take at least a half-day to complete. To add to his worries, Magruder had not received confirmation about Jackson's whereabouts. The pressure of protecting Richmond and semi-independent command triggered an anxiety attack. His subordinates noted that the general suddenly lost his relaxed manner and became peevish and irritable.[21]

Nervousness did not breed complacency. Magruder instructed his men to be vigilant and moved his headquarters to the front so he could closely monitor the enemy's movements. While Lee secured victory at Gaines's Mill on June 27, Magruder's troops resumed their deceptive tactics. One Union officer uncovered a typical Magruder ploy during a personal reconnaissance. Creeping just beyond Confederate lines he saw "a whole lot of niggers parading, beating drums, and making a great noise." McClellan disregarded such information because it challenged his cherished notion that he was under attack on both sides of the river. His official report asserted: "So threatening were the movements of the enemy on both banks of the Chickahominy that it was impossible to decide until the afternoon where the real attack would be made." Magruder's demonstrations and creative tactics prompted the excessively cautious Union commander to deem "it necessary to hold a considerable force in position to meet them."[22] Lee must have appreciated Magruder's important role south of the Chickahominy, but serious mistakes in the coming days would overshadow Prince John's impressive contributions.

Confederate victory at Gaines's Mill sent Porter's troops in full retreat across the Chickahominy, where they united with the rest of the Army of the Potomac. Lee's success placed McClellan's entire force against Magruder. Prince John's fears mounted as he mistakenly believed that all the bridges between the two Confederate wings had been destroyed. The prospect of confronting some 100,000 Federals nearly resulted in mental paralysis. He started to show signs of emotional fatigue, made worse by a bad attack of indigestion. His fears were somewhat relieved when Confederate engineers repaired the New Bridge, establishing communication with the Confederates north of the Chickahominy. Additional good news arrived when Lee determined late on June 28 that McClellan was retreating southward. The Union commander had decided to shift his supply base from the Pamunkey to the James River. With the Federal army in such a vulnerable position, Lee saw an opportunity to destroy it. Final success ultimately depended on a vigorous pursuit. Magruder heeded Lee's order to stay in close contact with the enemy. Not only did he direct his men to sleep on their arms, but he also rode along his lines during the evening of the twenty-eighth. His obsessiveness, however, further injured his health and thereby jeopardized the efficiency of his command. He should have rested, but, as he noted in his official report, "I passed the night without sleep." [23]

During the early morning hours of June 29, a weary Magruder conferred with Lee. As they rode down the Nine-Mile Road, the commanding general outlined the army's pursuit in explicit terms. Magruder would sweep down the Williamsburg Road, attacking the enemy when he made contact. To his left, Jackson would march south, repair and cross the Grapevine Bridge, and pressure the Federal rear. To Magruder's right, Huger would advance along the Charles City Road and hit the flank of the retreating Federal column. When the two officers reached Fair Oaks Station, Lee repeated Magruder's mission to make certain that his subordinate understood. More than anything else, the commanding general wanted aggressiveness from his lieutenant, a point that was not lost on Magruder. In his official report, he stated that Lee's orders required that he press the enemy "vigorously in front." His advance did not hinge on Jackson's or Huger's support, nor were his orders discretionary. [24]

As soon as Lee rode off to Huger's command, Magruder lost his sense of urgency and forgot the commanding general's insistence on a rapid advance. Light resistance from the Union rear guard brought Magruder's col-

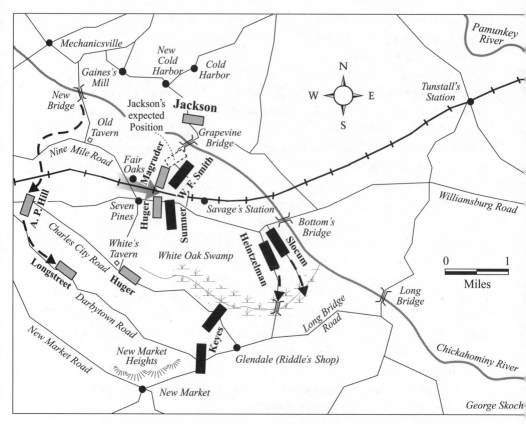

Battle of Savage's Station, June 29, 1862

umn to an immediate halt. Instead of attacking, as Lee instructed, Magruder
wasted precious time in scouting the enemy's position near Savage's Station
on the Richmond & York River Railroad. He determined that he faced a
numerically superior force and that the Federals had aggressive intentions.
He decided that he needed reinforcements, and Major Brent rode to Lee's
headquarters for help. When Brent explained Magruder's delay, Lee was in-
credulous. Every scouting report suggested that the enemy was in rapid retreat and that the rear guard would not attack. He asked Brent, "Major, have
you yourself seen and formed an opinion upon the number of the enemy?"
Brent replied that he had not made a personal reconnaissance. "But what
do you think?" Lee interjected. "Is the enemy in large force?" The question
caught Brent off guard. After some deliberation, he answered with care:
"Genl. Magruder has instructed me to say that he finds the enemy in strong
force in his front." Brent's response amused Lee, who seemed to appreciate
the staff officer's loyalty to Magruder because, as Brent put it, he refused "to
express an opinion contrary to the message that I bore." Just as the confer-

PETER S. CARMICHAEL

ence ended, Lee told Brent that Huger would reinforce Magruder with two brigades. "But if they are not actually engaged by 2 o'clock," he cautioned, "he must order them to resume their march and rejoin Genl. Huger." [25]

Meanwhile, Magruder searched for support on his left. Dispatching a staff officer to the Grapevine Bridge, he learned that Jackson's progress had been delayed and that he would not cross for another two hours. This report discouraged Magruder, who decided to call off his advance until Jackson and Huger could cooperate. With these commands in place, some 46,000 men, Magruder planned to envelop the enemy's rear guard. Lost in Magruder's new scheme was Lee's dictate to attack the enemy without hesitation, the crucial component in Lee's overall plan. When Huger arrived with his two brigades, Magruder told him that "the enemy were advancing in great force." To Huger's disbelief, Magruder assigned his reinforcements to a defensive position instead of pushing forward. The 2:00 P.M. deadline passed and Huger's troops remained idle, standing under a hot sun. Huger scanned the enemy's works and noticed that they had been abandoned. "I could not conceive their attack was a serious one," he later wrote, "but the demonstration was only to delay us." Huger informed Magruder "that under my order I had decided it was not necessary for me to stay," and his two brigades returned to the Charles City Road. [26]

Shortly after Magruder received Huger's message, more bad news arrived. A note from Jackson stated that he could not cooperate with Magruder because "he had been ordered on other important duty." The dispatch left Magruder's grand scheme in shambles. Without Jackson, "I was compelled to abandon the plan of capturing any large portion of the enemy forces," he wrote. [27] The promise of sending 40,000 men against the Federals had been reduced to Magruder's command of 14,000 soldiers. All day Prince John had been avoiding Lee's orders. With his tactical options exhausted, he finally decided to obey headquarters and attack the enemy.

Three Union corps maintained a defensive position near Savage's Station. Those Federals were to hold their ground until they could retreat under the cover of darkness. Magruder correctly estimated that he was outnumbered and cautiously advanced with two and a half of his six brigades. A stronger show of force probably would have achieved little except high casualties. Darkness and a fierce thunderstorm brought the inconclusive fighting at Savage's Station to an end. [28]

Lee probably considered the twenty-ninth his best opportunity to destroy the Army of the Potomac during the Seven Days because McClellan's rear guard had not escaped the confines of White Oak Swamp. In unusually harsh language, he rebuked Magruder: "I regret much that you have made so little progress today in the pursuit of the enemy. To reap the fruits of our victory the pursuit should be most vigorous. I must urge you, then, again to press on his rear rapidly and steadily. We must lose no more time or he will escape us entirely."[29]

Without a combined assault involving Jackson and Huger, Lee probably expected too much of Magruder. But Magruder deserved the harsh criticism for his blatant disobedience of orders. He controlled the trip wire that would have set Lee's plan into motion. If Prince John had followed his orders and aggressively pushed up the Williamsburg Road, he would have locked the Union rear guard around Savage's Station. With the Federals fixed in place, amid the bogs of White Oak Swamp, Huger could have sealed McClellan's escape by advancing down the Charles City Road while Jackson threatened the rear. Magruder's disobedience ruined any chance Lee had of trapping McClellan in White Oak Swamp. Although the odds of destroying a portion of the Union army did not favor Lee even if Magruder had executed his orders flawlessly, the commanding general recognized that a potential opportunity had been squandered. Armistead Long of Lee's staff captured the frustration that prevailed at army headquarters after Magruder's poor showing on June 29: "The audacity which was so conspicuous on the Peninsula seemed to abandon him [at Savage's Station] for he closely hugged his breastworks with thirty thousand men, while McClellan was in active preparations for retreat. The advantage thus gained [by McClellan] could never be overcome."[30]

Magruder's illusions of Yankee counterattacks continued throughout the night. Although the phantom legions never appeared, he again punished his body by riding his lines until the early morning hours of June 30. "General Magruder was known to us to have been unwell for a day or two," recalled Brent, "but it would not have been believed by any stranger who saw him. He was going to and fro and sending out orders and instructions as long as I remember." After a 3:00 A.M. meeting with Jackson, Magruder fell asleep — his first rest, he later wrote, in forty-eight hours. At sunrise, Lee informed his exhausted subordinate that Jackson would lead the pursuit of the enemy's rear guard. Magruder would follow Longstreet as a reserve and march to the Darbytown Road. Lee's decision to pull Magruder from the advance could be interpreted as indicating a loss of confidence.[31]

Events on June 30 nearly pushed the frazzled Magruder over the edge. He reached the Darbytown Road at 2:00 P.M., waiting a few hours behind Longstreet's command before new orders directed him to move to the New Market Road to support Theophilus Holmes. The march was hot and confusing. Neither local guides nor maps could untangle the complex road networks

PETER S. CARMICHAEL

east of Richmond. Just as his troops reached Holmes at dusk, headquarters recalled Magruder to Longstreet's position. His weary soldiers returned to the dusty roads and started to retrace their steps.

During the day, Magruder frantically rode up and down the line, reprimanding subordinates for minor infractions, assuming control of trivial matters that should have been left to others, and generally serving as an impediment to the movement he was so anxious to expedite. Brent's feelings "of mortification at the apparently nervous excitement of the General" prompted him to confront his superior. While their horses were drinking from a stream, Brent said to Magruder, "I am sorry to see that you are not feeling well this morning." "Why do you think so?" Magruder snapped. "Because," Brent continued, "I have never seen you act as you have this morning." Magruder did not seem to understand and asked for specifics. Brent reluctantly told him that he had lost his "usual calmness" because of "an extreme irritability, sometimes exhibited without any apparent cause, and hence I inferred that you must be feeling badly." "Well, Major, you are right," Magruder confided. "I am feeling horribly. For two days I have been disturbed about my digestion, and the doctor has been giving me medicine, and I fear he has given me some morphine in his mixture, and the smallest quantity of it acts upon me as an irritant. And beside that, I have lost so much sleep that it affects me strangely; but I fully appreciate your kindness in speaking to me, and I will endeavor to regain my self control." [32]

After some eighteen hours on the road, marching more than twenty miles and never firing a shot, Magruder's soldiers finally reached their destination near the Glendale battlefield. He then transferred his troops to Longstreet's front, the scene of the day's fighting. This duty required his personal attention until 3:00 A.M., after which he slept for another hour, his second in three days. Magruder again left camp before dawn, weary, sick, and famished. To his relief, a staff officer brought him some food, his first in nearly twenty-four hours. Magruder then straightened out his battle lines, advanced his skirmishers, and captured some Union soldiers before coming into contact with Jackson's troops. [33]

The inconclusive fighting at Savage's Station and Glendale did not divert Lee from his aggressive strategy. July 1 offered another chance to destroy part of the Army of the Potomac. McClellan had selected Malvern Hill to make his final stand. Thousands of northern infantrymen and more than a hundred artillery pieces occupied this impressive but not impregnable defensive position. Lee met with Magruder and Jackson to outline the attack. As the three men rode down the Long Bridge Road, the commanding general unrolled a map. Tracing the route with his finger, Lee said: "You, General

Jackson, will take the position on the left, . . . and you, Genl. Magruder advancing down the Quaker Road, will form our right." [34] The staff officer who overheard this important meeting did not recall any other details. The specific plan of attack, who would initiate it, and how much discretion Lee gave his subordinates were not recorded. Such information would go a long way in explaining the botched assaults later in the day. The conference ended at 10:00 A.M., and the generals returned to their respective commands.

Three local guides had been secured to lead Magruder to the Quaker Road, but nobody knew two Quaker Roads existed. As they directed the column to the west instead of the south, Magruder feared he was headed away from the enemy. It appeared that it was June 30 all over again, his troops meandering across the countryside without seeing any action. Already stinging from Lee's rebuke after Savage's Station, Magruder wanted to get his troops into position to attack as quickly as possible. He questioned his guides, but they insisted that "this was the only Quaker Road known to them." [35] Prince John remained unconvinced but continued along his present course until overtaken by Longstreet, who agreed that the troops were moving around Malvern Hill instead of toward it. Magruder requested orders to move back, but Longstreet replied that he lacked authority to issue them. A frustrated Magruder then gave instructions to countermarch, returning to what Lee's map identified as the Quaker Road, but which was in fact the Long Bridge Road. Confusion about the Quaker Road had delayed Magruder at least three hours. The time could have been better spent preparing for the assault, bringing up artillery, and coordinating the tactical arrangements. After the battle Magruder received much criticism for taking the wrong road, a patently unfair charge. His tardiness did not ruin chances of Confederate victory on July 1.[36]

When Magruder finally reached Malvern Hill at 4:00 P.M., he must have been in awe of McClellan's seemingly invincible position. A closer examination, however, revealed flaws. The narrowness of the 850-yard Union front made it vulnerable to a converging artillery fire as well as a concentrated infantry assault. McClellan's flanks rested on steep cliffs, and the deep valleys below afforded cover to attacking Confederates. Overall, Lee faced imposing but not insurmountable odds at Malvern Hill. A successful infantry assault depended on effective artillery fire and coordination among Lee's subordinates. The commanding general achieved neither, largely because of poor staff work and dangerously vague orders. Without strong direction from above, Magruder never achieved a concentration of artillery, a serious mistake compounded by his piecemeal infantry attacks. The haphazardness of Magruder's assaults, together with the general's previous record and peculiar behavior on the Malvern Hill battlefield, would lead some critics to accuse him of drunkenness on July 1.

The Confederate high command envisioned a powerful converging fire coming from Jackson's guns near the Poindexter farm and Magruder's on the right. Although this was an essential element of Lee's plans, only four cannon of Magruder's sixteen batteries opened fire. Stephen D. Lee, Magruder's chief of artillery and a man sympathetic to his superior, claimed that "he received no order from the Genl. during the action, except to place the Batteries . . . in rear of the Battlefield," where they received heavy fire from "the enemy during the evening without being able to return it." Magruder's failure to use his division artillery remains a mystery. Before the assault, he acknowledged that the infantry charge would be an "impossibility" unless supported by "thirty pieces of the heaviest caliber." The general did manage to collect a handful of guns from other commands, but unfortunately he sent those batteries to the front separately. In short order the Yankee cannon on Malvern Hill silenced them. When fresh Confederate guns replaced those raked by enemy fire, the cycle was repeated.[37]

Capt. Greenlee Davidson's Letcher Artillery participated in one of the first artillery bombardments, firing between thirty and forty minutes before twenty Union guns disabled the battery. Davidson denounced Magruder for sending his batteries forward in a piecemeal fashion. "If he had concentrated 30 or 40 guns upon the enemy's strong position at Crew's House as he could have done with ease," Davidson concluded, "he would have silenced the fire of the batteries, scattered the immense masses of infantry supporting them, and thereby saved many hundreds of valuable lives, which were lost in the impotent charges across the open field." Another subordinate complained that Magruder forwarded only a few guns, and they were "knocked into strips in ten minutes."[38]

Late in the afternoon, repeated orders from Lee initiated the desperate infantry charges at Malvern Hill, although the commanding general would later claim that he never ordered the attack. Lee probably interpreted this as further evidence that Magruder could not follow orders. Prince John actually wanted more time to prepare for the advance but did not feel "at liberty to hesitate under the stringency of my instructions."[39] Feeling pressure from headquarters created a sense of urgency that might explain why his attacks lacked coordination. Instead of funneling individual brigades toward Malvern Hill, he should have consolidated his troops and struck with one mighty blow. A lack of coordination forced Confederate attacking units to fight in isolation, their communications further hampered by the rugged terrain. Magruder persisted in this mode of attack with the predictability of an assembly

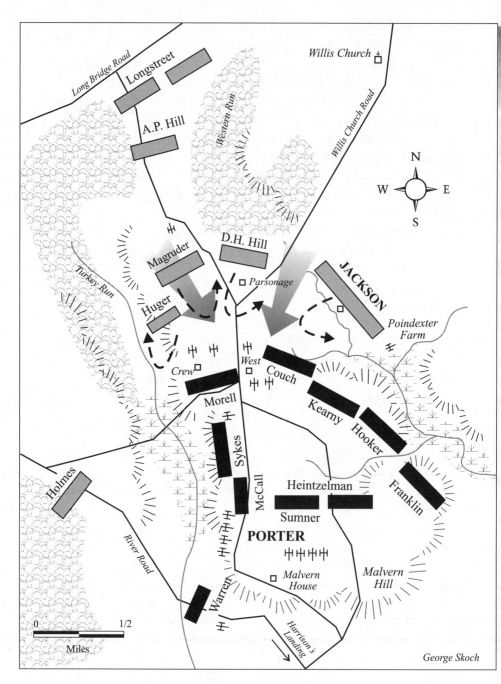

Battle of Malvern Hill, July 1, 1862

PETER S. CARMICHAEL

line. A brigade would rush forward, briefly sustain its momentum, then withdraw when Union batteries blasted it from the field. As soon as a new unit reached the front, Magruder would pitch it into the bloody morass at the base of Malvern Hill.

The experience of Joseph B. Kershaw's South Carolina brigade typified Magruder's deadly approach. After enduring the enemy's artillery fire for most of the day, Kershaw received a generic order from one of Magruder's staff officers to "advance and attack the enemy's battery." Kershaw later complained that he had "no knowledge of the ground or position of the enemy." Magruder should not have sent units into combat without briefing his subordinates of the situation and their place in the overall tactical scheme. In a wartime publication, a Mississippi soldier believed Magruder "was intent on killing his men by detachments, for there seemed to be no settled plan of action." This man could not understand why the general did not push "forward reenforcements to succor those in front" while his lead units "were compelled to stand before the enemy's pieces, without support, until decimated, and then retire as formerly." [40]

As Magruder's offensive fell apart on July 1, so did the general. The stress, lack of sleep, and allergic reaction to his medicine virtually disabled him. Again he lacked composure in front of the troops. He appeared agitated, almost frantic, unable to control his emotions. "While receiving my orders from General Armistead," wrote artillerist Greenlee Davidson, "my attention was attracted to General Magruder who seemed to be laboring under the most terrible excitement." "The wild expression of his eyes and his excited manner" especially disturbed Davidson, who thought the general "was under the influence of some powerful stimulant, spirits or perhaps opium." "He was certainly the most excited General officer I have ever met upon a battlefield and in my opinion was totally incapacitated for the high command he held," concluded Davidson. A captured Union soldier also observed Magruder "riding back and forth, swearing and raving like a madman, trying to reform his lines, but all in vain." [41]

Magruder's emotional instability and uncertain health partially explain his chaotic management of the Confederate right flank. He failed to facilitate the cooperative action essential to any offensive movement. Instead of a massed infantry assault, he used only about one-third of his 15,000 men in disjointed attacks. By the end of the day, the Confederate charges cost the army some 5,000 men.

Magruder's behavior fueled rumors that he was inebriated during the battle. A staff officer under Gen. David R. Jones reported that Magruder "was so drunk at the battle that two of his aides had to hold him up and that by orders he butchered many of our men." "Some of us must tremble in our shoes," he grimly concluded, "if such thorough work is going on." Col. Thomas R. R. Cobb informed his wife that "Old Magruder made no reputation in this battle. He lost rather than gained. He was depressed, and I fear was drinking." Another participant heard "that Gen. Magruder was *drunk*, and that he was accused on the battlefield by some of his Brig-Gens. of being a murderer." The strongest indictment came from Thomas Caffey, an Englishman who served in a Mississippi regiment. After Malvern Hill, he remembered that "curses were on every lip against Magruder." Caffey had "never heard a mortal man so despised and execrated among all classes of military men." "Was he tipsy?" Caffey asked. Although lacking conclusive proof, he wondered if Magruder "had returned to his old habits at such an important moment, to frustrate all our designs by passion and intoxication! Hundreds are willing to swear that he was unfit to command on that day."[42]

Only a handful of officers stood against the current of opinion that threatened to wash Magruder out of the army in disgrace. Surg. E. J. Eldridge of the 16th Georgia saw the general on three different occasions during the battle. He dismissed the charge that Magruder had sought a safe place on the battlefield, testifying that he "saw no disposition on his [Magruder's] part to screen himself from the enemy's fire. On the contrary, heard remarks about his fearlessness." Although Eldridge noted that the general expressed the normal anxiety experienced during combat, he stated without equivocation that if Magruder "was under the influence of liquor, I failed entirely to see it. . . . [I] am positive, as far as my judgment goes, that he had not even taken a drink — most certainly was not the least excited from any cause." Stephen D. Lee also considered the accusations of drunkenness "to be false." After the war, staff officer John Lamb published a strident defense of his superior, claiming that "General Magruder was perfectly sober the whole day."[43]

Testimony about his allergic reaction to morphine would have strengthened his case. Inexplicably, neither Magruder nor any of his defenders raised this issue during the war. Only staff officer Brent referred to the ill-advised medication in his recollections. The theory that morphine agitated Magruder's emotional state appears dubious. In most people, morphine would have the calming effect of a sedative. His hyperactive behavior on the battlefield, well documented and seen by many officers, cannot be explained with the available sources.[44]

On July 11, the controversy became more than harmless army gossip when Lee's chief of staff Robert H. Chilton wrote Confederate adjutant and inspector general Samuel Cooper about Magruder's conduct during the

PETER S. CARMICHAEL

Lt. Col. Robert H. Chilton
Francis Trevelyan Miller, ed., The Photographic History of the Civil War, *10 vols.*
(New York: Review of Reviews, 1911), 10:319

Seven Days. Upon reflecting on Prince John's pending transfer to the Trans-Mississippi, Chilton was "more strongly convinced . . . of the sad injustice to be inflicted upon the people of the South West by sending one so utterly incompetent and deficient as is Magruder." He added that Lee "concurs in my belief of his incompetency, but will not act unless directly asked by the President." When Chilton discovered that Jefferson Davis had read his indictment of Magruder, a letter that he considered personal and for Cooper's eyes only, he immediately tried to cover his tracks. In a dispatch to the president, he claimed that his letter to Cooper was not an official communiqué and that this correspondence occurred "without the knowledge of Genl Lee." "Any use of Genl Lee's name," he added, "was conjectural, on my part." Chilton's assumption about Lee's opinion of Magruder was "not based upon what I had heard Genl. Lee state, but my observation of facts which I knew must be within the knowledge of Genl Lee."[45]

After surveying the correspondence between Chilton and Cooper, Davis decided to recall Magruder, who had left for the Western Theater. The president wanted to resolve the questions surrounding his behavior before handing him the Trans-Mississippi command. A Mississippi officer welcomed the official inquiry but thought Magruder would escape conviction: "Magruder is under trial for *Drunkenness & Incompetency* and *Disobedience of Orders.* He has too many friends in civil life as well as the Army not to be acquitted, but we are done with him. Davis & Lee will never trust him again."[46]

When Magruder returned to Richmond, he prepared a thorough defense of his actions. By mid-August the report was in Lee's hands. After a quick examination, he informed Secretary of War Randolph that "General Magruder appears to have greatly exerted himself to accomplish the duty devolved on him, and I can bear testimony to the uniform alacrity he displayed in its execution. He had many difficulties to contend with, I know. I regretted at the time, and still regret, that they could not have been more readily overcome. I feel assured, however, that General Magruder intentionally omitted nothing that he could do to insure success." In classic Lee style, the commanding general offered a vague, noncontroversial response so as to dispense with the matter as quickly as possible. Even with Lee's approval, Magruder languished in Richmond for three more months, waiting until October 10 for Confederate authorities to approve his transfer. When he reached his new post, the Trans-Mississippi Department had been assigned to Theophilus Holmes. Magruder reluctantly accepted command of the District of Texas, Arizona, and New Mexico, although he would have preferred his original assignment.[47]

Lee's desire to maintain harmony in the Army of Northern Virginia largely explains why he neither offered a public defense of Magruder nor pressed for a full-blown court of inquiry. A master at controlling potentially disruptive problems of command in his army, Lee wanted to settle the affair quickly. His reluctance to defend Magruder also could have stemmed in part from legitimate concerns about his subordinate's drinking habits. To suspect a confirmed alcoholic of seeking refuge from the bottle during a time of duress was not unreasonable. Beyond the question of personal habits, Lee had just cause to censure Magruder. On June 29, he disregarded Lee's order for a rapid advance toward Savage's Station. At Malvern Hill, Magruder botched the attacks, showing little aptitude for offensive operations while nearly suffering an emotional collapse in front of the troops. That Lee took such failures seriously would be apparent less than two years later when he removed Richard S. Ewell from corps command after the battles at Spotsylvania for similar transgressions.[48] If Magruder's performance suffered because of poor health or a lack of sleep, he had the responsibility to turn command over to a subordinate. Lee had taken such precautions when he fell ill at Malvern Hill.

The commanding general did recognize that inadequate staff work, primitive maps, and an unwieldy organizational system had contributed to the difficulties of all his subordinates. Yet Lee appears to have been more forgiving with Jackson and Longstreet than with Magruder, though all three men made similar mistakes during the Seven Days. Lee perceived leadership qualities in Jackson and Longstreet that were lacking in Magruder. Prince John's constant anxiety, bouts of despondency, and dependency on alcohol revealed a man ruled by emotion. More than any other trait, Lee valued self-control. He knew officers could not gain the confidence of their troops without a calm demeanor and the look of self-assurance. Jackson and Longstreet possessed that essential element of leadership, but Magruder did not. Moreover, Lee believed that Magruder disregarded orders, an unforgivable sin that neither Jackson nor Longstreet had committed. Prince John would redeem himself in Texas, demonstrating that his performance outside Richmond was an aberration.[49] But he never removed the stain placed on his reputation by events during the Seven Days. Shortly after his death, an obituary in a New York historical magazine paid tribute not to his generalship but to his legendary excesses: "He could fight all day and dance all night. In the morning, a glass of brandy and strong cigar renewed his strength. . . . He loved magnificent uniforms, and magnificent horses, and magnificent women."[50]

NOTES

1. Joseph Lancaster Brent, *Memoirs of the War between the States* (New Orleans: Fontana Printing Company, 1940), 231.

2. Ibid., 230–31.

3. U.S. War Department, *The War of the Rebellion: A Compilation of the Official Records of the Union and Confederate Armies,* 127 vols., index, and atlas (Washington, D.C.: GPO, 1880–1901), ser. 1, 11(3):630 (hereafter cited as *OR;* all citations are to ser. 1).

4. On Magruder's drinking, see Paul D. Casdorph, *Prince John Magruder: His Life and Campaigns* (New York: Wiley, 1996), 2–3.

5. Gary W. Gallagher has speculated that Lee may have seen the character flaws of his father in Magruder; however, there is no hard evidence to prove such an interpre-

tation. See Gary W. Gallagher, "The Undoing of an Early Confederate Hero: John Bankhead Magruder at the Seven Days," in Gallagher, *Lee and His Generals in War and Memory* (Baton Rouge: Louisiana State University Press, 1998), 137–38.

6. The defense of Magruder at Savage's Station does not address his disobedience of Lee's orders. This critical issue has been sidestepped by some historians who focus on Jackson's failure to cross White Oak Swamp and poor staff work as the reasons Magruder did not inflict serious damage against the Federal rear guard on June 29. See Stephen Sears, *To the Gates of Richmond: The Peninsula Campaign* (New York: Ticknor & Fields, 1992), 274; Gallagher, "Undoing of an Early Confederate Hero," 128–29.

7. Betty Herndon Maury, *The Confederate Diary of Betty Herndon Maury, Daughter of Lieut. Commander M. F. Maury, 1861–1863,* ed. Alice Maury Parmelee (Washington, D.C.: Privately printed, 1938), 6. For a discussion of Magruder's place and date of birth, see Thomas Michael Settles, "The Military Career of John Bankhead Magruder" (Ph.D. diss., Texas Christian University, 1972), 5–6 n. 10.

8. A detailed examination of Magruder's experience at West Point and his service in the Mexican War can be found in Casdorph, *Prince John Magruder,* 13–25, 58–79.

9. On Magruder's fondness for extravagant entertainment and parties, see Gallagher, "Undoing of an Early Confederate Hero," 119–21; Daniel Harvey Hill, "Lee Attacks North of the Chickahominy," in *Battles and Leaders of the Civil War,* ed. Robert Underwood Johnson and Clarence Clough Buel, 4 vols. (New York: Century, 1887–88), 2:362n.

10. Excerpt of John Bankhead Magruder letter, May 15, 1840, in Gary Hendershott Catalogue (October 1993), Little Rock, Arkansas.

11. Casdorph, *Prince John Magruder, 30.* On Magruder's marriage, see Settles, "Military Career of John Bankhead Magruder," 21–22.

12. Settles, "Military Career of John Bankhead Magruder," 24–26.

13. Gallagher, "Undoing of an Early Confederate Hero," 121–22.

14. Brent, *Memoirs,* 159. For a favorable assessment of Magruder's activities on the Peninsula, see Sears, *To the Gates of Richmond,* chaps. 2–3.

15. Johnston's criticisms of Magruder can be found in his *Narrative of Military Operations, Directed during the Late War between the States* (1874; reprint, Bloomington: Indiana University Press, 1959), 111–13.

16. *OR* 11(3):537, 540, 551.

17. Terry L. Jones, *Lee's Tigers: The Louisiana Infantry in the Army of Northern Virginia* (Baton Rouge: Louisiana State University Press, 1987), 33–34.

18. Richard Leach to his father, February 5, 1862, James H. C. Leach Papers, Special Collections, William R. Perkins Library, Duke University, Durham, N.C. (repository hereafter cited as DU).

19. Sears, *To The Gates of Richmond,* 176, 195–96; Brent, *Memoirs,* 158–59.

20. Brent, *Memoirs,* 160; *OR* 11(2):661.

21. Brent, *Memoirs,* 167.

22. Sears, *To the Gates of Richmond,* 217; *OR* 11(2):661; (1):57.

23. Douglas Southall Freeman, *Lee's Lieutenants: A Study in Command,* 3 vols. (New York: Scribner's, 1942–44), 2:543; *OR* 11(2):662.

24. *OR* 11(2):494, 662.

25. Brent, *Memoirs,* 181.

26. *OR* 11(2):663, 789.

27. *OR* 11(2):664.

28. For an overview of the fighting at Savage's Station, see Sears, *To the Gates of Richmond,* 255–74, and Freeman, *Lee's Lieutenants,* 2:553–55.

29. *OR* 11(2):687.

30. A. L. Long, "Memoir of General John Bankhead Magruder," in J. William Jones et al., eds., *Southern Historical Society Papers,* 52 vols. (1876–1959; reprint with 3-vol. index, Wilmington, N.C.: Broadfoot, 1990–92), 12:110 (hereafter cited as *SHSP*).

31. Brent, *Memoirs,* 190; *OR* 11(2):666.

32. Brent, *Memoirs,* 191–92.

33. *OR* 11(2):667; Brent, *Memoirs,* 203.

34. Brent, *Memoirs,* 203.

35. Ibid., 206.

36. Freeman, *Lee's Lieutenants,* 1:590–91. Freeman thought Magruder bore responsibility for taking the wrong road and for the confused march: "Co-ordination was lost, in the second place, through a singular mistake on the part of General Magruder. . . . Apparently the galloping Magruder did not ask to examine Lee's map — the only one available — nor does he seem to have inquired of the commanding general where the road ran. . . . He had three guides from the neighborhood and, still without explanation, he bade them conduct him to the Quaker road."

37. Sears, *To The Gates of Richmond,* 320; Stephen D. Lee to [L. W.] Allen, August 2, 1862, in Compiled Service Record (hereafter cited as CSR) of Stephen D. Lee, Record Group M331, reel 155, National Archives, Washington, D.C. (repository hereafter cited as NA); *OR* 11(2):823.

38. Greenlee Davidson to [A. P. Hill], April 23, 1863, in Greenlee Davidson, *Captain Greenlee Davidson, C.S.A.: Diary and Letters, 1851–1863,* ed. Charles W. Turner (Verona, Va.: McClure Press, 1975), 71–72; Robert Toombs to Alexander H. Stephens, July 14, 1862, in *The Correspondence of Robert Toombs, Alexander H. Stephens, and Howell Cobb,* ed. Ulrich Bonnell Phillips (1913; reprint, New York: Da Capo, 1970), 600. D. H. Hill offered a biting commentary on Confederate artillery at Malvern Hill, writing that "instead of ordering up 100 or 200 pieces of artillery to play on the Yankees, a single battery (Moorman's) was ordered up and knocked to pieces in a few minutes. One or two others shared the same fate of being beat in detail. Not knowing

how to act under these circumstances, I wrote to General Jackson that the firing from our batteries was of the most farcical character" (*OR* 11[2]:628).

39. Douglas Southall Freeman, *R. E. Lee: A Biography,* 4 vols. (New York: Scribner's, 1934–35), 3:218; *OR* 11(2):669.

40. *OR* 11(2):728; An English Combatant, *Battle-Fields of the South, from Bull Run to Fredericksburg; with Sketches of Confederate Commanders, and Gossip of the Camps* (New York: John Bradburn, 1864), 374–75.

41. Greenlee Davidson to [A. P. Hill], April 23, 1863, in Davidson, *Captain Greenlee Davidson,* 71; John W. Urban, *Battle Field and Prison Pen, or through the War, and Thrice a Prisoner in Rebel Dungeons* (Philadelphia: Hubbard Bros., 1882), 171.

42. Henry Edward Young to his uncle, July 20, 1862, Robert Newman Gourdin Papers, DU; Thomas R. R. Cobb, "Extracts from Letters to His Wife, February 3, 1861–December 10, 1862," in *SHSP,* 28:293; William B. Bailey to Ned [?], July 21, 1862, Coco Collection, United States Army Military History Institute, Carlisle Barracks, Pennsylvania; An English Combatant, *Battlefields of the South,* 375, 373.

43. *OR* 11(2):682–83; CSR of Stephen D. Lee, NA; John Lamb, "Malvern Hill — July 1, 1862," in *SHSP,* 25:217.

44. For an overview of Magruder's medical history, see Jack D. Welsh, *Medical Histories of Confederate Generals* (Kent, Ohio: Kent State University Press, 1995), 151–52.

45. Robert H. Chilton to Samuel Cooper, July 11, 1862, Robert H. Chilton to Jefferson Davis, July 20, 1862, in Jefferson Davis, *The Papers of Jefferson Davis,* ed. Haskell M. Monroe, James T. McIntosh, and Lynda Lasswell Crist, 10 vols. to date (Baton Rouge: Louisiana State University Press, 1971–), 8:296–97, 297 n. 1. For a superb examination of the Magruder-Chilton controversy, see Richard Selcer, "Conduct Unbecoming," in *Civil War Times Illustrated* 34 (March–April 1995): 60–69.

46. Benjamin Grubb Humphrey to Richard Thomas Archer, July 29, 1862, Archer Family Papers, Virginia Historical Society, Richmond.

47. *OR* 11(2):679; Gallagher, "Undoing of an Early Confederate Hero," 137.

48. On Ewell's loss of corps command, see Donald C. Pfanz, *Richard S. Ewell: A Soldier's Life* (Chapel Hill: University of North Carolina Press, 1998), 397–403.

49. On Magruder's career in the Trans-Mississippi, see chapters 8–10 of Casdorph, *Prince John Magruder.*

50. "General John B. Magruder," Obituary in *Historical Magazine* 8 (1870): 249.

JAMES MARTEN

A Feeling of Restless Anxiety

Loyalty and Race in the Peninsula Campaign and Beyond

The 1st Delaware had settled pretty comfortably into garrison duty at Fort Monroe by early 1862. To pass the time, the troops had built a log theater, complete with curtains and footlights, where they held regular amateur theatricals. Eighty miles away, a different kind of playacting was going on in the Confederate capital, where a certain class of civilians had taken to wearing army uniforms and loitering around hotel bars. These "military dandies," as the Richmond *Examiner* called them, apparently hoped their faux uniforms would help them break into polite society.[1]

The make-believe ended in mid-March, when Maj. Gen. George B. McClellan shifted his army's base from northern Virginia to the Peninsula. His offensive against the Confederate capital commenced three weeks later. The Peninsula campaign opened the bloody second act of the war in the East, as two great armies, virtually silent since the previous July, converged on southeastern Virginia. The campaign also turned a spotlight on two crucial aspects of southern society: the loyalty of its white residents and the relationship between its masters and slaves. The presence in Confederate territory of many thousands of Union troops exposed sizable faults in Virginia society. As during the bitter debates over secession in early 1861, Virginians discovered that they were not necessarily united in a common purpose, and white southerners, northerners, and African Americans found themselves at odds over previous notions of race relations. This crisis — one ultimately faced by all southern communities, black and white — made many Confederates feel vulnerable to their own internal weaknesses.

Despite the long period of relative inactivity in Virginia since the previous fall, Richmond had already been deeply affected by the war. The influx of government officials, job-hunters, soldiers, and families of soldiers had caused the population of Richmond to grow suddenly, and it continued to

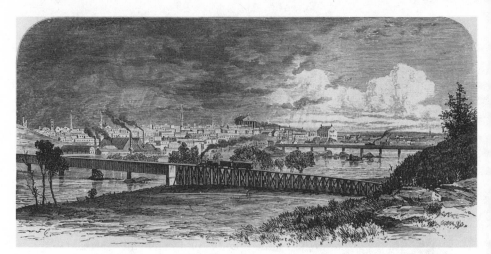

View of wartime Richmond from the right bank of the James River.
Robert Underwood Johnson and Clarence Clough Buel, eds., Battles and Leaders
of the Civil War, *4 vols. (New York: Century, 1887–88), 2:442*

soar throughout the war. The rise in the number of young, unattached men
brought increases in prostitution, venereal disease, and crime. The *Examiner* complained early in the new year about the transition of Richmond from
a quiet town to a metropolis, especially the apparently inevitable proliferation
of unlicensed taverns, brothels, and gambling houses. There were frequent
incidents of disturbing the peace and robbery and the occasional report of
an inebriated soldier exposing himself. Rumors flashed around the city a few
months before the campaign began that the gamblers and "plugs" of the city
had pooled their money to put up a candidate in the next mayoral election.[2]

Gambling also reached unprecedented levels in the capital, according to
one observer. "Impulsive by nature, living in an atmosphere of constant and
increasing artificial excitement, feeling that the money worth little today, perhaps, would be worth nothing tomorrow — these men of the South gambled
heavily, recklessly, and openly." At luxurious faro saloons, politicians, army
officers, and city leaders could smoke expensive cigars, drink rare liquors,
and gamble the night away. Other citizens chose to gamble on the open market by becoming "amateur speculators," buying up stocks of whiskey, flour,
fruit, boots — anything, in fact — and selling them for outrageous prices.
Another kind of gambling could be seen at the city's auction houses, where
private citizens sold personal goods, hoping to get something for furniture,
foodstuffs, dry goods, and any other possession before the Yankees arrived.[3]

There seemed to be a general loosening of peacetime inhibitions, which
was certainly reflected in the behavior of the city's boys. By January 1862,

"scores of youthful candidates for the penitentiary" were fighting regular Sunday afternoon battles with rocks and, on occasion, even shotguns. Some directed their stones at other targets, complained the *Examiner*, damaging the windows, shutters, and doors of numerous houses on Church Hill. The boys of the capital city, B. H. Wilkins recalled, "had all caught the fighting spirit." They "divided into as many clans as the seven hills" on which Richmond perched and challenged one another to rock battles in mimicry of the real-life soldiers defending the city.[4]

The raucous behavior of Richmonders belied the gloom that had fallen over the city long before Federal troops appeared on the Peninsula, at least according to one Richmond woman. Sallie Brock Putnam recalled shortly after the war that, at Christmastime 1861, "We had neither the heart nor inclination to make . . . merry with joyousness when such a sad calamity hovered over us." Seasonal salutations "were followed by anxious inquiries for dear boys in the field, or husbands or other whose presence had ever brought brightness to the domestic hall." The mood worsened as the Yankees approached in the spring.[5]

The immediate response of residents of the city to the threat of invasion was less than heroic. There were "many strange and humiliating spectacles," Edward Pollard wrote, and "the air was filled with those rumors of treason and disloyalty which seem invariably to grow out of a sense of insecurity." Formerly vociferous rebels "were now engaged in secreting their property" and distancing themselves from the rebellion. Fainthearted refugees crowded the railroad stations and shop owners began to pack their wares for escape. Pollard characteristically reserved his most severe judgment for the Confederate government, which displayed "the most abundant and humiliating signs of the panic." Indeed, after voting itself a pay raise on April 22, the Confederate Congress adjourned and many of its members went home. Upon learning that Federal gunboats had started up the James River, President Jefferson Davis sent his family to Raleigh, North Carolina, and Secretary of War George Wythe Randolph asked the heads of government bureaus to prepare vital records for evacuation. The Richmond *Dispatch* tried to ignore the growing concern. "The same feeling which pervaded the city on the eve of the fight at Manassas seems to be prevalent now," it argued on the day Congress left town. "It is of restless anxiety, not in the slightest degree tinged with fear."[6]

But many Richmonders seemed fearful. Judith McGuire reported the "panic" that seized Richmond in mid-April. "My mind is much perturbed," she confessed. "We can only go on doing our duty, as quietly as we can." Many men took the president's lead in sending their families away from the apparently doomed city. "It is distressing to see how many persons are leaving Richmond, apprehending that it is in danger; but it will not — I know it will not — fall. It is said that the President does not fear; he will send his family away, because he thinks it is better for men . . . to be free from private anxiety." John B. Jones's wife and most of his children journeyed to Raleigh, ostensibly to visit another daughter at school. "But it is in reality another flight from the enemy," Jones admitted. "No one, scarcely, supposes that Richmond will be defended. But it must be!" As the Union army advanced and the Confederate army retreated, one girl began "to feel like the prisoner of the Inquisition in Poe's story, cast into a dungeon with slowly contracting walls."[7]

Pollard argued that the panic soon subsided. Confederate spines were stiffened by brave resolutions from the Virginia state legislature and a public meeting of the residents of Richmond, after which "inert and speculative patriotism was aroused to exertion." After a few weeks of confusion and dismay, the Virginia General Assembly finally drew a line in the dust on May 14 by demanding that Richmond be defended. The next day Governor John Letcher held a mass meeting to organize companies for local defense. The legislature allocated $200,000 for river obstructions and another $200,000 to evacuate women, children, and older citizens from the city in case of shelling. Arrangements were made to gather and burn valuable tobacco stores, and women began making bedding for military hospitals. The city fathers of Richmond also sprang into action, appointing a committee to look into the river defenses and organizing a home guard to provide security for bridges and other public property (the unit was not actually mustered until August).[8]

Perhaps inspired by the brave front put on by the city council and legislature, John B. Jones recorded on May 19 that "a sullen, but generally a calm expression of inflexible determination" had appeared "on the countenances of the people, men, women, and children. . . . We have learned to contemplate death with composure." By the third week in May, the *Dispatch* could report that "it is indeed refreshing to witness the cool determination with which citizens and soldiers await the approach of the foe. There is no trepidation manifest, and on all hands there is the firmest resolution to contend for every inch of ground in defence of the city."[9]

The Virginians who lived in the counties coming under the control of the massive Union army displayed a rather different set of emotions. Yorktown fell on May 4, and Confederates evacuated Norfolk and Portsmouth on May 9 and 10 respectively. The presence of tens of thousands of enemy troops in

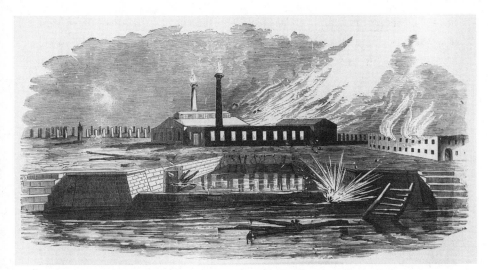

*Confederates burned the navy yard at Norfolk when they evacuated the city in
early May 1862, an event depicted in this wartime engraving.*
Frank Leslie's Illustrated Newspaper, *June 7, 1862*

the summer of 1862 and of a significant occupation force during the next
three years wreaked havoc on these towns and the surrounding area. The
Petersburg *Express* accurately stated in the summer of 1862 that Norfolk, her
"streets . . . deserted," was "now a city of gloom." [10]

In the occupied coastal cities, churches and schools closed, commerce
disappeared, newspapers ceased publication, and buildings decayed. Minis-
ters, physicians, lawyers, merchants, and their clerks were required to take
oaths of allegiance. Few Virginians in these depressed and depressing towns
found any reason to cheer up for many months. A few desperate local merchants did take the oath, hoping to rescue their failing businesses by trad-
ing with the Union army, but most refused, leaving northern merchants
and sutlers with army contracts to dominate commerce on the tip of the
Peninsula from the makeshift army village with streets named McClellan and
Ellsworth. [11]

The occupation of her hometown, Williamsburg, and the closing of her
church because the minister refused to pray for the president of the United
States so upset one young woman that she needed morphine to get to sleep.
Yet within a week, Harriette Cary and her fellow congregants were holding
secret prayer meetings in private homes and basements. Williamsburg, Cary
wrote less than a fortnight after its occupation, "begins to wear the garb of a
mourner — an air of neglect pervades this once happy little village. . . . The

most favored spots have been despoiled by the ruthless hands of these Yankee invaders. Our once beautiful greens are cut up and their lovely sward destroyed — the side walks preferred by equestrians, much to the annoyance of pedestrians." [12]

Confederate dismay followed the Union army wherever it went. George A. Townsend, a reporter for the *New York Herald,* recorded how the Union army had transformed the lower Peninsula. Men and horses and supplies choked the Federal beachhead at Fort Monroe: "One was startled at the prodigal outlay of means, and the reckless summoning of men." Sutlers worked from sloops anchored offshore or from shanties built of rough planks onshore; women and children from the neighborhood also got into the business of supplying troops. As Townsend accompanied the army's slow approach to Yorktown, he noted the furrows dug by artillery fire, the deserted houses and camps, the wrecked fences, and the scattered detritus of an army on the march. Townsend gave grudging respect to the tough old men — the younger ones had fled — who remained on the farms being ravaged by Union troops. They glared out of windows or walked aimlessly around their yards, "half-weakly, half-wrathfully," as "their gates were wrenched from the hinges, their rails used to pry wagons out of the mud, their pump-handles shaken till the buckets splintered in the shaft, and their barns invaded." [13]

Soldiers were both amused and angered by the steely glares and icy hatred that greeted them. "Our soldiers," wrote one New Yorker, "seemed to be the objects of curious and eager inspection" by the inhabitants of Norfolk, "who had evidently been led to believe that the Yankee soldiers were semibarbarous and lacking in everything appertaining to civilized life." The women mustered "a rather masculine and vicious spirit in their remarks and actions," and the boys "cheered shrilly for Jeff. Davis." The civilians must have wondered what manner of men had occupied their town when many members of the 10th New York shaved their heads; some left the number "10" or the initials "NY" on their otherwise bare skulls. [14]

A Delaware chaplain reported a "latent and cordial hatred of the old Government" among most of the residents of Norfolk, who tried to scare away Union troops by assuring the invaders that they would soon be carried off by epidemics of yellow fever, typhoid, and even measles. Some of the women took out their anger on Federal patients at the local military hospital, bringing food and delicacies only to sick and wounded Confederate prisoners and ignoring the Yankees in distress. Others expressed their displeasure by refusing to walk beneath the United States flag flying over one segment of sidewalk, preferring to cross to the other side. A squad of Union soldiers rigged the flag up to a pulley so it could be shifted from one side of the street to the other, forcing passing ladies to make sudden course corrections or to pass, defeated, underneath the hated banner after all.[15]

At the same time Virginians on the lower Peninsula confronted their world turning upside down, residents of Richmond braced to meet the foe. As they had throughout the late winter and spring, Richmond newspapers attempted to inspire confidence in their beleaguered readers with encouraging pronouncements. Virginians were rising to meet the challenge, the *Dispatch* promised in early March. "The whole population are inflamed to the highest pitch of patriotic resistance." If anyone still needed to be convinced, the editorial rhetoric, which might have signified either confidence or fear, soared to dizzying heights: "Descendants of the nobles who wrested Magna Charta from a tyrant, and of nobler men than they — of the immortal champions of American liberty in '76 — come to the RESCUE OF VIRGINIA, and if she must perish let it be in a blaze of martyrdom whose flames shall light up the whole heavens, and carry to every land, the illumination of her virtues and the sparks which shall set every human heart on fire with admiration of her name and devotion to the cause of liberty!" Suggestions to apply bold tactics and unconventional weapons followed. The *Daily Dispatch* printed a series of articles concerning the history and proper use of pikes and assured readers that Union gunboats could be defeated by pouring oil on the James River and setting it on fire. Very early in the campaign, the *Examiner* suggested that the northern troops could be defeated by luring them into the interior, far from their supply line, as the Russians had done to Napoleon half a century before.[16]

Raising civilians' morale was only one goal of such boisterously patriotic lines as the *Dispatch*'s assurance that southerners "can die with dignity and glory, but . . . will never live to be slaves." Civilians must also mobilize to help defend their city. To that end, newspapers frequently announced the need for specific contributions and sacrifices. With battle looming, ladies were asked to prepare "an ample supply of bandages and lint." On other occasions, women were urged to make huge quantities of coffee for the soldiers, to donate their vegetables and ice to local hospitals, and to help manufacture saltpeter; butchers were asked to contribute animal bladders for use as ice bags. Sometimes opportunities to support the war effort came without warning. As Confederate soldiers passed through the city on their way to the Peninsula late in June, women and children carried still-steaming dinners, along with pitchers of "Confederate lemonade" — made of sorghum or vinegar and water — to the street for the soldiers to consume. McGuire participated in the great spontaneous feeding of Confederate troops as they passed through town. "Every table in Richmond seemed to have sent its dinner to Broad Street," she observed, "and our dear, hungry gray coats dined to their hearts' content, filled their haversacks, shouted 'Richmond forever!' and went on their way rejoicing."[17]

Although memoirists tended to romanticize the sudden and spontaneous outpouring of aid from the women of Richmond, a contemporary broadside took a less admiring tone, browbeating females to put aside their "tinted dresses" and their jewels, to braid back their long hair, to come to the aid of the "dead and the dying." In graphic detail the poem described the bloody hospital wards, the shattered men, the hard work that lay before them. "What! Trembling and paling already," the author demanded. "Before your dear mission's begun?" In other words, the poem seemed to tell Richmond women, buck up and do your duty like the rest of us.[18]

Many of the women of Richmond did just that, swallowing their fears and going to work with the wounded, temporarily throwing aside notions of propriety, and exposing themselves to previously undreamed of sights and sounds. Sara Rice Pryor fainted when she first saw the bloody stump of an amputated arm, but she steeled herself with "spirits of camphor" and went back to work. Nevertheless, she wrote years later, she would "veil myself closely" while walking to and from her hotel, to "shut out the dreadful sights in the street, — the squads of prisoners, and, worst of all, the open wagons in which the dead were piled." Such scenes stamped horrid visions in the memories of anyone who witnessed them. Pryor once saw, raised from a pile of corpses in a dead wagon, "a stiff arm," shaking "as it was driven down the street, as though the dead owner appealed to Heaven for vengeance."[19]

The steadfast patriotism displayed by women like Pryor won admirers all over the South. "I wish I were one of the women in Richmond!" Betty Herndon Maury of Fredericksburg exclaimed to her diary. "They have made for themselves a name that will be handed down with praise and honour for many generations." The *Dispatch* copied a laudatory article from a Raleigh newspaper, which described the conditions faced by the "Noble Women of Richmond": "Sorely pressed by the enemy, with almost famine prices for nearly every edible they purchase, with but few if any luxuries and delicacies, with the sounds and alarms of war around them, and with their own sons and brothers and husbands in the army, these noble women are devoting themselves to the sick and the wounded from every State who are thrown among them, with a patience, fortitude, and unwearied particularity of attention."[20]

Yet from Richmond all the way to Norfolk, examples of grave — if isolated — disaffection, ranging from unpatriotic opportunism, to duties shirked, to outright disloyalty threatened to sap the energy with which Virginians met the invasion. Months before, rumors had spread that traitors lurked among the workers at Richmond munitions plants; apparently, most of the shells produced at the government factory in the city failed to explode. At about the same time, the *Examiner* accused unnamed individuals of spreading panic and rumors of invasion around the city and called on the government to do something about their actions before they completely destroyed civilian morale.[21]

Even worse, between February, when the *Examiner* reported smugglers and extortioners charging exorbitant prices for necessities like salt, and the end of May, economic disloyalty had become epidemic. "The extortion of the hucksters in the city markets," according to the *Dispatch,* was "growing worse daily." The merchants in the market — "principally . . . foreigners, exempt from military duty . . . from taxes, and feeling no interest in our Government other than it is a good place to make money" — allegedly doubled their prices in the course of a single night. Merchants and individuals were criticized or even arrested for refusing to accept — or even for merely criticizing the stability of — Confederate currency. Other forms of opportunism emerged in the swarms of substitute agents profiting from the desire of eligible men to escape military service, the slipshod workmanship of the contractors building fortifications around the city, and even the outrageous prices newsboys set for newspapers they sold to soldiers. By early summer, scam artists, claiming to be recently mustered out of the army, were offering themselves as substitutes and promptly deserting after being paid.[22]

As Union troops dug in outside Yorktown, the *Dispatch* announced, "The curse of this war is AVARICE." Almost as soon as the shooting had started, "monopolists and extortioners" began their careers of "heartless and unlimited extractions." The victims included the soldier, "who is exposing himself to death on the battlefield, and the worse death in the hospital"; the soldiers' families, "left penniless at home"; and the government. In their "fleecing and swindling operations" these unpatriotic individuals "wage war on all and weaken both Government and people to the full extent of their ability." The editor recommended expanding the price-fixing activities of the government to include "the whole catalogue of things indispensable for the sustenance and clothing of the people." "If there is a man on this earth for whom a special punishment of direct character is reserved, he is the extortioner," who "is now doing all in his power to help the invading army. He is sowing the seeds of discontent, and depressing the public spirit by his oppression of the people amongst whom he lives." Even worse, "he will be ready at any moment to swear allegiance to Lincoln, or to any one who for the time may have the power to protect or appropriate what is to him dearer than life or honor — *his property.*"[23]

Another sign of premature war-weariness was the growing list of advertisements for substitutes that appeared in local newspapers throughout the late winter, spring, and summer. Long lines of men gathered at the offices of the Board of Inquisition trying to coax exemptions from militia duty. In mid-March, when two companies of the militia, each supposedly totaling more than 150 men, were supposed to gather, only a handful of members appeared. One fed-up correspondent from the army, speaking for "All Old Volunteers" in a letter to the *Dispatch,* criticized the stay-at-homes who "have shown remarkable aptitude at finding fault with us for what we have not done" and suggested they "now give us an illustration of how the thing ought to be done." To those able-bodied men who thus far refused to serve their country, the author exclaimed, "Have you no pride of character? Are you not ashamed? If you are not, have you no wife, no sister, no father, no mother, to be ashamed for you?" It was about time for those "young gentlemen, who finger downy mustaches, twirl ivory-headed canes, smoke cigars, and lounge about barrooms" to "step out and set yourselves up along-side of better men, as targets to be shot at. . . . The country can as well afford to lose you as any class we know of."[24]

Although most of the men who had opposed secession in 1861 had changed their minds or gone underground, an outrageous example of Unionist sentiment — and nerve — occurred during the night of April 20, when someone scrawled Unionist graffiti on the exterior walls of several Richmond businesses. Although "the writer was an indifferent poet and an illiterate and blasphemous man," the *Examiner* recorded for its readers the nasty epithets, which included a teasing reference to Richmond ladies' attempts to raise money for a "petticoat gunboat"; "The Lord is on our side, but, in consequence of pressing engagements elsewhere, could not attend at Pea Ridge, Donelson, etc."; and "Southern boasters grasp the dust, / In the Lord you vainly trust, / For the Lord you fain would cheat / With halcyon lips and Pluto's feet."[25]

No one was more aware than John B. Jones of the competing interests that divided residents of the Confederate capital. During the crisis, he complained of tobacco owners — southerners as well as foreigners — striving to ensure that their investments would not be destroyed if the city was evacuated. His complaints against Gen. John H. Winder and his corrupt and ineffective "Baltimore detectives" continued throughout the spring and summer. During the fighting, he almost gleefully reported that those detectives had gone into the field to defend the city but had remained too far to the rear to do any good, actually firing into their own troops on one occasion; later they had stripped the body of a dead Union colonel.[26]

As Union troops slowly consumed more of southeastern Virginia during the laborious march up the Peninsula, the potential for disloyalty rose dramatically. Prewar conditions may have encouraged some residents to reconsider their support for the Confederacy. Commercial feuds between Norfolk and Portsmouth and inland cities and Portsmouth's economic dependence on the Federal Navy Yard carried over into secession-era politics. Voters in Norfolk and Portsmouth had voted overwhelmingly for John Bell in 1860, and each elected a Unionist as its delegate to the Virginia secession convention. Yet, like Unionists in most other parts of the South, residents of Norfolk eventually seemed resigned to the necessity for war and supported the Confederacy enthusiastically, even after its capture by Union troops. After the mayor and city council announced that they would neither take the oath of allegiance nor cooperate with Federal authorities, they were removed from office. And when an election was finally held in late 1862, only 1,400 voters — out of prewar totals of more than 10,000 — bothered to participate.[27]

The *Dispatch* assured its readers that "the respectable portion" of the residents of Norfolk and Portsmouth remained loyal to the Confederacy, "regardless of threatened imprisonment." Those taking the oath of allegiance to the United States were limited to "a few low Irish and Dutch," who "were never regarded as reliable, and their weakness in the knees which has now been made manifest has excited the surprise of none." A resident of Norfolk escaping to Richmond estimated that fewer than 150 had "manifested any submission to the Yankees." Few attended the Fourth of July celebration in Yorktown; the women who dressed to represent the states of the Union were, in fact, "women of the town!" A little later in the summer, the *Dispatch* was delighted to report another sign of the continuing loyalty of Virginians enduring Yankee occupation: the funeral procession for a Confederate soldier from Norfolk was so long that the local commander forbade the burial of any more dead rebels in his city. A Union army newspaper published a report of a rebel girl in Yorktown pleading in vain with local photographers to take her picture posed stamping on the stars and stripes.[28]

Yet there were bona fide Unionists among the citizens of Portsmouth especially. "Whilst the Union men of Norfolk are reserved and fearful," reported the *New York Times,* "those of Portsmouth . . . gave the most enthusiastic testimony" to their loyalty. Many had been employed in the Navy Yard and were dismayed when the Confederate government destroyed their livelihoods. When Union troops arrived, small boys were "parading the streets" waving homemade U.S. flags, and larger versions were seen hanging from some houses. Shortly afterward, a "large and enthusiastic meeting" of Portsmouth Unionists passed a series of resolutions denouncing secession, supporting a quick suppression of the "rebellion," declaring that a majority of Virginians actually favored the Union, urging the government to recognize West Virginia's application for statehood, and asking Federal authorities to remove from office any local officials who refused to take the oath of allegiance to the United States. The meeting ended with a band playing patriotic songs and a procession through the streets of the city.[29]

A few Unionists became informants, helping Yankees search the homes and open the mail of secessionists suspected of holding arms or communicating with Confederates outside the occupation zone. The commander of the North Atlantic Blockading Squadron reported to the secretary of the navy that one of his ships had picked up three white men, one accompanied by his wife and two children, escaping by boat from Norfolk, who reported on the status of the USS *Merrimack*/CSS *Virginia,* rumored to be under construction.[30]

Sufficient disaffection toward the Confederacy existed for one Portsmouth resident to write many years later that "between the Loyalist and the Secessionist a gulf yawned. Oh, it rankled deep! I don't know as I have outgrown it yet." During the occupation, rebel girls refused to wear red with blue clothes. "They shunned those that did wear the hated color, and so the barriers grew. Contempt was shown on all occasions possible, dearest friendships ruptured."[31]

If the war loosed tensions within the white community on the Peninsula, it unleashed liberating and terrifying forces on the black community. The war had affected Virginia slaves almost immediately. From the beginning, refugees had fled into the tiny haven of Union authority at Fort Monroe to escape hard labor on Confederate fortifications. Although their numbers fluctuated throughout the summer and fall, by June 1861, 176 free black men were laboring on the river batteries at Jamestown; another 50 were working at Yorktown. Because few slave owners were voluntarily offering their slaves to work on Confederate defenses by late 1861, the state and Confederate governments passed several laws regulating the impressment of slave laborers as well as the conscription of free African Americans. The latter could be required to work up to 180 days, subject to a fine of up to $100. With the onset of the campaigning season — and especially after Confederate strategists began to understand the vulnerability of the Peninsula to Federal at-

Northern sketch artist Edwin Forbes made this study of contrabands in
Virginia making their way to Union lines.
Frank Leslie's Illustrated Newspaper, *August 20, 1864*

tack — hundreds of slaves were put to work on the fortifications. In response
to Gen. John B. Magruder's frantic call for laborers, fourteen different counties sent a total of more than 1,300 impressed bondsmen to the Peninsula.[32]

Slave owners commonly complained of the harsh conditions their human
property had to endure, and accounts of poor and scanty rations, disease,
punishing work schedules, and abusive discipline appeared in Richmond
newspapers. Even before the crash building program of the spring and summer of 1862, a correspondent for the *Examiner,* the pages of which almost
always carried articles critical of the government, found appalling conditions
at the "Negro Engineer Hospital." "Stench and filth abound in intolerable
quantities," he reported, "and the poor Negroes are dying off like penned
sheep. . . . It is a disgrace to humanity to behold their utter neglect." A year
later, conditions had not improved. "We doubt if the government is aware of
the treatment of Negroes, sent by the patriotic planters of the counties to
work on fortifications around Richmond," the *Examiner* scolded. Fed only
a small amount of meat and unleavened bread and water three times a day,
the slaves were expected to put in long hours of heavy, sometimes dangerous
labor. Hunger drove some to snatch food from others' plates; some of the
rations meant for the afflicted slaves were being sent elsewhere. Many plant-

ers complained about the feeble condition in which their slaves returned home, while others castigated the government for failing to pay for those slaves who died.[33]

Slaves understandably hated the difficult, dangerous work and were soon streaming into Union army camps near Fort Monroe. Gen. Benjamin F. Butler initiated his famous policy of "confiscating" slaves as "contraband of war" at Fort Monroe during the war's first summer. Butler immediately put them to work — deducting the cost of their rations from their meager pay — and reported that removing them from the rebel work force had already paid direct dividends. He once boasted of the escape of a dozen black men who had previously been working on a Confederate battery that had just that morning fired on his men. Although at first the status of the escaped slaves was nebulous — apparently Butler thought of them not as free people but as temporarily confiscated commodities — it soon became clear that they would not be returned to their masters. As United States government policy evolved during the next two years, those African Americans who managed to get into Union lines were, for all intents and purposes, declared free men and women. By July 1861, at least 900 had run, walked, and rowed into Union lines in the area of Fort Monroe, and the flood of bondspeople flowing to freedom never crested.[34]

The opening of the 1862 campaign provided even more opportunities for freedom. Every Union patrol moving through contested territory seemed to bring in escaped slaves. One cavalryman, early in the war, got lost in the woods and was guided to Fort Monroe by a slave. For that "little piece of service," he wrote smugly, "I gave him his freedom." After a cavalry raid returned to Yorktown with a number of confiscated horses and fifty or sixty contrabands, an officer asked why they had brought the black people with them. "Why they followed us and we could not stop them," answered one of the men. Slaves took any opportunity, no matter how unexpected, to flee into Union lines, leaving plows standing in the fields and taking off with neither a hat nor a coat when the chance to join a band of Yankees presented itself.[35]

The way that the appearance of Union troops on the Peninsula drove a wedge between confident slave owners and their human property can be seen in the diary of Edmund Ruffin, one of the most ardent defenders of slavery and of the Confederacy. Ruffin's property lay in the path of the Federal army, and his diary includes often poignant descriptions of the depredations committed against his house and farms. Ruffin also carefully recorded the manner in which the war destroyed slavery in his rural neighborhood. As Yankee gunboats ascended the nearby river and Union forces occupied the farms

JAMES MARTEN

and plantations of his son and neighbors, slaves ran away or, at the very least, remained "at home idle, & in quiet rebellion." Only the oldest, the sickest, or those with newborn babies stayed behind, along with a handful of free blacks hired to help bring in the harvest.[36]

One former slave described a fairly typical experience to his interviewer many years after the war. Charles Grandy, a nineteen-year-old slave when the war began, grew up on a plantation near Hickory Ground, Virginia. Rumors that the Union army was enlisting soldiers sometime during 1862 inspired him and some other slaves to make a break for it. Upon reaching Norfolk, Charles spent a few days "wandering about the outskirts" of the city, subsisting on wild berries and pondering his next move. After stumbling across a friendly Union soldier, he accompanied him into camp and was soon working as a cook for the Federals. Later given a uniform and a gun, he served for a time with the 19th Wisconsin and subsequently reenlisted as a guard at Fort Monroe, where he served out the rest of the war. Long after, he attended reunions of Civil War veterans. Another young slave, Richard Slaughter, was thirteen when the Yankees landed on the Peninsula. He and his family were picked up near City Point by a gunboat and taken to Hampton. After a bout with the measles, he became a well-traveled "government water boy" on various Union ships, including one that carried President Lincoln to meet with Gen. Joseph Hooker. He joined the army as a cook in a Maryland regiment during the siege of Petersburg and proudly recalled the "day I walked up the road in Richmond" after its capture.[37]

The movement of slaves into the promised land of Union lines resembled a biblical exodus. A few months after the campaign ended, there were barely enough slaves left in Charles City County to do necessary farmwork. Yet not all slaves left their masters. Many were "refugeed" to places safely in the rear of the army, in an effort duplicated throughout the contested parts of the Confederacy to preserve the best and most productive slaves. Other African Americans, left behind by white families fleeing before the invaders, stayed on plantations and farms and actually operated them on their own. Still others, whose masters chose to stick it out on the Peninsula, stayed on because the mere threat of their leaving — the ease with which they could walk, in a day or two, to freedom — gave them leverage over their desperate owners. Finally, slavery was technically legal in those parts of the Peninsula that remained in Union hands throughout the war. The Emancipation Proclamation exempted occupied portions of the Confederacy, including Elizabeth City, York, Norfolk, and Princess Anne Counties, where, as late as the summer of 1863, there were still 5,000 slaves.[38]

Even as a war evolving into a fight for their freedom raged around them,

African Americans sampled the fruits of liberty. They did not have to run to the safety of Union forces to enjoy the sea change in race relations beginning to make itself felt on the Peninsula. Slaves refused to work — or at least refused to work as hard. They broke tools, faked illnesses, and in other ways resisted the orders of their masters. Runaway slaves sometimes banded together and foraged for subsistence from the farms of hard-pressed southerners and, on occasion, even attacked Union troops. Others established small colonies that were within the protection of Union gunboats but not under Federal authority. These settlements sometimes acted as way stations for fugitives seeking freedom. The escaped slaves maintained communication with their still-enslaved friends and families, often returning time and again to visit or to help others escape. A few brave souls ventured as far as Confederate Richmond. A northerner working with contrabands stated with admiration that "colored men will help colored men and they will work along the by paths and get through." They did not fear the white people and believed the risk of being recaptured was worth the chance to free their families.[39]

The enthusiasm with which slaves absconded from plantations and farms throughout the summer of 1862 and later in the war astonished and disappointed white southerners. Although it is difficult to establish the exact number of contrabands within Union lines at any given time, by 1864 there were 31,654 in southeastern Virginia and northeastern North Carolina.[40]

"They have not proven as faithful as we expected," complained the Richmond *Enquirer,* and even those "who have been tenderly treated by kind mistresses, have heartlessly deserted them to follow after strangers." Even crippled and elderly slaves, "maintained by their masters purely from humanity," have "deprived themselves of the comfort and shelter of their decrepitude by running away!" The *Enquirer* suggested that slaves assumed that the Yankees would care for them and that "their future will be nothing but fine clothes and holyday [*sic*]." But southerners must not be too harsh. These "poor deluded creatures . . . have been beguiled by our enemies, and seduced by every possible appliance to forsake their duty." They failed to realize that the Yankees' motive in encouraging them to escape "was not good to *them,* but evil to their masters." The article went on to catalog rumors of abuse and betrayal on the part of Federal authorities: Yankees shipped contrabands to Santo Domingo or Cuba; they put former slaves to work in iron foundries in Pennsylvania or the wheat fields of Ohio at starvation wages; when "the terrors of the Northern winter closes in upon them . . . they will suffer as they have never dreamed of," but "they will find that Abolition charity ended when it seduced them from their homes." In fact, the newspaper suggested, freedom had begun a "retrogradation towards their native barbarism" that was "both astonishing and painful." All of the weaknesses and foibles of their race were unleashed in the separation of slaves from their friends and teachers — their masters. "The frivolity, the low tastes, and the supreme indolence and improvidence of the African race, seem to assert their full sway." In the knowing tone with which white southerners often couched comments about the character of their slaves, the *Enquirer* assured its readers that "they wish no greater happiness than to lie about in the sun, gaze at a parade, and eat the rations which Lincoln has provided for them. They furnish swift proof that the negro is a parasitic being, destined to find his highest development and greatest happiness and usefulness under the shelter and control of a superior race."[41]

Former slaves discovered that many white northerners shared southerners' views on racial superiority, causing blacks and whites in the occupied portions of the Peninsula to form complex and ambiguous relationships. On the one hand, they found common cause in the war against the Confederacy. Union commanders soon discovered the value of the contrabands' knowledge of the local terrain, of Confederate troop dispositions, even of the white southerners' state of mind. In the first few months of the war, Federal patrols venturing out from their slice of the Peninsula near Newport News relied on black informants. One soldier reported that "we get all the information we desire from the niggers." Black spies warned Union officials of the building of the CSS *Virginia,* while a servant in the Confederate White House frequently spied on Jefferson Davis. During the Peninsula campaign, Yankee officers relied on escaped slaves for a great deal of military intelligence, ranging from the numbers of Confederate troops holding vital positions to the nature of their armaments and the best routes through enemy territory. McClellan apparently learned that Stonewall Jackson was nearing his flank from a "contraband servant" who had recently run away from the 20th Georgia.[42]

On the other hand, the officers and men of the invading army often expressed little interest in the well-being of the black men, women, and children they encountered. As early as 1861, the army had begun to feel overwhelmed by the large numbers of African American refugees flocking into its lines, and attempts were made to ship black laborers to other theaters of war — North Carolina, for instance — with dismal results. A year later, an appalled army officer reported that a number of contrabands had been placed on isolated farms with neither supplies nor supervision and claimed that many were "at the point of starvation." A year later, the new commander of the Department of Virginia, Gen. John A. Dix, who did not want to feed so many mouths and who doubted that the runaways would be of much use to the army, at first tried to ship contrabands north. Failing in this, he established them in a camp on Craney Island, at the mouth of the Elizabeth River, trying to isolate them and keep them out of his way.[43]

As happened elsewhere in the occupied Confederacy, tensions between African Americans and Union soldiers on the Peninsula foreshadowed post-war race relations as it became clear that the army was, in general, more interested in controlling than in assisting former slaves looking for help and protection. All able-bodied African Americans were put to work, but their pay came not in cash but in food and clothing — a system remarkably, and no doubt alarmingly, to many of the workers — like slavery.[44]

Relationships between the races worsened during the Union buildup and the early stages of the Peninsula campaign. Federal troops often rampaged through black settlements looting the people's sparse property, killing their livestock, and raping the women. Army quartermasters frequently sold on the black market supplies and rations meant to be distributed to freedpeople; paymasters withheld at least $10,000 of the wages appropriated for black laborers; and common soldiers sometimes took over the little houses built by freedmen next to the chimneys of the burned-out village of Hampton, leaving black families to fend for themselves.[45]

In groups and as individuals, Union troops practiced deliberate as well as almost casual cruelty against contrabands. Newspapers printed by and for Union soldiers serving on the Peninsula ran ads for runaway slaves, while a paper published by the 5th Pennsylvania at Williamsburg declared that only "white folks" belonged under the paper's motto of "Union" and "Freedom." Just to make sure his readers understood, the editor went on to say, "We do not wish it even insinuated that we have any sympathy with abolitionism." Readers got the point when they read a satirical article called "Lecture on Woman's Rights, by a Colored Lady," which was filled with racist — not to mention sexist — language and images. It began, "Good ebening, wite folk . . . I appear before you did ebening to lucidate and splainify to you de subjec of Woman's Rights," and went downhill from there. One unit went beyond racist declarations. In their spare time, officers and enlisted men in the 99th New York allegedly returned many escaped slaves to their masters for $20 to $50 a person.[46]

One day, members of the 5th Maryland grabbed a black child wandering through camp and began tossing him high into the air and catching him in a blanket, a favorite pastime of soldiers in camp. In this case, the blanket "must have been rotten," wrote a witness, "for when the poor fellow came down . . . he went through and fell on the ground, and broke his neck." The soldiers "were very sorry" — perhaps because "that broke up the blanket game for awhile." Less deadly but no less demeaning was the constant teas-

ing of the Union troops, who played on the alleged superstition and gulli-
bility of the slaves. A reporter with the army wrote that Yankees would play
"the game of astonishment," telling wide-eyed listeners that hundreds of
thousands of troops were advancing on the Peninsula from all directions.[47]

Observers were still reporting the abuse of free black people by the Yankees on the Peninsula two years later. A representative of the New England
Freedmen's Aid Society reported that an old woman had been "driven at the
point of the bayonet" into a contraband camp, that mothers were unjustly
jailed and prevented from seeing their children, and that respectable black
citizens were evicted from their homes for no reason. The treatment of free
blacks and contrabands was so bad, the report continued, that "many negroes who had had kind masters preferred to return to slavery rather than be
driven to the camps."[48]

Yet some Union troops took a closer, more compassionate look at African
Americans they encountered. Elisha Hunt Rhodes attended a "jubilee meeting held by the Negroes," describing a sermon in which the black preacher
argued that every man must seek his own salvation: "Brethren," he announced, "the Scripture says, 'Every man for himself. Every tub on its own
bottom.'" "Not exactly Scripture," wrote the bemused Yankee, "but it came
near the truth." At least one private appreciated how the newly freed blacks
must have felt. When his regiment disembarked at Fort Monroe, he recalled
years later, "Negroes were everywhere, and went about their work with an
air of importance born of their new-found freedom."[49]

Such expressions of sympathy and attempts to understand African Americans were unfortunately rare in the army. Less than three weeks after Union
troops occupied Norfolk and Portsmouth, a race riot broke out in the smaller
of the two towns. The violence occurred after a reign of terror by some of
the infamous slave-catchers of the 99th New York, who led the army in
atrocities committed against black Virginians. The tension burst into public
violence after a soldier in the 99th beat up a regimental cook, who shot and
killed his attacker. Members of the regiment rioted, killing at least three and
perhaps ten blacks and wounding dozens more. The Richmond *Dispatch*
reported up to a hundred casualties among the contrabands, with a half
dozen or more killed or mortally injured. Not surprisingly, the rebel paper
described with glee the "circumstances of atrocity and blood-thirstiness" of
the Yankees, who were "infuriated to madness" by the killing of their comrade by a black man.[50]

Along with the often dubious relationships they formed with Union
troops, black Virginians were soon introduced to northern missionaries who
came South to help prepare contrabands for their new lives as free men and

women. At a purely material level, they could use the help. Crowded into often informally organized and poorly administered "contraband camps," black families faced disease, death, and degradation that in some respects rivaled the conditions in the worst slave quarters. A few former slaves had the chance to become their own bosses by renting farms on the abandoned lands now controlled by the United States government, but most lived in the squalid camps. The experience must have seemed strange and confusing. The sheer numbers of people, black and white; the military personnel, missionaries, merchants, and other white northerners bustling to and fro; the conflicting and overlapping spheres of authority among military and civilian organizations operating in the area; and the expectations among ostensible friends from the North that all black people be obedient and hardworking made for a new and exciting but also challenging and sometimes dangerous world.

A Massachusetts missionary described newcomers to Craney Island as "almost wholly destitute of clothing" and "covered with vermin." Some were housed in newly built barracks, but most lived in makeshift quarters: tents propped against brick chimneys, with interior lighting provided only by pine knots or rags burning in heated fat. According to an inspector for one of the northern philanthropies, each black family in one of the freedmen's settlements was assigned one and one-quarter acres for their own cultivation as well as a cabin. Yet the "hovels" in which they lived — many measured only ten by twelve feet — had leaky roofs, no windows, and cheap log and stick chimneys. Cooking utensils were limited, and some families were forced to cook and eat out of tin cups. Although they relied on the government for many of their supplies, some of the more enterprising contrabands had established stores at which they sold flour, sugar, meat, and other necessities they had brought over from Fort Monroe.[51]

The emotional challenges of freedom — or the transition to freedom represented by residence in a contraband camp — were also difficult. When they arrived a few months after the campaign, Sarah and Lucy Chase, Quaker sisters from Massachusetts who worked as teachers, described the loneliness of wives whose husbands were off in the army; the unhappiness of women who, even in slavery, had not done the kind of field work expected of them on Craney Island; the despair of mothers whose children had died; and the confusion of everyone "made aware by painful experience, that, in these war-times, one knows not what a day will bring forth." Yet another source of constant concern was the health of the former slaves. Even the nearly 2,000 residents in the tightly controlled contraband camp on Craney Island suffered poor health. Consumption was "sadly prevalent" and particularly deadly to the "very delicate . . . African constitution." Sarah and Lucy Chase described residents as "half clad," and the exposure in the damp coastal winter brought "coughs and colds into every barrack." Every day, the Chases sadly reported, two or three patients in the camp hospital died.[52]

Not surprisingly, some contrabands wondered whether they had made the right decision in fleeing the only homes — albeit homes polluted by the institution of slavery — they had ever known for uncertain lives with these hard-to-fathom Yankees. The superintendent of contrabands at Fort Monroe reported that a delegation of black men from Suffolk had come to him, seeking guarantees that they would not be put in irons and chains, whipped — "just as in slavery" — and sent to Cuba. "That was the story up there, and they were frightened and didn't know what to do."[53]

Despite crushing hardships and emotional insecurity, freedpeople of all ages seemed to believe that the most treasured benefit of freedom was the opportunity to receive an education. The first school for African Americans on the Peninsula had opened in September 1861, when Rev. Lewis C. Lockwood, a representative of the American Missionary Association, established a Sunday school as well as a day school for the escaped slaves crowding into Fort Monroe. His first teacher was a local woman named Mary Peake, who soon began teaching evening classes for adult African Americans. A chaplain in a Massachusetts regiment reported an "exhibition" performed by two hundred schoolchildren for the soldiers, which included declamation pieces and singing. "Each child," wrote the clergyman, "seemed to look pleadingly at the soldierly group present, as if saying, 'Am I not worthy to be free?'"[54]

Adults and children alike combined schooling with work. Contrabands labored as stevedores, laundresses, cooks, and common laborers for $10 a day — half that for teenaged boys or sickly men. Some became orderlies for officers, while a few found jobs as blacksmiths and carpenters and many others worked on farms run by the government. But they all sought an education. Women studied large "ABC" cards hanging from walls as they sewed, while teenagers put in long days of backbreaking work for the United States Sanitary Commission before getting out their spelling books and primers for an evening of learning. A white teacher in Norfolk admiringly reported in the summer of 1864 that most of the African Americans who labored on a nearby farm came into school after work, studying until ten at night by candlelight, sitting in their ragged clothes on the floor when the desks in the crowded schoolroom filled up. They pored over such American Tract Society publications as *Advice for Freedmen, Friendly Counsels for Freedmen, Out of the House of Bondage,* and *The Ten Commandments Illustrated.* Other educational books and pamphlets included *The Lincoln Primer, The Freedmen's*

Spelling Book, and *The Freedmen's Primer.* In biblical extracts, short biographies, and other selections, the books demonstrated values like hard work, thrift, loyalty, and philanthropy. Slavery and secession were criticized, abolitionists were praised, and the argument was made that not all races were alike.[55]

As the area under Union occupation moved up the Peninsula, so did the establishment of schools for the slaves freed by the evacuation of their white masters. By late 1862, fifteen instructors taught twelve hundred pupils in Norfolk; two years later, the American Missionary Association employed more than sixty teachers in Norfolk, Portsmouth, and the surrounding area. Although most black people in southeastern Virginia would not have access to schooling until months or even years after the Peninsula campaign ended, they immediately made achieving an education their top priority. One northern teacher triumphantly began a letter home by exclaiming, "I am rejoicing with the happy negro in his greed for letters."[56]

Eventually, many of the northerners who worked among the contrabands came to admire them greatly. "They warm my heart, these warm-hearted people," wrote a woman missionary. "One almost worships the wealth of love with which God has blessed them, and willingly forgives the barbarous assaults they make on ones [*sic*] patience and forbearance, remembering that slavery alone is responsible for the scars which so disfigure them." But those sentiments came only after several months of contact. When the Chase sisters first arrived at Craney Island, they spoke rather harshly about the freedpeople. They believed that they were not yet fit for freedom, that they could not yet compete with white laborers, and that "to talk of them after the manner of ignorant, enthusiastic philanthropists, is giving undue praise to the barbarous teachings of slavery." One of their first direct experiences with their new black acquaintances was at a prayer meeting, where, the sisters clucked, "we saw a painful exhibition of their barbarism." The intensely Quaker women complained that "their religious feeling is purely emotional; void of principle, and of no practical utility." They believed their supervisor when he said that the blacks "will rise from prayer and lie or steal, if the way opens therefor." Their letter even attempted to recreate the dialect of the illiterate man leading the worship service: "ohuh Lorder! This afaternoonugh, hear our prayerer! . . . And dontuh let usuh take helluh by stormuh!" Such attitudes about blacks would be as difficult to dislodge in northern whites as in Confederate troops who had fought at Seven Pines.[57]

The aftermath of fighting on the Peninsula was, most immediately, a matter of accommodating the dead and wounded. After the more than 20,000

Confederate casualties of the Seven Days, the smell of death filled Richmond. Bloated bodies burst the cheap coffins in which they had been placed. There were so many funerals on any given day that attendance at individual ceremonies was sparse. And still the city swelled with the arrival of families of stricken soldiers, looking hopefully among the wounded and resignedly among the dead for loved ones. Even after the fighting moved farther north, sleeping soldiers cluttered Richmond sidewalks. The strain of the huge number of soldiers and other transients showed. Tobacco juice seemed to stain every inch of walkway; hotels were dirty and run-down and lacked soap. Among the troops coming into the city in the aftermath of the battles outside Richmond were the first conscripted Confederates. They were, according to one historian, "slouching, clay-faced, 'salt marsh' men from South Carolina and North Carolinians of equally poor physique." Wearing makeshift uniforms and grim frowns, they were preyed on by Richmond liquor dealers and gamblers.[58]

On another level, the hard-fought victories of May and June seemed to amplify the confidence that had begun to appear in the spring. After the battles, a Confederate wit issued a cheeky broadside explaining "The Reasons Why McClellan Did Not Capture Richmond": he had "two 'Hills' to pass," "a 'Stonewall' to mount," and "a 'Longstreet' to march through." However, "seeing the impossibility of attempting such a capture, he wisely concluded to 'SKEDDADLE.'"[59]

A different tone surfaced in a *Dispatch* editorial published during the confusing days after the vicious fighting of the Seven Days. Although echoing earlier, confident calls to arms, it also recognized that not all Confederates were pulling their weight. Calling on stragglers to return to duty, it urged civilians "to show the straggler no quarter." They should be ridiculed and "frowned down." No one should feed them or give them a bed to sleep in. The editor appealed to the women of Virginia — "more especially . . . the younger portion of them" — "to treat the renegades with the scorn they deserve; to drive them back to their colors with the scorn which nobody but a woman knows how to manifest." Virginians must force these men to do their duty, lest "their homes be pillaged, their daughters . . . outraged, their sons . . . made bond slaves, by the most detestable race that God ever permitted to breathe the air of life."[60]

This harsh brand of patriotism matched the mood of John B. Jones. The rather hard-to-please patriot complained in mid-July that "the people are too jubilant, I fear, over our recent successes near the city. A great many *skulkers* from the army are seen daily in the streets, and it is said there are 3000 men here subject to conscript duty, who have not been enrolled. The business of purchasing substitutes is prevailing alarmingly." The economic opportunism of the previous winter and spring continued unabated. When the Army of Northern Virginia marched through the capital city in mid-August, merchants turned the stirring generosity of Richmond residents when Confederate soldiers passed through the city a few weeks before on its head; they made a mint by selling the veterans food at greatly inflated prices.[61]

The potential for disaffection so clearly foreshadowed during the crisis in the early months of 1862 burst into violence against property and authority a year later, when women, men, and boys rioted through Richmond's downtown to protest high prices and shortages. Other factions also emerged in the city as the war dragged on. Not surprisingly, given contemporary attitudes about Judaism and Jews, that segment of the population was frequently blamed for the speculation in necessities and other goods. Just as it had in the weeks leading up to the Peninsula campaign, the Richmond city government frequently clashed with the Confederate government over goals and methods. And as the Confederacy collapsed, Richmond experienced the same doubt and disorder — residents did not distinguish themselves in the drunken riot that accompanied the fire on the night the Confederate forces evacuated the capital — that the rest of the Confederacy faced.[62]

Even as factions within the city struggled to shape the Confederate war effort, large swaths of the southeastern tip of the Peninsula remained contested territory. McClellan had taken most of his troops with him late in August when he headed north. But a significant, if not particularly threatening, Federal presence remained for nearly two years before the Army of the Potomac once again invaded the Peninsula. After Confederates and Federals settled into the uneasy quiet of the post-campaign stalemate, rebel raiders would dodge Yankee patrols, according to General Dix, "carrying off both white men and negroes to the army at Richmond."[63]

For the next couple of years, a ragged kind of war developed in the no-man's-land between the armies. Confederate as well as Union foraging parties plundered civilian property. When Confederate engineers drew a map of the area in 1863, they indicated scores of "ruins," especially in places where the Union army had dug in during the Peninsula campaign. In a typical operation during the second week of December 1862, Federal Brig. Gen. Henry M. Naglee led a reconnaissance by several regiments and a section of artillery out of Yorktown into Gloucester, Matthews, King and Queen, and Middlesex Counties. He met little resistance but seized sheep and hogs being driven to Richmond, burned a tannery making leather for the Confederacy, and captured more than a dozen Confederates — "rangers" he called them —

engaged in recruiting men for the rebel army, collecting supplies, and "catching runaway negroes." [64]

From time to time, Union soldiers stationed in Norfolk or Portsmouth, venturing beyond normally "safe" perimeters, were ambushed by Confederate irregulars. Hiding out in the Great Dismal Swamp, sheltering on the numerous farms and tiny backwoods villages in the area, taking advantage of the thinly spread Union line, guerrillas struck small groups of Union soldiers throughout 1863. Union commanders also fretted about the illicit mail sent between secessionists in occupied Norfolk and Richmond (some of which, the army feared, contained important military intelligence), the periodic cutting of the telegraph lines between Jamestown and other Union positions, and occasional attacks on Yankee vessels plying the James River. As late as 1864, when the massive Union army was approaching Petersburg to the west of Jamestown, a Union patrol was ambushed by Confederates, apparently irregulars, who were never tracked down.[65]

Sometimes rebel forces mustered the resources to attack northern strong points. Late in March 1863, Union pickets were attacked and an attempt made to burn the "public stores" at Fort Yorktown, and a few days later Confederates attacked Williamsburg, where they fought a sharp skirmish with Union troops. The Confederates lost eighteen men killed and wounded, while five Yankees were wounded, two "murdered" — and their boots stolen — and six still missing a day after the fight. A Union officer claimed that disloyal residents had "aided, if not planned," the Sabbath morning attack by guiding Confederates into the city, placing them in strategic positions along certain streets, and preparing packs of supplies to be taken out later. Perhaps because of the continuing danger of wearing blue uniforms on the ostensibly occupied Peninsula, Federal recruiters managed to induce fewer than one hundred men from the area to join the First Loyal East Virginia Infantry.[66]

The ongoing, low-level conflict between armed northerners and southerners was overshadowed by the far more dramatic transformations taking place in the lives of former slaves. White Virginians had feared that the increased freedom given to local African Americans would lead to intolerable disorder and crime. By the end of 1862, wrote one resident of Portsmouth, "The slaves seduced from their homes" had come into town, "idle impudent and thievish dreaming of freedom by first of January, and liable to be led to acts of disorder and violence by rabid Abolitionists." An alarming — at least to local white residents — example of the consequences of the new racial order occurred in October 1862, after some of the former slaves of William Allen, a Jamestown planter and the wealthiest man in Virginia, took over parts of his property and burned one of his houses. When a party of whites and a free African American stumbled across a group of those same slaves, they promptly got into what can only be called a misguided argument about the fact that the former slaves had left wheat in the field and had no right to burn down Allen's house. The black men consulted one another and then, after about one hundred contraband men, women, and children appeared to witness the proceedings, shot their captives. Although seriously wounded, the free black escaped; the three white men were killed.[67]

One of the most severe tests of the peaceful occupation of Norfolk — and an indication of the extent to which race relations would remain a thorn in the side of Federal administrators throughout the war — was the murder of Lt. A. L. Sanborn, a white officer in the 1st United States Colored Troops. Dr. David M. Wright shot and killed the Yankee while he was marching at the head of his troops down Main Street in July 1863. After a quick military trial and several appeals (President Lincoln refused to overturn the sentence), Wright was hanged in October.[68]

For the time being, violence took a back seat to the recognition of black people's legal rights. Certain moments punctuated that freedom: the establishment by African Americans of the Human Aid Society, the Temperance Society, and the Anglo-African Educational Society; the decision by a group of one hundred former slaves to divide an old plantation among themselves; the January 1, 1863, parade in Yorktown celebrating the Emancipation Proclamation — even though it failed to free a single one of the four thousand marchers. One moment came in 1863, when a black man was called to testify against a white woman in a civil trial near Fort Monroe. Another appeared in the form of a math problem in the *Freedman,* a monthly published by the American Tract Society and used in some of the schools for contrabands on the Peninsula: "If the freedmen should kill, or take prisoners, 394 of the rebels who numbered 462, how many would be left to run away?" The response — "Not many, I hope" (the answer was actually 68, of course, "but I don't believe the freedmen let them run far"). This problem represented an entertaining twist on Confederate arithmetic problems that exaggerated rebel battlefield prowess.

Yet another moment of victory came two years after the fury of the Seven Days marked the end of the Peninsula campaign, when Norfolk schools closed to celebrate the Fourth of July 1864. Twelve hundred people, mostly African Americans and some white teachers and officers, gathered to hear prayers, a sermon, and a letter from a northern benevolent society. Children sang, the Declaration of Independence and the Emancipation Proclamation were read, and an elderly freedman named Father Parker declared in a short speech: "This is the greatest Fourth of July I even knew. I have been here fifty years: I never saw a gathering of this kind before. The colored people to have a public library! The colored people to be educated! Thank God for what my eyes see, and my ears hear! I have often heard the white people talk of the day of Independence; but this is my first and your first one. . . . How can we thank the blessed Lord enough for permitting us to hold this day!"[69]

The forces unleashed by war in general and by the Peninsula campaign in particular had transformed southeastern Virginia. The institution of slavery had sustained irreparable damage. Despite the ambiguous relationships between African Americans and Yankees, slaves continued to flee their masters and to seek paid employment and a basic education from their northern allies. For white Virginians, cracks in Confederate unity that appeared in the months leading up to the worst military threat Richmond faced until 1864 would widen into fissures that, though not exactly crippling to the southern war effort, would undermine notions of nationalism and patriotism with which the fledgling nation had hoped to compensate for shortages of manpower and military resources. But these dramatic changes in the lives of the black and white residents of Richmond and the Peninsula are no doubt more apparent in hindsight than they were to the men and women struggling to adjust to the demands of freedom, to the exigencies of enforced occupation by enemy troops, or to the dreadful excitement of life in the Confederate capital. For them, the anticlimactic withdrawal of Federal troops from the Peninsula provided only a temporary reprieve from the "restless anxiety" that had dominated their summer.

NOTES

1. Samuel S. Thompson, *Some Personal Experiences at Fortress Monroe in 1862* (Philadelphia: n.p., 1915), 10; Richmond *Examiner,* January 27, 1862.

2. Emory M. Thomas, *The Confederate State of Richmond: A Biography of the Capital* (Austin: University of Texas Press, 1971), 68–69; Richmond *Examiner,* January 25, February 5, 13, 6, 1862.

3. T. C. De Leon, *Four Years in Rebel Capitals* (Mobile: Gossip Printing Co., 1890), 236–37.

4. Richmond *Examiner,* January 22, 1862; B. H. Wilkins, *"War Boy": A True Story of the Civil War and Re-Construction Days* (Tullahoma, Tenn.: Wilson Bros., 1990), 41.

5. Sallie A. Brock Putnam, *Richmond during the War* (New York: G. W. Carleton, 1867), 89.

6. Edward A. Pollard, *Southern History of the War: The Second Year of the War*

(New York: Charles B. Richardson, 1865), 32–33; Thomas, *Confederate State of Richmond,* 90, 92–93; Richmond *Dispatch,* April 22, 1862.

7. Judith W. McGuire, *Diary of a Southern Refugee during the War* (1867; reprint, Lincoln: University of Nebraska Press, 1995), 107, 110; John B. Jones, *A Rebel War Clerk's Diary,* ed. Earl Schenck Miers (New York: Sagamore Press, 1958), 75; Cary Harrison, "A Virginia Girl in the First Year of the War," *Century Illustrated Monthly Magazine* 30 (August 1885): 611.

8. Pollard, *Southern History of the War,* 33; Thomas, *Confederate State of Richmond,* 93–96; Louis H. Manarin, ed., *Richmond at War: The Minutes of the City Council, 1861–1865* (Chapel Hill: University of North Carolina Press, 1966), 167, 186.

9. Jones, *Rebel War Clerk's Diary,* 78; Richmond *Dispatch,* May 22, 1862.

10. Spencer Wilson, "Experiment in Reunion: The Union Army in Civil War Norfolk and Portsmouth, Virginia" (Ph.D. diss., University of Maryland, 1973), 43–45, 60–68 (quotation on p. 68).

11. Lenoir Chambers, "Notes on Life in Occupied Norfolk, 1862–1865," *Virginia Magazine of History and Biography* 73 (April 1965): 133–35, 138; Wilson, "Experiment in Reunion," 52–56, 72–91, 109–11; Yorktown *Cavalier,* July 30, 1862.

12. "Diary of Miss Harriette Cary, Kept by Her from May 6, 1862, to July 24, 1862," *Tyler's Quarterly Historical and Genealogical Magazine* 9 (October 1927): 106–7, 110–11.

13. George Alfred Townsend, *Rustics in Rebellion: A Yankee Reporter on the Road to Richmond* (Chapel Hill: University of North Carolina Press, 1950), 47–49, 60–61.

14. Charles W. Cowtan, *Services of the Tenth New York Volunteers (The National Zouaves) in the War of the Rebellion* (New York: Charles S. Ludwig, 1882), 79–80.

15. Rev. Thomas G. Murphey, *Four Years in the War: The History of the First Regiment of Delaware Veteran Volunteers* (Philadelphia: James S. Claxton, 1866), 57–58, 70–71, 64.

16. Richmond *Dispatch,* March 10, May 2, 5, 26, 19, 1862; Richmond *Examiner,* March 18, 1862.

17. Richmond *Dispatch,* March 6, May 5, 22, 26, June 3, 1862; Katharine M. Jones, *Ladies of Richmond, Confederate Capital* (Indianapolis: Bobbs-Merrill, 1962), 108–9; McGuire, *Diary,* 103.

18. "Ladies of Richmond," Confederate Broadsides Collection (on-line), Rare Books and Manuscripts, Z. Smith Reynolds Library, Wake Forest University, Winston-Salem, N.C. (repository cited hereafter as WFU).

19. Jones, *Ladies of Richmond,* 130–31.

20. Betty Herndon Maury, *The Confederate Diary of Betty Herndon Maury, Daughter of Lieut. Commander M. F. Maury, 1861–1863,* ed. Alice Maury Parmelee (Washington, D.C.: Privately printed, 1938), 87; Richmond *Dispatch,* July 5, 1862.

21. Richmond *Examiner,* February 21, 28, 1862.

22. Richmond *Examiner,* February 8, 27, January 10, 1862; Richmond *Dispatch,* April 11, 8, July 21, June 12, 20, 1862.

23. Richmond *Dispatch,* April 11, 1862.

24. Richmond *Examiner,* March 6, 14, 19, 1862; Richmond *Dispatch,* March 8, 1862.

25. Frank Moore, ed., *The Rebellion Record: A Diary of American Events,* 12 vols. (New York: Putnam [vols. 1–6] and Van Nostrand [vols. 7–12], 1861–68), "Poetry and Incidents" section, 5:21–22. Union troops also used graffiti as an outlet for political expression. After wrecking Edmund Ruffin's house, they scrawled phrases on his walls such as, "This house belonged to a Ruffinly son of a bitch," "Old Ruffin don't you wish you had left the Southern Confederacy to go to Hell, (where it will go) & had stayed at home?" and "You did fire the first gun on Sumter, you traitor son of a bitch." Ruffin carefully recorded each of the messages and, demonstrating more than a little compulsiveness, the thirty-one names that were also scribbled on the walls of his home (Edmund Ruffin, *The Diary of Edmund Ruffin,* ed. William Kauffman Scarborough, 3 vols. [Baton Rouge: Louisiana State University Press, 1972–89], 2:420, entry for August 17, 1862).

26. Jones, *Rebel War Clerk's Diary,* 76, 81–82.

27. Wilson, "Experiment in Reunion," 8–16, 22–26, 31, 59, 92–96, 101–3.

28. Richmond *Dispatch,* June 13, July 12, 19, 1862; Yorktown *Cavalier,* July 23, 1862.

29. Moore, ed., *Rebellion Record,* "Documents" section, 5:45, 340–41.

30. Stephen V. Ash, *When the Yankees Came: Conflict and Chaos in the Occupied South* (Chapel Hill: University of North Carolina Press, 1995), 121; L. M. Goldsborough to Gideon Welles, April 22, 1862, in U.S. War Department, *The War of the Rebellion: A Compilation of the Official Records of the Union and Confederate Armies,* 127 vols., index, and atlas (Washington, D.C.: GPO, 1880–1901), ser. 1, 11(3):122 (hereafter cited as *OR;* all references are to ser. 1).

31. Mrs. M. V. Rives, "Contraband Conscience," in [Charleston *News and Courier*], *"Our Women in the War": The Lives They Lived; the Deaths They Died* (Charleston, S.C.: News and Courier Book Presses, 1885), 67.

32. James H. Brewer, *The Confederate Negro: Virginia's Craftsmen and Military Laborers, 1861–1865* (Durham, N.C.: Duke University Press, 1969), 133, 6–7, 140–44.

33. Ibid., 153–54.

34. Ira Berlin et al., eds., *Freedom: A Documentary History of Emancipation, 1862–1867,* Series 1, Vol. 1: *The Destruction of Slavery* (New York: Cambridge University Press, 1985), 60–65 (hereafter cited as Berlin, *Freedom*); Benjamin F. Butler to Commander-in-Chief of the Army, May 27, 1861, ibid., 70–71.

35. *Harper's Weekly,* June 29, 1861, in *African American History in the Press, 1851–1899* (Detroit: Gale, 1996), 194; "Testimony by the Superintendent of Contrabands . . . ," in Berlin, *Freedom,* 90.

36. Ruffin, *Diary,* 2:301, 306, 307, 312, 337 (quotation), 349, 350, 356, 420.

37. George P. Rawick, ed., *The American Slave: A Composite Autobiography,* 41 vols. (Westport, Conn.: Greenwood, 1972–79), 16:22–23, 45–48.

38. John M. Coski, "All Confusion on the Plantations: Civil War in Charles City County," in James P. Whittenburg and John M. Coski, eds., *Charles City County, Virginia: An Official History* (Salem, Va.: Don Mills, 1989), 72; Leon F. Litwack, *Been in the Storm So Long: The Aftermath of Slavery* (New York: Knopf, 1979), 30–36; Berlin, *Freedom,* 66–67. Tens of thousands of slaves were taken to Texas from Louisiana, Mississippi, Arkansas, and states as far away as Tennessee and Virginia. See Randolph B. Campbell, *An Empire for Slavery: The Peculiar Institution in Texas, 1821–1865* (Baton Rouge: Louisiana State University Press, 1989), 243–46.

39. Ervin L. Jordan Jr., *Black Confederates and Afro-Yankees in Civil War Virginia* (Charlottesville: University Press of Virginia, 1993), 178; "Testimony by the Superintendent of Contrabands . . . ," in Berlin, *Freedom,* 89. For the chaos into which the institution of slavery was thrown by the war, see Litwack, *Been in the Storm So Long,* 45–63; Clarence L. Mohr, *On the Threshold of Freedom: Masters and Slaves in Civil War Georgia* (Athens: University of Georgia Press, 1986).

40. *Extracts from Letters of Teachers and Superintendents of the New England Freedmen's Aid Society* (Boston: John Wilson and Son, 1864), 11.

41. Richmond *Enquirer,* July 12, 1862, in *African American History in the Press,* 238–40.

42. *Harper's Weekly,* June 29, 1861, in *African American History in the Press,* 194; Jordan, *Black Confederates and Afro-Yankees,* 284–85; J. S. Missroon to Maj. Gen. George B. McClellan, April 14, 1862, Brig. Gen. E. D. Keyes to Maj. J. H. Taylor, April 21, 1862, McClellan to Maj. Gen. Ambrose Burnside, June 15, 1862, McClellan to Edwin Stanton, June 26, 1862, in *OR* 11(3):99, 117–18, 252, 257.

43. Wilson, "Experiment in Reunion," 145–46, 152; Berlin, *Freedom,* 66.

44. Francis Engs, *Freedom's First Generation: Black Hampton, Virginia, 1861–1890* (Philadelphia: University of Pennsylvania Press, 1979), 30–31. The classic account of the relationships among northern philanthropists, army officers, and freed African Americans is Willie Lee Rose, *Rehearsal for Reconstruction: The Port Royal Experiment* (Indianapolis: Bobbs-Merrill, 1964).

45. Engs, *Freedom's First Generation,* 31–35; Jordan, *Black Confederates and Afro-Yankees,* 133.

46. "Testimony by the Superintendent of Contrabands . . . ," in Berlin, *Freedom,* 90; Jordan, *Black Confederates and Afro-Yankees,* 265–66.

47. J. Polk Racine, *Recollections of a Veteran; or, Four Years in Dixie* (Elkton, Md.:

Appeal Printing Office, 1894), 25; Joel Cook, *The Siege of Richmond: A Narrative of the Military Operations of Major-General George B. McClellan during the Months of May and June, 1862* (Philadelphia: George W. Childs, 1862), 75.

48. *Second Annual Report of the New England Freedmen's Aid Society* (Boston: The Society, 1864), 43.

49. Elisha Hunt Rhodes, *All for the Union: The Civil War Diary and Letters of Elisha Hunt Rhodes,* ed. Robert Hunt Rhodes (New York: Orion Books, 1985), 65–66; Warren Lee Goss, "Yorktown and Williamsburg: Recollections of a Private," in *Battles and Leaders of the Civil War,* ed. Robert Underwood Johnson and Clarence Clough Buel, 4 vols. (New York: Century, 1887–88), 2:189.

50. Wilson, "Experiment in Reunion," 150–51; Richmond *Dispatch,* June 13, 1862.

51. Lucy and Sarah Chase "To Our Folks at Home," January 15, 1863, in Henry L. Swint, ed., *Dear Ones at Home: Letters from Contraband Camps* (Nashville, Tenn.: Vanderbilt University Press, 1966), 24; Engs, *Freedom's First Generation,* 71, 74–75; *Statistics of the Operations of the Executive Board of the Friends' Association of Philadelphia and Its Vicinity, for the Relief of the Colored Freedmen* (Philadelphia: Inquirer Printing Office, 1864), 27–28.

52. Lucy and Sarah Chase to "Dear Home Folks," April 1, January 20, 1863, in Swint, ed., *Dear Ones at Home,* 59, 27.

53. "Testimony by the Superintendent of Contrabands . . . ," in Berlin, *Freedom,* 89.

54. Robert D. Parmet, "Schools for the Freedmen," *Negro History Bulletin* 34 (1971): 128; New York *Weekly Anglo-African,* January 18, 1862.

55. Wilson, "Experiment in Reunion," 147; Lucy and Sarah Chase to "Dear Home Folks," January 20, 1863, in Swint, ed., *Dear Ones at Home,* 27; Jordan, *Black Confederates and Afro-Yankees,* 103; *Extracts from Letters of Teachers and Superintendents,* 7; Joe M. Richardson, *Christian Reconstruction: The American Missionary Association and Southern Blacks, 1861–1890* (Athens: University of Georgia Press, 1986), 42; *Fifth Annual Report of the New England Branch of the American Tract Society* (Boston: The Branch, 1864), 19–20.

56. G. K. Eggleston, "The Work of Relief Societies during the Civil War," *Journal of Negro History* 14 (1929): 291–92; Sarah and Lucy Chase to "Dear home folks," February 7, 1863, in Swint, ed., *Dear Ones at Home,* 41.

57. Lucy and Sarah Chase "To Our Folks at Home," April 1, January 15, 1863, in Swint, ed., *Dear Ones at Home,* 61, 21–22.

58. Alfred Hoyt Bill, *The Beleaguered City: Richmond, 1861–1865* (New York: Knopf, 1946), 138, 142, 143.

59. "The Reasons Why McClellan Did Not Capture Richmond," Confederate Broadsides Collection (on-line), WFU.

60. Richmond *Dispatch,* July 19, 1862.

61. Jones, *Rebel War Clerk's Diary,* 90; Richmond *Examiner,* August 22, 1862.

62. Michael B. Chesson, "Harlots or Heroines? A New Look at the Richmond Bread Riot," *Virginia Magazine of History and Biography* 92 (April 1984): 131–75; Myron Berman, *Richmond's Jewry, 1769–1976: Shabbot in Shockoe* (Charlottesville: University Press of Virginia, 1979), 184–89; Michael B. Chesson, *Richmond after the War, 1865–1890* (Richmond: Virginia State Library, 1981), 30–34. Gary W. Gallagher plays down the role of dissent as a factor in southern defeat, while at the same time showing the fault lines among Confederate soldiers and civilians that revealed the serious, if not fatal, disaffection that plagued the South. See Gallagher, *The Confederate War* (Cambridge, Mass.: Harvard University Press, 1997).

63. Maj. Gen. John A. Dix to Edwin Stanton, July 31, 1862, in *OR* 11(3):344–45.

64. Coski, "All Confusion on the Plantations," 73, 84; report of Brig. Gen. Henry M. Naglee, in *OR* 18:49–51.

65. Wilson, "Experiment in Reunion," 128–37; David F. Riggs, *Embattled Shrine: Jamestown in the Civil War* (Shippensburg, Pa.: White Mane, 1997), 78–79, 100–101.

66. Brig. Gen. Egbert L. Viele to Maj. Gen. John A. Dix, March 26, 1863, report of Brig. Gen. Richard Busteed, March 30, 1863, C. C. Suydam to Commanding Officer, Williamsburg, Va., March 29, 1863, in *OR* 18:568, 203, 204; Richard Nelson Current, *Lincoln's Loyalists: Union Soldiers from the Confederacy* (Boston: Northeastern University Press, 1992), 25–27. Military defeat on the Peninsula and guerrilla attacks waged against Union troops cracked the government's commitment to a policy of conciliation, leading to tougher confiscation policies and more aggressive actions against southern civilians. See Mark Grimsley, *The Hard Hand of War: Union Military Policy toward Southern Civilians, 1861–1865* (New York: Cambridge University Press, 1995), 67–76.

67. Ash, *When the Yankees Came,* 158; Riggs, *Embattled Shrine,* 82–86.

68. Chambers, "Notes on Life in Occupied Norfolk," 142–44.

69. Sing-Nan Fen, "Notes on the Education of Negroes at Norfolk and Portsmouth, Virginia, during the Civil War," *Phylon* 28 (1967): 201; Jordan, *Black Confederates and Afro-Yankees,* 103–4; Wilson, "Experiment in Reunion," 105, 177–78; *Freedman* 1 (August 1864): 30. For an example of patriotic math problems in Confederate texts, see L. Johnson, *An Elementary Arithmetic, Designed for Beginners* (Raleigh: Branson and Farrar, 1864).

WILLIAM A. BLAIR

The Seven Days and the
Radical Persuasion

Convincing Moderates in the North of the Need for a Hard War

====

Nearly two weeks after the Seven Days battles ended outside of Richmond, Abraham Lincoln revealed that he had changed his mind about emancipation. While traveling to a funeral with Secretary of State William Henry Seward, Mrs. Seward, and Secretary of the Navy Gideon Welles, Lincoln mentioned that he now believed emancipation "was a military necessity absolutely essential for the salvation of the Union, that we must free the slaves or be ourselves subdued." It was July 13, 1862. A surprised Welles interpreted the policy as a new departure for the commander-in-chief. Previously, Lincoln had denounced interference by the Federal government with slavery. Just two months before he had rescinded the order of Maj. Gen. David Hunter, who had tried to free slaves in South Carolina and Georgia. "But the reverses before Richmond," Welles noted, "and the formidable power and dimensions of the insurrection . . . impelled the Administration to adopt extraordinary measures to preserve the national existence."[1] Although stopping short of wholesale emancipation, the Second Confiscation Act and the Militia Act that passed in July signaled a new departure in Congress, which paved the way for slaves to be used not only as field laborers but also as soldiers.

This is partly an old story, for Welles's account is a standard part of the narratives of the war. Historians agree that the Seven Days convinced northerners to initiate a harder brand of warfare against the Confederacy, embodied in legislation to confiscate rebel property and empower Lincoln to recruit black soldiers. Yet the reasons for this tremendous change in moderate thinking have focused more on the battlefield than on the persuasion of radical editors and politicians at home. Battle front and home front both played roles in pushing the North toward greater punishment of the South. Capped by the Seven Days battles, the Peninsula campaign helped convince northerners that little hope existed for a significant loyalist groundswell within the Confederacy. The radicals, however, supplied the reasons and methods for conducting a harder war against a determined enemy. Lincoln himself would use their logic in justifying emancipation as a military necessity. In the process, abolitionist and antislavery rhetoric moved closer to moderate sensibilities in an effort to steer the war in a more radical direction.[2]

Within the first year of the conflict, the radicals in the Republican Party had shifted their rhetoric toward identifying emancipation as one part of a broader plan for achieving victory. As the Seven Days battles neared, they increasingly employed three lines of reasoning for bringing on a harder war. First, radicals claimed that the Union army was led by potentially traitorous men who did not want to defeat the South, as evidenced by the slow advance of the army and the respect shown to southern civilians. The generals not only favored slavery but also opposed enforcing loyalty oaths, letting the army feed off the southern countryside, and using slaves against their masters. Second, the radicals professed that the South contained very little Unionist support. To the contrary, its citizenry had proven itself to be deliberate traitors instead of essentially loyal masses duped by secessionists. Besides, the argument went, the South consisted of a barbarous people who committed atrocities on their own citizens, showing little respect for the property rights they claimed were their due. Finally, radical leaders said the Union needed to use slaves in the army to deprive the South of a weapon and to preserve white soldiers from menial chores that could be life-threatening in the hot southern climate. They adopted a racist approach that justified emancipation as benefiting white people more than African Americans.

This rhetorical strategy in itself represented a new departure in placing emancipation as a secondary goal, or the means for achieving reunion rather than the end. Before the war, antislavery advocates critiqued the peculiar institution either as a moral blight on the nation or a backward institution that had no place in a modernizing nation with a republican form of government. Within the older abolition circles revolving around William Lloyd Garrison and the *Liberator,* the moral emphasis never completely vanished, but it increasingly adopted a more practical justification for emancipation as a military necessity for saving the nation and punishing traitors. This new phase of the antislavery movement created some tensions within the abolitionist community. Garrison noticed that the cause after 1861 attracted antislavery people who had little regard for the rights of black people and who seemed to "distinctly declare themselves to be looking out for *Number One.*" But he and Wendell Phillips also recognized the opportunity that the new support for antislavery offered, even as they had to justify to hard-liners the

WILLIAM A. BLAIR

shift toward supporting a government they previously had vowed to repudiate. The questionable motivations of new believers and this new position of strong Unionism would matter little if the institution itself was destroyed. As Phillips put it, "When I see a man half-way down Niagara [Falls], I don't ask his intentions — [I know] he will go down."[3]

As might be expected, black abolitionists departed from white colleagues on their rhetorical strategy, especially concerning racial arguments. William Wells Brown, John Rock, and Frederick Douglass stressed the merits of African Americans as supporters of the Union and as an important resource for the military. They pointed out that slaves formed the only consistent base of Unionist support in the Confederate South. Black abolitionists also fought the notions that African Americans were not ready for freedom or would flood the North to compete with white labor. They preached the gospel of self-reliance — that black men and women would remain at home if they had the means to care for themselves.[4] Their logic did not find a home in the white press or Congress. Radical leaders instead focused on convincing northern white people that a harder war was needed to defeat the rebels, not to advance human rights. One of the newcomers to the abolitionist fold put it bluntly: "Men have tried for thirty years to appeal to humanity without success, for the Negro, and now let us try some other expedient. Let us regard him not as a man but as 'a miserable nigger,' if you please, and a nuisance. But whatever he be, if the effect of owning such creatures is to make the owner an intolerable fellow, seditious and insolent, it becomes pretty clear that such ownership should be put an end to."[5]

As the Peninsula campaign ground on, the differences between radicals and conservatives emerged with greater clarity. On the radical side, key leaders included Thaddeus Stevens, Charles Sumner, Benjamin Wade, and Zachariah Chandler in Congress; Horace Greeley, James Medill of the Chicago *Tribune*, Garrison, and other newspaper editors; and black abolitionists like Douglass. These persons and their allies tried to instill in the nation a greater sense of outrage and urgency about the rebellion. They kept reminding northerners about the enormity of what the rebels had done, decrying southerners as a people out to destroy the best government on Earth and solidify the power of slaveholders. Southerners were not, radicals would claim, a noble aristocracy fighting to protect state rights but traitors who had revoked protection under the Constitution. The radical persuasion thus favored putting down the rebellion with the strongest possible measures. While emancipation of slaves was a focal point, advocates of this position also had a broader prescription for handling the nation's ills. They wanted generals to confiscate property with warmaking potential, force civilians to take loyalty oaths, arrest those who did not, order the army to subsist off southern resources, and use slaves as soldiers. Without striking at the power base of these haughty slave owners, so the logic went, the North might not prevent future conflicts even if it reunited the country. "Should a peace soon be patched up, leaving the slaveholding oligarchy as strong as ever in their several States," observed Greeley's *New York Daily Tribune,* "it is very clear to our mind that the rebellion will only be smothered, not suppressed — the issue will be merely adjourned, not decided."[6]

On the other side of the debate stood self-proclaimed conservatives. In May 1862, fourteen Democratic members of the House of Representatives met to build support for their sentiments about how to fight the war. Key leaders hailed from the Border States, such as John J. Crittenden of Kentucky, and from Democratic areas of the Midwest. By July their number had grown to thirty-five spokesmen for the cause. They proclaimed that they remained loyal to the Union and wanted to remain above partisan politics. But they were alarmed by the clamor to punish the rebels through confiscation of their property, including slaves. The conservatives did not believe that slavery provided the reason for the crisis. According to them, the fighting began because of agitation by abolitionists and southern leaders who forced their section into the war. Conservatives professed that the U.S. government should grant amnesty to all the southern people, including full rights as citizens, while punishing only their leaders. They believed the Confederacy consisted of a large portion of Unionists who had never left the country and deserved protection under the Constitution. They opposed confiscating property, using slaves as soldiers, or breaching the "rights" of southern civilians in any way. A radical approach to the war threatened the fragile roots of the democracy that struggled to establish itself in a world still tending toward consolidated power.[7]

Maj. Gen. George Brinton McClellan provided the battlefield expression of the conservative cause. As commander of the Army of the Potomac, he sent a message to President Lincoln from Harrison's Landing on July 7, 1862, indicating how army policy meshed with this political position. He told Lincoln that the conflict was no longer a rebellion but had to be considered a war and thus needed to be conducted "upon the highest principles known to Christian Civilization." The Union should not subjugate the South or wage war on a population. Armed forces and political organizations should remain the target. This meant that the president should discourage confiscation of property, executions of civilians, and abolition of slavery. All private property and unarmed persons should be protected. If the military appropriated goods, it should pay for them. No civilians should face military arrests or oaths of loyalty. This policy of protecting constitutional freedoms, McClellan believed, would elicit support not only from the southern masses but also from foreign nations. If the government pursued the radical course, "especially upon slavery," warned the general, the army might not be willing to continue the fight.[8] This document not only represented the general's opinions but also perfectly captured the sentiments of key Democrats in Congress.

In the middle stood the moderates who were disgusted with the wrangling of both sides because they believed it drained energy from the more immediate objective of ending the conflict quickly. Now was the time to fight; the country could sort out constitutional niceties later. This group consisted primarily of Republicans but included a sprinkling of Democrats who had begun to depart from their more conservative colleagues over the means necessary to prosecute the war. Eventually, these men would earn the name War Democrats (versus the Peace Democrats, who advocated an armistice). As is so often the case, moderates found the extreme views of both sides distasteful, while finding some merit in both. War Democrats such as Brig. Gen. John White Geary hated treating rebels gently and enjoyed a reputation as an officer despised by southern civilians. Moderate Republicans like Lincoln shared the antislavery beliefs of the radicals but differed on the timetable for this social upheaval. Like Democrats, these Republicans interpreted the Constitution as protecting slavery and did not believe the war itself gave the power to set the document aside. In general, they looked for a smoother transition to a free society, possibly with compensation to slave owners and the colonization of the freedpeople in Liberia or elsewhere.

The moderate position was articulated well by the *New York Times*, which at this stage generally supported the Lincoln administration. The editor of the paper defined radicals by their desire to free and enfranchise slaves, as well as to confiscate rebel property. The continual carping on the need to emancipate slaves struck moderates as verging on fanaticism. Conservatives, however, seemed equally misguided in wanting to protect the southern masses and conserve the Constitution as it was. "What!" the editor fumed, "Talk of magnanimity to rebels — 'constitutional rights' of rebels — when they are leaping like bloodhounds at the throat of the nation — when they are slaughtering the sons of loyal fathers and mothers by tens of thousands under their disloyal banners? These suggestions, falling upon the popular ear at this hour of reverse and anxiety, seem akin to treason." To those in the middle, the best thing to do was fight the war and win it, then settle the status of southern rebels and slaves.[9] The proper course for winning the war was not as clearly articulated, other than the desire for harmony at home, less concern for the sentiments of southern civilians, and a more vigorous eastern army that won its battles.

A variety of obstacles prevented the war from taking a more radical course before the Seven Days battles. First was the impact of the Border States. More than a year into the war both Confederacy and Union still fought for the loyalties of the border region, which contained important material and human resources that would help the South significantly in its bid for independence. In Congress, men from Missouri, Kentucky, Maryland, and Delaware constituted the principal speakers who battled their radical colleagues on legislative issues. Besides Crittenden from Kentucky, they included Senator Willard Saulsbury of Delaware and Representative Charles A. Wickliffe of Kentucky. Second, common racial views often meant that people with antislavery tendencies might not favor immediate emancipation. Lincoln himself retained colonization as the solution for freeing slaves and avoiding racial strife. Third, most northerners remained hopeful that the South contained a sufficient number of Unionists. Like the British during the southern campaigns of the American Revolution — or the United States in Vietnam, for that matter — there was at least the hope that loyalist support would surface if the army stabilized areas. The majority of northerners had witnessed precious few signs of white Unionism in the intense fighting that occurred in the first year of war, yet they could not abandon the hope that most southerners would come back to the Union willingly.

Perhaps the most decisive reason for continuing a more conciliatory approach to the conflict was the simple fact that victory seemed within reach. In the Western Theater, the Union army achieved considerable success by penetrating much of Tennessee, controlling the upper stretches of the Mississippi, and capturing New Orleans. Large portions of the seacoast had come under Union control, and Union authorities at New Bern, North Carolina, had raised two regiments of soldiers from the Tarheel State. The outcome of McClellan's campaign on the Virginia Peninsula seemed equally promising. Hopes soared as the Army of the Potomac established itself at Yorktown, Virginia, in early May. Under the circumstances, it made no sense to moderate-minded people to push for something as extreme as upending the entire southern social system — and their own in the process — when reunion was only a matter of time. Before June 1862, the public press beyond the radicals continued to profess faith in the eastern army's leader. On May 10, the *New York Times* reported: "The most confirmed of croakers must certainly confess that Gen. McClellan has brilliantly redeemed the pledges [to push the enemy] which he gave the Department and the country." [10]

WILLIAM A. BLAIR

Horace Greeley
Francis Trevelyan Miller, ed., The Photographic History of the Civil War, *10 vols.*
(New York: Review of Reviews, 1911), 9:297

Despite strong resistance, radicals had begun building momentum for their agenda before and during the spring campaigns: through controlling key committees in Congress, through constant lobbying with the president, and through a persistent campaign in radical newspapers such as Horace Greeley's *New York Daily Tribune.* To a certain extent they had succeeded.

In March 1862, Lincoln had revealed a plan for gradual emancipation, with compensation to loyal members of the border region. Leaders from that area rejected the offer, but that it was made at all struck many at the time as a remarkable gesture. The trend continued in April, when Congress abolished slavery in the District of Columbia and enacted articles of war that prohibited the return of fugitive slaves to the enemy. Taken as a whole, these signs troubled most Democrats and would prompt them to form their caucus to reinvigorate the party a month later.

Radical leaders, though, remained frustrated by the lack of overall progress toward their goals. They worried about Lincoln's continuing desire to placate the Border States and the army's unwillingness to enforce measures established by the legislative branch. McClellan's movement on the Peninsula may have been too slow, but if he succeeded too quickly it could delay the emancipation of slaves. For the radicals to achieve their goals, the right kind of leaders had to direct the army, either supporters of their view or, at the least, soldiers inclined to push the enemy hard and leave the social and political decisions to Congress. It grew increasingly urgent to show why the military was misled by inept commanders, if not outright traitors.

The radical assault on the army's commanders coalesced over the winter of 1861–62 in the Joint Committee on the Conduct of the War. Begun as an arm of Congress to investigate the debacle at Ball's Bluff of October 1861, the committee expanded its role in an attempt to determine what frustrated northern victory. The effort quickly became an ongoing examination of the overall Union war effort, involving everything from leadership to supply. As the Thirty-seventh Congress convened in December 1861, Republicans enjoyed a majority in both houses and radicals dictated the thrust of the investigation. Not surprisingly, the committee pursued a partisan agenda. Although beginning its examination with Bull Run and the competency of Maj. Gen. Irvin McDowell, the committee had turned most of its energies toward McClellan by the time the Army of the Potomac fought the Confederates on the approach to Richmond.[11]

The process presented a rather bizarre spectacle for a nation at war. During a sensitive time for military affairs, a parade of officers made their way from the battlefield to Washington, where they invariably had to assess the conduct of a superior. The committee ostensibly met in secret sessions; however, the witnesses knew that their testimony could become public. Committee members had little compunction about leaking information or releasing reports of their findings to partisan journals. Through these sessions, public officials on the committee gathered ammunition that they used in public addresses on why the war needed to enter a new, more radical phase.

The first inquiry into McClellan's behavior concerned his decision to invade the Confederacy by water instead of marching his soldiers to Richmond by land. Lincoln and other thoughtful moderates shared the anxieties of the radicals. Officials around Washington were not sure that dividing the army was a good thing. Many believed that the maneuver exposed the capital to a rebel raid. Lincoln consented to the plan grudgingly, with the proviso that the general leave enough soldiers behind to protect the city. McClellan gave only halfhearted attention to this directive, reserving a requisite number of troops but leaving them throughout Virginia in a way that limited their coordination. When Lincoln discovered the true nature of the troop dispositions, he halted the transfer of additional soldiers to his general. This unintentionally opened the door for McClellan to argue later that he had failed to take Richmond because he was not sufficiently supported by the Lincoln administration.

Through the Seven Days battles and beyond, the radicals on the committee continued to question military officers about the wisdom of McClellan's plan to move on Richmond from the Peninsula. Brought in after the battles on July 8, Maj. Gen. John Pope openly criticized McClellan for dividing the army, claiming that an overland campaign made the most sense. Montgomery C. Meigs, quartermaster general of the army, supported Pope's opinion. So did Maj. Gen. E. A. Hitchcock, who told the committee that the capital was so important that to let it be captured would allow Confederates to claim victory. But the radicals on the committee wanted more than the critique of general officers about a colleague's strategic vision. They hoped to find evidence that McClellan had disobeyed orders from Lincoln to guard Washington. Although members were not satisfied that the general acted with sufficient regard for the capital's safety, they could not uncover enough wrongdoing to justify a court-martial.[12] Yet the hearings served a propaganda purpose. If they could not find cause for removing the general, radicals could try to raise outrage against his kind of warfare by alleging that McClellan was more interested in coddling traitors than taking care of his own soldiers.

McClellan helped the radical cause not only by treating southern civilians with great respect but also by protecting the property of none other than Robert E. Lee. When the Army of the Potomac landed in Virginia, its commander had issued strict orders against committing depredations upon the persons and property of the residents. The order extended to using fence rails as firewood. In many instances, civilians could secure a military guard over their home and crops if they petitioned a sympathetic officer. In following this course, the general's beliefs matched those of many top commanders in his army. The Committee on the Conduct of War, for instance, had charged McDowell with guarding the crops of a rebel farmer near Fredericksburg, which he happily admitted without apology. Provost marshals in the region under McDowell's control had acted in a similar fashion, and military commanders Rufus King and John F. Reynolds pursued the same policy when they supervised the area. Many generals at this time considered acts against civilians as vandalism that would demoralize the troops, making it more difficult to exact discipline if they became lawless brigands.[13]

Some people in the country, however, believed that McClellan crossed a line by stationing a guard over the home known as the White House. The estate on the Pamunkey River had been owned by Mary Custis Lee's father, the adopted son of George Washington, who willed the property to one of the Lee sons. Mary Lee herself had lived in the home, vacating it just ahead of the Federal soldiers who established a supply depot in the region. She was captured not far from the place but granted an escort to Confederate lines. Before leaving, she had posted the following notice on the door: "Northern soldiers who profess to reverence Washington, forebear to desecrate the home of his first married life, the property of his wife, now owned by her descendants."[14] McClellan honored the request. Later, when Mrs. Lee again found herself behind Union lines, he assigned more soldiers to lead her to Confederate territory. The gestures were very much in keeping with his view on conducting a civilized warfare that would enlighten the southern masses that the North offered no threat to their way of life.

Radicals characterized McClellan's gesture as proof that the general valued southern lives above those of his own soldiers. Newspaper correspondents touring the battlefield in early June after the battle of Seven Pines were appalled at seeing the wounded lying on the swampy ground under the hot sun. They viewed the White House as a perfectly good hospital going to waste while men suffered. McClellan maintained that the house was a small frame building consisting of six rooms that could not hold many wounded. He adamantly defended his decision to the secretary of war, claiming that he protected no homes that were needed by the sick or wounded soldiers. The explanation did not slow down the opposition. Radical correspondents continued to focus on the guards who kept these men from shelter in the home of a notorious rebel. Good Union men who committed the ultimate sacrifice suffered while other soldiers protected the property of traitors.[15]

The Committee on the Conduct of the War stepped up its inquiry into this particular army activity, its members routinely grilling witnesses on the

White House on the Pamunkey River. Initially protected by order of
General McClellan, this residence was burned when the Federals
changed base to the James River.
Francis Trevelyan Miller, ed., The Photographic History of the Civil War, *10 vols.*
(New York: Review of Reviews, 1911), 1:275

treatment of rebel property. A reporter from the Philadelphia *Inquirer* testified on July 10 that McClellan even used troops to guard "negro" homes.
Asked similar questions, a colonel offered that the practice of guarding
homes annoyed soldiers, adding that he believed good treatment did not
necessarily make good friends. Representatives took to the field to see conditions with their own eyes with a correspondent in tow from Greeley's *New
York Daily Tribune.* At one point, Senator Benjamin Wade of Ohio confronted Maj. Gen. Edwin V. Sumner: "He informed the General that this
farce of placing guards over the property of Rebels and taking vastly more
care of it than was done with the property and persons of Union men must
come to an end, and that speedily." As luck would have it, some members of
this same congressional party later tried to seek shelter from a storm in the
house of a woman whose husband was fighting in the Confederate army.
The correspondent claimed that a Union guard would not let the politicians in.[16]

More outrageous to the radicals was the practice of returning fugitive
slaves that continued sporadically in various places despite the order against

it. On May 17 the *New York Daily Tribune* reported that military authorities returned fifty fugitive slaves to masters in Maryland. The story was not verified, but that did not matter. Coupled with the treatment of southern civilians, the events provided radicals with a powerful indictment against the military commanders who endorsed conciliatory measures. Privately, a supporter wrote Salmon P. Chase: "The reason the war has made such slow progress is because our anti slavery soldiers have been placed under the command of proslavery Generals." Publicly, Representative Thaddeus Stevens of Pennsylvania issued a more stinging critique shortly after the close of the Seven Days battles. "I cannot approve of sitting generals who sympathize with slavery at the head of armies," he told Congress on July 5, "or setting our generals, under express orders, to pursue and return fugitives from traitors. I cannot consent to that portion of the conduct of the war which sets our armies to watch the property of rebel soldiers in arms against us, rather than allow it to be occupied by our own troops, while, in the mean time, our soldiers, sick and wounded, are placed in swamps filled with deadly miasma, which destroys health and unfits our men to meet the enemy." [17]

As powerful as this line of reasoning was, it alone could not do the job. Radicals understood that they had to convince the northern masses that the Union faced a determined foe, a traitor who undermined republican government. Worse, the Confederates were gruesome barbarians who preyed on the corpses of soldiers and punished good Unionists by seizing their property.

Nothing better demonstrates the naïveté of northern conservatives about their southern foe than the remarks of a member of McClellan's staff just before the Seven Days battles. After closing negotiations for exchanging prisoners, Col. Thomas M. Key rode back toward Union lines with another officer. "'Those leaders on the other side talk as if they would fight,'" the colonel commented. "'Do you think,' continued he, 'that they, the leaders, reflect the sentiments of the great mass of the people South?'" His companion believed the question to be a moot one — that the only way to find out was to kill all the leaders. "'But,' continued he, 'do you not think it would be better to raise the masses to their legitimate authority, and thus sink these fellows?'" Key's companion thought the conversation was remarkable considering that the Confederates had resisted the Union army at Yorktown, fought a battle at Williamsburg, and fallen upon the advancing forces with great fury at Fair Oaks.[18] To the officer the answer was obvious: long, hard fighting was necessary to end the war. Yet the staff officer reflected the opinion of many conservatives, and not a few moderates, who could not relinquish the hope that the Confederacy contained pockets of loyalists awaiting a liberating army.

The war helped the radicals convince northerners otherwise. As the Union army occupied portions of the Confederacy, newspaper correspondents flocked into the areas, with one of their missions to uncover the status of southern Unionism. Radicals in Congress took their lead, especially from the reporting of the *New York Daily Tribune*, which charted rebel behavior in Memphis, New Orleans, and occupied Fredericksburg, Virginia. The southern masses in those places did not welcome the Federal soldiers. In New Orleans, Union officers met with an unwelcome greeting when women dumped the contents of chamber pots on them. Confederate civilians in several places tore down the national flag. Few southerners rushed to take oaths of loyalty to the United States or showed any signs of apology. To the contrary, the radical press reported that civilians in Fredericksburg issued a statement that they remained loyal to Jefferson Davis and the southern cause.[19]

Radicals capitalized on this behavior further by showing that the few Unionists who did exist suffered persecution. In Fredericksburg, the Confederate populace had forced the editor of the *Christian Banner* to shut down his newspaper and flee to the North in May 1861. Others reported being beaten or intimidated into keeping quiet about their opposition to secession. Most of these reports were true, as was the charge in reverse that northerners treated signs of dissent harshly. As an example of the treatment of Unionists, the radical press cited the case of William Nisson, a German immigrant who lived in New Orleans. In retaliation for confiscation laws in the North, the Confederate government had allowed for confiscation of property belonging to people judged as alien enemies. Authorities had arrested the man a few months earlier because he would not take the oath of loyalty to the Confederacy. Allegedly, the man was beaten, robbed of his cash and gold watch, and thrown in jail for a month. Those who wanted to know about life under rebel rule, an editor observed, would find the experience instructive. "And if there be any who believe that the South (we mean the white South), is unanimously Rebel," he continued, "his treatment will show you how it became and was kept so — that is, by knocking down and throttling all who dared to avow themselves Unionists."[20]

Through these reports back home the newspapers built an image of a South either devoid of Unionists or with the loyal stuffing knocked out of them by rebel mistreatment. The main point to all of this was to show that reconciliation was a doomed strategy because southerners did not want to return to the fold. A correspondent touring northern Alabama for the Chicago *Tribune* noted: "Let the North become reconciled to the fact that in order to restore the Union as it was, the South must be subjugated, and act accordingly."[21]

The southern behavior had an impact, especially on some Democrats and moderate Republicans. At home in New York City, Maria Lydig Daly heard confirmation of the newspaper accounts about rebel behavior from a family friend. Daly favored Democrats and was married to a common pleas court judge prominent in party affairs. Her visitor in the spring of 1862, Capt. Adam Badeau, would later become a military secretary to Ulysses S. Grant. He had returned recently from the military front, where he had talked with Confederate soldiers in the garrison at Fort Pulaski. Badeau was openly despondent over the lack of loyalty demonstrated in the population. The enemy had told him that the Union "might take their forts and seaports, but they would retreat inland and keeping up an incessant guerilla warfare, defy us." Even worse for those preaching conciliation was the latter part of his message: "Some allowed that they knew the North did not wish to take their slaves, but they did not care. They were fighting for independence." The moderate *New York Times* could not help but notice the same thing. "With feelings of surprise and disappointment we read in the story of Nashville, Norfolk and New-Orleans captured, of the nonappearance of that Union sentiment, upon the existence of which the nation has counted with confidence."[22]

The radicals pressed the case that with few white people supporting the national cause, the section consisted primarily of traitors who deserved the wrath of the government. Column after column and speech after speech raised the cogent point that the Constitution did not apply to people who waged war on the United States. By becoming insurrectionists, Confederates had revoked their rights as citizens. "Remember, they are traitor states at war with the Union," one member of the U.S. House told his colleagues. "And the question to be settled is, shall we permit that treason to vindicate itself by success, and that Confederated rebellion to culminate in political independence?" Representative Thomas D. Eliot of Massachusetts then tried to prove that the Constitution itself, contrary to the claims of conservatives, allowed for confiscation of rebel property. Under the war powers provisions, "an enemy may be rightfully deprived of whatever gives to him power and strength." In this case, a planter's real estate could be seized because the estate of a rebel was an instrument for making war. This was especially true of slaveholders who could fight with the army while their chattel produced the goods that maintained the rebellion.[23] President Lincoln later would use the same logic when issuing his proclamation of emancipation.

WILLIAM A. BLAIR

Garrison's *Liberator* laid bare the contradictions contained within the conservative desire to fight a conciliatory war. The executive committee of the American Anti-Slavery Society wondered how one could muster any kind of warfare without infringing on life, liberty, and property. As long as a war was fought, it seemed only logical that confiscation would follow. The committee reasoned: "If there are no constitutional scruples against sacking the towns, ravaging the fields, and destroying the lives of the rebels of the South, why should there be any against transferring four millions of slaves from the side of the rebellion to that of the Union, the Constitution, the Government, and breaking all their fetters."[24] The Chicago *Tribune,* meanwhile, added a pecuniary twist. Its editor mused that if either the innocent or the guilty must pay for this war, it might as well be the guilty: "Those who break the laws and commit crime should pay the damages inflicted on the community." Confiscation of rebel property could ease the tax burden on northerners.[25]

Radicals had a more compelling ally for their cause than abstract constitutional arguments or issues affecting the pocketbook. Northern newspaper correspondents and witnesses testifying before the Joint Committee on the Conduct of the War painted gruesome portraits of a barbaric enemy who committed atrocities on the living and the dead. Through such reports, they tried to curb the inclination to admire the South as a region of gentlemen who embodied the perfect expression of gentility. Previously the abolitionist critique of the South had tried to dismiss this ideal by highlighting as much as possible the brutal nature of southerners in the punishment of slaves and the separation of families through slave auctions. After the Union army advanced into the South, especially in the Virginia theater, the radicals still drew attention to the mistreatment of slaves by masters but added the Union soldier as a target of rebel barbarity to incite even greater vengeance within the white populace.[26]

One of the earlier incidents seized by the press and radical speechmakers involved the use of torpedoes by the Confederate military to protect the retreat from Williamsburg on May 4. In Civil War parlance, torpedoes described something more like today's land mines than propeller-driven explosives. Confederates had used these devices to guard against being overrun in the fortifications around the area. Four of them placed by Brig. Gen. Gabriel J. Rains incited the controversy. In charge of the rear guard, he had grabbed abandoned artillery shells, rigged them as torpedoes, and placed them along the road under trees to slow the Union advance so the Confederate sick and wounded could make their escape. Unsuspecting members of the 52nd Pennsylvania triggered the shells, which killed one soldier and wounded six others. While these were the most notorious torpedoes, a few others exploded as well. All told, the army lost four or five men killed and a dozen wounded because of these weapons.[27]

For once, radicals and Democrats were on the same side. To most northerners, these torpedoes provided evidence of a barbaric people unschooled in civilized warfare and, perhaps worse, aristocrats whose manliness should be questioned. This form of war seemed cowardly. Democratic members of the military committee of the Senate went to investigate and returned from Yorktown full of wrath against the rebels, "whose Satanic torpedoes they found at all points." Greeley's newspaper was happy to find a common sense of outrage and happier still that the committee encountered captured rebel officers forced to dig out the remaining projectiles. The captives received little sympathy when complaining that the use of prisoners in this activity was against the rules of war. They were told that planting torpedoes did not exactly fit the rules either. The *Tribune* summed up the situation: "New cases required new rules."[28] Even more remarkable, McClellan himself had encouraged using prisoners to do this job. In a letter to the War Department he claimed the Confederates had hidden the shells in wells, springs, near magazines, flagstaffs, telegraph offices, and other likely places for soldiers to search while secreting the weapons in carpetbags and barrels of flour. He ended by saying, "I shall make the prisoners move them at their own peril."[29]

The use of torpedoes troubled the Confederate high command enough to warrant a review by the secretary of war. The issue divided military officers. A week after the first incident, Maj. Gen. James Longstreet, Rains's superior, expressly ordered that no more torpedoes be planted on a future retreat. But Rains's immediate commanding officer, D. H. Hill, had endorsed the weapons, echoing the tone of northern radicals in adding: "In my opinion all means of destroying our brutal enemies are lawful and proper." The issue landed on the desk of Secretary of War George W. Randolph, who ruled it appropriate to use torpedoes for defense against assaults, to check enemy pursuit to save troops, or as obstacles in harbors. "It is not admissible," Randolph continued, "to plant shells merely to destroy life and without other design than depriving your enemy of a few men, without materially injuring him." His ruling supported Longstreet's position against the indiscriminate use of the weapon. To make this clear, Randolph wrote Rains that if he did not like the decision he could be reassigned to river defenses, "where such things are clearly admissible."[30]

As the northern public heard about torpedoes, radicals fed the frenzy against the enemy by releasing a report of the Joint Committee on the Conduct of War about rebel atrocities after the battle of First Bull Run. Dated April 30, 1862, the report coincided perfectly with the advance on the Peninsula. No less a figure than Senator Benjamin F. Wade, a leading Radical Republican from Ohio and chairman of the committee, provided the introductory comments. The report alleged that prisoners were treated terribly by Confederate guards. Gen. P. G. T. Beauregard reportedly wanted to use one officer as a hostage. Other Union prisoners suffered from scanty provisions, insufficient shelter, and poor medical care. We understand these complaints today as a standard assessment of prisoner treatment for both sides; however, civilians were still learning what to expect from their enemy.

Wade was merely warming to the task. He shifted the emphasis from crimes against the living to those against the dead. "Inhumanity to the living has been the leading trait of the rebel leaders," he said in referring to masters' treatment of slaves, adding, "but it was reserved for your Committee to disclose, as a concerted system, their insults to the wounded and their mutilation and desecration of the gallant dead." Soldiers were buried naked, meaning that they were stripped of their clothing. Some were placed face down rather than in the appropriate position. These actions indicated a lack of respect on the part of the enemy. Yet these men were the lucky ones. Corpses, Wade alleged, were also burned and mutilated. Other bodies of the nation's patriots lay neglected in the open with "their bones being carried off as trophies, sometimes, as the testimony proves, to be used as personal adornments." For instance, one witness saw the head of an officer cut off by a secessionist who used the skull as a drinking cup on his wedding day. Another skull of a Union soldier allegedly was in the possession of the sergeant at arms in the Confederate House of Representatives. Wade left no doubt about the impact he hoped the disclosures would have: "They should inspire these people [of the loyal states] to renewed exertions to protect our country from the restoration to power of such men. They should, and we believe they will, arouse the disgust and horror of foreign nations against this unholy rebellion."[31]

Abolitionist newspapers had disclosed these outrages before the committee's official report appeared, suggesting that congressmen leaked the news to serve the overall propaganda effort. The Boston *Congregationalist* had reported that Confederates bayoneted and scalped Federal troops in their last agony, buried corpses face down, used skulls for soap dishes, and mistreated prisoners. On April 17, the abolitionist Wendell Phillips delivered a speech on this issue. Phillips welcomed the news as a tonic to the delusion that the South contained graceful, chivalrous, and picturesque slaveholders. "That delusion goes out at Manassas — the skulls of brave men used for drinking vessels. It goes out at Fort Donelson and Pittsburg [Landing], when chivalry took to its heels before the men whom it had affected to despise. Never again will the North sit down blind worshippers of a civilization supposed to be better than their own." [32]

As incredible as these things sound today, branding southerners as barbarians who desecrated bodies and drank from their enemy's skulls did not seem so outlandish at the time. Civilians read about these atrocities in most newspapers and heard speeches to this effect. In May, reporters printed any rumors they could find indicating that rebels had goulish tendencies. In these accounts, bound Union prisoners had their throats cut. Flags of truce were allegedly violated. Not even good loyal women were safe from the barbarians. Confederate authorities, according to the *New York Daily Tribune*, arrested six women suspected as Union loyalists near Williamsburg. When released, the women reportedly complained to Union officials that "their persons had been violated" by Maj. Gen. John B. Magruder and other high-ranking officers. [33] In Congress, a representative from Pennsylvania picked up the theme and proclaimed about Confederates, "In the prosecution of their rebellion they have committed barbarities upon our living and our dead which make humanity shudder." Among the complaints he charged was that rebels had strewn the bones of dead Union soldiers about the ground rather than bury the corpses. Not surprisingly, this persistent campaign had a telling effect on some Democrats. "Stragglers from our army," Maria Lydig Daly noted in her diary at the end of May, "are found tied by their feet to the trees with their throats cut, and it seems that what was said of their barbarities after the battle of Bull Run was only too true; that they did boil the flesh and carry away the bones of our poor soldiers as trophies." [34]

Still, it was a large leap for northerners to make from increasing their hatred of rebels to embracing the help of slaves. Despite good propaganda material for turning up the heat against the enemy, it would take more to convince the country to use African Americans in the fight.

A reporter at Yorktown watched as members of the 93rd Pennsylvania extended a redoubt in the warm June sun. The observer had seen the men earlier when they were fresh-faced recruits. Now they appeared pale-faced, their shrunken muscles barely able to push their shovels through the wet, reluctant clay. On a rest break, one soldier gazed emptily at the horizon, perhaps thinking of home. After a large African American rode by on a horse to fulfill a mission for a staff officer, the eyes of the weary soldier blazed in anger, especially as they then fell upon the shovel, regarding its "non-military surface from blade to handle." As he stood erect and looked at the heavens, the soldier's demeanor validated the radicals' message. Why degrade an army of invading soldiers as diggers of ditches "when the Heaven-appointed digger of ditches by hundreds of thousands, are all around, praying for the privilege of taking the tools out of the hands of our troops, and of casting in their labor with our fighting[?]" Then the reporter burst out, "Invasion and conquest by shovels and pickaxes, wielded by black Virginia's plantation laborers, or by Northern infantry soldiers!!!"[35]

As the radicals sensed the country's sentiments against the enemy hardening, they used racial arguments to convince fellow citizens that using slaves in the army would be good for white people. Why, they asked, waste good white soldiers on work better handled by black folks? The thrust of this message was that slaves offered many talents that could be turned against the enemy. They could serve as scouts, perform menial labor, and in some cases fight. Perhaps if the administration offered freedom in exchange for these services, the slaves might turn on their rebel masters and force the Confederacy to deal with internal insurrection.

Anyone who wanted proof of the value of the African Americans needed only to look at the Confederacy. At Yorktown in early May it became widely known that the southern army used slaves to build the fortifications that blocked the Union advance. It frustrated radicals that so many people dragged their feet when the benefits of employing black labor seemed so apparent. One report in the *New York Tribune* had a reporter watching through a telescope the progress of slaves working on the entrenchments. When the reporter snapped shut his telescope, an artilleryman standing nearby allegedly commented, " 'Pretty hard, Sir, that President Lincoln won't let us use negroes against them, while they use negroes against us.' " In this way, the reporter tried to indicate that the army had widespread support for using the slaves. The reporter also characterized the soldier as wanting more. The enlisted man said that the soldiers had made up their minds on two things. The first was that every man should have 160 acres of land confiscated from southern estates: "The officers may do as they please, but we rank and file are determined to have our share of the lands we are reconquering into the Union." Second, the men in the ranks understood "that we are fighting for the Nigger. Now the Nigger has just got to fight for us. That is all there is about it."[36]

Most of these reports were distortions, but the basic message that the rebels were using slaves did hit home. Slaves dug entrenchments and performed other work for the enemy. "The rebels employ them as cooks, nurses, teamsters, and scouts," reported the *Liberator,* adding, "shall we decline such services in order to spare slavery?" The paper hinted that the rebels organized some units of African Americans as soldiers. Whether true or not, the public could not deny that African Americans had proven their value to the Union military. The black population of the South provided the only trustworthy, willing Unionists. Consequently, wherever the army advanced, officers could use these residents as guides through unfamiliar terrain. Some also could serve as spies, to extend the army's military vision farther. This happened enough times to add currency to the reasoning.[37]

As the Seven Days battles came and went, the radical persuasion increasingly targeted the northern public's sense of white supremacy to underscore why the army needed African Americans. Black people, so the reasoning went, were not only more suitable to manual labor but also more resistant to the hot southern climate. Radical leaders warned that more white soldiers would die of disease as the army penetrated deeper into the Confederacy. If soldiers believed the Upper South was hot, just wait until they penetrated into Mississippi or Alabama. African Americans were already acclimated to the weather. In the Senate, Morton S. Wilkinson of Minnesota said that he objected to the young men of his state being wasted by digging trenches while plenty of African Americans wanted to do the work. Representative William Windom of Minnesota voiced a similar attitude on May 20. "The sickly season at the South is rapidly approaching, when exposure and toil will be almost certain death to northern soldiers," he observed. "Why not employ the services of those who are acclimated and save the lives of our friends and neighbors?" Thaddeus Stevens of Pennsylvania joined in this chorus, which also attracted doughface Democrat Henry M. Rice. Stevens told his colleagues: "You must put acclimated soldiers, men whose peculiar constitutions will bear the climate, to be your sentinels amid the fogs and damps of the southern summer nights. If you put a white man to stand sentinel there for a single night, it is certain death to him."[38]

Although Democrat and Republican might agree on the need to save white soldiers by employing black laborers, the radicals needed additional ammunition to counter the resistance against using slaves as soldiers. The radicals employed history to remind the country that slaves had fought in prior wars. Although this was no secret — and was consistent with the argument of black abolitionists — the fact that the United States had resorted to slaves in wartime still came as a surprise to some. Thaddeus Stevens caught at least one conservative colleague off guard by claiming that most civilized nations resorted to using slaves as soldiers, adding: "It is the usage of every nation at war with another to liberate their slaves and take them into the service to war with their former masters." The United States did this during the Revolutionary War, he continued, and Andrew Jackson did the

WILLIAM A. BLAIR

same to repulse the British at the battle of New Orleans during the War of 1812. This last fact raised the eyebrows of Representative Wickliffe of Kentucky. He demanded that his colleague produce Jackson's proclamation to use slaves, which Stevens said he would gladly do. Jackson had owned slaves, making his use of them in battle a real problem to the opposition.[39]

Horace Greeley recognized the usefulness of citing Jackson's behavior, while continuing to play on northern racism. "Gen. Jackson lost no dignity," the *Tribune* noted, "by the presence of 'colored fellow-citizens' behind his breastworks at New-Orleans." The column observed that the British used "colored" troops to put down the Sepoy Rebellion and for various problems in the West Indies. But Greeley's newspaper recognized the concerns among white northerners that African Americans might not fight well because they were used to being led by masters or were not civilized enough to kill in the manner of soldiers subject to discipline. The column indicated that slaves made perfect soldiers precisely because of the liabilities attributed to their race. Instead of turning away savages, the North should use these people. "A savage can fight about as well as a philosopher," the newspaper observed, later adding that "a man of however great a genius in the ranks of the army is worth mainly his might, strength and agility." In other words, brains did not matter as much as brawn in combat.[40]

Garrisonian abolitionists did not adopt this racist tactic, but they increasingly pressed the need to use slaves in the army as a military necessity. The *Liberator* featured a speech by Representative George W. Julian of Indiana that at first took the classic, moralistic approach in referring to slavery as a guilt shared by northerners and southerners. Later in his address, Julian said that the time had come to employ emancipation as a military necessity. Slavery, he said, boosted the strength of the Confederacy. African Americans tilled the ground and supplied the enemy army with provisions. Multitudes joined the army to help with entrenchments and other military labors. Julian saw the slave population as a potential source for Union arms. "They cannot be neutral," the congressman declared. "As laborers, if not as soldiers, they will be the allies of the rebels, or of the Union." He added that slaves and free blacks fought in both the Revolution and the War of 1812, acquitting themselves well. "I do not say that any general policy of arming the slaves should be avowed; but that in some capacity, military or civil, according to the circumstances of each particular case, they should be used in the necessary and appropriate work of weakening the power of their owners."[41] Lincoln could not have said it better.

The militia bill enacted July 17, 1862, indicated that the radical message — coupled with the lack of results on the battlefield — had begun to score. As

McClellan's troops languished at Harrison's Landing after the Seven Days, moderates in Congress tired of the conciliatory approach and recognized that the time had come to allow the president to enroll African Americans as soldiers. Lincoln needed more troops. On July 1 he called on Union governors for 300,000 men to put down the rebellion. But the militia law severely restricted his power to mobilize the country. Passed in 1795, it no longer matched the needs of 1862 because it empowered the federal government to organize troops for only ninety days. Congress amended the act to grant broader powers to the president, including the ability to draft men for nine months and enlist persons of African descent for "any war service for which they may be found competent." Theoretically, this meant using African Americans in any capacity, ranging from laborers for the military to soldiers in combat.

Reactions to this act followed partisan lines, with supporters employing the radical explanations for the change. They stressed the need for the extra labor, the historical precedent, and the racial advantages of such an act. When he went back to his home state to meet constituents at Harrisburg, the secretary of the Senate portrayed the bill as a measure to prevent widespread emancipation. John Forney reportedly sparked applause when he mentioned that Lincoln told him that the government would use whatever means possible to end the conflict. "He thought it proper," Forney told the People's State Convention, "to put arms in their hands to save the lives of the Whites." Forney added that General Washington had used the "colored men of the South" in the Revolutionary War. Conservatives such as Senator Saulsbury of Delaware, however, sneered at the effort as designed "to elevate the miserable nigger." Moderate Republican Senators John Sherman of Ohio and William Pitt Fessenden of Maine saw it differently. Sherman believed the time had come to use all necessary force to put down the rebellion. Fessenden agreed, indicating that the Union should abandon "kid-glove warfare." The editor of the Chicago *Tribune* took notice. When Fessenden moved, he wrote, "it signifies that the whole glacier has started." [42]

Fessenden's reaction provides an indication of the success and failure of the radical critique. The militia act offered the means to wage a harder war but did not signal a movement toward all-out emancipation. Nor for that matter did the sentiment exist in either the Congress or the executive branch to begin a concerted effort to enlist slaves as soldiers. The senator echoed the radical reasoning in an address to the Senate on July 9. He had become convinced that conciliation with Confederates would not work. Southerners showed no tenderness toward the Union, "except that of the wolf toward the lamb." Soldiers increasingly hated guarding the property of the rebels who shot at them. Worse yet, the government's policy may have hurt future recruitment. The senator also noted a decline in enthusiasm for volunteering in his state, which he attributed to the unhappiness with soldiers who volunteered to fight instead being forced to dig entrenchments in swampy conditions. In the meantime, stated Fessenden, they recognized that an abundance of men existed who were acclimated to these conditions and who wanted to do the work that would save "our soldiers." Why not turn this weapon against traitors? If people thought he advocated emancipation, Fessenden emphatically denied it. "We are simply proposing to use those means in the army which are best for us, and to use those best able to perform a particular kind of service. Did anybody ever hear of a nation that was at war with any other country that would sacrifice the lives of their own men by making them do a kind of work when there were about them friends who were willing and anxious to relieve them from that work?" For the moment, the country would accept African Americans as military laborers to save white lives. The glacier had started to move, but it had miles yet to travel.[43]

It would be a mistake, however, to dismiss the changing mood of the North. The impact of the Seven Days was meaningful. Before those battles, legislation for the confiscation of rebel property had stalled. In July, the deadlock broke. The militia bill passed, allowing greater executive authority in raising troops, including black soldiers. Gone too was the notion that the South was filled with repressed Unionists awaiting the arrival of Union soldiers to renew their loyalty to the United States. Winfield Scott, former general-in-chief of the army and a Virginian, changed his own mind after seeing the resistance of the Confederates. After Scott visited Judge Daly in New York, the judge's wife entered in her journal: "Scott thinks the war now is one of conquest. He says the Southerners are a united people now, which they were not at first." More startling was a proslavery Democrat who came to the White House to meet with Lincoln in July. Francis Brockholst, a New York attorney, urged that slavery be wiped out to weaken the enemy and rally the increasing number of antislavery people in the North. In the Midwest, the Chicago *Tribune* took heart at the new mood of the country: "Lo, what a change! The whole country is at this moment almost abreast of the *Tribune*."[44] Of course, not all white northerners shared such attitudes. Elizabeth Blair Lee, a member of one of the most influential political families in the nation, could still write sympathetically about the South, indicating that she did not yet feel alien to the Confederates.[45] This opinion, however, was becoming a minority as the war took a radical turn.

Lincoln himself shoved the conflict in this direction with decisions in July that increased the control of the army and turned up the heat on the Confederacy. First, he changed the command structure of the army by promoting Maj. Gen. Henry Wager Halleck to general-in-chief. Next, on July 21 he issued several directives to his cabinet. One ordered the army to begin using African Americans as laborers. He was employing the power granted by the Militia Act, although admittedly within moderate limits. Also in that meeting he ordered the army to subsist on the countryside, showing himself in complete accord with the policies of Maj. Gen. John Pope in northern Virginia. (Had Robert E. Lee known of this, he might have included Lincoln in the outburst against the "miscreant" John Pope.) The next day the president revealed his emancipation plan to his cabinet. The draft of July 22 was a much shorter version of the final proclamation. It opened with a paragraph that justified the president's authority based on the confiscation bill that the radicals had engineered to deal with traitors who tried to bring down the government. Although members of the cabinet convinced him not to issue the proclamation in July, a considerable change in policy had occurred. The president was taking the gloves off, which put him increasingly at odds with the conservative general who led the major army in the East and with the Democratic Party that could now more clearly present itself as an option for dissatisfied voters in the forthcoming elections.[46]

So what was the impact of the radical argument? Did it, in fact, persuade? It seems doubtful that radicals in the Republican Party would have carried the nation to a harder brand of warfare based on force of argument alone. The battlefield in this case contained the decisive proof that turned moderates toward more demanding measures to subdue the rebellion. As the advancing Army of the Potomac encountered stiff resistance instead of Unionist support, much of the northern public reconsidered its position of leniency toward the southern masses. The Seven Days cemented the image of Confederates as a united, determined enemy who would not come back into the fold unless beaten. The radical critique, however, provided northerners both with justification for this changing mood and with the blueprint for how the country should fight the war. Moderates were for the most part in agreement with their radical colleagues in this explanation, although they would endorse using African Americans only as laborers and not soldiers. Union authorities now had a freer hand to seize certain kinds of property from traitorous civilians who no longer deserved protection from the Constitution. Lincoln himself borrowed from the radical persuasion when he crafted the Emancipation Proclamation. The version read to the cabinet on July 22 based his powers on the confiscation act that had just passed the Congress and that contained much of the radical prescription for how to deal with traitors. He may have arrived at the same conclusions independently, but he

WILLIAM A. BLAIR

lived in a moment when these debates filled the air, giving him a chance to assess the power of the logic on both sides. This context provided a useful exercise for a sharp attorney who understood the value of a good argument.[47]

In some respects, then, the Union accomplished more in the Seven Days by losing than it might have through winning. Had the war ended with McClellan's siege of Richmond, it is unclear whether slavery would have died immediately or continued as part of a conciliatory peace won by the conservative prescription for war and reunion. Germinating in the hot, sandy soil of Virginia's Peninsula were the seeds of emancipation, a sterner northern resolve, increased political opposition internally, and the military coordination needed to bring the conflict to a close. The South could still win, but the Seven Days changed the North in ways important for achieving future success. The radical argument was beginning to have an effect, even if still held in check by moderates. In strange ways the South itself contributed to these momentous changes through its continued resistance. Lee had succeeded in this round of battles outside of the capital, but that very victory would help cost the Confederacy the very thing it had gone to war to preserve.

NOTES

1. Gideon Welles, *Diary of Gideon Welles: Secretary of the Navy under Lincoln and Johnson,* ed. Howard K. Beale, 3 vols. (New York: Norton, 1960), I:70–71.

2. Studies that examine the pressure applied by radicals typically deal with the Emancipation Proclamation and largely ignore an extended analysis of radical rhetoric. James McPherson's work on the abolitionists devotes some attention to that rhetoric but remains focused on strategies surrounding emancipation. McPherson does show the impact of radicals on Lincoln, crediting them with the phrase "military necessity" and the justification of the president's powers under the war powers provisions of the Constitution. Hans Trefousse makes a similar point, indicating that Lincoln was not far from the radical position but portraying the president as skillfully manipulating the radicals to spur on generals and other politicians. See James M. McPherson, *The Struggle for Equality: Abolitionists and the Negro in the Civil War and Reconstruction* (Princeton: Princeton University Press, 1964); Hans Trefousse, *The Radical Republicans: Lincoln's Vanguard for Racial Justice* (New York: Knopf, 1968), 182; James Brewer Stewart, *Holy Warriors: The Abolitionists and American Slavery* (New York: Hill & Wang, 1976). For key works that highlight the importance of the Seven Days battles, see Mark Grimsley, *The Hard Hand of War: Union Military Policy toward Southern Civilians, 1861–1865* (New York: Cambridge University Press, 1995); James M. McPherson, *Battle Cry of Freedom: The Civil War Era* (New York: Oxford University Press, 1998), 496.

3. *Liberator,* February 14, March 21, April 25, 1862. For changes in abolition, see Stewart, *Holy Warriors,* 179–85; McPherson, *Struggle for Equality,* 99–106.

4. John Rock's address in *Liberator,* February 14, 1862; Frederick Douglass, "The Slaveholders' Rebellion: An Address Delivered in Himrod's, New York, on 4 July 1862," in Frederick Douglass, *The Frederick Douglass Papers,* Series One: *Speeches, Debates, and Interviews. Vol. 3, 1855–63,* ed. John W. Blassingame (New Haven: Yale University Press, 1979), 521–43.

5. Quotation in McPherson, *Struggle for Equality,* 92.

6. *New York Daily Tribune,* May 12, 1862. For other reports that articulated the differences between radicals and conservatives, see the *New York Daily Tribune,* May 9, 28, June 30, 1862. For scholarly distinctions that are particularly useful, consult Alan Bogue, *The Earnest Men: Republicans of the Civil War Senate* (Ithaca, N.Y.: Cornell University Press, 1981), 92–124; Trefousse, *Radical Republicans,* 3–33; Fawn M. Brodie, *Thaddeus Stevens: Scourge of the South* (New York: Norton, 1959), 187–89.

7. *New York Herald,* May 11, 1862; *New York Daily Tribune,* May 9, June 30, July 5, 1862. On the notion that southern leaders had hoodwinked the masses into war, see Grimsley, *Hard Hand of War,* 8–9.

8. George B. McClellan to Abraham Lincoln, July 7, 1862, in George B. McClellan, *The Civil War Papers of George B. McClellan: Selected Correspondence, 1860–1865,* ed. Stephen W. Sears (New York: Ticknor & Fields, 1989), 344–45.

9. *New York Times,* July 7, 1862.

10. For a sampling of how high hopes remained in the North, see Maria Lydig Daly, *Diary of a Union Lady, 1861–1865,* ed. Harold Earl Hammond (New York: Funk & Wagnalls, 1962), 126–27; George Templeton Strong, *Diary of the Civil War, 1860–1865,* ed. Allan Nevins (New York: Macmillan, 1962), 225; Elizabeth Blair Lee, *Wartime Washington: The Civil War Letters of Elizabeth Blair Lee,* ed. Virginia Jeans Laas (Urbana: University of Illinois Press, 1991), 140–41; Benjamin Brown French, *Witness to the Young Republic: A Yankee's Journal, 1828–1870,* ed. Donald B. Cole and John J. McDonough (Hanover, N.H.: University Press of New England, 1989), 396–97; *New York Times,* May 5, 6, 10, 1862.

11. Bruce Tap, *Over Lincoln's Shoulder: The Committee on the Conduct of the War* (Lawrence: University Press of Kansas, 1998), 21–37; Trefousse, *Radical Republicans,* 185.

12. *Report of the Joint Committee on the Conduct of the War* (Washington, D.C.: GPO, 1863), 260–69, 276, 295–97, 302–9.

13. McClellan's orders in U.S. War Department, *The War of the Rebellion: A Compilation of the Official Records of the Union and Confederate Armies,* 127 vols., index, and atlas (Washington, D.C.: GPO, 1880–1901), ser. 1, 11(2):161 (hereafter cited as *OR;* all references are to ser. 1). McDowell's and other officers' attitudes in William A. Blair, "Barbarians at Fredericksburg's Gate: The Impact of the Union Army on Civil-

ians," in *Decision on the Rappahannock: The Fredericksburg Campaign,* ed. Gary W. Gallagher (Chapel Hill: University of North Carolina Press, 1995), 147-48.

14. Emory M. Thomas, *Robert E. Lee: A Biography* (New York: Norton, 1995), 230.

15. Tap, *Over Lincoln's Shoulder,* 120; George B. McClellan to Edwin Stanton, June 7, 1862, in McClellan, *Civil War Papers,* 290-91.

16. *Report of the Joint Committee on the Conduct of the War,* 286-87, 301; *New York Daily Tribune,* June 21, 1862.

17. J. Medill to S. P. Chase, May 30, 1862, in Salmon P. Chase, *The Salmon P. Chase Papers,* ed. John Niven, 5 vols. to date (Kent, Ohio: Kent State University Press, 1993-), 3:206; Thaddeus Stevens, *The Selected Papers of Thaddeus Stevens,* ed. Beverly Wilson Palmer, 2 vols. (Pittsburgh: University of Pittsburgh Press, 1997), 1:310.

18. *OR* 11(1):1059-60.

19. *New York Tribune,* May 12, 21, 1862; *Congressional Globe,* 37th Cong., 2nd sess., 2342.

20. *New York Daily Tribune,* June 7, 1862.

21. Quoted in *New York Daily Tribune,* May 7, 1862. For similar arguments, see *Congressional Globe,* 37th Cong., 2nd sess., 2342, 2527.

22. Daly, *Diary,* 122; *New York Times,* May 27, 1862.

23. *Congressional Globe,* 37th Cong., 2nd sess., 2233-35.

24. *Liberator,* May 9, 1862.

25. Chicago *Tribune,* May 28, 1862.

26. For examples of the continuing citation of barbarity against slaves, see *New York Daily Tribune,* May 5, June 13, 1862, and Boston *Congregationalist* account in *Liberator,* April 25, 1862.

27. *OR* 11(1):511, 557-58; (3):511, 516-17. See also Charles S. Wainwright, *A Diary of Battle: The Personal Journals of Colonel Charles S. Wainwright, 1861-1865,* ed. Allan Nevins (New York: Harcourt, Brace & World, 1962), 45.

28. *New York Daily Tribune,* May 13, 1862.

29. *OR* 11(3):135.

30. *OR* 11(3):509-10.

31. For Wade's introductory comments, see *Liberator,* May 9, 1862.

32. Boston *Congregationalist* and Phillips speech quoted in *Liberator,* April 25, 1862.

33. *New York Daily Tribune,* May 15, 1862.

34. *Congressional Globe,* 37th Cong., 2nd sess., 2292; Daly, *Diary,* 139.

35. *New York Daily Tribune,* July 14, 1862.

36. George Alfred Townsend, *Rustics in Rebellion: A Yankee Reporter on the Road to Richmond, 1861-65* (Chapel Hill: University of North Carolina Press, 1950), 70; *New York Daily Tribune,* May 6, 1862.

37. *Liberator,* May 2, 1862; *New York Daily Tribune,* May 31, 1862. For another

report that the Confederates organized black units, see Chicago *Tribune*, May 29, 1862.

38. *New York Daily Tribune*, July 12, 1862; *Congressional Globe*, 37th Cong., 2nd sess., 2246; Stevens, *Selected Papers*, 1:313; Bogue, *Earnest Men*, 162.

39. Stevens, *Selected Papers*, 1:311–12.

40. *New York Daily Tribune*, July 10, 1862.

41. *Liberator*, May 2, 1862.

42. *New York Daily Tribune*, July 19, 1862; McPherson, *Battle Cry of Freedom*, 500; *New York Times*, July 10, 1862; Bogue, *Earnest Men*, 161–62.

43. Fessenden's address in *New York Times*, July 10, 1862.

44. Daly, *Diary*, 162; Benjamin P. Thomas and Harold M. Hyman, *Stanton: The Life and Times of Lincoln's Secretary of War* (New York: Knopf, 1962), 238–39; Chicago *Tribune*, July 23, 1862.

45. Lee, *Wartime Washington*, 162.

46. Salmon P. Chase, *Inside Lincoln's Cabinet: The Civil War Diaries of Salmon P. Chase*, ed. David Donald (New York: Longmans, Green, 1954), 95, 99; Grimsley, *Hard Hand of War*, 87–92.

47. Lincoln's most recent biographer portrays the president as testing the arguments for and against emancipation with various visitors throughout June 1862. See David Herbert Donald, *Lincoln* (New York: Simon & Schuster, 1995), 364. See also in Stewart, *Holy Warriors*, 185, the argument that abolitionists did not originate emancipation sentiment but capitalized on it and channeled it into politics using new methods.

R. E. L. KRICK

The Men Who Carried This Position Were Soldiers Indeed

The Decisive Charge of Whiting's Division at Gaines's Mill

T he battle of Gaines's Mill is memorable as the first real victory in the Confederate career of R. E. Lee. It was there that Lee launched his largest single attack of the war. The triumph at Gaines's Mill triggered a long series of Confederate victories that increased southern resolve. It was, claimed an Army of Northern Virginia veteran after the war, "the battle of all others which inspired our troops with confidence in themselves and their great commander, General Lee." [1]

The little division of William H. C. Whiting did much to help Lee and the army win those prizes. The nine regiments of Whiting's division, by direct frontal assault, broke three consecutive lines of Union infantry that day. They captured several batteries and succeeded where dozens of regiments before them had failed. Their achievement was a watershed event for the army, an almost alchemical moment that brought together circumstance, opportunity, and some of R. E. Lee's ablest soldiers to produce a unique compound. It was the birth of the Army of Northern Virginia as a great fighting organization.

The situation looked cautiously promising to the Confederate commander on the morning of June 27, 1862. His thoughtful plan to rid central Virginia of George B. McClellan's Federal army had commenced reasonably well the day before, despite its awful execution. The greater part of McClellan's force still menaced Richmond, admittedly, and the Chickahominy River still lay between the city and the bulk of Lee's own force. But "Stonewall" Jackson's army from the Shenandoah Valley had arrived and stood poised to sever the Richmond & York River Railroad, the exposed and vulnerable artery that supplied the Federal army in front of Richmond. Lee knew that the loss of the rail line would force McClellan to abandon his approach to Richmond and seek a new base from which to operate or concentrate his army away from the city and fight a decisive contest for control of the railroad. The Confederates welcomed either option as a major improvement on the situation.

McClellan had, in fact, already chosen to leave the Richmond area in favor of a new base on the James River. He assigned his most trustworthy deputy the task of keeping Lee at arm's length while the army commenced its withdrawal. Fitz John Porter had not commanded the Fifth Corps long, but he enjoyed McClellan's confidence. There were three excellent divisions in Porter's corps, each of which featured a large contingent of able officers. The Fifth Corps was to spend the afternoon of June 27 by itself, with its back to the Chickahominy River, blocking Lee's advance along the north side of that waterway.

Although Lee was not aware of it at the time, the six divisions he brought to the battlefield on June 27 gave him nearly twice as many troops as General Porter. The day's orders called for Jackson to take four of the six divisions and move to the vicinity of Old Cold Harbor, a location Lee inaccurately thought was behind the Federal position. The divisions of James Longstreet and A. P. Hill were to drive whatever enemy they encountered into Jackson's arms. Lee framed this greatly flawed plan based on an imperfect understanding of the geography and road network above the Chickahominy.[2]

Of the six divisions in Lee's army that day, none was smaller than that of William Henry Chase Whiting. A native of Mississippi, the thirty-eight-year-old brigadier general had a reputation for brilliance based on a stellar academic career at West Point. Somewhat contentious and outspoken, "Chase" Whiting offered a direct contrast to Stonewall Jackson, in whose command he served. Whiting's demi-division included only two brigades. Both were commanded by men destined to win fame and reputation as fighters, beginning with their good work at Gaines's Mill. Col. Evander M. Law had four regiments in his brigade, while Brig. Gen. John Bell Hood commanded five regiments. The efforts of Confederate president Jefferson Davis to establish homogeneity by state in the army's brigades seems not have reached Whiting's division by June. Law's command had two regiments from Mississippi (the 2nd and 11th), one from Alabama (the 4th), and one from North Carolina (the 6th). Hood's foot soldiers also came from far-flung corners of the South, with three regiments from Texas (the 1st, 4th, and 5th) and one each from Georgia and South Carolina (the 18th and the Hampton Legion, respectively).

Law's brigade was the more seasoned of the two. The 4th Alabama had seen service atop Matthew's Hill at First Manassas a year earlier and incurred heavy loss there. The 6th North Carolina also survived that day's ordeal, arriving on the battlefield in time to earn combat experience on Henry Hill.

Brig. Gen. William Henry Chase Whiting
Francis Trevelyan Miller, ed., The Photographic History of the Civil War, *10 vols.*
(New York: Review of Reviews, 1911), 1:342

The Hampton Legion was the only unit in Hood's brigade with a comparable record, but one year into the war it already bore little resemblance to the elite regiment of 1861. Its cadre of officers had broken apart in the spring of 1862 during an acrimonious reorganization, and the unit now served only as a small infantry regiment.[3]

Subsequent events showed that the 18th Georgia and the three Texas regiments were arguably the finest fighters in Lee's entire army, but in June 1862 that distinction seemed unlikely. None of the four had seen much action. For the Texas regiments, the extreme distance between the Lone Star State and Virginia made furloughs virtually impossible, and the attendant effect on morale posed a potentially thorny problem. "This regiment has completely played out," reported a soldier in the 1st Texas Infantry in May. He blamed

Col. Evander M. Law (photographed later in the war as a brigadier general)
Francis Trevelyan Miller, ed., The Photographic History of the Civil War, *10 vols.*
(New York: Review of Reviews, 1911), 10 : 107

the trauma of reorganization and the election of new officers for his regiment's sorry condition.[4]

The 4th Texas Infantry was destined to play the key role at Gaines's Mill, yet it too had experienced unrest before the campaign. Like many Confederate units that spring the 4th was riven by internal politics. Col. John Marshall commanded the regiment but did not enjoy its confidence. His appointment "was not altogether satisfactory" to the regiment, admitted the 4th's chaplain, even though "we had no braver man in our army than he was." The official history of the brigade echoed those remarks: Marshall "was not deemed competent to direct the regiment in battle." His close connections with President Davis and various politicians in Richmond, however, often enabled the 4th "to procure all the necessaries and comforts for the campaign," and "the Regiment soon learned to appreciate his value." [5]

Lt. Col. Bradfute Warwick was Marshall's second in command. A native of Richmond, Warwick had seen European service under Garibaldi in the 1850s before settling in Texas. He and his brigade commander, General Hood, both courted the same girl in Richmond, though perhaps at different times. No man would cut a more conspicuous figure on the Gaines's Mill battlefield than Warwick. [6]

The 18th Georgia Infantry may have been the most interesting regiment of them all. Thrown in with a crowd of rowdy Texans, the Georgians quickly won the allegiance of their sister regiments. Soon, "through love," they were known as the "3rd Texas." William T. Wofford was the unit's superb colonel, but he was at home sick during the Seven Days battles. Lt. Col. Solon Z. Ruff commanded the 18th at Gaines's Mill in Wofford's stead. Ruff possessed the outspoken confidence prized by Texans. Writing to his father on June 15, Ruff boasted that "our men can whip Yankees two to one all the time." The fighting around Richmond cemented an alliance between the Texans and Georgians that lasted until the 18th left the brigade after Sharpsburg. [7]

The assortment of weapons known to be carried in the division during the Seven Days battles helps to confirm the traditional perception of a hastily patched together, makeshift southern army. Some units certainly had rifles, though most apparently did not. The 5th Texas carried Enfield rifles at Gaines's Mill. Company D of the 4th Alabama — "the Canebrake Rifles" — also carried rifles, yet no one in the company had a bayonet. Most and possibly all of the other companies in the 4th carried smoothbore muskets, leaving the Canebrake Rifles the onerous chore of going to the front as skirmishers on every field. In the 11th Mississippi's "Van Dorn Reserve" (Company I, from Aberdeen), the men probably carried the rare breechloading 5-shot Colt's Rifle. Despite these exceptions, there is little doubt that most of Whiting's men breasted the storm of battle carrying smoothbore muskets — weapons of little value outside one hundred yards. [8]

Whiting's division had been very active in the weeks preceding the Seven Days battles. Lee had chosen it to reinforce Stonewall Jackson's army in the Shenandoah Valley. General Whiting had been in favor of the trip to join the

Brig. Gen. John Bell Hood, an engraving published in the Confederacy
eight months after the Seven Days campaign.
Southern Illustrated News, *February 28, 1863*

famous Jackson, but Hood had protested, apparently thinking that the battle
for Richmond would offer him more opportunities. Nonetheless, the journey
westward commenced on June 11. Within hours of its arrival in Staunton on
the seventeenth, the division received new orders to retrace its steps toward
Richmond with the rest of Jackson's force. Together they would form the
key element of Lee's elaborate plan to maneuver the Union army away from
Richmond.[9]

Hood's brigade led the march of Jackson's column on June 26 as it veered southeastward from Ashland toward McClellan's vulnerable railroad. The Texans played an important role in the frequent scuffles with enemy cavalry that interrupted the column's progress. At the bridge over Totopotomoy Creek, Jackson worked with some men of the 4th Texas to drive off Union skirmishers and secure a bridgehead on the steeply carved southern bank. Whiting and Jackson saw much of each other that day, and their relations seem to have been cordial enough, although one of Whiting's friends wrote later that Jackson's customary reticence, even with important subordinates, annoyed Whiting, who was "somewhat sore" about the whole thing.[10]

On the morning of June 27, Whiting's men brought up the rear of Jackson's long column, a fateful assignment that placed them in the right spot for their history-making charge that evening. The division was ready to march before daylight. "Everybody expected to find a rough day ahead of us," remembered John Coxe of Hampton's Legion. Once the march began, Col. Evander Law noticed that the column's progress was "strangely slow." "We seemed to be feeling our way instead of moving promptly upon well-known points," he wrote. That sluggishness may have been the only evidence Whiting's men saw of the now-famous wrong turn that the head of Jackson's column took above Gaines's millpond midway through the day's march. An impatient General Hood encountered Jackson about then and asked for something to do, to which Jackson characteristically replied, "Press on, sir — press on."[11]

Eventually the front of Jackson's column approached Old Cold Harbor crossroads and became the left of the Confederate army's position. D. H. Hill's division, acting that day as part of Jackson's command, began establishing its position south of the intersection by building up a line of artillery. In time, Richard S. Ewell's division, followed by Jackson's old division, entered the fight in the woods to the west of D. H. Hill. This left only Whiting's division still in column north of the battlefield. Jackson sent an officer to direct Whiting toward the right of Jackson's line near New Cold Harbor, in the general vicinity of James Longstreet's division. Geography dictated that Whiting's two brigades would have to venture across broken terrain.[12]

Some of the Texans came under fire long before catching their first glimpse of the battlefront. Poorly aimed shells from Union batteries periodically overshot the battlefield and instead plowed through Whiting's marching men. It seemed to Granville Crozier of the 4th Texas that "those screaming, shrieking shells bursting around us would never stop." Jim Smilie of the 4th Texas became the brigade's first casualty. Several men in the regiment observed a solid shot come "crashing through the trees." Bennett Wood, marching beside Smilie, saw it just in time to drop to the ground. This exposed poor Smilie, and the ball decapitated him. Word of the spectacular casualty soon passed to the next company in the column, speeding its march still more until the whole regiment was in a steady trot. A deep stream astride the route slowed and further disarranged the Texans. Shorter soldiers in the ranks had to hold their cartridge boxes high in the air to keep them dry.[13]

Other obstacles soon appeared. Stragglers, hundreds of them, began choking the line of march. Joe Polley of the 4th Texas wrote of seeing "regiments of them that were seemingly beyond the control of their officers." Some of Arnold Elzey's brigade, badly cut up, shouldered through the men of the 5th Texas. The uninspiring appearance of Elzey's soldiers discouraged some of Whiting's men, who felt they were too late to help win the battle. "I never dreamed of such confusion," wrote a Texas officer; "men deserted their colors, Colonels lost their commands, and God only knows how far off were a rout and panic." Hood's men also began to lose sight of their surroundings. Enormous clouds of dense black powder smoke drifted around the lines. "The air was stifling," and unsettling gloom supplanted bright sunshine. Chase Whiting and John Hood ignored these distractions, consistently urging the men to push forward toward the sound of the guns.[14]

When Whiting finally arrived at New Cold Harbor Tavern, the outlook was poor. A. P. Hill's division had been entirely deployed and now lay motionless; Longstreet was ready to advance but understandably was chary of exposing his men to an enfilading fire from across the river; and Jackson's other two divisions were snared in the woods on the eastern end of the battlefront. Lee likely also realized that he was fighting the sun as much as Fitz John Porter. The onset of darkness would allow Porter's escape and ruin an opportunity to drive him into the river. Whiting's division was the army's last intact reserve that evening, and its deployment deserved special care to ensure maximum effect. With everyone clamoring for support, General Lee himself decided where Whiting's men could be most useful. The nine fresh regiments would march directly ahead, uniting their weight with other commands in one last attempt to carry the Federal position. Perhaps they would galvanize Hill's fought-out brigades. At the very least, Whiting's men could provide support for Longstreet's left flank and allow that general's troops at last to add their muskets to the fight.

If Lee knew much about the geography of this battlefield, he must have been disheartened. The Federal Fifth Corps occupied a plateau ideally suited for defense. At its base ran Boatswain's Creek, a shallow and narrow stream with steeply scarped sides and a sticky, clay-like bottom. A ribbon of woods, varying in width from a few yards to nearly one-third of a mile, extended on

R. E. L. KRICK

both sides of the creek. At the spot where Whiting's men attacked, the hill defended by Porter's Federals rose almost at once. Its ascent was so precipitous that in most places several parallel lines of infantry could cling to the slope, firing over one another's heads. This terraced arrangement gave Porter's defense some depth and tripled his firepower. Farther to the south, atop the hill, a line of cannon lobbed shells over Boatswain's Creek and into the Confederate formations near New Cold Harbor.

George Morell's division defended the section of line opposite Whiting. His men had improved their circumstances in places by felling trees, dragging in fence rails, piling up knapsacks, and otherwise improvising shelter. A selective prebattle thinning of the woods created lanes of fire for the hilltop artillery. From New Cold Harbor southward to Boatswain's Creek the ground sloped gently. An enormous field extended across the Confederate front (the same field in which A. P. Hill's brigades lay in line, pinned down by Federal fire), running parallel to the stream. Any attacks directed against Morell's division would have to brave several hundred yards of barren slope before reaching the shelter of the creek's bed. With a layered defense and virtually unlimited fields of fire, this section of Porter's line was especially well sited. Even its flanks were secure. Morell's men had no worries about being turned on their left because Federal artillery on the south bank of the Chickahominy River protected that open ground. In the other direction more soldiers from the Fifth Corps secured Morell's right.[15]

Lee greeted Whiting's division when it arrived at the Telegraph Road. A Texan wrote a few weeks later that Lee hurried the men forward, "as if the fate of mankind depended upon our coming." Whiting joined Lee and together they sought out General Hood for a consultation. After a brief conference Lee and Whiting rode off, leaving Hood to sort out his line of battle. Some time later, Lee returned in search of Hood. The two men spoke earnestly. Hood learned that the Union line in front of New Cold Harbor remained unbreached. "Can you break his line?" Lee asked. Hood promised to try. Lee doffed his hat to Hood and rode off to orchestrate the movements of the other troops on the field. The men of the 18th Georgia watched with interest this last conference between their brigadier and R. E. Lee and saw the hat-raising. Maj. John C. Griffis told those around him that he thought the polite general was Lee, but no one was sure, "as none of us have seen him."[16]

As a result of this conference, Hood rode off on a reconnaissance to scout the ground he would traverse. By this time both he and Law had deployed their brigades into lines of battle and the men were scattered along the axis of the Telegraph Road, stolidly enduring long-range artillery fire. Off to their left front they could hear the rest of Jackson's Valley army throwing its full weight into the fight. Colonel Law wrote in 1887 about the "deafening" noise of musketry and judged it "the heaviest I have ever heard on any field." [17]

The two brigades had a difficult wait in the minutes before they entered the fight. The 18th Georgia found itself assigned briefly to support one of the ineffectual Confederate batteries posted near New Cold Harbor. Lying flat to avoid the flying iron, the Georgians watched as Federal shells silenced two consecutive batteries. In less than thirty minutes of this terrifying duty the 18th lost between twenty and thirty of its men killed and wounded. Union artillery performed effectively against other units too. A pair of men in the 5th Texas made a practice of stooping and twisting to avoid the deadly missiles until finally they both dodged directly into the path of one that tore them apart. Somewhere nearby (and presumably beyond the range of the artillery), Capt. William M. Robbins of the 4th Alabama assembled the regiment and led it in prayer, the entire body of men momentarily subduing the passions of battle to kneel for an incongruous moment of worship in an incredibly violent setting. Officers in the 4th Texas likely engaged in more swearing than praying. Colonel Marshall somehow had fumbled a command, got the regiment "entangled," and caused the men needless fatigue while marching around trying to find the rest of the brigade. He and Lieutenant Colonel Warwick spent the lull squabbling over control of the regiment. Another officer in the 4th entertained those around him by "drawing his sword and waving it over his head" while he recited lines from Walter Scott's poem "Marmion." [18]

As the time for the charge neared, the alignment of Whiting's division became more clear. Hood's brigade would attack on the left, Law's brigade on the right. No doubt the latter had instructions to look for any of Longstreet's men and knit together the flanks of the two divisions if possible. Shortly before stepping off, Hood received a messenger from Gen. Richard S. Ewell. That voluble warrior was managing the fight near the Confederate center. Future general John M. Jones, serving on Ewell's staff, brought word to General Hood that Ewell needed help in the woods. This news caused Hood to align his units so that his easternmost regiments would hit the front lines where Ewell needed them. The Hampton Legion served as Hood's left during the attack, with the 5th Texas on the Legion's right, followed by the 1st Texas and the 4th Texas. Brigade historian Joe Polley visited the battlefield after the war and estimated the length of the line at more than one-third of a mile. The 18th Georgia was not part of this arrangement, having been detained in its chore of supporting the artillery. The four front-line units gathered at the edge of the crowded woods in front of New Cold Harbor.

R. E. L. KRICK

Beside them on the right were two of Law's four regiments, the 11th Mississippi and the 4th Alabama. Both of those regiments were in the eastern edge of the big field at New Cold Harbor. The 2nd Mississippi and 6th North Carolina formed a second line parallel to Law's two front regiments.[19]

A mixture of disorganized and terrified stragglers continued to clog the piney woods and embarrass the field officers' efforts to prepare for battle. The 5th Texas found its line repeatedly fractured by clusters of walking wounded and panic-stricken skulkers emerging from the trees. "They would implore us not to go as it was certain death, the place was impregnable," wrote R. A. Brantley. On Evander Law's front the problem was exactly the opposite: immobile soldiers — Virginians, thought W. A. Love of the 11th Mississippi — who blocked the line of advance and could not be induced to move either forward or rearward.[20]

Senior officers associated with the division understood the importance of the moment. Evander Law supposed that failure to breach the Union line "would be equivalent to a Confederate disaster, and would involve the failure of General Lee's whole plan for the relief of Richmond." In fact, the Union army already was in the preliminary stages of abandoning the lines east of Richmond, but no Confederate officer at Gaines's Mill suspected that on June 27. To the army it was a critical moment, demanding the greatest effort possible. The full drama of a Civil War battlefield provided the proper backdrop to those thoughts. A private in Law's brigade could not believe the visual drama unfolding around him and labeled the scene "the reality of the pictures given us by artists."[21]

Such high stakes and emotional scenes stirred the usually reticent Chase Whiting to oratory. Riding his dapple gray horse among Law's brigade, the general did his best to inspire the men. The 6th North Carolina cheered him as he rode along its line. Wheeling his horse, Whiting pointed toward the Union batteries visible atop the distant hill and triggered the charge by yelling: "Boys, you can take it!" He also addressed the 11th Mississippi briefly, urging it to "Come on!" An officer in the 4th Alabama's Tuskegee Zouaves saw Whiting "far in advance of us, waving his hat and exclaiming, 'To the charge.'"[22]

While Law's men moved forward at Whiting's urging, the most significant tactical event of the battle occurred. General Hood, riding with the 4th Texas, saw an opportunity to improve the 4th's chances. The large field, with Law's men tucked into its easternmost corner, offered excellent room for maneuver. So Hood took the 4th diagonally across the rear of Law's line, eventually arriving more or less on that brigade's right. This move separated Hood from the rest of his brigade and left a gap between Law and the

1st Texas, but it also helped close the seam between Law and Longstreet and freed the 4th Texas from the woods, allowing it to build momentum in its charge. The 18th Georgia arrived just in time to hook on to the end of the 4th's column, and together the two regiments arrived in the field that was destined to be their avenue to fame.[23]

In this field Hood found the Parson house — probably not much of a structure since almost no one mentioned it — and most of the remnants of A. P. Hill's division. It was "an old field" of the sort commonly seen in war-torn Virginia, covered with weeds. The moment Hood's men entered the field in a great wheeling movement from the woods, they took casualties. Among the first to fall was Colonel Marshall, who was shot in the neck and killed. He fell from his horse while his men pivoted into line. Granville Crozier, the smallest man in the 4th Texas's Tom Green Rifles, fell about the same time, wounded by a bullet that glanced off the hammer of a comrade's gun. The regiment soon aligned itself in perfect formation, looking as if it were on dress parade. General Hood then rode out of the woods, climbed off his horse, and addressed the 4th in a manner and tone long remembered with pride by every survivor.[24]

Hood "made us a little talk," recollected Bennett Wood. "Surely no one who ever heard that voice could forget it," wrote J. T. Hunter of Hood's staff. The general "looked sublime," thought another soldier, and "every man in the regiment was watching him." Driven to haste by the steady stream of shells dropping in Parson's field, Hood merely reminded his audience that he had promised to lead them in their first big battle and urged the men to keep their eyes on their flag as a guide and not to move too fast. Val Giles remembered Hood remarking, "The time has come and I am here." Nearly everyone heard the general say specifically that there was to be no firing until he gave the order; they would save their volley for closer range, when it would count more. Hood then walked some six paces ahead of the 4th, snatched off his hat with his left hand, hoisted his sword in his right, and bellowed: "Forward! Guide right!" and the regiment launched its charge.[25]

The other three regiments in Hood's brigade, deprived of their general, had already reached the firing line, as had Evander Law's men. The 5th Texas encountered both thick brush and mire on its way to join some of Ewell's troops on a wooded hilltop about one hundred yards short of Boatswain's Creek. There the 5th lay prone and blasted away, apparently awaiting explicit orders from anyone. The major of the 5th, thirty-nine-year-old John C. Upton, impressed his men with hard-nosed leadership. His battle dress consisted of a ragged pair of pants, scuffed cavalry boots, an ancient cotton shirt, a black slouch hat, and "a huge sabre, with a pair of six shoot-ers." The entire package made him look "less like an officer than any of his men." During the firefight Upton paced along the line, encouraging the men steadily: "My brave boys, give it to them." Then he would "wave his saber over his head and give a yell." Pvt. Robert Campbell watched in amusement as one of Ewell's staff officers raced up to the 5th and called out, "stand my men, for God's sake stand — or the day is lost." This unnecessary rallying ignited Upton's temper, and he confronted the unfamiliar officer brusquely: "Who in hell and damnation are you?" Upon learning the stranger's identity, Upton banished him: "Leave here, you damn coward, these are my men, these are Texans, and they *don't know* how to run — and sir, if you don't leave here immediately, I will teach you how to run." After thirty minutes of inconclusive action, someone came up and called for the 5th Texas to fix bayonets, then General Ewell ordered a charge across the creek. The officers of the 5th could not see any other regiment in the brigade.[26]

In front of Law's two leading regiments the situation seemed worse. Their line of attack was more open, and the trees where Union infantry lurked were thicker and concealed a less visible enemy. Between Law and the creek lay more of A. P. Hill's men, thought to be Charles W. Field's Virginia brigade. Those Confederates' "straggling" line sheltered "behind a gentle ridge that ran across the field." The attack would have to move directly over their prostrate forms. Col. Owen K. McLemore of the 4th Alabama backpedaled in front of his regiment and called out drill steps to his men to keep them in formation as they trampled Hill's line. But on reaching the crest of the ridge Law's men encountered a blast of fire so devastating it stopped them in their tracks. McLemore fell wounded, the 4th Alabama and 11th Mississippi both wavered, and despite General Whiting's orders to stop for nothing the brigade stalled. For more than thirty minutes the 4th Alabama confronted what one soldier termed "all the black rays of Death." Visibility dwindled to only ten feet at times, and once the 4th Alabama even fell back for some sixty or seventy yards, its fine scorn for A. P. Hill's men now forgotten. Rufus Hollis of the 4th remembered lying on his back to load, with his gun wedged between his feet, and rolling over to fire at the distant Union line. This ended when a bullet clipped the back of Hollis's neck. Others complained of taking friendly fire from Field's brigade nearby. Like the 5th Texas, Law's two forward regiments seemed to be looking for some compelling reason to move ahead once more.[27]

The arrival of the 4th Texas provided the missing motivation. It thundered past Law's right flank, screeching the rebel yell. "Forward, boys! Charge them!" cried Law, and the Alabamians and Mississippians pushed down the hill toward the creek with ever-increasing speed. "The ground

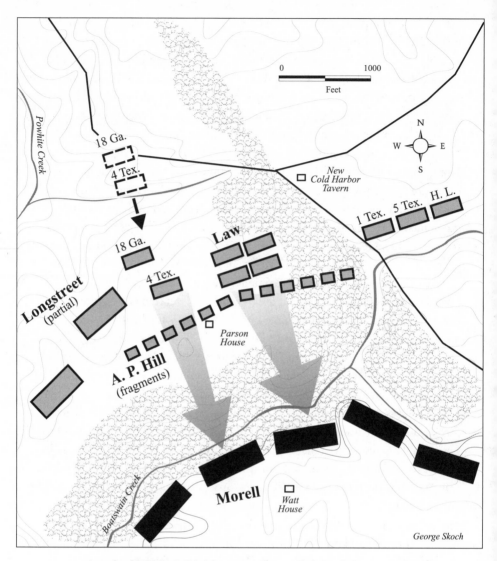

Assault of Whiting's Division across Boatswain's Creek, June 27, 1862

in rear of the advancing column was strewn thickly with the dead and wounded," recorded Law, but momentum kept the brigade headed in the correct direction. Thirty yards short of the creek the brigade let out "a wild, mad shout." [28]

The 4th Texas, followed by the 18th Georgia — barely 1,000 men — had pushed through the peach orchard beside the Parson house and on across the field, moving rapidly but not at a "double quick." "It was when we first came in view of the Federals that we suffered our heaviest loss," reported the brigade history. Lt. James L. Lemon of the 18th Georgia saw four of his men cut down in the first fifty yards. William Hamby of the 4th likened the fall of bullets to "drops of rain from a passing cloud," and the memorably named Decimus et Ultimus Barziza reported that the Federals opposite the 4th delivered well-disciplined volleys. "Oh, the slaughter as we charged!" lamented Bennett Wood, a Texan in Company C. "We understood why Gen. Hood wanted us to go . . . without firing, for in piles all around us were other Confederates, who [had] stopped to load their guns . . . dead and dying." Facing an invisible foe only added to the terror of the experience. It was not until the 4th reached the crest of what Hood called "the bald ridge," about 150 yards short of the creek, that the men got their first glimpse of the Union line, and only then by peering between distant tree trunks.[29]

Under a "very hot sheet of musketry," Lieutenant Colonel Warwick tried to stop the 4th and return the fire. This was precisely the mistake Hood wanted to avoid. Most of the men fired their weapons across the creek once, but Hood soon had the regiment in hand again and ordered it to fix bayonets and make for the gully. With Warwick in front waving a flag he had found abandoned on the field and Sgt. Ed Francis "right gallantly" carrying the 4th's own colors, the Texans made their final rush for the creek and "plunged right into the deep branch," "yelling like madmen."[30]

At no point is Boatswain's Creek impassable. The spot where the Texans and Georgians reached it was less swampy and more narrow than elsewhere, and some survivors pointed out later that the relatively easy crossing improved their chances of success. Where the 4th Texas hit the creek it was "of steep banks & mirey channel," with felled trees on both sides adding a further encumbrance. Lieutenant Lemon of the 18th Georgia found that he needed both hands to climb up the southern bank and had to holster his pistol for the maneuver; but the stream was not particularly deep, and few others in the two regiments recorded much difficulty in getting across.[31]

Piles of very large logs on the southern bank of the creek greeted the attackers once they got across. A few bullets buzzed in from the rear — apparently fired by ill-disciplined soldiers in A. P. Hill's division — toppling some men of the 4th as they scaled the obstructions. From there it was thirty or forty yards to the first semientrenched line of Union infantry. The Texans continued to shout wildly, their noise at the creek drowning out the roar of battle in that confined space. Nearly all Confederate sources agree that once Hood's two regiments crossed the creek, the momentum of their charge permanently altered the nature of the fight. Union infantry in the first line broke almost at once after firing a few scattering shots and "fled like a flock of sheep." The 4th Texas unloosed one rippling volley into the backs of the

An early postwar depiction of Hood's brigade attacking at Gaines's Mill.
R. G. Horton, A Youth's History of the Great Civil War, from 1861 to 1865
(New York: Van Evrie, Horton, 1867), opposite p. 211

retreating Federals and continued on up the hill, dodging among occasional large oak trees that had escaped the axes of Union infantry. The unraveling of this first line "was not simply complimentary and encouraging," thought Joe Polley of the 4th, "it was also inspiring and persuasive." "On we went, yelling, shooting, seeing men fall and die, up, up to the top of that murderous hill," wrote Bennett Wood. Lieutenant Barziza relished the memory: "We flew toward the breastworks, cleared them, and slaughtered the retreating devils as they scampered up the hill." Hood's momentum could not be blunted. It built upon itself, frantic and frenzied.[32]

Reaching the second line of makeshift breastworks, the Texans again let out a roar, one which, said Chaplain Nicholas A. Davis of the 4th, "will long be remembered by those who heard it." Lieutenant Colonel Warwick was conspicuous here with his flag, shouting, "Come on!" The regiment continued to load and fire repeatedly as it surged up the hill, the men "yelling, shouting and swearing." They watched in appreciation as the first Union line trampled the second and third lines of infantry, creating a roiling mass of fugitives. This crowd burst onto the open plateau atop the hill, where the Watt house sat as a centerpiece to the action.[33]

The Texans followed closely, their eyes fixed on an isolated cluster of

The earliest known photograph of the Sarah Watt house, centerpiece of the battlefield at Gaines's Mill, was taken forty-two years after the battle. The camera's view is toward the southwest.

New York Monuments Commission, In Memorium Henry Warner Slocum, 1826–1894 (Albany: J. B. Lyon, 1904), opposite p. 70

Union cannon posted very close to the crest of the hill. Lieutenant Barziza saw a Union officer on horseback unsuccessfully trying to rally men around the guns by waving his sword with a hat perched atop it. Val Giles of the 4th fell wounded by a canister ball some fifty yards before reaching the top — excellent evidence of how far forward that Union battery had been pushed to depress the muzzles of its guns down the steep slope. The Texans overran the battery and left it in their wake, their attention drawn to choicer targets in the distance. William Barry of Company G professed to know later that a total of twenty-eight minutes elapsed during the operation, from the charge's beginning until the capture of the four cannon.[34]

Several hundred yards to the east, the other half of Hood's brigade, with the regiments of Law's brigade on its right, conducted a simultaneous battle.

They encountered many of the same obstacles as their friends in the 4th, but the denser woods on that part of the battlefield added another layer of both difficulty and protection. Unlike the regiments under Hood's direct eye, the 5th Texas exhibited no fire discipline and allowed itself three volleys before beginning its descent toward the creek bottom. Robert Campbell remembered giving "a leap and a yell" on the way down the hill. R. A. Brantley of the same regiment identified the 5th's battle cry as "the old Indian war hoop, now called rebel yell." Its stirring notes sustained the 5th as it tumbled down the slope and into the water. Boatswain's Creek assumed a somewhat different character where the 5th and 1st Texas crossed. Its approaches proved swampier and the lip of the embankment steeper. Private Campbell lost a shoe in the bottom of the creek but could not afford to pause and continued the charge uphill semishod, slicing through Federal soldiers who "were thick as black birds." Stunned by the ferocity of the attack, some of the Union infantry would not raise their heads above the logs, making the 5th's chore much easier. The adjacent 1st Texas also met dwindling resistance. Reaching the open crest of the plateau, it encountered crowds of Union infantry and "had nothing to do but shoot them as they went panic stricken." [35]

The two front units of Law's command, wedged between the separated wings of Hood's brigade, reached the creek in good order. Many survivors were shocked at the perfection of the Union position in their front. The ravine in which the creek ran was about four feet deep and six feet wide in front of the 4th Alabama, and when the 11th Mississippi reached its crossing point the men found they had to help each other struggle out of the little gorge. Once across, Law's men encountered a line of "serviceable breastworks of green logs" piled three feet high. Midway up the slope the second Federal line also enjoyed partial security behind a line of logs and fence rails, and the entire hillside was "covered with low timber and bushes." Writing the next day, an unidentified man in the brigade still marveled at what he had seen: "This position was, perhaps, the most formidable of the kind that was ever built. Scaling ladders and boarding pikes would have been far better adapted to its reduction than bayonets." [36]

The 4th Texas had roared past already and probably was nearing the top of the plateau when Law's brigade got across the creek. Colonel Law confirmed after the war that his men faced an indifferently conducted resistance and that the Federals in their front broke and ran when the cheering Confederates approached. "Then we had our 'innings,'" wrote Law. "As the blue mass surged up the hill in our front, the Confederate fire was poured into it with terrible effect. . . . Scarcely a shot fired into that living mass could fail of its errand." None of the numerous accounts from Hood's and Law's sur-

R. E. L. KRICK

vivors speaks of hand-to-hand fighting on the hillside, and the inference is clear that many of the northern defenders fled in haste. Law's two regiments emerged onto the plateau very close to the Watt house.[37]

One chore remained to block Whiting's division from a total success. Several batteries of Federal artillery dotted the last crest of the plateau, their backs at the steep descent to the floodplain of the Chickahominy River. Emerging from the timber on the heels of Morell's division, the Confederates immediately felt the presence of those batteries off to the southeast and southwest. Isolated fragments of Morell's infantry continued to contest Hood's progress in places, but for the most part the Confederates were left alone to contemplate the hideous task confronting the artillery. The 4th Texas pushed about one hundred yards beyond the Watt house and halted in an orchard (variously described as consisting of peaches, pears, or apples) south of the main building. There General Hood found it and attempted to reconfigure its remnants for the final attack against the cannon. The 18th Georgia joined the right of the 4th. Some of Law's men — primarily from the 11th Mississippi but with other regiments sprinkled into the mixture — came up and affixed themselves to the 18th's right flank. Hood then wheeled the entire mass obliquely to its left some forty-five degrees, facing southeastward. About five hundred yards distant the men could see at least three batteries of Federal artillery on a conspicuous knoll. A deep, waterless ravine bisected the intervening area.[38]

Heavy and accurate fire from the batteries produced "frightful terror" and made the delay at the orchard very brief. Joe Polley of the 4th figured that it was less than five minutes. Hood gave his final orders with such calmness that his demeanor buoyed up the spirits of one Texan: "I just determined that if he could stand it, I would." Hood could muster aplomb more readily, perhaps, because he did not accompany the men in the final charge against the artillery. In fact, no officer seemed to have had direct control of the movement. All three field officers in the 4th had been hit. What little organization the participants claimed for themselves afterward they attributed to lower-level leadership. "Every man was his own commander," was how C. C. Chambers of the 11th Mississippi phrased it. A man in the 18th Georgia wrote of "the clear shrill voices" of the unit's major and adjutant as they strove to keep the men in line. In Company C of that regiment (the Jackson County Volunteers), the lieutenant commanding the company dropped, "terribly mangled" by a shell. His replacement fell a few seconds later. In Company H every officer went down, leaving a sergeant commanding the company. The picture in the 4th Texas seemed even more bleak to Lieutenant Barziza: "On, on we go, with not a field officer to lead us, two thirds of the Company

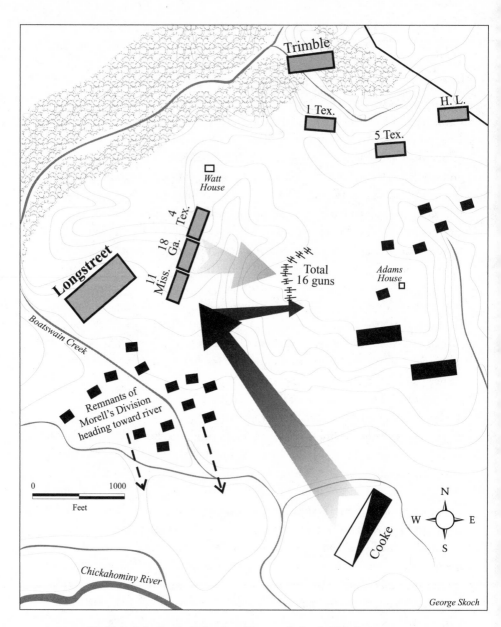

Twilight fight for the Federal artillery at Gaines's Mill, June 27, 1862

officers and half the men already down — yelling, shouting, firing, running straight up to the death-dealing machines."[39]

Mercifully, the intervening depression — "a steep-banked, tortuous gully" — provided shelter for the men to regroup before their final rush, though they found the ditch clogged with "fugitive Yankees." Peeking over the lip, they could see the blue-clad cannoneers ramming down charges of canister; seconds later "a long, blazing flame issued from the pieces," and then came the peculiar whistling sound of the projectiles. Drifting dust dimmed everyone's vision, but it was minor compared to the black powder smoke that by now had "settled down upon the field in thick curtains, rolling about like some half solid substance." [40]

A fateful congruence of three events now brought affairs to a climax. The Georgians, Texans, and Mississippians braced themselves for crossing the final three hundred yards up the hill to the guns. Directly behind them the summer sun shone its final, weak rays, reminding anyone with enough detachment to observe such things that darkness was imminent. Into this scene barged several companies of United States cavalry in an ill-advised charge that stunned everyone on the field. The commander of the Federal cavalry, Gen. Philip St. George Cooke, ordered the charge into the teeth of the Confederate advance as a diversion, hoping to buy a few minutes during which the threatened artillery could limber up and drive away. William Hamby of the 4th described the impressive scene later: "In a short while we felt the ground begin to tremble like an earthquake and heard a noise like the rumbling of distant thunder." The sunlight glistening on waving sabers and the thundering of the horses "was a spectacle grand beyond description, and imparted a feeling of awe in the bravest of hearts." [41]

Some of the Texans helped break up the cavalry charge, but the bulk of the work fell to the 18th Georgia and the 11th Mississippi. "This was an altogether unexpected assault," wrote W. A. Love of the 11th, and the cavalrymen appeared "remarkably bold." By far the best Confederate account of this episode was written by Jim Lemon of the 18th while the circumstances were fresh in his mind. He reported that the first he knew of it was when someone yelled out, "Cavalry!" Lemon saw the horses angling toward the right wing of the 18th Georgia. He and other skilled company officers were able to bend the three right companies of the regiment obliquely to their right rear and thus faced the cavalrymen head-on. One precise volley served to destroy the cohesion of the charge, knocking down most of the leading horses and littering the field with frightened animals dragging dead and wounded riders. A few brave cavalrymen rushed onward, however, and one Confederate witness even saw an attacker bayoneted. Another horse rode off the field with a bayoneted Confederate musket sticking from its side.

Lemon's company anchored the right of the 18th Georgia during the charge, and he barely escaped death at the hands of a bold horseman. The entire company had fired its volley and was reloading when one Federal rode directly up to Lemon and tried to shoot the lieutenant, whose pistol re-

Confederate advancing to the capture of disabled guns Gaines [mill]

Alfred R. Waud's dramatic sketch depicts the moment when Confederate infantry overran Union guns near the Watt house at Gaines's Mill.

Library of Congress

mained in its holster where he had stuffed it while climbing the banks of Boatswain's Creek. Luckily for Lemon, the gun of his brother-in-law William Davenport had misfired during the volley. Davenport quickly recapped the piece and shot the Federal soldier, saying afterward, "I could not allow that Yank to make Sis' a widow." Moments later another stray horseman rode up and tried to shoot Davenport, but Lemon's pistol repaid the debt. Lemon found the whole thing "a most embarrassing incident which if not for its singularity would most certainly remain unrecorded."[42]

While the three companies of the 18th Georgia beat back the cavalry, the rest of the regiment, together with the 4th Texas and some of Law's men, captured most of the artillery atop the hill. At least two men in the 11th Mississippi shot at the battery horses and claimed success in that tactic. Climbing up the hill the Confederates soon came in range of some of the cannon, but the contours of the ground exposed them to only part of the menacing line of artillery. Nonetheless, the final few yards proved terrible. A few feet short of one gun a blast of canister ripped through Company K of the 18th, killing and wounding seven men. Here Col. Solon Z. Ruff of the 18th ran to the front of his men, waved his hat in the air, and led the way into the batteries. Unionist gunners fell at their pieces, several shot in the process of loading. Tom Rawls of the 11th Mississippi climbed on one of the trophies to celebrate, "but his rear becoming painfully hot he was compelled to retire in quick order amid shouts of laughter from his amused comrades." Two men bearing flags of the 18th Georgia climbed atop different guns to wave the emblems, and a great cheer erupted. From different points all across the vast rolling landscape, men saw in the growing darkness those fluttering flags and knew that the keystone of the Federal position had fallen.[43]

Some of the cannon barely escaped, but apparently the Confederates were able to secure about fourteen guns. Scattered Union infantry continued to snipe at the captors from the shelter of the Adams house, forcing the Confederates to halt their self-congratulations, reform, and push onward in the twilight. The 4th Texas and 18th Georgia saw no more combat in the few minutes remaining before complete darkness, but their comrades in the 5th Texas achieved a significant capture of a different sort. The 5th had been fooling around in a cluster of tents the men discovered when emerging onto the plateau after crossing Boatswain's Creek and driving off the Union infantry. They saw the capture of the artillery on the high ridge in front of them and pushed on up the hill for a reunion with their friends in the 4th Texas. For some ten minutes the 5th lay down on the ground and rested or wandered among the 4th's trophies. Sporadic Federal fire dropped there yet, and regimental commander Jerome B. Robertson fell wounded. But everyone was shocked when suddenly a few bullets came up the hill from the north. George N. Woods of Company F fell mortally wounded, shot in the back. The men roused themselves, squinted down the hill, and discovered a huge mass of blue-clad infantry emerging from the treeline. "The boys gave a whoop," and eccentric Major Upton led the way down the hill to arrange the surrender of the 4th New Jersey Infantry, an intact unit of Henry W. Slocum's division that had become disoriented and cut off in the woods. Upton's arms soon became so full of surrendered cutlery from the Jersey officers that he had to discard the frying pan he normally carried into battle. Gleeful Texans disarmed about 440 disgusted New Jerseyites and sent them off to Richmond as prisoners.[44]

By this time Whiting's regiments were scattered all over the dark battlefield. The division commander had sent the 2nd Mississippi Infantry to support Reilly's Battery while it lobbed long-range shells into the masses of Union survivors making for the Chickahominy River. Part of the 4th Texas, led by Capt. William P. Townsend, found itself in the timber bordering the river. An attempt to call the roll ended in dismay when only seventy-two men could be found; others straggled in during the night. The 18th Georgia also advanced toward the river, and when it became too dark to see the men just lay down where they were and went to sleep.[45]

Many men from Hood's brigade retraced their steps that night over the incredibly long route of their attack. Most were looking for missing friends or relatives. "Glimmering lights scattered far and wide over the field" showed the extent of the army's loss. "I know it was the most miserable night of my life," wrote Samuel Hankins of the 2nd Mississippi. General Hood patrolled the field, assisting his men in collecting casualties. His voice could be heard in the darkness all night long, calling for stretchers to carry off the injured. Bennett Wood of the 4th Texas, who was hunting for his mortally wounded brother, encountered Jake Smilie. Hood had given his own horse to Jake so that Smilie could collect the bodies of his two dead brothers and bury them together. The emotional trauma of the battle and its aftermath finally overwhelmed Hood; a staff officer found the sturdy general in the darkness, "sitting on a cracker-box, crying."[46]

Dawn revealed the full scope of the division's loss. "So horrid, so gloomy, so terribly horrible is the scene," wrote an 11th Mississippi officer in his diary, "that the imagination could never so far lose all sense of humanity as to depict it." A curious soldier in A. P. Hill's division traced the path of Hood's charge and found the descent to Boatswain's Creek "literally strewed with the dead." Every company had some particular tragedy to mourn. The men of Company B, 4th Texas, discovered their missing dog Candy lying "cuddled up under the arm of poor John Summers, who was killed the evening before." Members of the 4th Alabama's Canebrake Rifles located their own John Pitts and buried him in the Watt house orchard. He had been killed there just one day past his nineteenth birthday. Both brigades took time out from these dolorous scenes to listen to speeches praising them. For Law's brigade it was Jefferson Davis who spoke, doubtless drawn there by the presence of two heroic Mississippi regiments. In Hood's brigade the orators were Hood himself and Senator Louis T. Wigfall. Hood's remarks are not on record, but W. H. Gaston of the 1st Texas discovered that "he is a better soldier than speaker." The hard-drinking Wigfall had commanded the Texans early in the war before returning to politics and by the summer of 1862 had established himself as a sort of besotted mascot for the brigade. His eloquent speech on the morning of the twenty-eighth, delivered in Parson's field near where Colonel Marshall had been killed, did much to intensify the burgeoning pride many of the Texans felt. The greatest praise of all came from Stonewall Jackson, who rode over the battlefield on June 28 and re-

marked of Whiting's regiments, "The men who carried this position were soldiers indeed!"[47]

The cost of Whiting's magnificent charge proved substantial. The 11th Mississippi and 4th Alabama suffered heavily, losing 180 of 521 and 132 of an unknown strength respectively. In the second layer of Law's brigade, the 6th North Carolina sustained 51 casualties while the 2nd Mississippi quietly amassed 100 killed and wounded during the fight. In the Hampton Legion losses were relatively light — only 20. The 1st Texas lost 78 out of 440 by nightfall, and beside it the 5th Texas incurred 75 more out of 503 taken into battle. The two primary sufferers, of course, were the 18th Georgia and 4th Texas. The former unit seems to have carried 507 men into the fight and lost about 145 of them in action. In the 4th, the sum was between 250 and 261, out of an estimated strength of between 530 and 546. These losses bring the division casualty figure to approximately 1,035. One wartime source assigned the division a strength of 5,300 before the battle, but a total of nearly 590 men per regiment seems far too high. Even presuming Whiting's division was weaker than 5,300, the day's losses reached about 20 percent, a figure not as awful as the accounts would make one believe.[48]

Inevitably controversy emerged regarding the details of the charge. With so much glory at stake — it was, after all, the army's first sweeping tactical success in Virginia since First Manassas — many claimants appeared to dispute one another's boasts. For a time after the war the debates raged with unusual heat. R. A. Brantley of the 5th Texas went to extraordinary lengths to prove that the flag of his regiment (with himself as color-bearer) reached the top of the hill before the 4th Texas. Texas Brigade historian Joe Polley defended the brigade against the "tardy but clamorous" claims of men in Pickett's Virginia brigade. Happily for historians, Polley returned to the battlefield in the 1890s and measured precise distances between key points associated with his brigade's activities on June 27. He used his findings to help rebuff the Virginians' graceless and ill-formed argument. The men of Evander Law's brigade seem to have possessed the most legitimate arguments for equality, yet their accounts mostly are silent on the matter. Enough firsthand material survives from widely disparate sources to make it clear that the claims of the 4th Texas are legitimate.[49]

One other bit of related controversy deserves notice. Whiting's division was so far from Jackson's personal presence when it entered the battle that "Old Jack" could not really be credited for its feats. General Lee seems to have determined the division's general route of attack, and there is no evidence that anyone higher than Whiting exerted tactical control of the division after that. But immediately after the war James Longstreet, whose troops

*Lt. William D. Rounsavall of Company K, 4th Texas Infantry, was one of hundreds
of Texans shot on June 27 at Gaines's Mill. He lost an arm; his brother John
was mortally wounded that same afternoon.*
Debra Rounsavall Mulholland

abutted Whiting's, protested to Lee that the army commander's official report had failed to notice Longstreet's role. Whiting's troops "were under my
orders and handling," wrote Longstreet, and were found wandering the field
just before the final attack. "Gen. Whiting reported to me that he had lost
his way and did not know where to find Gen Jackson," Longstreet contin-

ued, and it was only through quick thinking that "Old Pete" found a place for Whiting's men "a little behind Pickett's Brigade." Even if the broader argument of Longstreet's control is accepted (and there is not a single piece of proof to support it), it is plain that the details are askew. Whiting's division never was lost, and Lee greeted it when it arrived and selected the spot for its attack. Jackson deserves no more credit for this than does Longstreet and, significantly, neither man claimed it at the time. It appears merely to be an unusually early example of the gasconade for which Longstreet is now famous.[50]

Whiting's charge burnished the reputation of its survivors in many ways. The division commander "won imperishable fame" that sustained his reputation through subsequent failures in 1864 and 1865. The same was true for Hood. He already was popular with his men, but his leadership on the field at Gaines's Mill gave the relationship permanence. "Old Hood is a brave fellow," wrote Jim Lemon of the 18th Georgia in his diary. Three weeks after the battle Lemon bought a silver star from a man in the 4th Texas and affixed it to his own hat as a demonstration of unity with his comrades from the Lone Star State.[51]

The Texas Brigade as an entity proved to be the greatest beneficiary of all. With its charge at Gaines's Mill, the brigade took an important step toward establishing its place in Confederate history. Within days Hood had identified his men as heroes, asserting that "too much cannot, or ever will, be said in their praise." Postmaster John H. Reagan, the most prominent Texan in the Confederate government, testified that R. E. Lee's enormous faith in the brigade could be traced directly to its heroics at Gaines's Mill. "After that on different occasions," Reagan wrote, "General Lee urged me to aid him in getting a division of Texans for his command, remarking that with such a force he would . . . break any line of battle on earth in an open field." Although that claim seems a bit optimistic, the record of the Texas Brigade at Second Manassas, Sharpsburg, Gettysburg, Chickamauga, the Wilderness, and New Market Heights at least verifies the judgment. Though it could choose from among many memorable anniversaries, the Texas Brigade Association almost always held its annual reunions after the war on June 27. The veterans liked to say that at Gaines's Mill their brigade made a reputation that "nearly exhausted them to achieve, and nearly finished them to maintain."[52]

Hindsight shows that the charge of Whiting's division at Gaines's Mill was a defining moment in the history of the Army of Northern Virginia. Confronted with a new commander, a gloomy semisiege of the capital city, and no marked tactical victory in nearly a year, the army simply had to achieve a major triumph. Whiting's men produced one in the most dramatic circumstances imaginable. Ignoring the presence of disheartened troops along the route, unfavorable terrain, menacing Union defenses, and the complete absence of artillery support, Whiting's nine regiments broke the Federal line and triggered the victory. Their reliance on high morale, sound tactics, and superb leadership among junior officers became a blueprint for the army. A veteran of the Texas Brigade speculated after the war that Gaines's Mill "was the battle which taught the Confederate troops in Virginia how to win." Perhaps the assault at Gaines's Mill differs from those at other battlefields only in its particulars, but Whiting's men set the standard. The legendary bond between R. E. Lee and the Army of Northern Virginia was born that afternoon.[53]

NOTES

1. "General Hood's Brigade," *Southern Historical Society Papers,* ed. J. William Jones et al., 52 vols. (Richmond, Va.: Southern Historical Society, 1876–1959), 29:297 (hereafter cited as *SHSP*).

2. U.S. War Department, *The War of the Rebellion: A Compilation of the Official Records of the Union and Confederate Armies,* 127 vols., index, and atlas (Washington, D.C.: GPO, 1880–1901), ser. 1, 11(2):492 (hereafter cited as *OR;* all references are to ser. 1). It is likely that Lee never understood the specifics of the Federal situation at Gaines's Mill, as illustrated by his comment nine months later: "The principal part of the Federal Army was now on the north side of the Chickahominy." In fact, Lee faced no more than 25 percent of McClellan's army on the field at Gaines's Mill.

3. William C. Davis, ed., *The Confederate General,* 6 vols. (Harrisburg, Pa.: National Historical Society, 1991), 6:132; Judith N. McArthur and Orville Vernon Burton, eds., *"A Gentleman and an Officer": A Military and Social History of James B. Griffin's Civil War* (New York: Oxford University Press, 1996), 224–27, 234–41. Griffin's letters nicely summarize the unrest plaguing the Hampton Legion in June 1862.

4. Harold B. Simpson, ed., "Whip the Devil and His Hosts: The Civil War Letters of Eugene O. Perry," *Chronicles of Smith County, Texas* 6 (Fall 1967): 40.

5. Donald D. Everett, ed., *Chaplain Davis and Hood's Texas Brigade* (San Antonio, Tex.: Principia Press of Trinity University, 1962), 157; J. B. Polley, *Hood's Texas Brigade: Its Marches, Its Battles, Its Achievements* (New York: Neale, 1910), 46. Polley's books are cited repeatedly in this essay and are essential sources (see note 30 below for the first citation of Polley's other title). A good biographical sketch and photograph of the posterity-minded Polley can be found in Thomas F. Harwell, *Eighty Years under the Stars and Bars Including Biographical Sketches of "100 Confederate Soldiers I Have Known"* (Kyle, Tex.: n.p., 1947), 24. For classic examples of Colonel Marshall's polit-

ical pandering, see John Marshall to Louis T. Wigfall, December 29, 1861, February 2, 1862, Confederate Research Center, Hill Junior College, Hillsboro, Texas.

6. Robert K. Krick, *Lee's Colonels: A Biographical Register of the Field Officers of the Army of Northern Virginia*, 4th ed. rev. (Dayton, Ohio: Morningside, 1992), 387–88; Mary Chesnut, *Mary Chesnut's Civil War*, ed. C. Vann Woodward (New Haven: Yale University Press, 1981), 431, 442.

7. Janet B. Hewett et al., eds., *Supplement to the Official Records of the Union and Confederate Armies*, 98 vols. to date (Wilmington, N.C.: Broadfoot, 1994–), pt. 1, 2: 431 (hereafter cited as *ORS*); P[eter] W[ellington] A[lexander], "Army Correspondence of the Savannah Republican," Atlanta *Southern Confederacy*, December 12, 1862; Gerald J. Smith, *"One of the Most Daring of Men": The Life of Confederate General William Tatum Wofford* (Murfreesboro, Tenn.: Southern Heritage Press, 1997), 36–38; Solon Z. Ruff to father, June 15, 1862, extract in Fall 1987 catalog of manuscript dealer Len Rosa.

8. Polley, *Hood's Texas Brigade*, 65; *ORS*, pt. 2, 1:274; George W. Elkin to "Dear Sister Mattie," May 25, 1862, Aberdeen *Examiner*, March 15, 1918 (typescript at Evans Memorial Library, Aberdeen, Mississippi). The Elkin letter states specifically that his company carried the Colt's Rifle in late May, but there is no definite proof it still retained that weapon two months later. An ordnance return for Hood's division in December 1862 showed that of the 32,500 rounds of ammunition "Expended + Lost in Battle of Fredericksburg," 25,000 were of .69 caliber — smoothbore rounds. More than half of the regiments in Whiting's division at Gaines's Mill were in Hood's division six months later, and it is extremely unlikely that any of them had downgraded from rifled pieces to smoothbores in the interim. This roundabout logic reinforces the conclusion that most of Whiting's men carried smoothbores on June 27 (Compiled Service Record of Beverley Randolph, M331, roll 206, National Archives, Washington, D.C.).

9. E. M. Law, "The Fight for Richmond in 1862," *Southern Bivouac* 11 (April 1887): 652. For a full discussion of this round-trip, see Douglas Southall Freeman, *Lee's Lieutenants: A Study in Command*, 3 vols. (New York: Scribner's, 1942–44), 1:466–68. Freeman concluded that Lee took advantage of Whiting's meanderings to deceive McClellan only as an afterthought. John B. Hood, writing after the war, offers contrary evidence, stating that Whiting told him before reaching Jackson that they would return to Richmond (J. B. Hood, *Advance and Retreat* [Philadelphia: Press of Burk & McFetridge, 1880], 24).

10. Law, "The Fight for Richmond," 653. Nearly all of the Texas sources cited subsequently in this essay contain valuable material on the June 26 march. One of the best is J. B. Polley, "Hood's Brigade and the 'Bucktails,'" *Confederate Veteran* 24 (February 1916): 73.

11. John Coxe, "Seven Days' Battles around Richmond," *Confederate Veteran* 30

(March 1922): 92; Law, "The Fight for Richmond," 655; Polley, *Hood's Texas Brigade,* 64. The generally accepted version of the story of Jackson's wrong turn is in R. L. Dabney, *Life and Campaigns of Lieut.-Gen. Thomas J. Jackson* (New York: Blelock, 1866), 443.

12. *OR* 11(2):562; Hood, *Advance and Retreat,* 25.

13. Granville H. Crozier, "A Private with General Hood," *Confederate Veteran* 25 (December 1917): 556; Burnell L. Aycock, *A Sketch of the Lone Star Guards* (n.p., n.d.), 7; Mamie Yeary, ed., *Reminiscences of the Boys in Gray, 1861–1865* (Dallas, Tex.: Press of Wilkinson Printing Company, 1912), 815; [Decimus et Ultimus Barziza], "Graphic Description of the Battle of Gaines' Mill," Richmond *Daily Whig,* August 4, 1862. Barziza's outstanding eyewitness account of the battle was later published in the Houston *Tri-Weekly Telegraph,* April 3, 1865, and in Decimus et Ultimus Barziza, *The Adventures of a Prisoner of War,* ed. R. Henderson Shuffler (Austin: University of Texas Press, 1964), 26–28.

14. Polley, *Hood's Texas Brigade,* 41; John W. Stevens, *Reminiscences of the Civil War* (Hillsboro, Tex.: Hillsboro Mirror Print, 1902), 28; Barziza, "Graphic Description"; Crozier, "A Private with General Hood," 556.

15. *OR* 11(2):273, 291, 296, 307; George T. Todd, *Sketch of History the First Texas Regiment, Hood's Brigade, A.N.Va.* (Jefferson, Tex.: Jefferson Jimplecute, 1909), unpaginated leaves; "Richmond" [pseud.], "Battle of Gaines' Mill," Richmond *Daily Whig,* March 6, 1863. Certain sections of Morell's front had abatis in addition to the other defenses.

16. Barziza, "Graphic Description"; Everett, *Chaplain Davis,* 86; William R. Hamby, "Fourth Texas in Battle of Gaines' Mill," *Confederate Veteran* 14 (April 1906): 183–84; Hood, *Advance and Retreat,* 25; James L. Lemon diary, July 11, 1862, in possession of Mark Lemon, Acworth, Georgia. The chronology of these events is reconstructed from several sources. The only discordant account among them is J. T. Hunter, "At Yorktown in 1862 and What Followed," *Confederate Veteran* 26 (March 1918): 113. Hunter makes no mention of Lee and instead relates an implausible story about Whiting and Hood. I am grateful to Mark Lemon for kindly sharing the diary of his relative. It is one of the two best Confederate sources on Whiting's division at Gaines's Mill.

17. Everett, *Chaplain Davis,* 86; Law, "The Fight for Richmond," 656.

18. "Chickahominie" [pseud.], "The Eighteenth Georgia Regiment," Richmond *Daily Whig,* July 10, 1862; W. A. Fletcher, *Rebel Private, Front and Rear* (Beaumont, Tex.: Press of the Greer Print, 1908), 27–30; Robert T. Coles, *From Huntsville to Appomattox,* ed. Jeffrey D. Stocker (Knoxville: University of Tennessee Press, 1996), 48; "Austin" [pseud.], "Enquirer's Correspondence," Richmond *Enquirer,* July 4, 1862; Everett, *Chaplain Davis,* 86; Hamby, "Fourth Texas in Battle of Gaines' Mill," 183.

19. *OR* 11(2):568; Chickahominie, "Eighteenth Georgia"; Polley, *Hood's Texas Brigade,* 64; Law, "The Fight for Richmond," 657.

20. R. A. Brantley, "The 5th Texas, Seven Days Battle around Richmond," undated typescript in author's possession; *Confederate Veteran* 7 (August 1899): 357; Robert Campbell memoir in the possession of George Skoch, Cleveland Heights, Ohio. Readers of this series will recognize George Skoch as the deft cartographer whose maps enhance all of these essays. I thank him for giving me a prepublication view of the excellent Campbell memoir. W. A. Love ("History and Romance: Recollections of a Charge at Gains' Mill," *Alabama Soldier,* December 26, 1891) identified these petrified soldiers as Pickett's Virginians. That seems unlikely. If the men in question truly were from the Old Dominion, then Gen. Charles W. Field's brigade is a more probable candidate, based on its position relative to Whiting.

21. Law, "The Fight for Richmond," 657; Walter Clark, ed., *Histories of the Several Regiments and Battalions from North Carolina in the Great War, 1861–'65,* 5 vols. (Raleigh, N.C.: E. M. Uzzell, 1901), 1:304 (hereafter cited as Clark, *N.C. Regiments*).

22. Samuel Hankins, *Simple Story of a Soldier* (Nashville, Tenn: Confederate Veteran, 1912), 25–27; Clark, *N.C. Regiments,* 1:304; letter of "B" dated July 3, 1862, published in an unidentified wartime newspaper, a typescript of which is in the file labeled "4th Alabama Infantry," Alabama Department of Archives and History, Montgomery (repository hereafter cited as ADAH). The author of that letter may have been Robert G. Lewis. C. C. Chambers of the 11th Mississippi left two accounts of Whiting's actions ("Mississippians at Gaines Mill," *Confederate Veteran* 19 [November 1911]: 511; and "The Coahoma Invincibles," *Confederate Veteran* 31 [November 1923]: 422), but both seem unreliable and serve only to confirm Whiting's presence with that regiment.

23. Law, "The Fight for Richmond," 657; Hood, *Advance and Retreat,* 26.

24. *Confederate Veteran* 6 (December 1898): 570; Barziza, "Graphic Description"; Everett, *Chaplain Davis,* 68, 157; Val C. Giles, "The Tom Green Rifles," *Confederate Veteran* 26 (January 1918): 21; Crozier, "A Private with General Hood," 557; Aycock, *Lone Star Guards,* 7; Yeary, *Reminiscences of the Boys in Gray,* 9; Austin, "Enquirer's Correspondence." Chaplain Davis reported that Colonel Marshall was shot 555 yards from the Federal lines. If literally true, that would mean Marshall was killed on ground that is now squarely in the middle of a large housing development just west of New Cold Harbor.

25. Yeary, *Reminiscences of the Boys in Gray,* 815; Hunter, "At Yorktown in 1862," 113; J. M. Polk, *The North and South American Review* (Austin, Tex.: Press of Von Boeckman-Jones Co., 1914), 16; Everett, *Chaplain Davis,* 87; Crozier, "A Private with General Hood," 557; Giles, "The Tom Green Rifles," 21; Austin, "Enquirer's Correspondence"; William E. Berry, "Three Glorious Regiments," in *Unveiling and Dedication of Monument to Hood's Texas Brigade,* comp. F. B. Chilton (Houston, Tex.:

F. B. Chilton, 1911), 103; Hood, *Advance and Retreat,* 26; George L. Robertson to "Dear Ma," July 12, 1862, Robertson Papers, Center for American History, University of Texas, Austin. Nearly every writer in the 4th Texas mentioned the general's order to the regiment not to allow itself to be lured into a premature firefight. One of the classic accounts of this charge is in John W. Thomason Jr., *Lone Star Preacher* (New York: Scribner's, 1941). This work of historical fiction is gracefully written and doubtless based on its author's close ties — both personal and familial — to survivors of the battle.

26. G. L. Robertson to "Dear Ma," July 12, 1862; Brantley, "The 5th Texas"; *ORS,* pt. 1, 2:432; Krick, *Lee's Colonels,* 378; Robert Campbell memoir, George Skoch Collection; *Confederate Veteran* 7 (August 1899): 357. Upton was promoted to lieutenant colonel after the Seven Days and was killed two months later at Second Manassas.

27. "Wauzee" [pseud.] in Richmond *Daily Whig,* July 2, 1862; Coles, *From Huntsville to Appomattox,* 47; letter of "B" in unidentified newspaper typescript, ADAH; "Reminiscences of the Fourth Alabama," Marion (Ala.) *Commonwealth,* January 10, 1867; Rufus Hollis, *Confederate Veteran* (Scottsboro, Ala.: Press of the Scottsboro Citizen, n.d.), 8.

28. Aycock, *Lone Star Guards,* 8; Barziza, "Graphic Description," Wauzee letter, Richmond *Daily Whig,* July 2, 1862; Law, "The Fight for Richmond," 658.

29. Polley, *Hood's Texas Brigade,* 55; Lemon diary, July 11, 1862; Val C. Giles, *Rags and Hope: The Recollections of Val C. Giles, Four Years with Hood's Brigade, Fourth Texas Infantry, 1861–1865,* ed. Mary Lasswell (New York: Coward-McCann, 1961), 110; Hood, *Advance and Retreat,* 27; Hamby, "Fourth Texas in Battle of Gaines' Mill," 183; Barziza, "Graphic Description"; Yeary, *Reminiscences of the Boys in Gray,* 815; Everett, *Chaplain Davis,* 86; Polley, *Hood's Texas Brigade,* 46–47.

30. Lemon diary, July 11, 1862; Everett, *Chaplain Davis,* 88; J. B. Polley, *A Soldier's Letters to Charming Nellie* (New York: Neale, 1908), 55; Aycock, *Lone Star Guards,* 8; Polley, *Hood's Texas Brigade,* 47; Hamby, "Fourth Texas in Battle of Gaines' Mill," 184; Barziza, "Graphic Description"; Robert Campbell memoir, George Skoch Collection. It is possible that the doctrine of charge first and shoot later was a philosophy Hood purposely inculcated in the minds of the brigade's officers. Capt. Ike Turner of the 5th Texas wrote to a newspaper seven weeks later, "In making a charge, men should never stop to fire a gun, until the enemy is routed" (I[ke] N. T[urner], "Letter from a Texas Captain," *Countryman* [Eatonton, Ga.], August 16, 1862). General Hood claimed in *Advance and Retreat,* 27, that he ordered the 4th Texas to fix bayonets *south* of the creek, a contention that stands in direct opposition to most other accounts.

31. Polley, *Hood's Texas Brigade,* 47–48; Everett, *Chaplain Davis,* 88; Robert Campbell memoir, George Skoch Collection; Lemon diary, July 11, 1862; Austin, "Enquirer's Correspondence." Polley estimated that the band of woods was only fifty yards wide where the 4th Texas crossed, though most other sources have it a bit thicker.

32. Austin, "Enquirer's Correspondence"; Barziza, "Graphic Description"; Edward H. Cushing, *The New Texas School Reader* (Houston, Tex.: E. H. Cushing, 1864), 99–100; Polley, *Hood's Texas Brigade,* 47; Polley, *Charming Nellie,* 55; Everett, *Chaplain Davis,* 83; Yeary, *Reminiscences of the Boys in Gray,* 815. The section on Gaines's Mill in *The New Texas School Reader* is Lesson 44. Its author was an unidentified soldier in A. P. Hill's division. He walked the field on June 28 and wrote that "an old snake fence" lined the southern bank of Boatswain's Creek.

33. Everett, *Chaplain Davis,* 85; Polley, *Charming Nellie,* 299; Giles, *Rags and Hope,* 110.

34. Giles, *Rags and Hope,* 110; Barziza, "Graphic Description"; Yeary, *Reminiscences of the Boys in Gray,* 815; Berry, "Three Glorious Regiments," 103. There is some confusion about the capture of these guns. Barziza and Wood (in Yeary) write of them, but Polley's brigade history is strangely silent on the subject. I am fairly certain that the 4th *did* capture some guns close to the Watt house before regrouping for the final charge against the larger concentration of Federal artillery.

35. Polley, *Hood's Texas Brigade,* 65; Robert Campbell memoir, George Skoch Collection; Brantley, "The Fifth Texas"; O. T. Hanks, *History of Captain B. F. Benton's Company, Hood's Texas Brigade, 1861–1865* (Austin, Tex.: Morrison Books, 1984), 9–10. Col. Jerome B. Robertson, commanding the 5th Texas, wrote two days later about his unit's capturing a Union battery in the edge of the field. His is the only source on this episode, and the vague language he used casts uncertainty on the claim (*ORS,* pt. 1, 2:433). The almost complete absence of source material from the Hampton Legion makes it difficult to track its activities on June 27.

36. Letter of "B" in unidentified newspaper, typescript at ADAH; *Confederate Veteran* 6 (December 1898): 570; Law, "The Fight for Richmond," 657; Austin, "Correspondence of the Enquirer"; Wauzee letter, Richmond *Daily Whig,* July 2, 1862.

37. Law, "The Fight for Richmond," 658–59.

38. Polley, *Charming Nellie,* 56, 296–98, 300; Polley, *Hood's Texas Brigade,* 49, 53; Lemon diary, July 11, 1862; Chickahominie, "Eighteenth Georgia." Colonel Law ("The Fight for Richmond," 658) was alone in his scorn for the accuracy of the cannon fire, labeling it "rapid but rather ineffective." The powerful concentration of Union guns apparently stood atop a knob near the Joseph Adams house. Joe Polley surveyed the ground after the war and determined that the artillery was three-eighths of a mile left (east) of the Watt house. The dry ravine between the Watt house and the artillery today is covered in dense growth, and the scene of the charge is just off the tiny part of the battlefield preserved by the National Park Service.

39. Everett, *Chaplain Davis,* 89, 163; Polley, *Charming Nellie,* 57, 300; Chickahominie, "Eighteenth Georgia"; Barziza, "Graphic Description"; Chambers, "Mississippians at Gaines' Mill," 511. The mortal wounding of Lieutenant Colonel Warwick provides a perfect example of a historian's frustrations. Most sources cannot agree on

the simplest particulars of Warwick's injury. Polley states that Warwick was struck by a shell fragment at the beginning of the charge out of Watt's orchard. Chaplain Davis puts the event at the crest of the plateau, about where the first battery was captured. Furthermore, Davis says Warwick was hit not by a shell fragment but by a bullet in the right lung. The regimental adjutant reported within days that Warwick was hit "just before capturing the first battery" (Richmond *Enquirer,* July 10, 1862).

40. Polley, *Hood's Texas Brigade,* 49–50; Chickahominie, "Eighteenth Georgia"; Barziza, "Graphic Description."

41. Hamby, "Fourth Texas in Battle of Gaines' Mill," 184; Barziza, "Graphic Description."

42. Love, "History and Romance"; Lemon diary, July 11, 1862; Barziza, "Graphic Description"; Chickahominie, "Eighteenth Georgia." Numerous sources from Pickett's and Wilcox's brigades speak of their role in stopping the cavalry charge. Their positions just to the right and rear of the 18th Georgia seem to match the terrain and the circumstances.

43. Chambers, "Mississippians at Gaines' Mill," 511; Polley, *Hood's Texas Brigade,* 50; Polley, *Charming Nellie,* 300; Love, "History and Romance"; Chickahominie, "Eighteenth Georgia"; Lemon diary, July 11, 1862. As with most large battles, there is inconsistency here in the sequence of events. Joe Polley's two books state quite clearly that the cavalry charge occurred after the capture of the cannon. But "Chickahominie," Lemon, and others are equally insistent that the charge hit them between the Watt house and the cannon. Primacy is given here to the latter sources because they were written within two weeks of the battle, and Polley's were postwar. Once past the cavalry, the Confederates apparently captured fourteen guns atop the hill, either eight or nine by the 18th Georgia and five or six by the 4th Texas. The identity of those guns probably can be deduced from a careful perusal of Federal source material.

44. Polley, *Hood's Texas Brigade,* 66, 69–70; Fletcher, *Rebel Private,* 27–30; Robert Campbell memoir, George Skoch Collection; Polley, *Charming Nellie,* 58; *OR* 11(2): 34; Barziza, "Graphic Description."

45. *OR* 11(2):564; Polley, *Hood's Texas Brigade,* 51; Hamby, "Fourth Texas in Battle of Gaines' Mill," 184; Chickahominie, "Eighteenth Georgia."

46. Barziza, "Graphic Description"; Hankins, *Simple Story of a Soldier,* 25–27; Everett, *Chaplain Davis,* 91; Stevens, *Reminiscences of the Civil War,* 29; Yeary, *Reminiscences of the Boys in Gray,* 815; J. W. Ratchford, *Some Reminiscences of Persons and Incidents of the Civil War* (Richmond, Va.: Whittet & Shepperson, 1909), 25.

47. John H. Graham diary, Schoff Civil War Collection, Clements Library, University of Michigan, Ann Arbor; Cushing, *The New Texas School Reader,* 101; Giles, "The Tom Green Rifles," 22–23; Philip Henry Pitts diary, typescript graciously provided by Pitts's descendant Mrs. Kitty Long of Uniontown, Alabama; Love, "History and Romance"; Brantley, "The 5th Texas"; Robert W. Glover, ed., *"Tyler to Sharpsburg"*

(Waco, Tex.: W. M. Morrison, 1960), 19; Hood, *Advance and Retreat*, 28. Four days later Wigfall spent the battle of Malvern Hill passed out drunk on a surgeon's amputating table while many of the same men he had impressed with his oratory died of their wounds around him (James R. Boulware diary, July 1, 1862, South Caroliniana Library, University of South Carolina, Columbia).

48. Sources for the 11th Mississippi are the Richmond *Enquirer*, July 2, 1862, and the author's correspondence with the regiment's diligent historian, Steven Stubbs, of Philadelphia, Mississippi, whose figures are based on compiled service records and anything else he could find. Sources for the 4th Alabama are *OR* 11(2):973 and Coles, *Huntsville to Appomattox*, 49. Figures for the 6th North Carolina, 2nd Mississippi, and Hampton Legion are derived only from *OR* 11(2):973; those for the 1st Texas and 5th Texas come from *OR* 11(2):973 and *Hood's Brigade Historical Papers* (n.p., n.d.), unpaginated leaves (this pamphlet, completely without bibliographical clues, looks to date from about 1910 and seems to be based on the muster rolls). The sources used to calculate the 18th Georgia's losses are *OR* 11(2):973; Chickahominie, "Eighteenth Georgia"; and the Lemon diary. The Atlanta *Southern Confederacy*, July 11, 1862, reported 240 casualties, but this seems to have been nothing more than a wild guess. Casualties for the 4th Texas were estimated using Everett, *Chaplain Davis*, 91; Richmond *Enquirer*, July 10, 1862 (which has a company-by-company breakdown); *OR* 11(2):973; *Hood's Brigade Historical Papers;* and James Campbell to "dear Martha," July 16, August 2, 1862, in the John Campbell Papers at Rice University, Houston, Texas. An early estimate of division casualties is in Richmond [pseud.], "Battle of Gaines' Mill," Richmond *Daily Whig*, March 6, 1863.

49. "Caxton" [pseud.], "The Storming of Gaines' Hill — The Texas Brigade," Richmond *Daily Whig*, July 18, 1862; Brantley, "The 5th Texas"; Yeary, *Reminiscences of the Boys in Gray*, 77–79; Polley, *Charming Nellie*, 293–306. William B. Shields of the 11th Mississippi provided one of the few arguments against the 4th Texas from Law's brigade, writing on June 29: "We were first in their fortifications, [and] first on their batteries" (W. B. Shields to "My dear Bonnie," June 29, 1862, in Shields-Jennings Papers, Mitchell Memorial Library, Mississippi State University, Starkville). General Whiting officially identified the 4th as the first regiment to break the Union lines (*OR* 11[2]:564).

50. James Longstreet to R. E. Lee, March 30, 1866, Lee Headquarters Papers (series 10, Reminiscences), Virginia Historical Society, Richmond; James Longstreet, *Manassas to Appomattox: Memoirs of the Civil War in America* (Philadelphia: Lippincott, 1896), 127–29. Longstreet's official report (*OR* 11[2]:757), written in July 1862, takes no direct credit for Whiting's assault. The accuracy of his memory in the 1866 letter is further discredited when Longstreet notes that the brigades of Anderson and Kemper made an important counterattack after the breakthrough, else the enemy "would have recovered his position I think." This Federal resurgence is not on record anywhere

else, and Longstreet forgot by 1866 that Kemper's brigade did not fire a shot on June 27. He may have been mixing the events of Gaines's Mill and Frayser's Farm (three days later) somehow, as Anderson and Kemper at least fought together on that latter field. Whiting (*OR* 11[2]:563) obliquely confirms Longstreet's confusion.

51. Richmond *Daily Whig,* June 28, 1862; Lemon diary. One interesting dissenting voice to all the praise directed at Hood came from Gen. Cadmus M. Wilcox, whose excellent Alabama brigade did the best work in Longstreet's division at Gaines's Mill. Writing after the war, Wilcox professed to know that Hood was safely in the rear during the charge and that the distortions in Hood's official report had unfairly shaped historians' interpretations of the battle. As documented above, there is overwhelming evidence to dispute Wilcox's claim (Cadmus Wilcox Papers, Library of Congress, Washington, D.C.).

52. *OR* 11(2):569; John H. Reagan, *Memoirs, with Special Reference to Secession and the Civil War* (New York: Neale, 1906), 145; Mrs. A. V. Winkler, *The Confederate Capital and Hood's Texas Brigade* (Austin, Tex.: Eugene von Boeckmann, 1894), 78. See Chilton, *Unveiling and Dedication of Monument,* for repeated examples of the brigade's faithful observance of the June 27 anniversary. General Hood attended the fifteen-year anniversary at Waco on June 27, 1877.

53. "General Hood's Brigade," *SHSP* 29:297.

KEITH S. BOHANNON

One Solid Unbroken Roar of Thunder

Union and Confederate Artillery at the Battle of Malvern Hill

n *The Long Arm of Lee,* a history of the artillery of the Army of Northern Virginia, Jennings C. Wise wrote that "one involuntarily thinks of Malvern Hill as an engagement that typifies the great power of concentrated artillery fire." L. Van Loan Naisawald, who wrote the standard study of the Army of the Potomac's artillery, believed that McClellan's force "escaped probable defeat and destruction at Malvern Hill by the massed fire of its artillery." Wise, Naisawald, and all others who have written about Malvern Hill, the final battle of the 1862 Seven Days campaign, have attributed great importance to the Federal artillery's participation in that engagement. What factors allowed the Union cannoneers to dominate their opponents at Malvern Hill, resulting in one of the best performances of the Civil War for the artillery arm of the Army of the Potomac?[1]

When the Union Army of the Potomac reached Malvern Hill on June 30, 1862, it had been retreating toward the James River for three days, fighting several engagements to stave off Confederate pursuers. The narrow Malvern Hill plateau, located a little more than a mile north of the James, provided the beleaguered Federals with a fine defensive position. Reaching roughly 150 feet at its highest elevation, the plateau was one and one-quarter miles wide from north to south and three-quarters of a mile deep from east to west. Steep bluffs formed the western edge of Malvern Hill, and the wooded banks of Western Run delineated the plateau's eastern boundaries. To the south, a marshy stretch of ground and Turkey Island Creek separated Malvern Hill from the James River.[2]

The Army of the Potomac fought at Malvern Hill, noted Gen. Fitz John Porter, "to prevent the enemy from turning our flank and getting in our rear" and to protect the trains of provisions, baggage, artillery, and ammunition that had preceded it to Haxall's Landing on the James. Union army commander George B. McClellan certainly thought that Malvern Hill was important. In his official report of the campaign, McClellan stated that "although our force was small for so extensive a position it was necessary to hold it at any cost."[3]

Despite McClellan's desire to establish a temporary position at Malvern Hill, he inexplicably spent little time there with his army. The fatigued and depressed commander inspected the position on June 30 but left in the afternoon for his headquarters at Haxall's Landing. At 4:45 P.M. that day, Mc-Clellan and his staff boarded the ironclad USS *Galena,* the flagship of the James River Flotilla, and steamed upriver to shell a Confederate column approaching Malvern Hill on the River Road from the west.

McClellan again inspected his lines at Malvern Hill at dawn on July 1 before returning to Haxall's and boarding the *Galena* for a trip downstream to examine Harrison's Landing, the point he had designated as the army's ultimate destination. Although McClellan returned to Malvern Hill late that afternoon, he remained on his army's far right flank some two miles from the fighting. Fitz John Porter, McClellan's trusted subordinate and commander of the Fifth Corps, directed the Union forces engaged on June 30 and July 1 at Malvern Hill.[4]

Porter arrived on Malvern Hill on the morning of June 30, 1862, accompanied by several officers, including Col. Henry J. Hunt. Described as "a small grizzly man with a high-pitched voice," Hunt was a well-known and respected artillerist from the Old Army. Hunt had graduated from West Point in the class of 1839, compiled a distinguished record during the Mexican War, and been one of three officers who revised the army's system of light artillery tactics in 1860.[5]

Hunt commanded the Army of the Potomac's Artillery Reserve during the Seven Days campaign. While roughly two-thirds of the Union batteries had been assigned to individual infantry divisions or the corps artillery reserves, the remaining guns in the army's Artillery Reserve provided "a source of artillery supply, whence the divisions could draw batteries for their needs." Roughly twenty batteries made up the Artillery Reserve, most of them understrength U.S. Regular units rather than volunteer organizations raised by the states. Hunt's Artillery Reserve also included the Army of the Potomac's siege train of heavy guns and the horse artillery.[6]

Throughout the morning of June 30, Hunt rode over the Malvern Hill plateau, under orders from McClellan "to examine and report on its capabilities for battle." Fitz John Porter also surveyed the position, concluding that "it had certain elements of great strength, and was the best adapted for field-artillery of any with which we have so far been favored." Hunt's Artil-

Col. Henry J. Hunt

Robert Underwood Johnson and Clarence Clough Buel, eds., Battles and Leaders
of the Civil War, 4 vols. (New York: Century, 1887–88), 3:320

lery Reserve, accompanied by other batteries assigned to infantry divisions, moved into position on the Malvern Hill plateau alongside infantrymen from Porter's corps beginning in the late morning on the thirtieth.[7]

Hunt posted his guns, numbering roughly thirty-six pieces, along the steep western bluffs of Malvern Hill, facing westward over open lowland toward the River Road. Several batteries went into position around Porter's headquarters, the venerable brick Malvern house, located at the southern end of Malvern Hill. Around 4:00 P.M. that day, the Federals came under fire from five rifled guns the Confederates had placed along a wood line in the lowland approximately a thousand yards west of Malvern Hill. An observer noted that after the first enemy shell landed in the Federal position, Malvern Hill "was cleared, as if by magic, of wagons and of stragglers, that went down the hill together" and continued by the hundreds to Haxall's Landing on the James.[8]

The southern cannon were the advance element of a Confederate column commanded by Gen. Theophilus H. Holmes. Holmes had heard earlier from an engineer officer that the Federals were "retreating in considerable confusion along the road leading over Malvern Hill." As Holmes's cannon moved through dense timber and underbrush to unlimber astride the River Road, he rode forward to reconnoiter and encountered Confederate army commander Robert E. Lee. Lee had just completed a reconnaissance of the enemy's position and approved of the actions taken by Holmes, directing "that, after infantry supports had moved into position, fire should be opened on the enemy's column."[9]

Federal artillerists on Malvern Hill opened on the Confederates with approximately twenty-eight guns, at least eight of them 20-pounder Parrott rifles. On the James River two and one-half miles to the south, naval gun crews on the *Galena* and the gunboat *Aroostook* added the firepower of their 100-pounder Parrott rifles and 9-inch Dahlgrens to the Federal barrage. After a dreadfully unequal one-hour contest, the overwhelmed Confederate artillerists and their infantry supports retreated westward, the five-gun battery having lost seventeen men and fifteen horses killed and wounded and at least one limber blown up.

The performance of Capt. Edward Graham's Virginia battery, left in the rear in reserve that afternoon, undoubtedly made the Confederate defeat even more bitter. Graham's artillerists "completely stampeded" when the enemy barrage began, getting their pieces and caissons "entangled among the trees." They abandoned two guns and six caissons, which the Federals retrieved later that night.[10]

The left flank of the Union line on July 1 rested on the western bluffs of Malvern Hill roughly a mile south of the white frame Crew house. At the Crew house and outbuildings, the line ran eastward for a mile, crossing the Willis Church Road and continuing past the West house before encountering the wooded banks of a stream known as Western Run. At Western Run the line turned southeast toward the James for roughly a mile. Between the Crew and West houses, open farm fields filled with wheat (both standing and in shocks) stretched northward at a gentle downward slope for roughly four

The Malvern Hill battlefield. 1880s view of the Crew farm looking southwest toward the Union position. The building in the cluster of trees on the far left is the West house. The three buildings in the center are the slave quarters (the same ones that appear in the 1880s image reproduced on page 222 below) and a barn. The cluster of buildings on the far right of the photograph includes the Crew house and outbuildings.

hundred yards, providing a perfect field of fire for the Federal batteries stationed on the crest and their infantry supports.

Gen. Charles Griffin, a recently appointed Union infantry brigade commander who had been an artillery officer and instructor in the Old Army, took charge at Porter's request of the half dozen batteries from Hunt's Artillery Reserve and Gen. George Morell's division stationed between the Crew and West houses.[11] The size and composition of Griffin's command varied during the day as batteries exhausted their ammunition and retired while others took their places, but he probably had around twenty-five guns during the morning and early afternoon. The majority of these pieces were

The Malvern Hill battlefield. 1880s view of the Crew farm looking northwest from the Union artillery position toward the wood line where the Confederates deployed artillery batteries and formed their infantry to charge. The two frame buildings to the left of center are slave quarters.

Gilder Lehrman Collection on deposit at the Pierpont Morgan Library, New York. GLC 5111.11.320

3-inch ordnance rifles, 10-pounder Parrott rifles, and 12-pounder Napoleons. Larger guns, including 20- and 30-pounder Parrott rifles and 4½-inch Rodmans from the army's siege train, stood in support to the south.[12]

While Griffin's batteries made their final preparations for battle on the morning of July 1, Confederate captain James Reilly rode over the large wheat fields of the Poindexter farm northeast of Malvern Hill. An experienced artillerist from the Old Army, Reilly had orders from Gen. W. H. C. Whiting to conduct a thorough reconnaissance of the enemy's position. Reilly reported to Whiting, his division commander, that the Federals had thirty guns posted on ground commanding the Poindexter fields. The captain also pointed out that the Confederate guns, except for captured pieces, were in-

KEITH S. BOHANNON

ferior in size and number to those of the enemy. Reilly suggested that the Confederates compensate for their weakness by sending eight batteries into action at the same time. Whiting concurred, noting that the Poindexter field "afforded a good view of the enemy's position and fair opportunities for artillery." [13]

Gen. James Longstreet also reconnoitered that morning, following orders from General Lee to examine the Confederate right flank on the Crew farm. Longstreet and Gen. John B. Magruder, an infantry division commander, decided that the Confederates should mass batteries at the northern end of the Crew field opposite Griffin's Federal guns. Magruder told their guide, Col. Edward C. Edmonds of Gen. Lewis A. Armistead's brigade, that southern infantrymen could not attack Malvern Hill successfully unless supported in the Crew field by thirty artillery pieces "of the highest caliber."

Longstreet soon reported back to Lee, suggesting that the Confederates concentrate artillery in the northern ends of the Crew and Poindexter fields. Converging fire from these positions would throw the Federals on Malvern Hill into confusion. Lee assented and issued orders to implement the plan, including the dispatch of pioneers to the Crew field to cut a road for the advancing batteries.

Later that morning, Lee told his division commanders that "batteries have been established to rake the enemy's lines." If the Federals broke, as Lee thought probable, General Armistead's brigade of Virginians would advance with a yell across the Crew field against the Federal battery in its front. Armistead's attack would be the signal for a general assault. [14]

General Whiting responded to Lee's directive to mass artillery by ordering up several batteries. As Captain Reilly's Rowan Artillery and the Staunton Artillery moved through a farm gate on the Willis Church Road and into a narrow wooded lane leading eastward into the Poindexter fields, "Stonewall" Jackson rode up with his staff. Jackson went out alone into the Poindexter field and upon returning ordered Whiting to send the two batteries out to engage the Federals. Whiting protested: "I understood we were not to enter the field until fifty guns arrived," he stated. "These few guns will not be able to live in the field five minutes." When Jackson told Whiting to "obey your orders . . . willingly and promptly," Whiting replied, "I always obey orders promptly but do not obey these willingly." Jackson then told the battery commanders to instruct their gunners "to cut four shells for 400 yards, so as to be ready to fire as rapidly as possible as soon as they get in position." [15]

Captain Reilly's North Carolinians entered the Poindexter field first, Jackson helping to push one of their cannon through the standing wheat and

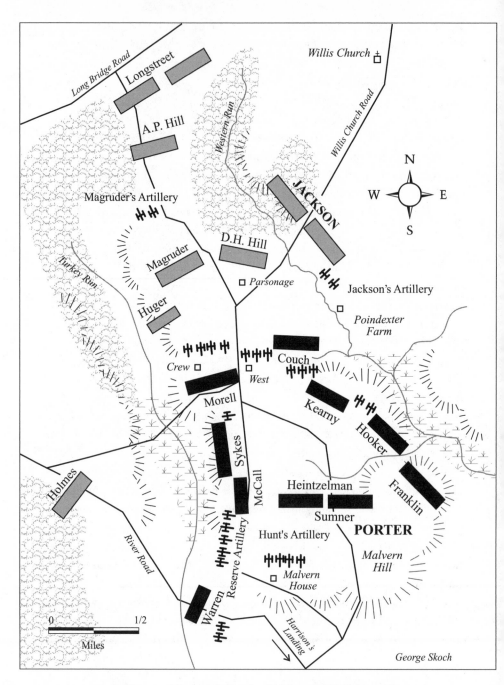

Artillery positions at the Battle of Malvern Hill, July 1, 1862

KEITH S. BOHANNON

direct it into position. As the North Carolinians unlimbered their guns, Union cannoneers opened with "a vastly superior cross-fire." Whiting ordered Reilly to withdraw after only fifteen or twenty minutes, the North Carolinians having lost twelve men wounded and eight horses. The fate of Reilly's command, one of eight southern batteries engaged that day in the Poindexter field, portended things to come for other Confederate artillerists.[16]

Union cannoneers first fired into the Crew field around 10:00 A.M. on July 1 in response to the advance of Confederate skirmishers. Charles Griffin's gunners had orders to fire slowly and deliberately once every few minutes, an edict obeyed except during the heaviest southern infantry assaults. A more rapid rate of fire, as expended by the rifled guns of Capt. Walter M. Bramhall's battery during an early morning Confederate infantry attack, resulted in "two shot[s] a minute from each piece."[17]

As Confederate skirmishers traded shots with their Union counterparts, Longstreet returned to the Crew field with orders from Lee to supervise the placement of batteries. Although only a few guns arrived at first, Magruder promised that Col. Stephen D. Lee, his chief of artillery, would bring up more as soon as possible.[18] The first two Confederate cannon sent into the Crew field belonged to Capt. Cary Grimes's Virginia battery. Grimes's artillerists moved their 10-pounder Parrott rifles roughly fifty yards into the Crew field around 11:00 A.M., immediately coming under a torrent of enemy artillery fire. The Virginians lost four men and three horses killed and wounded before unlimbering. Grimes kept his guns in action about two hours, carrying on an uneven duel with Federal artillerists eleven hundred yards away on the crest of Malvern Hill. When the Virginians retired they were unable to haul off one of their guns because of the loss of so many horses.[19]

Portions of four other Confederate batteries advanced into the Crew field on July 1.[20] Gen. Lewis A. Armistead, whose infantry regiments supported these batteries, claimed that he repeatedly asked several officers for more and heavier guns. Longstreet promised to let Armistead have what he required, but Longstreet's and Magruder's efforts to concentrate artillery in Armistead's front failed miserably. The southerners never had more than eight guns in action at once, and that number for only a short period of time.[21]

One of the hardest hit Confederate batteries in the Crew field was the Purcell Artillery commanded by Capt. William R. J. Pegram. After dueling with the Federals for two and one-half hours, twenty men and as many horses in Pegram's command had been killed and wounded and all but one of the battery's four Napoleons disabled. Pegram displayed incredible courage (and enjoyed even greater luck in avoiding injury) throughout the contest, cheering his depleted crews and assisting them in loading and firing the guns.[22]

Three guns of the 1st Richmond Howitzers eventually entered the Crew field to support an impending Confederate infantry charge and assist Pegram's lone operating gun. As the Howitzers ran to get into position, John Van Lew McCreery remembered being "raked from the head of the column to the end by solid shot, case and shell." While exchanging fire with the Federals, one of the Virginia battery's 6-pounders had its muzzle face "injured very much by a 12-pound ball" and another sustained such extensive damage to its carriage that it was left on the field. Robert Stiles of the Howitzers recalled that his battery's guns "were several times fired by fragments of Federal shell striking them after the lanyard was stretched and before it was pulled." McCreery and Stiles undoubtedly agreed with their comrade R. W. Royall, who wrote his mother of the battery's losses and claimed that it was "almost miraculous how any of us escaped."[23]

Around noon on July 1 a small group of Confederate infantrymen made the first serious attempt to break the Federal lines in the vicinity of the Crew house. Union artillerists turned their attention from the southern batteries to the infantry charge, pouring a frontal and enfilade fire into the Confederate line and breaking it apart. Up to this time the Union infantrymen had remained unengaged and sheltered behind their artillery. As Fitz John Porter explained, "Our desire was to hold the enemy where our artillery would be most destructive, and to reserve our infantry ammunition for close quarters to repel the more determined assaults."[24]

The small swales and ridges that sheltered Union infantrymen also offered protection to some Confederate artillerists in the Crew and Poindexter fields. Slight depressions allowed southern cannoneers to load their pieces under cover before advancing them by hand to fire at the enemy's batteries. Federal artillery fire proved devastating even with such protection, as testified by Confederate captain William T. Poague and two enlisted men from the Rockbridge Artillery. Poague, whose guns fought in the Poindexter field against Federal batteries located roughly twelve hundred yards to the south, noted that the Union barrage "was most terrific, and in the main very accurate." Young Randolph Fairfax wrote home that "shot and shell seemed to pour over us in one successive stream, and burst in our midst." Thomas M. Wade told his wife that "we soon got to where one of our battery had stood . . . & we were to take its place . . . it had attracted a hot fire which we had to go into."[25]

Shortly after Poague's guns and several other Confederate batteries began firing, word circulated that they had orders to withdraw. Unable to discover the rumor's source, Poague commanded his men to continue firing. Capt. Alfred R. Courtney's Henrico Artillery, positioned adjacent to Poague's battery, limbered up and left. Courtney later claimed that he had received, via a courier from General Whiting, instructions to withdraw, "which turned out to have been intended for another battery." The men of the Staunton Artillery also left the field, having exhausted all their ammunition.[26]

A sense of alarm quickly spread through the remaining Confederate batteries in the Poindexter field. Poague admitted that the withdrawal of an adjacent battery "in unseemly haste . . . made things look panicky." When a member of the Rockbridge Artillery repeated the order to withdraw, Edward Moore noted that "before it could be corrected, eight or ten of the company, joining in the rout, beat a retreat to the woods."[27]

The rout also influenced the Rockbridge Artillery's sister battery, the Alleghany Artillery. Lt. John C. Carpenter, commander of the Alleghany "Roughs," had been looking for a position to post his guns when he met two batteries withdrawing from the field. Discovering that his own battery was retiring, he asked who had told them to do so. His men could not identify the officer, noting only that "he rode up and told them to move back in the woods." With help from General Whiting, Carpenter moved his guns back into position next to Poague's battery.[28]

The Confederate artillerists in the Poindexter field (never firing more than six cannon at a time, according to one southern staff officer) faced between twenty and thirty Union guns from Hunt's Artillery Reserve and the Third Corps Artillery Reserve occupying elevated ground on the right of Fitz John Porter's line. Gen. Joseph Hooker noted that these Federal artillerists had "an enfilading fire from my position, a direct one from [Gen. Philip] Kearney['s], and a diagonal one from several other batteries, which soon resulted in driving the rebel gunners from their pieces." An officer in the 5th New Jersey Infantry watching the artillery duel noted that Confederate cannoneers located near the Poindexter barn and cattle pen "did not even get their guns unlimbered before our guns drove them like the flock of frightened sheep into the woods."[29]

Union captain Alonzo Snow, commanding a Maryland battery, also testified to the punishment meted out by the Federal gunners to Confederates in the Poindexter field. When a southern battery "well masked by stacked and standing grain" opened fire, the Federals replied for half an hour, inflicting noticeable damage on the enemy's teams and gun crews and forcing them to retire. Several Confederate batteries, including the Baltimore Light Artillery, unlimbered in the Poindexter field and hastily withdrew two or three times before ending their efforts for the day.[30]

Despite the unequal nature of the contest, the southern cannon fire was not without effect. Most postbellum accounts of Malvern Hill virtually ignore the Confederate afternoon bombardment, but Union infantry officers and men writing shortly after the battle were not so dismissive. Federal officers repeatedly refer in their official reports to the enemy's "furious cannonade," "heavy enfilading fire," and "incessant shower of shell and round shot." Many of these shells were undoubtedly "overshots" aimed at Union artillerists. The official reports further indicate that Confederate batteries in the Crew and Poindexter fields achieved a converging fire against the Federal center. Union division commander Gen. George W. Morell reported that the Confederate artillerists produced "a serious cross-fire over my two rear brigades." One of Morell's regimental commanders, Col. Charles W. Roberts of the 2nd Maine, remembered lying for three hours "under an incessant and extremely hot artillery fire, both from the right, left, and front."[31]

Fortunately for the Federals, the rolling terrain at Malvern Hill provided many infantrymen with shelter from the enemy shells. The Confederate barrage "plowed up and tore the earth and trees in all directions," wrote a Pennsylvania officer, but did not significantly alter the troop dispositions along Porter's front lines. This was not the case in the Union rear, where Gen. Edwin V. Sumner sent most of the Second Corps to the protection of wooded bluffs southeast of the Malvern house. Sumner then ordered Porter to move his troops back to the Malvern house but withdrew the command after Porter refused to obey it without first obtaining permission from McClellan.[32]

The danger of being struck from the rear by friendly fire added to the ordeal of Union soldiers at Malvern Hill. Sometime before 4:00 P.M., the 30-pounder Parrotts stationed near Porter's headquarters at the Malvern house fired into the woods immediately west of the Crew house. One shell landed in the midst of Battery C, 1st Rhode Island Artillery, killing two men and two horses and wounding three other artillerists. A Rhode Islander noted that "the explosion was stunning" and that with shells falling onto their position "from Right, Rear, and Left . . . we were ordered to retire." Another shell from the rear landed in the midst of the 3rd U.S. Infantry, causing three casualties.[33]

Cannoneers of the 1st Connecticut Heavy Artillery manning the siege guns near the Malvern house also received friendly fire. Their only casualties during the day came from a massive shell fired in the late afternoon by one of the Union vessels standing at anchor in the James near the mouth of Turkey Run Creek. At least two of these vessels, the side-wheel steamer USS *Mahaska* and the ironclad *Galena,* participated in the naval bombardment on

July 1. The *Mahaska* opened fire around noon and continued intermittently throughout the afternoon and early evening, discharging a total of fifty-six shells from its 100-pounder Parrott and 9-inch Dahlgren rifle. The *Galena* first came to anchor at 4:50 P.M. and fired until 5:40 P.M. Fifty minutes later the *Galena* anchored astern of the *Mahaska* and the two vessels opened fire, their hulls careening as they kept up the bombardment until a little before 8:00 P.M.[34]

Because of their distance from the battlefield, officers aboard Union vessels looked to a signal officer stationed on the fore-topmast of the *Mahaska,* who communicated with a signal station at the Malvern house, for the results of their fire. In the wake of the afternoon explosion that killed and wounded several of the Connecticut artillerists, Fitz John Porter sent a frantic written message to the gunboats, stating, "For God's sake, stop firing, you are killing & wounding our men — The dust and smoke is so dense — we cannot signal you." The message temporarily suspended the naval barrage.[35]

The overall effect of the Union naval fire on July 1 is difficult to gauge. Although northern newspapers praised the navy's role in aiding McClellan's army at Malvern Hill, Fitz John Porter claimed that "not one of their projectiles passed beyond my headquarters" at the Malvern house. Porter's statement seems hard to believe, given that the 100-pounder Parrott rifles easily could send a shell into the Confederate lines at Malvern Hill and as far north as the Long Bridge Road. The gunboat shells certainly had a demoralizing effect on many Confederates but also rattled the nerves of many Federals. Union officer Thomas W. Osborn wrote that the gunboats "threw a few shell here and there . . . with . . . no beneficial results," adding that the Federals "feared them quite as much as the enemy."[36]

At roughly 3:00 P.M. a lone Confederate infantry brigade charged out of the woods opposite the center of the Union line. The southerners got to within 150 yards of the Federals before being driven back in confusion by discharges of case shot and canister from two Union batteries and the fire of several infantry regiments. A foreboding silence reigned on the battlefield afterward, the Federals taking advantage of the lull to replace batteries that had exhausted their ammunition and to bring up additional infantrymen. Fitz John Porter ordered three fresh batteries into a gorge in the Willis Church Road behind his front lines, "instructing them to join in the fight if necessary, but not to permit the advance of the foe, even if it must be arrested at the risk of firing on friends."[37]

The silence ended around 4:30 P.M. when Confederate gunners opened fire along the entire front of the Union line. The bombardment neither disabled enemy batteries nor substantially weakened the Federal position. At

Union artillerists repulsing a Confederate infantry charge up the slopes of Crew Hill.
Robert Underwood Johnson and Clarence Clough Buel, eds., Battles and Leaders of the Civil
War, *4 vols. (New York: Century, 1887–88), 2:417*

least a few Confederate officers, including Gen. D. H. Hill, sensed the cannonade's futility. Hill wrote Stonewall Jackson asking what to do, stating that
the artillery effort "was of the most farcical character." Hill's subordinate
Gen. Samuel Garland observed that the southern cannon fire "was so wild"
that his party of observers dispersed with the impression "that no movement
of infantry would be ordered." Gen. Lafayette McLaws, who was on another
part of the battlefield, remembered years later "the utter hopelessness of success, which was apparent to any casual observer."[38]

James Longstreet claimed in his memoirs that Robert E. Lee, like McLaws,
Harvey Hill, and others, realized the failure of the Confederate bombardment
and canceled the conditional orders for a general attack. Longstreet's official
report, written only weeks after the battle, seemingly reinforces his postwar
assertion. "A little after 3 p.m.," stated Longstreet in the report, "I understood we would not be able to attack the enemy that day, inasmuch as his

position was too strong to admit of it." Longstreet observed in his memoirs that Lee, being "under the impression that his officers realized the failure and abandonment of his original plan . . . failed to issue orders specifically recalling the appointed battle." The climactic afternoon assaults began by mistake, Longstreet concluded, when the noise of a small southern attack in the Crew field "was taken as the signal for assault under the original order of the day."[39]

In *Military Memoirs of a Confederate*, Confederate artillerist Edward Porter Alexander effectively challenged Longstreet's postwar interpretation. Alexander argued that the battle did not commence as a mistake but instead was "begun by a direct order from Lee given hastily under the influence of a misapprehension of fact." During the afternoon, Lee and Longstreet rode to the Confederate left flank in search of a route to turn the enemy's position. As they returned, Lee received word from Whiting at the Poindexter field of "the movement of baggage and troops in retreat by the Turkey Bridge Road." (This Federal movement was undoubtedly Sumner's Second Corps troops pulling back.) The Confederate commander also received news that Lewis Armistead's Virginians had driven off enemy skirmishers and advanced farther in the Crew field. Believing that the enemy was in retreat, Lee sent Magruder orders "to advance rapidly . . . it is reported the enemy is getting off. Press forward your whole line and follow up Armistead's success."[40]

As Magruder's long lines of gray-coated infantry charged across the open Crew field and then Harvey Hill's men burst out of the woods near the Federal center "with a quick, long swinging stride," Union artillerists opened fire. Lt. Charles Phillips of the 5th Massachusetts Battery noted how northern gunners filled the air over the Confederates "with the smoke of bursting shells whose fragments plowed the ground in front." When the southerners got halfway across the field, Federal artillery rounds began plowing wide gaps in their lines. "They got within 800 yards," noted Phillips, "when out rushed the [Federal] infantry on our left, and the rattling of musketry mingled with the roar of cannon." The Massachusetts artillerists fired as fast as they could get new limbers full of ammunition, "piling up our canister alongside of the gun, so as to be ready for them."[41]

A cannoneer in Battery G, 1st New York Artillery, remembered that during a break in the Confederate attacks "orders were given to the chiefs of pieces to fire low at the advancing lines, [and] to aim at the feet of the enemy." The New Yorkers were told not to waste time sponging the bores of their cannon; at every discharge they "cut huge gaps" in the Confederate lines. Capt. John D. Frank, commanding the New Yorkers, reported that his battery of eight 10-pounder Parrotts fired a total of 981 rounds (400 of shell, 515 of spherical case, and 66 of canister) in a little more than two hours, a very rapid rate of fire.[42]

Despite the scathing artillery fire, Confederate infantrymen came close to breaking the Federal lines near the Crew house around dusk. Capt. John Edwards, commanding Battery L & M, 3rd U.S. Artillery, related the intensity of the fighting there and the problems faced by numerous batteries positioned along the crowded Union battle lines. During the southern attacks, Edwards first ordered the crews of his four 10-pounder Parrott rifles to fire case shot. As the Confederates advanced farther, the captain had his men switch to double canister, a command "reserved for critical and dangerous moments." Eventually the southerners got so close to Edwards's guns that one of his corporals killed an attacker with a pistol shot.[43]

When it appeared that the Confederates would capture Edwards's pieces, the 9th Massachusetts Infantry cheered and moved up into a position immediately behind the battery's line of limbers. There the Massachusetts men opened fire, placing the artillerists and horses of Edwards's command in extreme jeopardy. When the 9th eventually advanced beyond the cannon, Edwards ordered his artillerists to limber up and move to the rear.

Many if not most of the 3,000 Federal casualties incurred at Malvern Hill were in infantry regiments like the 9th Massachusetts that charged onto the open slopes in front of their own batteries to engage the Confederates at close range. These costly advances undoubtedly saved the day for the Federals. Despite the Union artillery's frightful effectiveness, the batteries alone could not have repulsed the massed southern infantry attacks.[44]

At dusk, while the Confederate attacks remained "fierce and persistent," Henry Hunt brought his last artillery units forward under orders from Porter. This force included the army's Horse Artillery Brigade and a contingent of 32-pounder howitzers from Lt. August Grimm's battery of the 1st Battalion New York Light Artillery. At least one of the horse artillery batteries commanded by Capt. John C. Tidball advanced over ground where the Union infantry had fought. To keep from crushing dead and wounded Federal soldiers, Tidball's gunners dismounted and cleared paths through the carnage.

Shortly after dusk, Captain Tidball rode over to Grimm's battery, an organization composed entirely of German immigrants. The large howitzers manned by the Germans soon began roaring as the cannoneers fired at will and the officers rode about "swinging their sabres and giving the most voluminous orders." When Colonel Hunt galloped up and repeatedly endeavored to stop the rapid firing, "the 'Dutch' officers ordered it to continue, they evidently thinking he meant for it to be continued." Hunt soon became

Capt. James M. Robertson's Battery B and L, 2d United States Artillery.
Francis Trevelyan Miller, ed., The Photographic History of the Civil War, *10 vols.*
(New York: Review of Reviews, 1911), 1:281

frantic, his voice rising "to a piping shreak." According to Tidball, a bilingual soldier from his battery defused the situation by riding up to one of the German officers, grabbing him by the collar, and delivering "a little speech in their native tongue" that silenced both the yelling officers and their battery.[45]

Around 10:00 P.M. all the Federal batteries ceased firing. The late evening and nighttime Union bombardment had caused considerable havoc behind the Confederate lines; mention of it appears in practically every southern account of Malvern Hill. Col. Marcellus Douglass noted that the bursting of shells over his position was "so incessant as to render it almost impossible for commands to be heard." Chaplain Nicholas A. Davis of the Texas Brigade watched in awe as the Federal projectiles "gleamed and flashed streams and sheets of burning fire." Davis believed that "one could easily imagine, while witnessing this bursting storm of human passion, that he was within one step of the council chamber of his Satanic Majesty." Gen. Charles S. Winder, commander of the famed Stonewall Brigade, wrote how his men endured "a continuous stream of shot, shell, and balls for some two hours."[46]

Winder's command suffered heavily from the Federal fire, but losses were even higher among those units that charged up the exposed slopes of Malvern Hill. Lee's army suffered more than 5,000 casualties at Malvern Hill. D. H. Hill claimed in an oft-cited statement that more than half of them were from artillery fire, "an unprecedented thing in warfare." Although Hill's statement is probably an exaggeration, the Federal artillery nonetheless dealt a sizable physical and psychological blow to the Army of Northern Virginia at Malvern Hill.[47]

Sometime around 9:00 P.M., Fitz John Porter sent a message to McClellan stating that after "a hard fight for nearly four hours against immense odds, we have driven the enemy beyond the battle field." Porter knew that he had won a defensive victory and told his commander that with reinforcements and additional ammunition "we will hold our own and advance if you wish." But McClellan had decided to continue the retreat, and before Porter's message reached him he sent orders to set the army marching, with the Artillery Reserve in the lead, to Harrison's Landing on the James River. Porter successfully completed this operation before dawn on July 2.[48]

Numerous factors explain the Union artillery's domination on the Malvern Hill battlefield. Henry J. Hunt deserves enormous credit for his leadership and skillful disposition of Federal batteries on June 30 and July 1. At the critical moment of the fighting on the first, Hunt led forward his reserves to bolster the Federal lines, stating that "not a gun remained unemployed and not one could have been safely spared." Hunt exposed himself to enemy fire throughout the day, having two horses shot from under him.[49]

Gen. Charles Griffin also stood out for his tireless exertions. A Union infantryman watching Griffin remembered that "as fast as our batteries came galloping up from the right and rear he would ride up swiftly at their head and lead them into good positions." Griffin personally directed each new arrival into place, seemingly indifferent to the Confederate fire. Admiring infantrymen commented repeatedly on the likelihood of Griffin's being hit, "but he bore a charmed life it seemed." Griffin's "knowledge and experience as an officer of artillery," noted Gen. George W. Morell, "contributed materially to our success."[50]

The performances of Hunt and Griffin stand in dramatic contrast to those of the Confederate artillery commanders. On June 30 and July 1, Robert E. Lee's army suffered from uniformly poor leadership on the part of those entrusted with the artillery. Much of this stemmed from inexperience; very few Confederate officers had learned and practiced how to bring masses of artillery into action on time. Even experienced artillerists found themselves handicapped by the southern practice of assigning individual batteries to infantry brigades, an administrative choice that made the effective deployment and concentration of artillery extremely difficult. (The Union army's assignment of batteries to infantry divisions and corps artillery reserves also created problems, but the chiefs of artillery were usually well-trained regulars from the Old Army.)[51]

William Nelson Pendleton, Lee's chief of artillery and commander of the Confederate Artillery Reserve, exercised little or no control over events on July 1. Pendleton, who served only three years in the army after graduating from West Point in 1830, had been unwell with a slight fever and dysentery during much of the Seven Days campaign. In his official report, he stated that he spent July 1 "seeking for some time the commanding general, that I might get orders, and by reason of the intricacy of routes failing in this." He then supposedly scouted the field but found no good firing positions for the batteries of his powerful Artillery Reserve. "To remain nearby," he concluded, "and await events and orders, in readiness for whatever service might be called for, was all I could do."[52]

Pendleton's inability or unwillingness to employ the batteries assigned to the Artillery Reserve angered numerous officers in that command. Many of the Artillery Reserve batteries were close enough to the fighting on July 1 to come under hostile artillery fire but never received orders to go into battle. Maj. J. Thompson Brown's command "had no opportunity to do anything amid the great superabundance of artillery and the scanty use that was made of it." One of the most vocal critics of Pendleton and the Artillery Reserve was Lt. Col. Allen S. Cutts. Cutts reported that "although I am sure that more artillery could have been used with advantage in this engagement, and also that my command could have done good service, . . . I received no orders." Cutts confronted Pendleton a few weeks later, vowing that he would leave the Artillery Reserve "either by death resignation or desertion," pointing out "that the corps never had fought any and never would fight any, [and] that it was an absolute disgrace to the army."[53]

Much had gone wrong at Malvern Hill, admitted Pendleton, who commented frankly in his official report about some of the problems that plagued Confederate artillerists. He described the rough terrain and "the prevalence of woods and swamps" that made it difficult to move and deploy the guns. The Confederates had also thrown too little artillery into action at one time and left too much in the rear unused. "We needed more guns taking part," wrote Pendleton, "for our own protection and for crippling the enemy." Pendleton did not, however, accept any blame for what had happened, remaining silent about the damning fact that not one of the eighteen batteries in the Confederate Artillery Reserve saw action on July 1.[54]

Pendleton had many critics during and after the Civil War, one of the

Brig. Gen. William Nelson Pendleton
Robert Underwood Johnson and Clarence Clough Buel, eds., Battles and Leaders
of the Civil War, *4 vols. (New York: Century, 1887–88), 3:329*

harshest being Edward Porter Alexander. Alexander believed that the army's
chief of artillery was "too old and had been too long out of army life to be
thoroughly up to all the opportunities of his position." Pendleton's Malvern
Hill report, thought Alexander, convicted him "of having practically hidden
himself out all day where nobody saw him, and no orders could reach him."
The "extensive" Poindexter and Crew fields, Alexander further claimed,
provided ample space to have deployed the powerful Artillery Reserve.[55]

KEITH S. BOHANNON

Several of the Confederate division chiefs of artillery also exercised little control over their commands on July 1. Stonewall Jackson's chief of artillery Col. Stapleton Crutchfield was absent sick and apparently failed to designate a replacement. Gen. W. H. C. Whiting may have filled Crutchfield's place. Whiting ordered batteries up from the rear and claimed that he and his staff received orders, probably from Jackson, "to direct the artillery fire," which they did during the afternoon. Jackson also assisted with the guns. A youth in the Charlottesville Artillery remembered seeing the former artillery officer and instructor riding "time and time again back and forth from one edge of the woods to another" sending batteries into the Poindexter field.[56]

Lt. Col. Stephen D. Lee stated in his official report that he received no orders to send his batteries of Magruder's division into the Crew field. In a private letter written several weeks after the battle, Lee noted that his guns had been placed around the Carter house north of the Crew field, where all but four of them remained during the battle. Lee claimed that the four rifled guns from his command that saw action went in under orders from one of Magruder's aides. Magruder's report confirms that he sent a staff member back late in the day to bring up two batteries but also claims that he had earlier ordered Lee "to bring up from all the batteries thirty rifled pieces if possible."[57]

The training and skill of the battery commanders and gun crews in the opposing armies contrasted almost as starkly as the battlefield performances of the high-ranking artillery officers. At least half a dozen of Henry Hunt's battery commanders were graduates of the U.S. Military Academy, where they took ordnance and gunnery classes and conducted extensive artillery drills. Almost all of the officers had served for several years in the artillery branch of the antebellum U.S. Army and gone through the army's school of instruction in field batteries.[58]

An examination of the muster rolls of most of the U.S. Regular batteries engaged at Malvern Hill reveals that a large percentage of the enlisted men and especially the noncommissioned officers (the sergeants and corporals in charge of individual gun detachments) had entered the U.S. Army before 1861, usually for a period of five years. Although many of these artillerists had spent lengthy periods before the war serving as infantrymen at isolated posts, the men "as a whole," wrote one observer, "might have been considered well qualified in the various duties of artillerymen."[59]

Several of the Union army's volunteer batteries at Malvern Hill were also extremely well trained. Capt. William B. Weeden's Battery C, 1st Rhode Island Artillery, was "almost perfectly drilled," according to a contemporary account. Even U.S. Regular officers, including Charles Griffin, "were astonished and delighted" at the battery's proficiency in executing orders. Although a volunteer, Captain Weeden so impressed his superiors that he received an appointment as chief of artillery for Gen. George Morell's division.[60]

The results of the intensive training received by the U.S. Regulars and many of the Federal volunteer batteries were evident at Malvern Hill and noted in official reports and personal accounts. Lt. Adelbert Ames, who won praise from superiors for his performance on July 1, noted that his noncommissioned officers "made themselves conspicuous by their bravery and skill in handling their guns." Lt. Henry Kingsbury of the West Point Battery, Battery D, 5th U.S., offered similar accolades, noting that the accuracy of his men's fire "could not be excelled." Lt. John B. Hyde of the 5th Massachusetts Battery observed with contempt how a Confederate battery made a "very ridiculous" attempt to silence the Union guns before being silenced by his gunners within fifteen minutes of firing their first shot.[61]

Among the fifteen Confederate battery commanders at Malvern Hill, only one had served in the antebellum U.S. Army and two others had received training in southern military schools, one at the Virginia Military Institute and one at the Citadel. The rest of these citizen-soldiers had been lawyers, students, farmers, and a master painter before the war. Some of them undoubtedly found themselves in positions similar to that of William T. Poague, a prewar lawyer and captain of the Rockbridge Artillery. Poague had been in charge of his poorly disciplined battery for only a little more than two months at the time of Malvern Hill and keenly felt his deficiencies. Capt. James M. Carrington of the Charlottesville Artillery had even less experience than Poague. Carrington's battery had received its guns only weeks earlier, and the captain "hardly knew how to load a cannon."[62]

Union artillerists testified that Captains Poague and Carrington were not alone in their deficiencies; few southerners had mastered the difficult skills of gunnery by the early summer of 1862. A Rhode Island artillerist whose battery dueled with the Confederate guns posted in the Poindexter field noted that "although the shot and shrapnel fell in showers about us . . . few fell near enough to do any harm." The Rhode Islander concluded that the Confederates "must have been poorly supplied with good gunners." Another Rhode Islander engaging southerners in the Crew field wrote that most of the enemy's shells "overreached and did comparatively little damage."[63]

The Union artillerists also had a distinct advantage in the number and type of guns they employed at Malvern Hill. Henry Hunt ordered into action on July 1 twenty-two batteries totaling approximately 107 cannon. Well more than half of these guns were 3-inch ordnance rifles and 10-pounder Parrott rifles, both extremely accurate weapons capable of firing a $9\frac{1}{2}$-pound projectile a little more than a mile. The Federals also had at least a dozen 12-pounder Napoleons and a number of larger pieces, including 20- and 30-pounder Parrotts and $4\frac{1}{2}$-inch Rodman siege rifles.[64]

Henry Hunt also made sure his batteries had ample ammunition. On June 30 he had the foresight to place the Artillery Reserve's one hundred ammunition wagons close to Porter's headquarters at the Malvern house. Thus all Union batteries had access to ammunition, although the ammunition wagons for many of the batteries assigned to infantry divisions had been mixed up with the baggage trains and sent to the rear.[65]

A total of only fifteen Confederate batteries numbering probably between forty and forty-five guns saw action on July 1 at Malvern Hill. Fragmentary southern ordnance records make it impossible to determine the armament of most of these batteries, but at least half of them had one or two obsolete Model 1841 6-pounders. These smoothbore guns, already gone from the Army of the Potomac, lacked the hitting power, range, and accuracy needed to duel effectively with the Federals. Most Confederate battery commanders and their superiors sent into action only 12-pounder Napoleons or rifled guns, mainly 10-pounder Parrotts and 3-inch rifles.[66]

The lack of uniform armaments in many Confederate batteries contributed to already serious problems concerning the quantity and quality of artillery ammunition. Some Confederate batteries that fought at Malvern Hill suffered throughout the day for a lack of sufficient ammunition. General Whiting, for instance, claimed that the artillerists in the Poindexter field "labored under much disadvantage from want of ammunition, both as to kind and quantity."[67]

Robert E. Lee's official report of Malvern Hill made no mention of unskilled artillerists, outmatched and obsolete cannon, or insufficient ammunition, although he was undoubtedly aware of these handicaps. Instead he focused almost solely on the terrain as the reason for his artillery's failure. The woods and swamps, he stated, "made it impracticable to bring up a sufficient amount of artillery to oppose successfully the extraordinary force of that arm employed by the enemy." He further claimed that the fields "afforded us few positions favorable for its use and none for its proper concentration."[68]

The accuracy of Lee's assessment of the terrain is difficult to gauge. Several other Confederate officers left conflicting testimony on the subject. E. P. Alexander claimed that he went over the field after the battle and found "short, easy & covered roads in every way favorable" for bringing up batteries. James Longstreet wrote in the *Century Magazine* that after suggesting the placement of sixty guns in the Crew field he found that the approaches to the position were so "rough and obstructed" that only one or two batteries could unlimber there at a time. Longstreet makes no mention of rough terrain in his memoirs, however, stating only that forty to sixty guns could have been massed in the Crew field with "a hundred or more" in front of Jackson's position on the Poindexter farm.[69]

Capt. Greenlee Davidson of the Letcher Artillery also offered conflicting observations about the terrain in the Crew field. Davidson stated in his official report that there was not enough room at the northern end of the Crew field for him to place his six guns at their proper intervals. (The guns, limbers, and caissons of such a battery, aligned according to the army regulations, would cover a space nearly equivalent to a football field.) In the spring of 1863, however, Davidson claimed in a personal letter to Gen. A. P. Hill that the Confederates could easily have concentrated thirty or forty guns in the Crew field.[70]

While the number of Confederate guns that could have operated in the Crew and Poindexter fields is debatable, one thing is clear: southern batteries sustained extremely high casualties at the hands of their Federal counterparts. An officer in the 7th South Carolina Infantry was one of many witnesses who commented on the carnage marking the southern artillery positions. "I came upon numbers of dead and dying horses," this officer wrote, "who with the drivers and gunners, laid in a pile together, their several dismounted guns, their caissons, fired and blown up by the enemy's balls — all presenting an aspect of desolation and ruin." The fifteen Confederate batteries that saw action on July 1 lost approximately one hundred men killed or wounded. The toll in horseflesh was also high, amounting to more than seventy animals.[71]

The Union victory at Malvern Hill was undoubtedly the finest day of the Civil War for the Army of the Potomac's Artillery Reserve. Henry J. Hunt, recognizing that much of the credit belonged to captains and lieutenants commanding individual batteries, recommended promotions for seventeen of them based on their performances on July 1. Although most of these officers went on to distinguished careers, the Artillery Reserve declined in size and importance in the months following the Seven Days because the Union high command reassigned many of its batteries to newly created infantry commands.[72]

George B. McClellan acknowledged the important role Hunt and his command had played at Malvern Hill. An ardent McClellan supporter, Hunt told a friend several days after the battle that the army commander was "in every way and in all respects thoroughly satisfied with me and my work." McClel-

KEITH S. BOHANNON

lan also praised Hunt in his official report, noting that "so destructive was the fire of our numerous artillery" at Malvern Hill and "so heroic the conduct of our infantry, and so admirable the dispositions of Porter that no troops could have carried the position." Gen. Darius Couch, whose Union infantry division saw some of the heaviest fighting at Malvern Hill, offered one of the more succinct and accurate assessments of the performance of the Union field artillery on July 1 when he stated: "This arm did brilliant service. It could not have been excelled."[73]

ACKNOWLEDGMENTS

The author wishes to acknowledge the generous assistance of the following individuals for their help with this essay: John Coski, Noel Harrison, John Hennessy, Robert E. L. Krick, Robert K. Krick, Eric Mink, Michael Musick, James Ogden III, Mike Redding, and David Slay.

NOTES

1. Jennings C. Wise, *The Long Arm of Lee, or, The History of the Artillery of the Army of Northern Virginia . . .* , 2 vols. (Lynchburg, Va.: J. P. Bell, 1915), 1:221; L. Van Loan Naisawald, *Grape and Canister: The Story of the Field Artillery of the Army of the Potomac, 1861–1865* (New York: Oxford University Press, 1960), vii.

2. Douglas Southall Freeman, *Lee's Lieutenants: A Study in Command,* 3 vols. (New York: Scribner's, 1942–44), 1:593–95; Robert Underwood Johnson and Clarence Clough Buel, eds., *Battles and Leaders of the Civil War,* 4 vols. (New York: Century, 1887–88), 2:409, 412 (hereafter cited as *B&L*).

3. Fitz John Porter to John C. Ropes, March 19, 1895, John C. Ropes Papers, Papers of the Military Historical Society of Massachusetts, Boston University Library (collection hereafter cited as PMHSM-BU); U.S. War Department, *The War of the Rebellion: A Compilation of the Official Records of the Union and Confederate Armies,* 127 vols., index, and atlas (Washington, D.C.: GPO, 1880–1901), ser. 1, 11(2):23 (hereafter cited as *OR;* all references to ser. 1).

4. Stephen W. Sears, *George B. McClellan: The Young Napoleon* (New York: Ticknor and Fields, 1988), 219–22; William F. Biddle to John C. Ropes, March 27, 1895, John C. Ropes Collection, PMHSM-BU. One of McClellan's staff officers, Biddle said that on the afternoon of July 1 the general's party "heard artillery firing away off to the left" but "were too far to hear the musketry distinctly."

5. Fitz John Porter, "The Battle of Malvern Hill," in *B&L,* 2:409; Edward G. Longacre, *The Man Behind the Guns: A Biography of General Henry J. Hunt, Commander of the Artillery, Army of the Potomac* (South Brunswick, N.J.: A. S. Barnes, 1977): 22–74; Naisawald, *Grape and Canister,* 28.

6. "Army of the Potomac, Artillery Reserve, Orders and Circulars Issued, Septem-

ber 1861–May 1863," entry 872, part 2, RG 393, National Archives, Washington, D.C. (repository hereafter cited as NA); Naisawald, *Grape and Canister,* 45, 123; William E. Birkhimer, "The Third United States Artillery," *Journal of the Military Service Institution of the United States* 14 (March 1893): 477; H. W. Hubbell, "The Organization and Use of Artillery during the War of the Rebellion," *Journal of the Military Service Institution* 11 (March 1890): 401; William E. Birkhimer, *Historical Sketch of the Organization, Administration, Material and Tactics of the Artillery, United States Army* (1884; reprint, New York: Greenwood, 1968), 80. As of June 4, 1862, the Army of the Potomac's Artillery Reserve needed 259 men to bring its units, especially the consolidated U.S. Regular batteries, up to full strength.

7. *OR* 11(2):229.

8. Porter, "Malvern Hill," in *B&L,* 2:410–11; Henry J. Hunt to Thomas T. Gantt, October 7, 1888, folder marked "General Correspondence, 1880–1885," box 3, Henry J. Hunt Papers, Library of Congress (repository hereafter cited as LC); *OR* 11(2):238–39, 910; J. Willard Brown, *The Signal Corps, U.S.A. in the War of the Rebellion* (Boston: U.S. Veteran Signal Corps Association, 1896), 318. The six southern guns came from Thomas H. Brem's (N.C.) battery, James R. Branch's (Va.) battery, and Thomas B. French's (Va.) battery.

9. *OR* 11(2):907.

10. *OR* 11(2):119, 242, 262, 265–66, 269, 318, 350, 357, 380, 796, 907–8, 910–11; U.S. Navy Department, *Official Records of the Union and Confederates Navies in the War of the Rebellion,* 30 vols. (Washington D.C.: GPO, 1894–1927), ser. 1, 7:699, 709; ser. 2, 1:39, 90 (hereafter cited as *ORN*); Walter Clark, ed., *Histories of the Several Regiments and Battalions from North Carolina in the Great War, 1861–'65,* 5 vols. (Goldsboro, N.C.: Nash Brothers, 1901), 3:162, 165 (hereafter cited as Clark, *N.C. Regiments*); Brown, *Signal Corps,* 317–18. Fitz John Porter referred to this engagement as the action of Turkey Bridge or Malvern Cliff.

11. Porter, "Malvern Hill," in *B&L,* 2:413; Ezra J. Warner, *Generals in Blue: Lives of the Union Commanders* (Baton Rouge: Louisiana State University Press, 1964), 190–91. Porter stated in a postwar account that he placed the artillery under Griffin's command on the morning of July 1, but the guns assigned to Morell's infantry division remained "under the care" of Capt. William B. Weeden, the division's chief of artillery.

12. *OR* 11(2):105, 166–67, 227, 238, 270, 260, 271, 283, 287, 314, 357. Battery E, 2nd U.S. Artillery (Capt. J. Howard Carlisle) occupied the gorge in the road behind the Union lines (Porter, "Malvern Hill," in *B&L,* 2:420). The principal Union batteries engaged on July 1 along Griffin's line west of the Quaker Road included Battery L & M, 3rd U.S. Artillery (Capt. John Edwards); Battery F & K, 3rd U.S. Artillery (Capt. La Rhett L. Livingston); Battery A, 5th U.S. Artillery (Lt. Adelbert Ames); Battery E, 5th Massachusetts Artillery (Lt. John B. Hyde), and Battery C, 1st Rhode Island Artillery (Capt. William B. Weeden). The principal Union batteries engaged east of the

Quaker Road on July 1 were Battery D, 5th U.S. Artillery (Lt. Henry W. Kingsbury); 6th Independent New York Battery (Capt. Walter M. Bramhall); Battery A, Maryland Light Artillery (Capt. J. W. Wolcott); Battery B, Maryland Light Artillery (Capt. Alonzo Snow); Battery D, 1st New York Artillery (Capt. Thomas W. Osborne); Battery G, 1st New York Artillery (Capt. John D. Frank); 2nd New Jersey Light Artillery (Capt. John E. Beam); and Battery K, 4th U.S. Artillery (Lt. Francis W. Seeley) (*OR* 11[2]:52, 103, 107, 105, 119, 266–67, 325).

13. *OR* 11(2):566; Clark, *N.C. Regiments*, 2:567, 569.

14. James Longstreet, *From Manassas to Appomattox: Memoirs of the Civil War in America* (Philadelphia: Lippincott, 1896), 142–43; James Longstreet, "The Seven Days," in *B&L*, 2:403; *OR* 11(2):677, 823. There is some conjecture about when Lee issued these orders; the paucity of sources on the Confederate high command at Malvern Hill makes it extremely difficult to reconstruct the events.

15. "Recollections of Captain [William L.] Balthis," reel 39, Jedediah Hotchkiss Papers, LC; F. Carter Berkeley, undated account of Malvern Hill, reel 39, Jedediah Hotchkiss Papers, LC.

16. George Lewis, *History of Battery E, First Rhode Island Light Artillery* (Providence, R.I.: Snow & Farnham, 1892), 68; *OR* 11(2):558, 566; Clark, *N.C. Regiments*, 2:569; D. H. Hill, "McClellan's Change of Base and Malvern Hill," in *B&L*, 2:392. The Confederate batteries engaged in the Poindexter field on July 1 included the Staunton (Va.) Artillery (Lt. William L. Balthis); the First Rockbridge (Va.) Artillery (Capt. William T. Poague); the Alleghany (Va.) Artillery (Lt. John C. Carpenter); the Danville (Va.) Artillery (Capt. George W. Wooding); the Charlottesville (Va.) Artillery (Capt. James M. Carrington); the Rowan (N.C.) Artillery (Capt. James Reilly); the Baltimore (Md.) Light Artillery (Capt. John B. Brockenbrough), and the Henrico (Va.) Artillery (Capt. Alfred R. Courtney). At least one gun of the Jackson (Va.) Artillery, also known as Cutshaw's Battery, was probably engaged in the Poindexter field. For evidence regarding Cutshaw's Battery, see James H. Beeler diary, July 1, 1862, Handley-Page Library, Winchester, Va.

17. "Head Quarters Artillery Reserve Camp Lincoln, Va, June 20, 1862," Orders and Circulars Issued, Chief of Artillery, September 1861–May 1863, entry 872, part 2, RG 393, NA; *OR* 11(2):105. On June 20, 1862, Hunt issued an order to the Artillery Reserve stating that "firing will be deliberate and the greatest care will be taken to secure accuracy. Under no circumstances will it be so rapid that the effect of the shot and shell can not be noted when the air is clear."

18. Longstreet, *Manassas to Appomattox*, 143.

19. *OR* 11(2):287, 802, 812–13; n.a., "From the Southern (S.C.) Guardian, Richmond July 7, 1862," Lexington (Va.) *Gazette*, August 7, 1862.

20. *OR* 11(2):697, 747, 798, 812–13, 818–19, 839. The Confederate batteries engaged in the Crew field on July 1 included the Portsmouth (Va.) Artillery (Capt. Carey F.

Grimes); the Lynchburg Beauregard (Va.) Artillery (Capt. Marcellus N. Moorman); the Purcell (Va.) Artillery (Capt. William R. J. Pegram); the Letcher (Va.) Artillery (Capt. Greenlee Davidson); the Washington (S.C.) Artillery (Capt. James F. Hart); and the First Richmond (Va.) Howitzers (Capt. Edward S. McCarthy).

21. *OR* 11(2):669, 818; Greenlee Davidson, *Captain Greenlee Davidson C.S.A.: Diary and Letters,* ed. Charles E. Turner (Verona, Va.: McClure Press, 1975), 40. Although Armistead did not specify the number of guns he required, he supposedly told Magruder that Longstreet had promised two batteries, which Magruder deemed inadequate. Little evidence exists regarding Longstreet's efforts to concentrate artillery in the Crew field other than his ordering forward the six guns of the Letcher Artillery.

22. *OR* 11(2):813; "The Purcell Battery in the Seven Days' Battles before Richmond," in *Southern Historical Society Papers,* ed. J. William Jones and others, 52 vols. (1877–1959; reprint with 3-vol. index, Wilmington, N.C.: Broadfoot, 1990–92), 21: 364 (set hereafter cited as *SHSP*); "The Purcell Battery," Richmond *Enquirer,* July 4, 1862; Peter S. Carmichael, *The Purcell, Crenshaw, and Letcher Artillery* (Lynchburg, Va.: H. E. Howard, 1990), 18–19.

23. Lee A. Wallace Jr., *The Richmond Howitzers* (Lynchburg, Va.: H. E. Howard, 1993), 18; *OR* 11(2):747; John Van Lew McCreery memoirs, Mss 5:1, M 13781, Virginia Historical Society, Richmond; Robert Stiles, *Four Years under Marse Robert* (New York: Neale, 1903), 103; "Howitzers' Camp, 5th July 1862," Richmond *Enquirer,* July 15, 1862; R. W. Royall to mother, July 9, 1862, typescript in author's possession; Janet B. Hewett et al., eds., *Supplement to the Official Records of the Union and Confederate Armies,* 98 vols. to date (Wilmington, N.C.: Broadfoot, 1994), pt. 2, 70:372 (hereafter cited as *ORS*).

24. *OR* 11(2):203, 270; Porter, "Malvern Hill," in *B&L,* 2:415.

25. *OR* 11(2):558, 566, 573; Philip Slaughter, *A Sketch of the Life of Randolph Fairfax* (Richmond, Va.: Enquirer Job Office, 1864), 29; Thomas M. Wade to "Dear Lou," July 3 1862, Thomas M. Wade Letters, Stonewall Jackson House, Lexington, Va.; Wilbur F. Davis, "Recollections of my life — especially during the War, 1861–5 for my children," Acc. #7396, Special Collections Department, Alderman Library, University of Virginia, Charlottesville (repository hereafter cited as UVA). The southern batteries that remained in the Poindexter field the longest, earning praise in Stonewall Jackson's official report, were the Staunton, Rockbridge, and Alleghany batteries. Wilbur F. Davis claimed that his unit, the Charlottesville Artillery, was the last Confederate battery sent into Poindexter field on July 1, where it fired for roughly fifteen minutes.

26. *OR* 11(2):573, 618; William Thomas Poague, *Gunner with Stonewall: Reminiscences of William Thomas Poague,* ed. Monroe F. Cockrell (Jackson, Tenn.: McCowat-Mercer, 1957), 29; Lancelot M. Blackford to "My Dear Mother," July 14, 1862, folder labeled "Confederate Letters, 1862–1863," box 3, Blackford Family Papers, Acc #6403, UVA.

27. *OR* 11(2):573, Poague, *Gunner with Stonewall,* 573; Edward A. Moore, *Story of a Cannoneer under Stonewall Jackson* (Lynchburg, Va.: J. P. Bell, 1910), 89–91.

28. *OR* 11(2):574.

29. *OR* 11(2):116; Terry L. Jones, ed., "Down the Peninsula with Richard Ewell: Captain Campbell Brown's Memoirs of the Seven Days Battles," in *The Peninsula Campaign of 1862,* ed. William J. Miller (Campbell, Calif.: Savas Woodbury Publishers, 1997), 63; Mary A. Hammond, ed., "'Dear Mollie': Letters of Captain Edward A. Acton to His Wife, 1862," *Pennsylvania Magazine of History and Biography* 89 (January 1965): 31.

30. *OR* 11(2):209, 267; William W. Goldsborough, *The Maryland Line in the Confederacy* (Baltimore: Guggenheimer, Weil, 1900), 279. Several Union artillery commanders complained about the fire of Confederate sharpshooters coming from the large wooded ravine created by Western Run.

31. Edward Porter Alexander, *Fighting for the Confederacy: The Personal Recollections of General Edward Porter Alexander,* ed. Gary W. Gallagher (Chapel Hill: University of North Carolina Press, 1989), 160; Wise, *Long Arm of Lee,* 1:231; *OR* 11(2): 64, 68, 72, 81, 93, 275, 297, 305, 319, 346; Lewis, *History of Battery E,* 68; Charles B. Haydon, *For Country, Cause and Leader: The Civil War Journal of Charles B. Haydon,* ed. Stephen W. Sears (New York: Ticknor and Fields, 1993), 261; Alfred Bellard, *Gone for a Soldier: The Civil War Memoirs of Private Alfred Bellard,* ed. David Herbert Donald (Boston: Little, Brown, 1975), 103. Confederate artillerist Edward Porter Alexander, among others, noted the effects of the converging southern fire.

32. *OR* 11(2):81, 90, 95, 203, 229; Porter, "Malvern Hill," in *B&L,* 2:416.

33. *OR* 11(2):283; 1885 note by William Weeden in Porter, "Malvern Hill," in *B&L,* 2:417; "Correspondence of the Journal, Battery C, Harrison's Bar, Va., July 8, 1862," Providence (R.I.) *Journal,* July 17, 1862.

34. *ORN,* ser. 1, 7:709, 712–13; ser. 2, 1:132; U.S. Naval History Division, comp., *Civil War Naval Chronology* (Washington, D.C.: GPO, 1971), 75.

35. *OR* 11(2):971–72; Porter, "Malvern Hill," in *B&L,* 2:422; *ORS,* pt. 2, 2:465; undated note from Fitz John Porter "for the comdg offr of Gun Boats," container A 72 (reel 29), George B. McClellan Papers, LC; Brown, *Signal Corps,* 320; *Civil War Naval Chronology,* 75; Edward S. Allen, "Near Harrison's Bar, James River, Va. July 23d, 1862," *Daily Courant* (Hartford, Conn.), July 30, 1862.

36. "Gen. McClellan's Army," *New York Times,* July 8, 1862; "The Battle of Malvern Hill," [excerpted from the July 4, 1862, Richmond *Examiner*], *New York Times,* July 10, 1862; Porter, "Malvern Hill," in *B&L,* 2:422; *Ordnance Instructions for the United States Navy Part II* (Washington, D.C.: GPO, 1864), lxxiii; Thomas Ward Osborn, *No Middle Ground: Thomas Ward Osborn's Letters from the Field,* ed. Herbert S. Crumb and Katherine Dhalle (Hamilton, N.Y.: Edmonston Publishing, 1993), 62–63.

37. *OR* 11(2):203; Porter, "Malvern Hill," in *B&L,* 2:420.

38. *OR* 11(2):628; 643; Lafayette McLaws to "Dear General," November 30, 1885, James Longstreet Papers, #210, Special Collections, Emory University, Atlanta, Ga. (repository hereafter cited as EU).

39. Longstreet, *Manassas to Appomattox,* 144–45; James Longstreet, "The Seven Days," in *B&L,* 2:403; *OR* 11(2):760. In his article on the Seven Days in *Battles and Leaders,* Longstreet stated that "the fire from our batteries failing of execution, General Lee seemed to abandon the idea of an attack."

40. Edward Porter Alexander, *Military Memoirs of a Confederate: A Critical Narrative* (New York: Scribner's, 1907), 161–62; *OR* 11(2):677–78.

41. *History of the Fifth Massachusetts Battery* (Boston: Luther E. Cowles, 1902), 375; Daniel G. MacNamara, *History of the Ninth Massachusetts Volunteers* (Boston: E. B. Stillings, 1899), 155.

42. Nelson Ames, *History of Battery G, First Regiment New York Light Artillery* (Marshalltown, Iowa: Marshall Printing Company, 1900), 35; *OR* 11(2):52, 107, 260, 267, 288. According to Lt. Adelbert Ames, Battery A, 5th U.S. Artillery, fired 1,392 rounds on July 1, probably more than any other Federal battery on the field.

43. *OR* 11(2):357, 724.

44. *OR* 11(2):203, 357; William E. Birkhimer, "Has the Adaptation of the Rifle-Principle to Fire-Arms Diminished the Relative Importance of Field Artillery?" *Journal of the Service Institution of the United States* 6 (September 1885): 235; Porter, "Malvern Hill," in *B&L,* 2:419; MacNamara, *Ninth Massachusetts,* 156. Darius Couch noted that the advance of numerous northern infantry regiments during this time masked the fire of the Federal artillery.

45. *OR* 11(2):229, 238, 242, 245, 250–51, 269, 567; Henry J. Hunt to "My Dear Colonel," July 6, 1862, folder titled "May–June 1862," box 7, Henry J. Hunt Papers, LC; John C. Tidball memoirs, 617–36, U.S. Military Academy Library, West Point, N.Y. The two horse artillery batteries brought up by Hunt were Battery A, 2nd U.S. Artillery (Capt. John C. Tidball) and Battery B & L, 2nd U.S. Artillery (Capt. James M. Robertson). Fitz John Porter had ordered up the third element of the Horse Artillery Brigade, Battery M, 2nd U.S. Artillery (Capt. Henry Benson), earlier in the afternoon. Capt. J. Howard Carlisle's Battery E, 2nd U.S. Artillery, also participated in the evening barrage.

46. *OR* 11(2):572–73, 578, 591, 601; Donald E. Everett, ed., *Chaplain Davis and Hood's Texas Brigade* (San Antonio: Principia Press of Trinity University, 1962), 96.

47. D. H. Hill, "McClellan's Change of Base," in *B&L,* 2:394; "The Battle of Malvern Hill," [excerpted from the July 4, 1862, Richmond *Examiner*] *New York Times,* July 10, 1862.

48. For a defense of McClellan's decision to retire to Harrison's Landing, see Wil-

liam H. Powell, *The Fifth Army Corps* (1896; reprint, Dayton, Ohio: Morningside, 1984), 177–78; Sears, *McClellan*, 222.

49. *OR* 11(2):238–39.

50. McNamara, *Ninth Massachusetts*, 152; *OR* 11(2):277.

51. Wise, *Long Arm of Lee*, 1:237, 239. For Stonewall Jackson's support of assigning batteries to infantry brigades, see Robert K. Krick, *Conquering the Valley: Stonewall Jackson at Port Republic* (New York: Morrow, 1996), 338–39. For problems with the organization of the Union army's artillery, see Naisawald, *Grape and Canister*, 227–31; Longacre, *Man Behind the Guns*, 99–100, 104.

52. *OR* 11(2):536, 539; Susan P. Lee, *Memoirs of William N. Pendleton* (Philadelphia: Lippincott, 1893), 194. Maj. Charles R. Richardson, commanding a battalion in the Artillery Reserve, received orders from Pendelton on the morning of July 1 to return with his guns to a camp in the Confederate rear.

53. *OR* 11(2):539, 547, 549, 550; James A. Blackshear diary, September 8, 1862, MS #302, EU.

54. *OR* 11(2):537.

55. Alexander, *Fighting for the Confederacy*, 112, 158, 336; Alexander, *Military Memoirs*, 158–59. Douglas Southall Freeman, *Lee's Lieutenants*, 1:614, 617, agreed with Alexander's criticisms of Pendleton but noted that Lee had few other officers with Pendleton's experience in directing large numbers of cannon. For a spirited defense of Pendleton's role at Malvern Hill, see Wise, *Long Arm of Lee*, 1:225–27.

56. *OR* 11(2):562, 571, 573–74; Wilbur F. Davis, "Recollections of My Life," UVA; Leroy Cox memoir, Albemarle County Historical Society, Charlottesville, Va. See criticism of Crutchfield in Jones, ed., "Campbell Brown's Memoirs," 63.

57. *OR* 11(2):669, 671, 694, 747; Stephen D. Lee to Mr. Allen, August 2, 1862, Stephen D. Lee file, Compiled Service Records of Confederate General and Staff Officers, M331, NA. The possibility exists that Magruder's orders to mass thirty guns never reached S. D. Lee.

58. Francis B. Heitman, *Historical Register of the U.S. Army* (Washington, D.C.: National Tribune, 1890), 87, 251, 414, 579, 642, 680; James L. Morrison Jr., *The Best School in the World: West Point in the Pre–Civil War Years, 1833–1866* (Kent, Ohio: Kent State University Press, 1986), 100, 118–19; testimony of Henry J. Hunt in *Report of the Joint Committee on the Conduct of the War at the Second Session Thirty-eighth Congress*, 3 vols. (Washington, D.C.: GPO, 1865), 1:91; William B. Skelton, *An American Profession of Arms: The Army Officer Corps, 1784–1861* (Lawrence: University Press of Kansas, 1992), 253–54; Longacre, *Man Bbehind the Guns*, 101–3.

59. Regular Army Muster Rolls: box 1278, 2nd United States Artillery, Battery E, Muster Roll for June 30–August 31, 1862; box 1308, 3rd United States Artillery, Battery K, Muster Roll for June 30–August 31, 1862; box 1310, 3rd United States Artillery,

Battery L, Muster Roll for June 30–August 31, 1862; box 1310, 3rd United States Artillery, Battery M, Muster Roll for June 30–August 31, 1862; box 1310, 4th United States Artillery, Battery K, Muster Roll for June 30–August 31, 1862, RG 94 (Adjutant General's Office), NA. On the decision to dismount light artillery batteries in the antebellum U.S. Army and its deleterious effects, see comments of Henry J. Hunt in Birkhimer, "Has the Adaptation of the Rifle-Principle to Fire-Arms Diminished the Relative Importance of Field Artillery?," 230; H. W. Hubbell, "The Organization and Use of Artillery," *Journal of the Military Service Institution* 11 (March 1890): 396, 397.

60. John R. Bartlett, *Memoirs of Rhode Island Officers* (Providence: Sidney S. Rider & Brothers, 1867), 398.

61. *OR* 11(2):167, 260, 288; *Fifth Massachusetts Battery*, 375.

62. Poague, *Gunner with Stonewall*, 4, 21; Krick, *Conquering the Valley*, 79; Robert K. Krick, *Lee's Colonels: A Biographical Register of the Field Officers of the Army of Northern Virginia* (Dayton, Ohio: Morningside, 1991), 69, 102, 278, 307, 317; Robert J. Driver, *The Staunton Artillery* (Lynchburg, Va.: H. E. Howard, 1988), 51; John H. Thompson, "Shaft to Portsmouth Artillery, Unveiling of June 8, 1906," *SHSP,* 34:150; Keith S. Bohannon, *The Giles, Alleghany, and Jackson Artillery* (Lynchburg, Va.: H. E. Howard, 1990), 103; Carmichael, *Purcell, Crenshaw, and Letcher Artillery*, 161; Robert H. Moore III, *The Danville, Eighth Star New Market and Dixie Artillery* (Lynchburg, Va.: H. E. Howard, 1989), 57.

63. Lewis, *History of Battery E,* 68; "Correspondence of the Journal," Providence (R.I.) *Journal,* July 17, 1862; *OR* 11(2):167, 357.

64. *OR* 11(2):52, 105, 238, 283, 390; Porter, "The Battle of Malvern Hill," in *B&L,* 2:411, 417. The author determined the identity of ninety-one Federal cannon engaged at Malvern Hill on July 1, including thirty 10-pounder Parrotts, twelve 20-pounder Parrotts, twelve Napoleons, four 32-pounder howitzers, twenty-three 3-inch rifles, one 12-pounder howitzer, five 30-pounder Parrotts, and four $4\frac{1}{2}$-inch Rodmans.

65. A few Union battery commanders whose units expended large numbers of rounds reported difficulties being resupplied. See *OR* 11(2):260, 288; Birkhimer, *Historical Sketch,* 101; Porter, "The Battle of Malvern Hill," in *B&L,* 2:411; Naisawald, *Grape and Canister,* 148.

66. *OR* 11(2):560, 573, 694, 798; Curt Johnson and Richard C. Anderson Jr., *Artillery Hell: The Employment of Artillery at Antietam* (College Station: Texas A&M University Press, 1995), 87–89, 93–95, 101, 103, 104; Krick, *Conquering the Valley,* 79; Carmichael, *Purcell, Crenshaw, and Letcher Artillery,* 18, 128; Clark, *N.C. Regiments,* 2:563, 567–68; Robert J. Driver, *The First and Second Rockbridge Artillery* (Lynchburg, Va.: H. E. Howard, 1987), 25. Stapleton Crutchfield stated that during the early stages of the June 27, 1862, battle at Gaines's Mill there were not enough "guns of a suitable character" among the batteries assigned to Richard Ewell's division (Courtney's, Carrington's, and Brockenbrough's batteries) to engage the enemy.

67. *OR* 11(2):568, 628; 21:1046; Freeman, *Lee's Lieutenants,* 1:617; "Hardaway's Rifle Battery," Columbus (Ga.) *Daily Sun,* July 14, 1862. For comments on the poor quality of Confederate artillery ammunition, see Alexander, *Fighting for the Confederacy,* 61, 248. The batteries assigned to Harvey Hill's division had exhausted their ammunition in the fighting at White Oak Swamp on June 30 and were unable to replenish their limber chests in time to participate on July 1.

68. *OR* 11(2):496. Wise, *Long Arm of Lee,* 1:230, supported Lee's position. For evidence that Lee was aware of the problems in his artillery arm, see *OR* 21:1046.

69. Alexander, *Fighting for the Confederacy,* 11; Alexander, *Military Memoirs,* 158; Longstreet, *Manassas to Appomattox,* 143; James Longstreet, "The Seven Days," in *B&L* 2:403. Porter Alexander was "occupied all day" on July 1 "with Ammunition Trains, bringing them up & posting them conveniently to the troops" (Edward Porter Alexander to father, July 4, 1862, Edward Porter Alexander Papers, Southern Historical Collection, University of North Carolina, Chapel Hill).

70. Davidson, *Greenlee Davidson,* 72; John Tyler, "Letcher Artillery Has Proud War Record," Richmond *Times-Dispatch,* July 22, 1917. Lt. John Tyler of the Letcher Artillery supported Davidson's official report, stating that the space in the Crew field was not sufficient "to operate a six-gun battery at full distance, as our front was reduced to half distance."

71. Unidentified officer of the 7th South Carolina Infantry, probably Capt. John S. Hard, "A Letter from the Battlefield," Charleston *Courier,* July 24, 1862; *OR* 11(2):567, 574, 594, 802, 975; "The Letcher Artillery," Richmond *Enquirer,* July 5, 1862; Robert H. Moore III, *Chew's Ashby, Shoemaker's Lynchburg and the Newtown Artillery* (Lynchburg, Va.: H. E. Howard, 1995), 68; "The Howitzers' Camp, 5th July 1862," Richmond *Enquirer,* July 15, 1862; "The Purcell Battery in the Seven Days' Battles before Richmond," in *SHSP,* 21:364; Driver, *Staunton Artillery,* 22; Lewis T. Nunnelee (Lynchburg Battery) memoir, 46, Museum of the Confederacy, Richmond, Va.

72. "List of Officers Recommended for Brevets for Gallant Conduct," folder titled "May–June 1862," box 7, Military Papers, 1841–62, Henry J. Hunt Papers, LC; Naisawald, *Grape and Canister,* 182, 229, 270. For Hunt's opposition to artillery batteries being assigned to infantry commands, see Hunt to General S[eth] Williams, March 17, 1863, box 7, Henry J. Hunt Papers, LC.

73. *OR* 11(2):23, 204; Henry J. Hunt to "My Dear Colonel," July 6, 1862, Hunt Papers, LC.

George B. McClellan's campaign against Richmond in 1862 has been less intensively studied than more famous operations such as the Confederate invasions that climaxed in the battles of Antietam and Gettysburg. Still, as with almost any important event during the Civil War, the Richmond campaign has inspired a sizable literature. In addition to the titles listed in this brief overview, readers should look to the notes accompanying the essays in this collection for important published items and manuscript collections.

The best source for printed primary material on the 1862 Richmond campaign is U.S. War Department, *The War of the Rebellion: The Official Records of the Union and Confederate Armies,* 127 vols., index, and atlas (Washington,D.C.: GPO, 1880–1901), ser. 1, vol. 11, pts. 1–3. These imposing volumes contain more than three thousand pages of official reports, correspondence, and other documents. Volume 2 of part 1 of *Supplement to the Official Records of the Union and Confederate Armies,* ed. Janet B. Hewett et al., 98 of a projected 100 vols. published to date (Wilmington, N.C.: Broadfoot, 1994–), contains additional material about both armies. For those interested in particular military units, the several dozen volumes in part 2 of the *Supplement* reprint "Record of Events" information from the National Archives that includes a wealth of information about personnel and movements.

Several large collections of testimony shed light on the Confederate side of the campaign, including *Southern Historical Society Papers,* ed. J. William Jones et al., 52 vols. (1876–1959; reprint, with 3-vol. index, Wilmington, N.C.: Broadfoot, 1990–92); *Confederate Veteran,* 40 vols. (1893–1932; reprint, with 3-vol. index, Wilmington, N.C.: Broadfoot, 1984–86); and Walter Clark, ed., *Histories of the Several Regiments and Battalions from North Carolina in the Great War, 1861–'65,* 5 vols. (Raleigh: E. M. Uzzell, Printer and Binder, 1901). For similar Federal material, readers should consult the *Papers* of the Military Order of the Loyal Legion of the United States (MOLLUS), 66 vols. and 3-vol. index (Wilmington, N.C.: Broadfoot, 1991–96). Many of these papers, which were read before the state commanderies of the MOLLUS, shed light on the 1862 Richmond campaign. For northern testimony delivered in a highly charged political setting, see U.S. Congress, *Report of the Joint Committee on the Conduct of the War,* 3 parts (Washington, D.C.: GPO, 1863). Additional useful material from former Federals and Confederates is in volume 1 of *Papers of the Military Historical Society of Massachusetts,* 14 vols. (1895–1918; reprint in 15 vols. with a general index, Wilmington, N.C.: Broadfoot, 1989–90), and volume 2 of *Battles and Leaders of the Civil War,* ed. Robert Underwood Johnson and Clarence Clough Buel, 4 vols. (New York: Century, 1887–88).

The best narrative treatment of the overall campaign is Stephen W. Sears, *To the Gates of Richmond: The Peninsula Campaign* (New York: Ticknor & Fields, 1992). As is true of all of Sears's books, this one combines solid research and felicitous prose and places military events within a broader political framework. Other useful campaign studies include Clifford Dowdey, *The Seven Days: The Emergence of Lee* (Boston: Little, Brown, 1964), an undocumented, engagingly written book that betrays the author's well-known sympathy for Lee and his army; Joseph P. Cullen, *The Peninsula Campaign 1862: McClellan and Lee Struggle for Richmond* (Harrisburg, Pa.: Stackpole, 1973), a brief treatment that highlights McClellan's and Lee's different styles of command; and William J. Miller, ed., *The Peninsula Campaign of 1862: Yorktown to the Seven Days,* 3 vols. (Campbell, Calif.: Savas Woodbury Publishers [vols. 1–2] and Savas Publishing [vol. 3], 1993–97), which covers the pre–Seven Days phase of McClellan's drive against Richmond. A pair of studies by participants remain worthwhile. Alexander S. Webb, who served as a Union staff officer during the campaign, offers an unsparing evaluation of his army commander in *The Peninsula: McClellan's Campaign of 1862* (New York: Scribner's, 1881); William Allan, a member of Stonewall Jackson's staff, allocates a good deal of attention to the Richmond campaign in his perceptive *The Army of Northern Virginia in 1862* (Boston: Houghton Mifflin, 1892).

For the role of artillery during the Richmond campaign, two general studies are the obvious places to begin: Jennings C. Wise, *The Long Arm of Lee: or, The History of the Artillery of the Army of Northern Virginia . . . ,* 2 vols. (Lynchburg, Va.: J. P. Bell, 1915); and L. Van Loan Naisawald, *Grape and Canister: The Story of the Field Artillery of the Army of the Potomac, 1861–1865* (New York: Oxford University Press, 1960).

Those seeking pictorial material can select from a number of choices. Four titles from Time-Life Books are especially good. *The Peninsula* and *The Seven Days* (Alexandria, Va., 1997, 1998), volumes in the "Voices of the Civil War" series, provide excellent color and black-and-white reproductions and an array of excerpts from primary accounts. *Forward to Richmond: McClellan's Peninsular Campaign* and *Lee Takes Command, from Seven Days to Second Bull Run* (Alexandria, Va., 1983, 1984), both in "The Civil War" series, offer collections of wartime and retrospective images knit together by serviceable narratives. For period photographs, readers should consult volume 1 of Francis Trevelyan Miller, ed., *The Photographic History of the Civil War,* 10 vols. (New York: Century, 1911), and volume 2 of William C. Davis, ed., *The Image of War, 1861–1865,* 6 vols. (Garden City, N.Y.: Doubleday, 1981–84).

George B. McClellan's role in the Richmond campaign can be traced through a number of important works. The general's often disingenuous memoir, *McClellan's Own Story* (New York: Charles L. Webster, 1887), and *The Civil War Papers of George B. McClellan: Selected Correspondence, 1860–1865*, ed. Stephen W. Sears (New York: Ticknor & Fields, 1989), are indispensable primary sources. The best biography is Stephen W. Sears's *George B. McClellan: The Young Napoleon* (New York: Ticknor & Fields, 1988), which sketches a commander who imagined himself beset by Confederate enemies in his front and political enemies in his rear and who avoided a decisive contest with the enemy. Warren W. Hassler's *George B. McClellan: Shield of the Union* (Baton Rouge: Louisiana State University Press, 1957) presents a far more positive portrait of "Little Mac," as do Thomas J. Rowland's *George B. McClellan and Civil War History: In the Shadow of Grant and Sherman* (Kent, Ohio: Kent State University Press, 1998) and Joseph L. Harsh's "On the McClellan Go-Round" (*Civil War History* 19 [June 1973]: 101–28). T. Harry Williams's *Lincoln and His Generals* (New York: Knopf, 1952), in which McClellan figures prominently, has little positive to say about the "Young Napoleon."

Robert E. Lee did not write his memoirs, but many of his letters and other documents relating to the Richmond campaign are in *The Wartime Papers of R. E. Lee,* ed. Clifford Dowdey and Louis H. Manarin (Boston: Little, Brown, 1961). The most detailed discussion of Lee during the Seven Days is in Douglas Southall Freeman's *R. E. Lee: A Biography,* 4 vols. (New York: Scribner's, 1934–35). Joseph L. Harsh, *Confederate Tide Rising: Robert E. Lee and the Making of Southern Strategy, 1861–1862* (Kent, Ohio: Kent State University Press, 1998), gives Lee high marks for his strategic conduct, if not his tactical execution, during the late spring and early summer of 1862. For a less positive reading of Lee's generalship during the Richmond campaign that emphasizes his aggressive strategy and tactics, see Alan T. Nolan, *Lee Considered: General Robert E. Lee and Civil War History* (Chapel Hill: University of North Carolina Press, 1991).

All of Stonewall Jackson's many biographers have evaluated the enigmatic Virginian's controversial role in the campaign. Two of the more impressive studies are James I. Robertson Jr.'s massively detailed *Stonewall Jackson: The Man, the Soldier, the Legend* (New York: Macmillan, 1997), which treats its subject gently in June and early July 1862, and Frank E. Vandiver's *Mighty Stonewall* (New York: McGraw-Hill, 1957), which is a bit harder on "Old Jack."

Letters, diaries, and reminiscences contain a mass of invaluable material on the Richmond campaign. Although just a handful of titles can be mentioned here, they will serve to convey a sense of what is available in published form. Robert McAllister's *The Civil War Letters of General Robert McAllister,* ed. James I. Robertson Jr. (New Brunswick, N.J.: Rutgers University Press, 1965), gives the perspective of an observant officer in the 1st New Jersey Infantry. Philip Kearny's *Letters from the Peninsula: The Civil War Letters of General Philip Kearny,* ed. William B. Styple (Kearny, N.J.: Belle

Grove Publishing, 1988), includes biting criticism of McClellan's handling of the campaign. Excellent accounts by witnesses of various ranks include Robert Goldthwaite Carter, *Four Brothers in Blue; or, Sunshine and Shadows of the War of the Rebellion: A Story of the Great Civil War from Bull Run to Appomattox* (1913; reprint, Austin, Tex.: University of Texas Press, 1978); Alfred Bellard, *Gone for a Soldier: The Civil War Memoirs of Private Alfred Bellard,* ed. David Herbert Donald (Boston: Little, Brown, 1975), which reproduces wonderful illustrations by Bellard; Wesley Brainerd, *Bridge Building in Wartime: Colonel Wesley Brainerd's Memoirs of the 50th New York Volunteer Engineers,* ed. Ed Malles (Knoxville: University of Tennessee Press, 1997); and Charles B. Haydon, *For Country, Cause and Leader: The Civil War Journal of Charles B. Haydon,* ed. Stephen W. Sears (New York: Ticknor & Fields, 1993).

From the Confederate perspective, James Longstreet's *From Manassas to Appomattox: Memoirs of the Civil War in America* (Philadelphia: Lippincott, 1896) is flawed but nonetheless essential. Edward Porter Alexander's *Military Memoirs of a Confederate: A Critical Narrative* (New York: Scribner's, 1907) and *Fighting for the Confederacy: The Personal Recollections of General Edward Porter Alexander,* ed. Gary W. Gallagher (Chapel Hill: University of North Carolina Press, 1989), boast splendid analysis as well as some of the most pointed criticism of Stonewall Jackson's performance to be found among southern sources. Thomas J. Goree, *Longstreet's Aide: The Civil War Letters of Major Thomas J. Goree,* ed. Thomas W. Cutrer (Charlottesville: University Press of Virginia, 1995), includes several important letters relating to the Richmond campaign, as do Shepherd G. Pryor, *A Post of Honor: The Pryor Letters, 1861–63, Letters from Capt. S. G. Pryor, Twelfth Georgia Regiment and His Wife, Penelope Tyson Pryor,* ed. Charles R. Adams Jr. (Fort Valley, Ga.: Garrett Publications, 1989), and Ujanirtus Allen, *Campaigning with Old "Stonewall": Confederate Captain Ujanirtus Allen's Letters to His Wife,* ed. Randall Allen and Keith S. Bohannon (Baton Rouge: Louisiana State University Press, 1998). Two classic narratives (both first published during the war) that include excellent sections on the Richmond campaign are Nicholas A. Davis, *The Campaign from Texas to Maryland, with the Battle of Fredericksburg* (1863; reprint, Austin, Tex.: Steck, 1961), and [Thomas E. Caffey], *Battle-Fields of the South, from Bull Run to Fredericksburgh; with Sketches of Confederate Commanders and Gossip of the Camps* (1864; reprint, Alexandria, Va.: Time-Life, 1984).

Four general works deserve careful attention from anyone interested in the maneuvering and fighting outside Richmond in 1862. Bruce Catton's *Mr. Lincoln's Army* (Garden City, N.Y.: Doubleday, 1951) relates the Army of the Potomac's activities in memorable prose. Volume 2 of Douglas Southall Freeman, *Lee's Lieutenants: A Study in Command,* 3 vols. (New York: Charles Scribner's Sons, 1942–44), employs key Confederate commanders as a vehicle to analyze the campaign; the first volume of Kenneth P. Williams, *Lincoln Finds a General,* 5 vols. (New York: Macmillan, 1949–59), pursues the same end using McClellan and other Federal commanders. Herman

Hattaway and Archer Jones, *How the North Won: A Military History of the Civil War* (Urbana: University of Illinois Press, 1983), places the Richmond campaign within the larger strategic picture of the war.

Some ways in which northern political and military affairs intersected during McClellan's Richmond campaign stand out in Bruce Tap's *Over Lincoln's Shoulder: The Committee on the Conduct of the War* (Lawrence: University Press of Kansas, 1998). On the process by which emancipation moved to the fore in 1862, see *Freedom: A Documentary History of Emancipation, 1861–1867*, Ser. I, Vol. 1: *The Destruction of Slavery*, ed. Ira Berlin et al. (New York: Cambridge University Press, 1985).

Finally, three wartime accounts illuminate life behind the lines in Richmond. John Beauchamp Jones's *A Rebel War Clerk's Diary at the Confederate States Capital*, 2 vols. (Philadelphia: Lippincott, 1866), deservedly one of the most quoted civilian diaries from the war, charts the ebb and flow of morale in the city as McClellan's army approached in the spring and summer of 1862. Sallie Brock Putnam's *Richmond during the War: Four Years of Personal Observation* (1867; reprint, Lincoln: University of Nebraska Press, 1996), includes memorable passages relating to how civilians reacted to thousands of dead and wounded soldiers. Judith W. McGuire's *Diary of a Southern Refugee during the War* (1867; reprint, Lincoln: University of Nebraska Press, 1995) offers the perspective of one of the many thousands of Confederates who sought safety in Richmond during the course of the conflict.

CONTRIBUTORS

William A. Blair is a member of the Department of History and director of the Civil War Era Center at Penn State University. His publications include *A Politician Goes to War: The Civil War Letters of John White Geary*, *Virginia's Private War: Feeding Body and Soul in the Confederacy, 1861–1865*, and several articles and essays on mid-nineteenth-century subjects.

Keith S. Bohannon earned an M.A. in history from the University of Georgia and received his doctoral training in American history at Penn State University. He is the author of *The Giles, Alleghany, and Jackson Artillery* and of essays and articles, and co-editor of *Campaigning with "Old Stonewall": Confederate Captain Ujanirtus Allen's Letters to His Wife.*

Peter S. Carmichael is a member of the Department of History at the University of North Carolina at Greensboro. The author of *Lee's Young Artillerist: William R. J. Pegram*, as well as several essays and articles in popular and scholarly journals, he is completing a study of Virginia slaveholders' sons and the formation of southern identity in the late antebellum years.

Gary W. Gallagher is the John L. Nau III Professor in the History of the American Civil War at the University of Virginia and editor of the Civil War America series at the University of North Carolina Press. He has edited *The Third Day at Gettysburg and Beyond*, *The Fredericksburg Campaign: Decision on the Rappahannock*, *Chancellorsville: The Battle and Its Aftermath*, *The Wilderness Campaign*, *The Spotsylvania Campaign*, and *The Antietam Campaign*, six previous titles in the Military Campaigns of the Civil War series.

John T. Hubbell is a member of the Department of History at Kent State University, director of the Kent State University Press, and former editor of the scholarly journal *Civil War History*. His publications include *Biographical Dictionary of the Union: Northern Leaders of the Civil War*, which he co-edited with James W. Geary, and *Battles Lost and Won: Essays from Civil War History.*

R. E. L. Krick, a Richmond-based historian, was reared on the Chancellorsville battlefield. The author of *The Fortieth Virginia Infantry* and of essays and articles, he is completing a biographical register of the staff officers of the Army of Northern Virginia.

Robert K. Krick grew up in California but has lived and worked on the Virginia battlefields for more than twenty-five years. He has written dozens of articles and ten books, the most recent being *Stonewall Jackson at Cedar Mountain* and *Conquering the Valley: Stonewall Jackson at Port Republic.*

James Marten is a member of the Department of History at Marquette University. His published work includes *Texas Divided: Loyalty and Dissent in the Lone Star State, 1856–1874, The Children's Civil War,* and numerous essays and articles.

William J. Miller, editor of *Civil War: The Magazine of the Civil War Society* for several years, is the author of *The Training of an Army: Camp Curtin and the North's Civil War* and *Mapping for Stonewall: The Civil War Service of Jed Hotchkiss,* editor and co-author of the 3-volume *The Peninsula Campaign: Yorktown to the Seven Days,* and editor of a forthcoming volume of Jed Hotchkiss's Civil War letters.

INDEX

Barnard, John G., xii, 37, 45–52, 54, 56, 58–59, 62–63, 64 (n. 33)

Barry, William, 197

Barziza, Decimus et Ultimus, 195–97, 199

Baton Rouge, La., 6

Beam, John E., 243 (n. 12)

Beaufort, N.C., 6

Beauregard, P. G. T., 12, 22–23 (n. 1), 33, 169

Beaver Dam Creek, battle of, 104

Bell, John, 131

Benson, Henry, 246 (n. 45)

Bernard, Helen Stuart, 12

Big Bethel, battle of, 100

Blackford, William M., 12

Blair, Frank, 18

Blair, Montgomery, 18

Blue Ridge Mountains, 66

Boatswain's Creek, 188–89, 192, 195, 198, 202–4, 213 (n. 32)

Boatswain's Swamp, 76

Border States, 156, 158, 160

Boston *Congregationalist*, 169

Boswell, J. Keith, 76

Bottoms Bridge, 48–49, 52, 57

Bramhall, Walter M., 243 (n. 12)

Brantley, R. A., 191, 198, 205

Brent, Joseph L., 101–2, 106–9, 114

Broad Street, 128

Brockenbrough, John B., 243 (n. 16), 248 (n. 66)

Brockholst, Francis, 175

Brown, G. Campbell, 94 (n. 57)

Brown, J. Thompson, 235

Brown, William Wells, 155

Bruce, George A., 5

Buell, Don Carlos, 6

Bull Run, battle of. *See* Manassas

Butler, Benjamin F., 134

Caffey, Thomas, 114

Campbell, Billy, 101–2

Campbell, Robert, 193, 198

Cannae, battle of, 4

Carlisle, J. Howard, 246 (n. 45)

Caroline County, Va., 12

Carpenter, John C., 227, 243 (n. 16)

Carrington, James M., 238, 243 (n. 16), 248 (n. 66)

Carter house, 237

Cary, Harriette, 125

"Casey's Redoubt," 58

Catton, Bruce, xv (n. 1)

Century Magazine, 239

Chamberlaine, William W., 78

Chambers, C. C., 199

Chancellorsville, battle of, xiv, 22, 82

Chandler, Zachariah, 16, 155

Charles City County, Va., 135

Charles City Road, 105, 107–8

Charleston, Va., 13

Chase, Lucy, 140–42

Chase, Salmon P., 16, 164

Chase, Sarah, 140–42

Chicago *Tribune*, 155, 165–67, 174–75

"Chickahominy fever," 62

Chickahominy River, xii, 15, 32–35, 44–45, 49, 50–51, 53, 56–58, 61–62, 78, 91 (n. 35), 102–5, 181–82, 189, 199, 203, 208 (n. 2)

Chickamauga, battle of, 207

Chilton, Robert H., 114–16, 120 (n. 45)

Church Hill, 123

Citadel, the, 238

City Point, Va., 135

Civilians, xiii

Cobb, Thomas R. R., 114

Cold Harbor, Va., 76

Colt's Rifle, 185, 209 (n. 8)

Columbia, S.C., 20

Gasparin, Agenor-Etienne de, 19

Gaston, W. H., 204

Geary, John W., 157

Georgetown, D.C., 15

Georgia, 153, 182

Georgia troops: 15th Infantry, 91 (n. 35); 16th Infantry, 114; 18th Infantry, 182–83, 185, 189–90, 192, 194–95, 199, 201–5, 207, 214 (nn. 42, 43), 215 (n. 48); 20th Infantry, 137; 38th Infantry, 69

Gettysburg, battle of, xiv, xv (n. 1), 207

Giles, Val, 192, 197

Gilmer, Jeremy F., 86

Glendale, battle of, x, 37–38, 79, 81, 109

Glorieta, battle of, 6

Gloucester County, Va., 144

Golding's farm, 50, 58

Gooney Manor Road, 79

Gorgas, Josiah, 6–7

Grandy, Charles, 135

Grant, Ulysses S., 6, 22 (n. 1), 31; 40 (n. 2), 62–63, 166

Grapevine Bridge, 52–53, 57, 64 (n. 20), 105, 107

Great Britain, 19

Great Dismal Swamp, 145

Greeley, Horace, 155–56, 159, 163, 168, 173

Griffin, Charles, 221, 234, 237, 242 (n. 12)

Griffis, John C., 189

Grimes, Carey F., 243–44 (n. 20)

Grimm, August, 232

Guerrilla warfare, 145, 152 (n. 66), 166

Gulf of Mexico, 6

Halleck, Henry W., 6, 16–17, 39–40, 176; *Articles of War*, 77

Hamby, William, 195, 201

Hampton, Wade, 80–81

Hampton, Va., 135, 138

Hanover County, Va. 74, 79, 89 (n. 23)

Hanover Court House, Va., 51; battle of, 32

Harman, John A., 68, 77

Harrisburg, Pa., 174

Harrison's Landing, x, 5, 14–16, 38, 96, 174, 218, 234, 246 (n. 48)

Hart, James F., 244 (n. 20)

Hattaway, Herman, 4; *How the North Won*, 4

Hawkins, Samuel, 204

Haxall's Landing, 37, 217–18, 220

Haydon, Charles B., 15

Heintzelman, Samuel P., 32, 37

Henrico County, Va., 92 (n. 36)

Henry Hill, 182

Henzel, H. W., 93

Hickory Ground, Va., 135

Hill, A. P., 79, 86, 102, 104, 182, 240

Hill, D. H., 67, 94 (n. 57), 102, 104, 119 (n. 38), 168, 187, 230, 234

Hill's (A. P.) division (Army of Northern Virginia), 102, 182, 188–89, 192, 195, 204, 213 (n. 32)

Hill's (D. H.) division (Army of Northern Virginia), 102, 187, 231, 249 (n. 67)

Hitchcock, E. A., 161

Hogan house, 58

Hollis, Rufus, 193

Holmes, Emma, 13

Holmes, Theophilus, 108–9, 116, 220

Homestead Act, 8

Hood, John B., 68, 73, 182, 185–92, 195, 199, 204, 207, 210 (n. 16), 212 (n. 30), 216 (nn. 51, 52)

Hood's (Texas) brigade (Army of Northern Virginia), xiv, 69, 73, 183, 187, 190, 192, 197–98, 204–5, 207–8, 233

U.S. Congress, ix, 7–8, 17–18, 45, 153, 155, 157–60, 164–65, 170, 174, 176

U.S. House of Representatives, 156, 166

U.S. Military Academy, 40–41 (n. 2), 45, 47, 98–99, 118 (n. 8), 182, 218, 235, 237

U.S. Sanitary Commission, 15, 141

U.S. Senate, 16, 168, 172, 174

U.S. War Department, 18, 168

University of Virginia, 98

Upper South, 172

Upper Trestle Bridge, 54, 58

Upton, John C., 192–93, 203, 212 (n. 26)

Valley Pike, 72

Van Dorn, Earl, 6

Venable, Charles S., 74, 86, 90 (n. 24)

Vicksburg, Miss., 6, 11; siege of, xv (n. 1)

Vietnam, 158

Virginia, ix–x, xiii, 3, 6–7, 11–12, 19, 21–22, 67, 69, 71, 100–101, 121, 131–32, 136, 142–43, 146–47, 150 (n. 38), 158, 161, 167, 171, 176–77, 181, 183, 192, 205, 208

Virginia, CSS, 7, 24 (n. 5), 29, 132, 137

Virginia General Assembly, 124

Virginia Military Institute, 238

Virginia troops: 31st Infantry, 72; 33rd Infantry, 72; 37th Infantry, 79; 4th Cavalry, 89 (n. 23); Letcher Artillery, 111, 240, 244 (nn. 20, 21), 249 (n. 70); 1st Loyal East Virginia Infantry (U.S.), 145; Graham's battery, 220; Staunton Artillery, 223, 227, 243 (n. 16), 244 (n. 25)Grimes's battery, 225; Purcell Artillery, 225, 244 (n. 20); 1st Richmond Howitzers, 226, 244 (n. 20); Rockbridge Artillery, 226–27, 238, 243 (n. 16), 244 (n. 25); Alleghany Artillery, 227, 243 (n. 16), 244

(n. 25); Henrico Artillery, 227, 243 (n. 16); Charlottesville Artillery, 237–38, 243 (n. 16), 244 (n. 25); Branch's battery, 242 (n. 8); French's battery, 242 (n. 8); Cutshaw's Battery, 243 (n. 16) Danville Artillery, 243 (n. 16); Portsmouth Artillery, 243 (n. 20); Lynchburg Beauregard Artillery, 244 (n. 20)

Von Kapff, Esther H., 99

Waco, Tex., 216

Wade, Benjamin, 155, 163, 169

Wade, Thomas M., 226

Walnut Grove Church, 75

Ware, Thomas L., 91 (n. 35)

War of 1812, 173

Warwick, Bradfute, 185, 190, 195–96, 213–14 (n. 39)

Warwick River, 31

Washington, George, 19–20, 162, 174

Washington, D.C., xi, 10, 18, 30, 32, 35–36, 39–40, 41 (n. 3), 44–45, 51, 58, 100, 160–61

Watt house, xiv, 199, 204, 213 (nn. 34, 38), 214 (n. 43)

Watt's orchard, 214 (n. 39)

Webb, Alexander, 34

Weeden, William B., 237–38, 242 (nn. 11, 12)

Welles, Gideon, 26 (n. 21), 153

Western Run, 217, 220, 245 (n. 30)

Western Theater, 6, 12, 96, 116, 158

West house, 220–21

West Indies, 173

West Point. *See* United States Military Academy

West Virginia, 132

White House (Lee), 162

White House (U.S.), 62, 175

White House Landing, 48

White Oak Swamp, 37, 58, 79–83, 92 (n. 39), 107–8, 118 (n. 6); battle of, xii, 66, 249 (n. 67)

Whiting, William H. C., 76, 85, 181–82, 185, 187–89, 191, 205–6, 209 (n. 9), 210 (n. 16), 211 (n. 20), 222–23, 225, 227, 231, 237, 239

Whiting's division (Army of Northern Virginia), xiii, 181–82, 185–90, 199, 205–8, 209 (n. 8), 210 (n. 16)

Wickliffe, Charles A., 158, 173

Wigfall, Louis T., 204, 215 (n. 47)

Wilcox, Cadmus M., 216 (n. 51)

Wilcox's brigade (Army of Northern Virginia), 214 (n. 42), 216 (n. 51)

Wilderness, battle of the, 207

Wilkins, B. H., 123

Wilkinson, Morton S., 172

Williams, Kenneth P., 33, 42 (n. 25)

Williamsburg, Va., 7, 101, 125, 138, 145, 167, 170; battle of, 23 (n. 3), 31, 44, 164

Williamsburg Road, 105, 108

Willis Church Road, 220, 223, 229

Winchester, first battle of, 13, 76

Winder, Charles S., 233

Winder, John H., 130

Windom, William, 172

Wisconsin troops: 19th Infantry, 135

Wise, Jennings C.: *The Long Arm of Lee*, 217

Wofford, William T., 185

Wolcott, J. W., 243

Wood, Bennett, 187, 192, 195–96, 204

Woodbury, Daniel P., 47–48, 54, 57

Woodbury-Alexander Bridge, 57

Wooding, George W., 243 (n. 16)

Woods, George N., 203

Wright, David M., 146

York County, Va., 135

York River, 48, 100

Yorktown, Va., 7, 15, 31, 41 (n. 14), 61, 101, 124, 126, 129, 131–32, 134, 144, 146, 158, 164, 168, 170–71; siege of, 44, 100, 103